D1483923

Happy
Sugar
Life 8

Tomiyaki Kagisora

Lifelog ★

Happy Sugar Life

Tomiyaki Kagisora

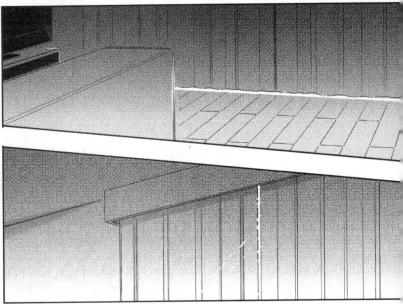

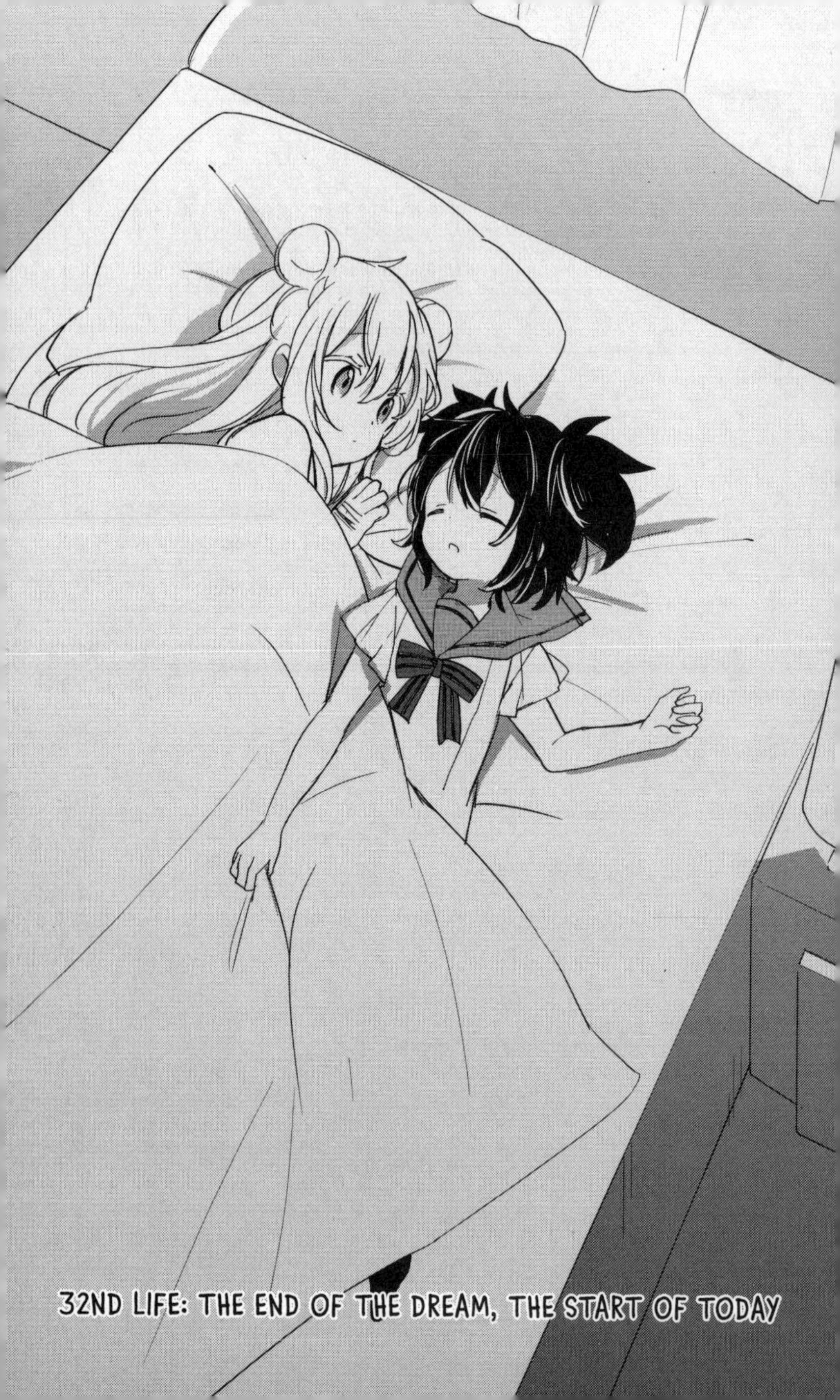
32ND LIFE: THE END OF THE DREAM, THE START OF TODAY

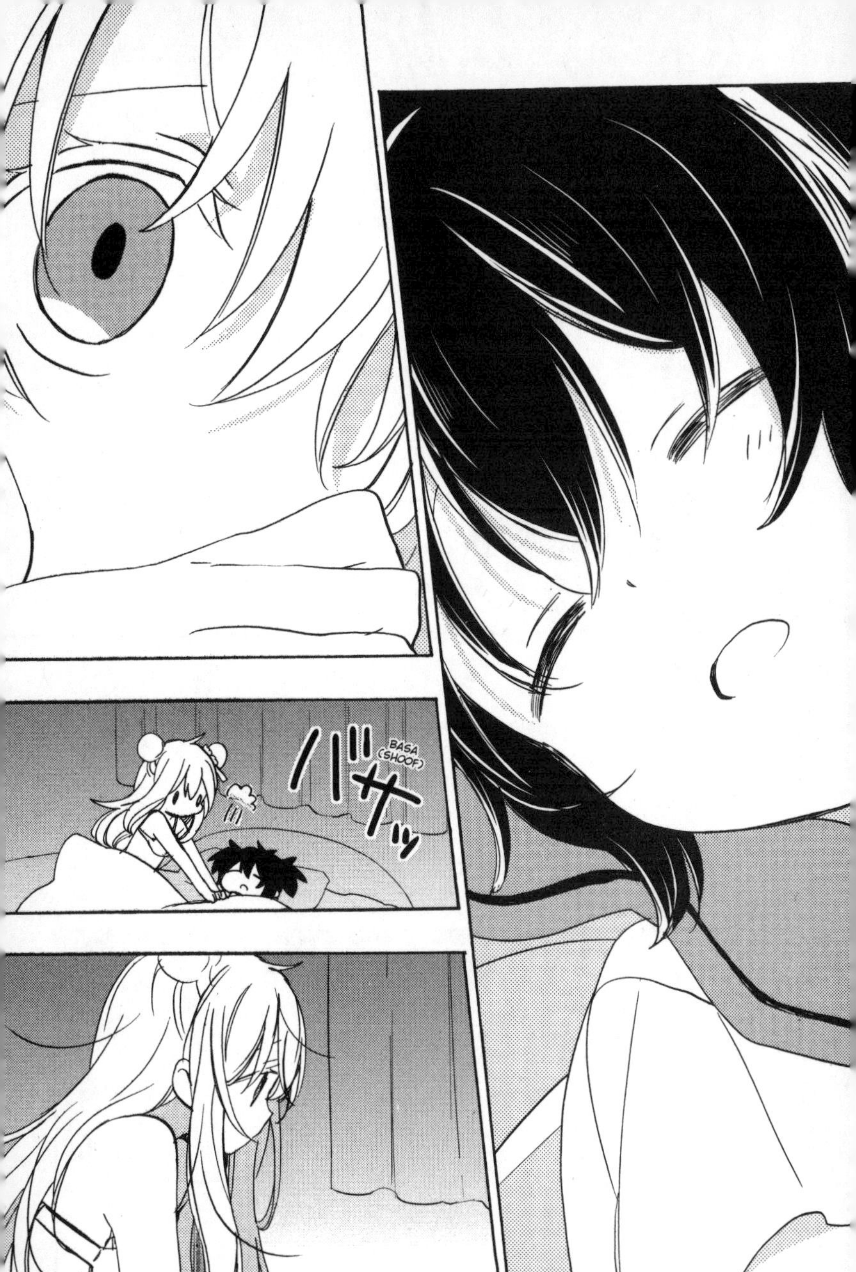
バサッ
BASA (SHOOF)

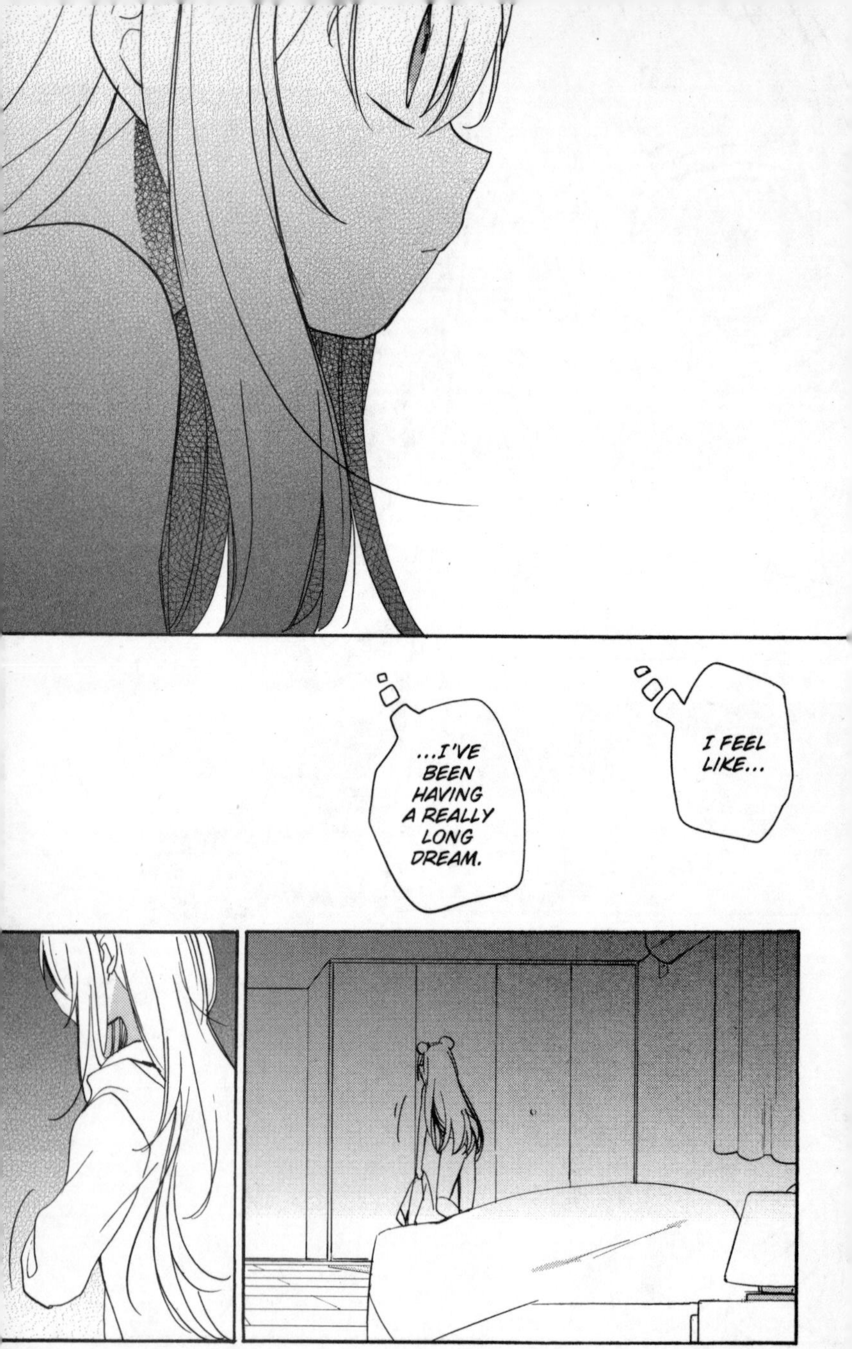
I FEEL LIKE...
...I'VE BEEN HAVING A REALLY LONG DREAM.

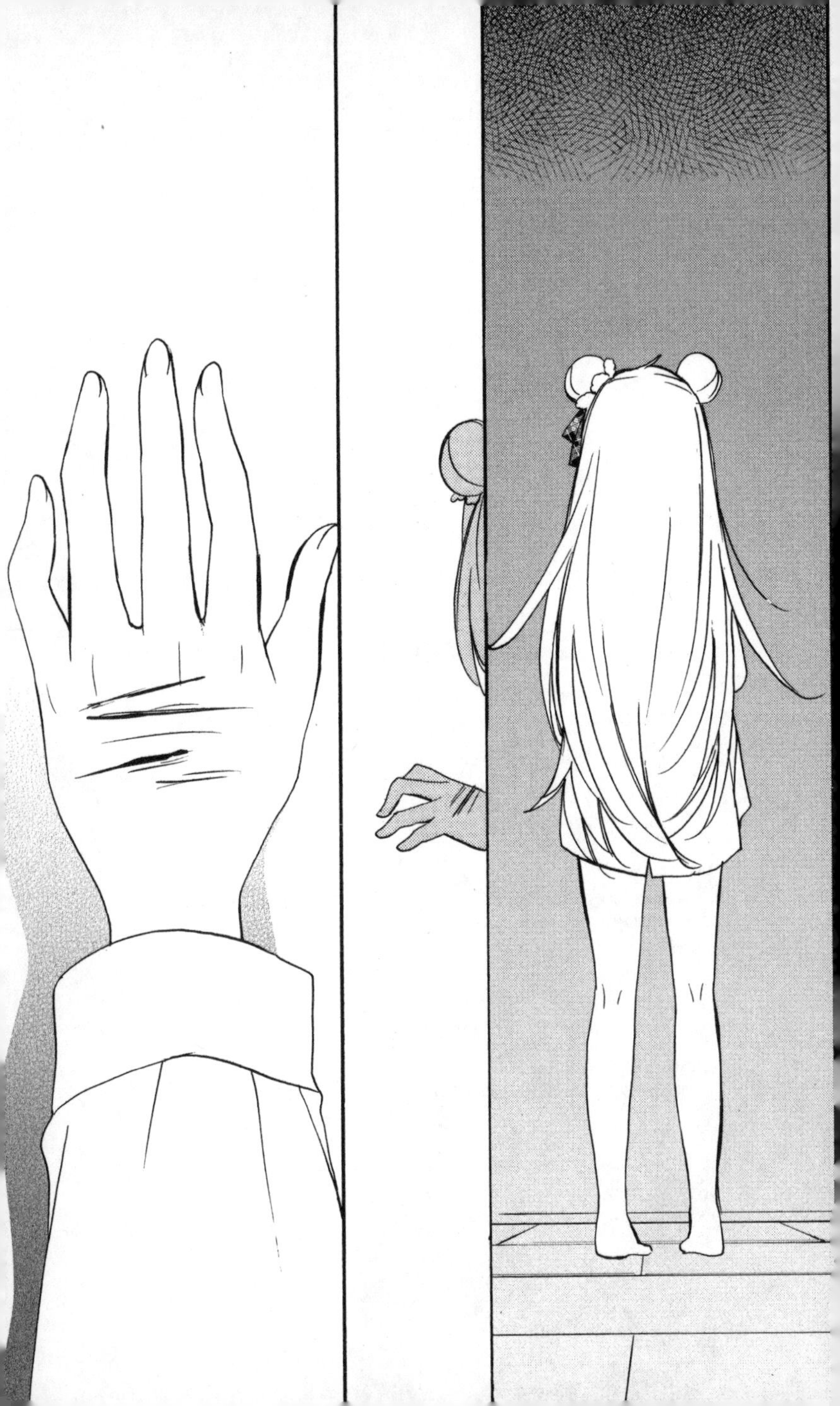

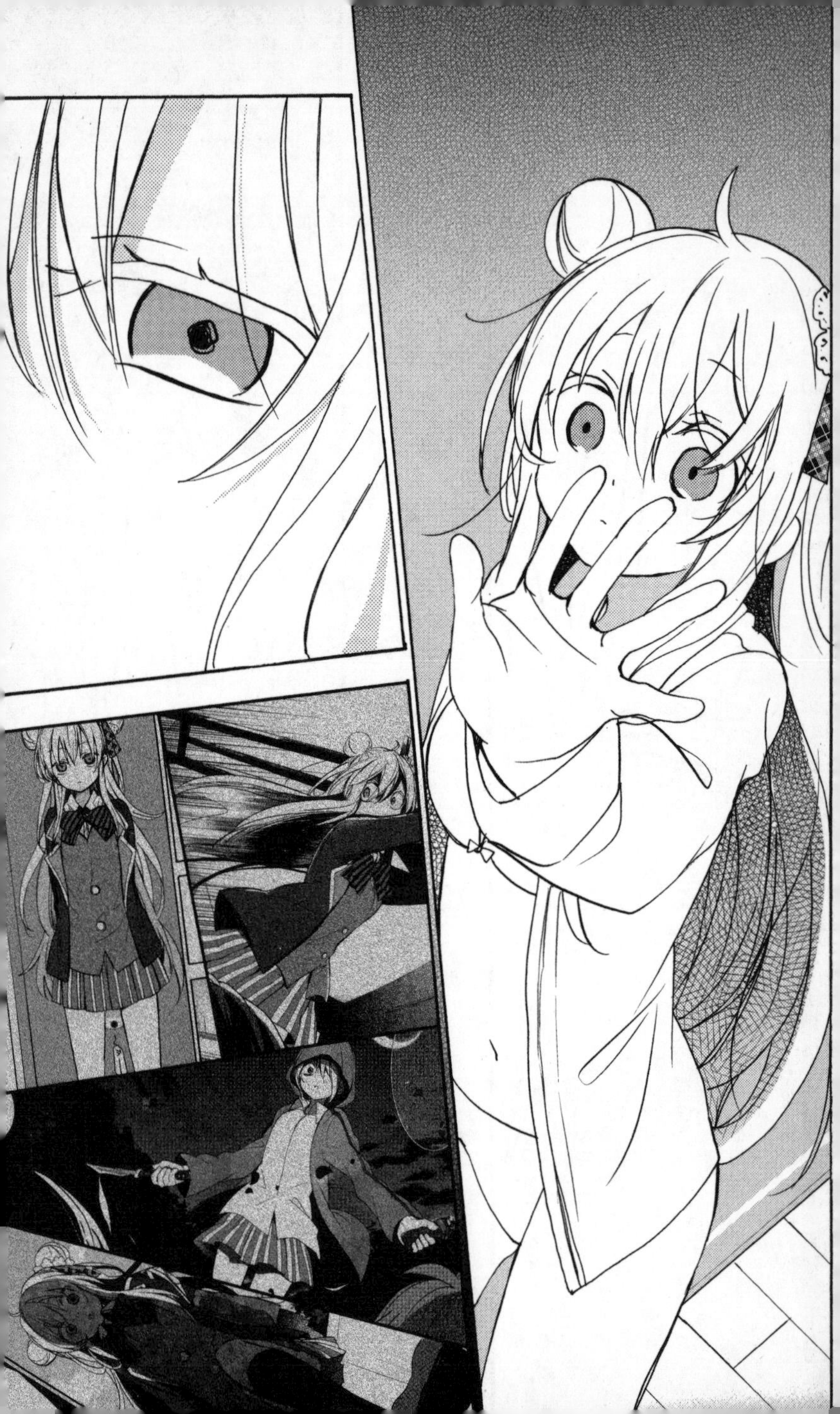

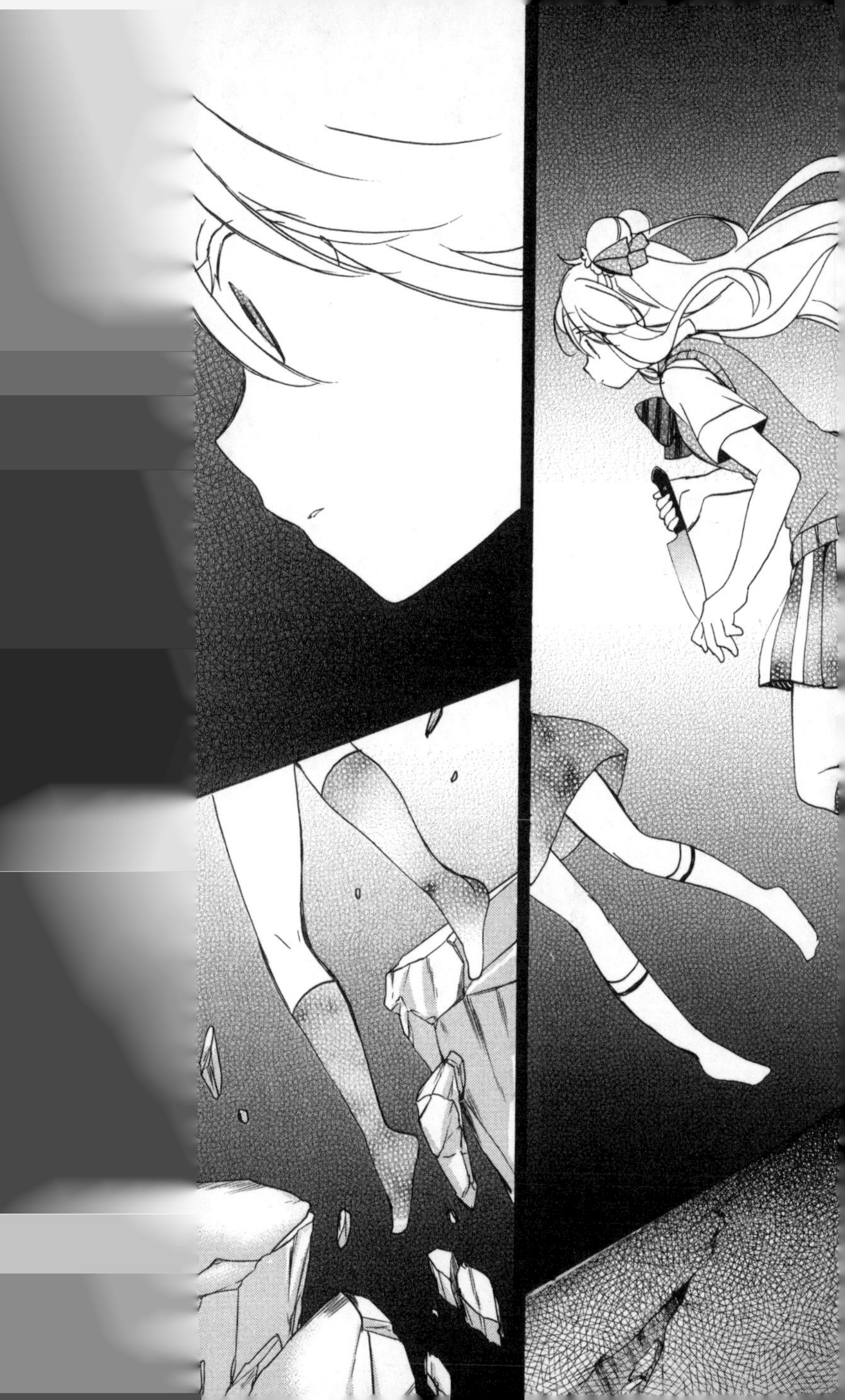

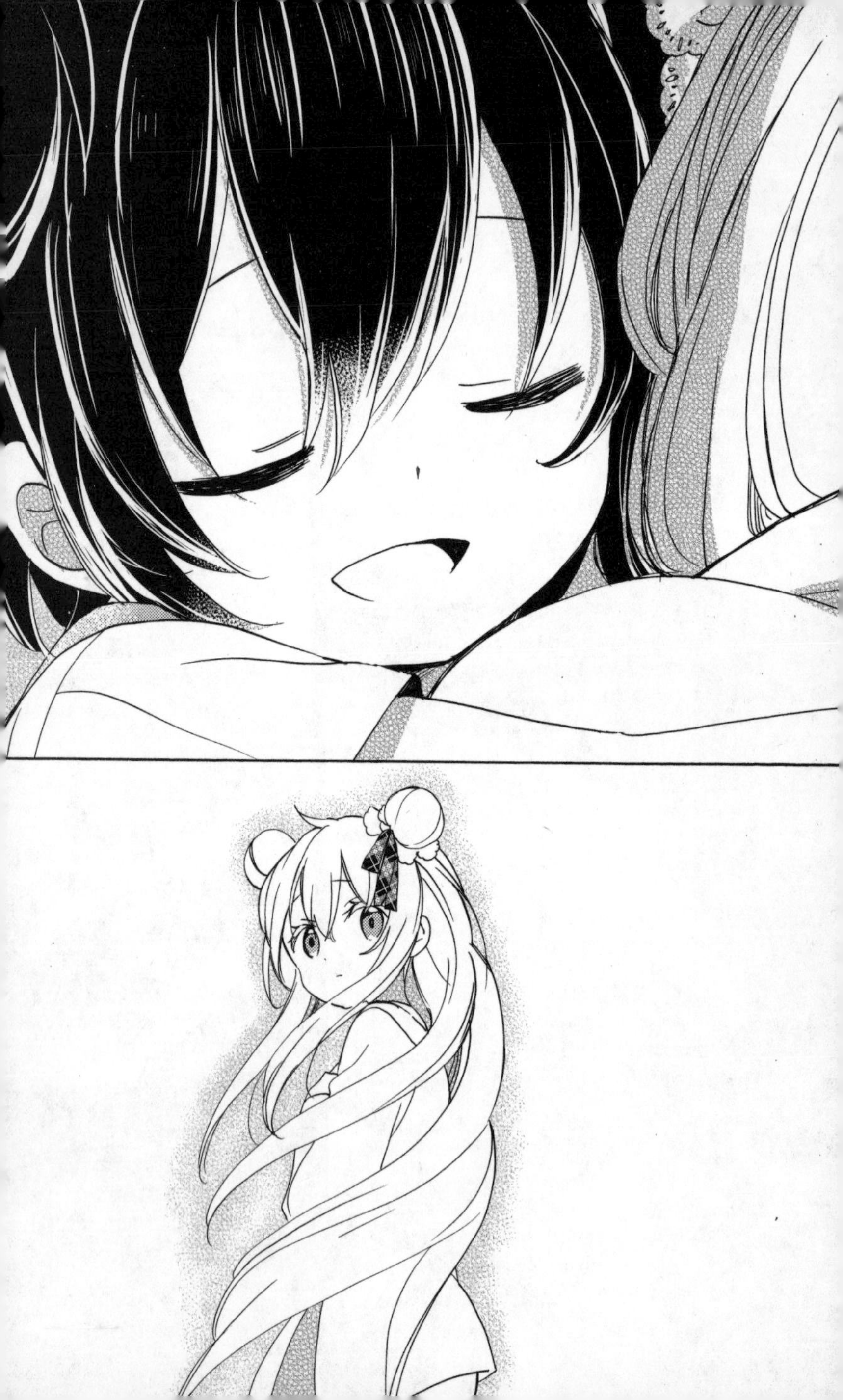

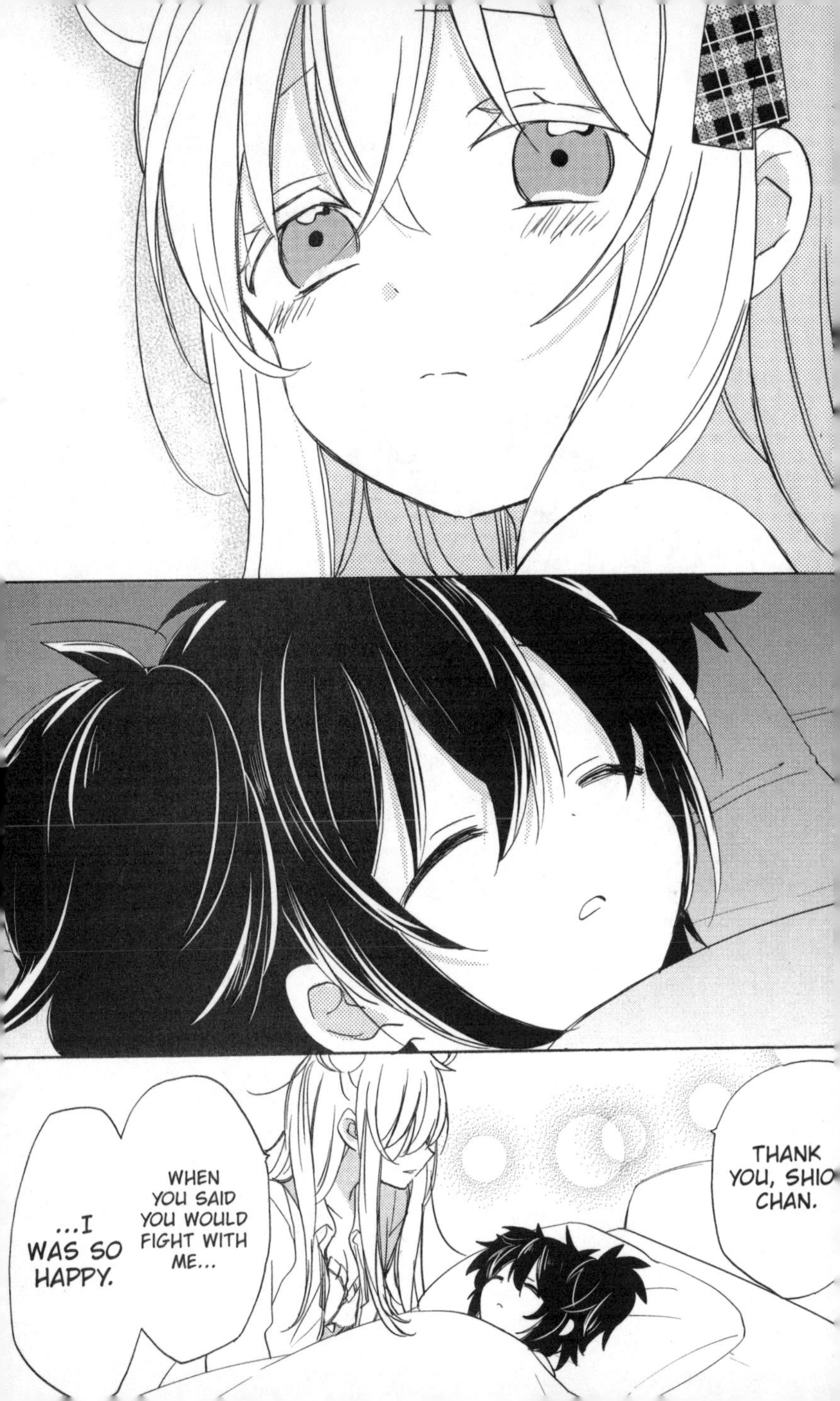
THANK YOU, SHIO CHAN.
WHEN YOU SAID YOU WOULD FIGHT WITH ME...
...I WAS SO HAPPY.

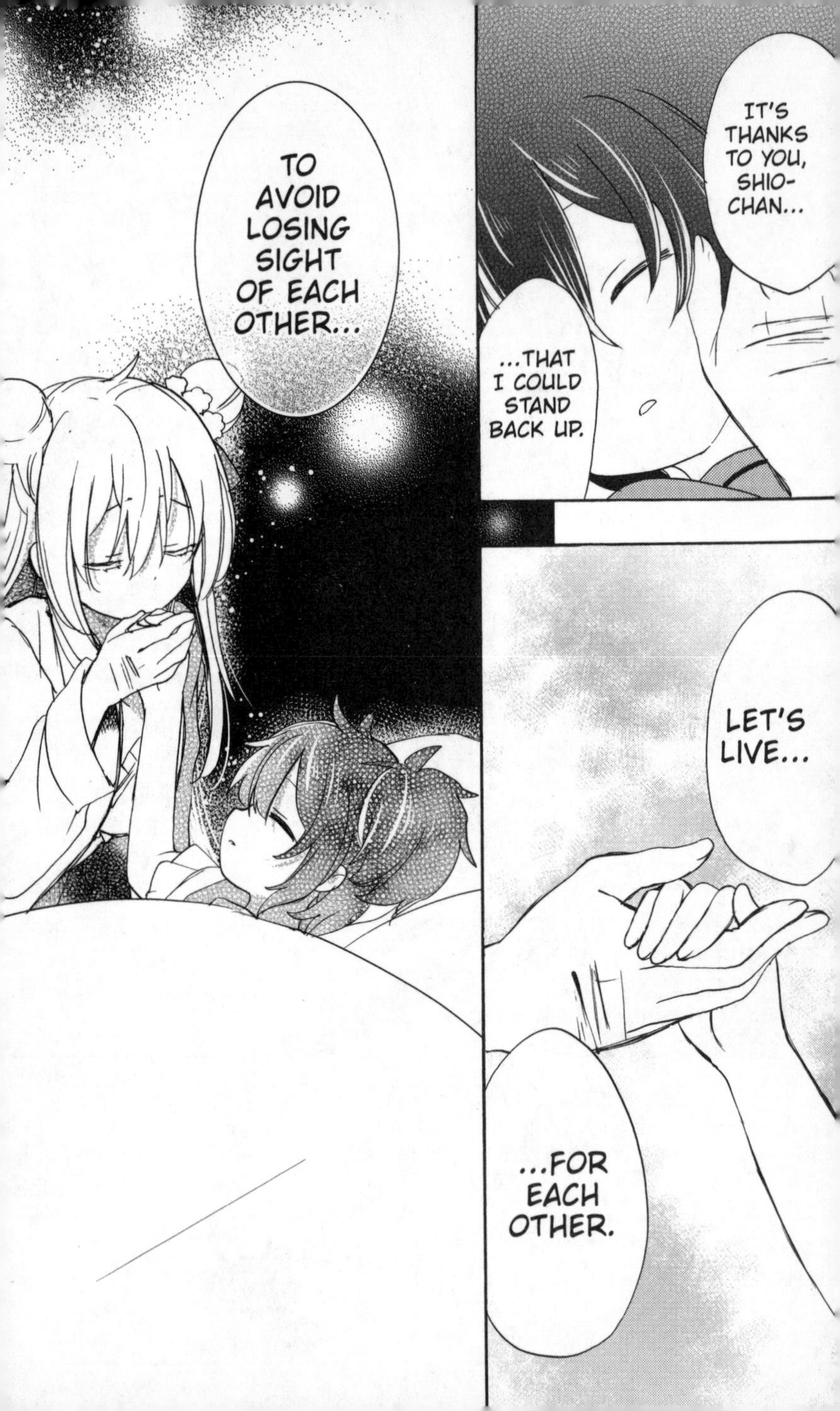
IT'S THANKS TO YOU, SHIO-CHAN...
...THAT I COULD STAND BACK UP.
LET'S LIVE...
...FOR EACH OTHER.
TO AVOID LOSING SIGHT OF EACH OTHER...

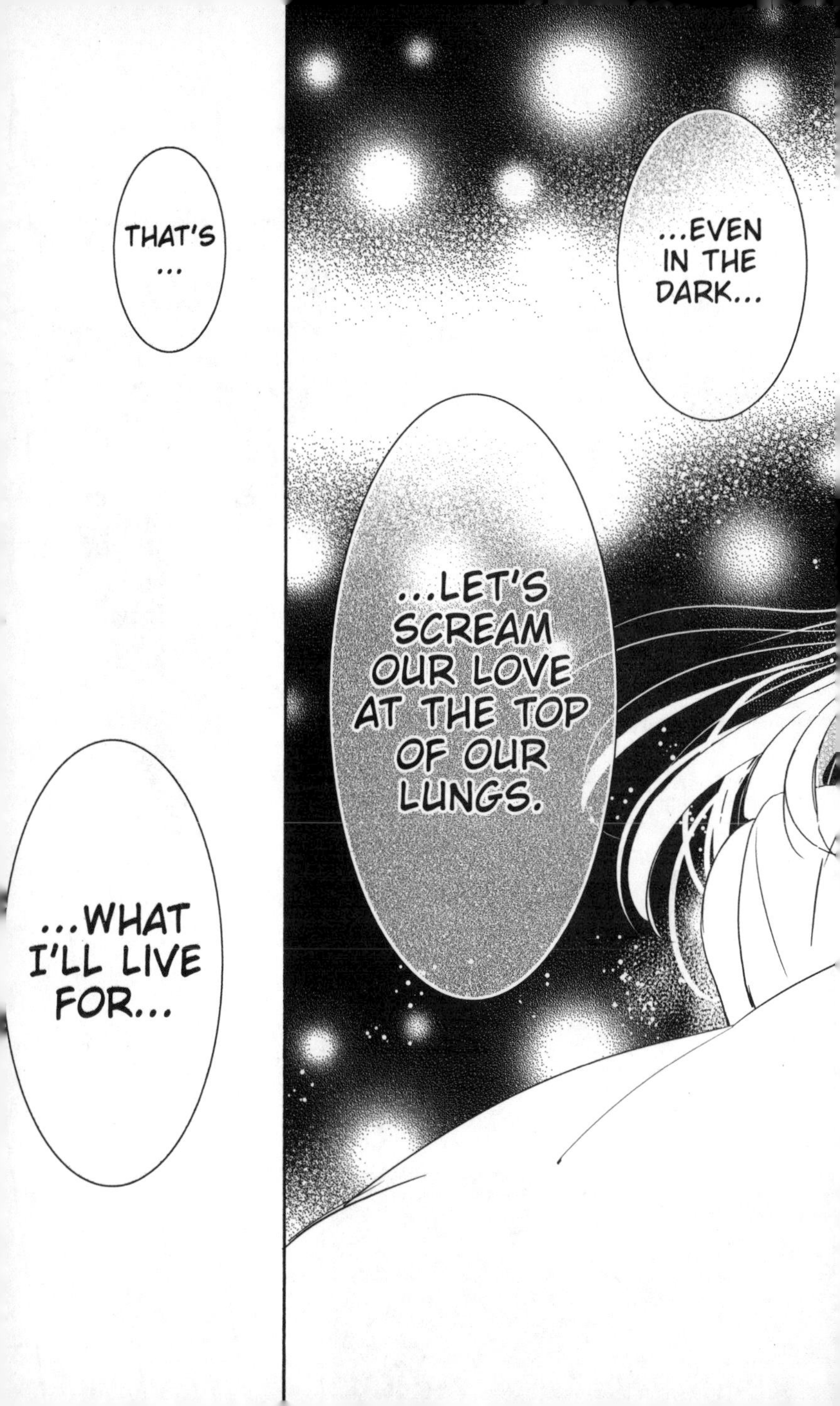
...EVEN IN THE DARK...
...LET'S SCREAM OUR LOVE AT THE TOP OF OUR LUNGS.
THAT'S ...
...WHAT I'LL LIVE FOR...

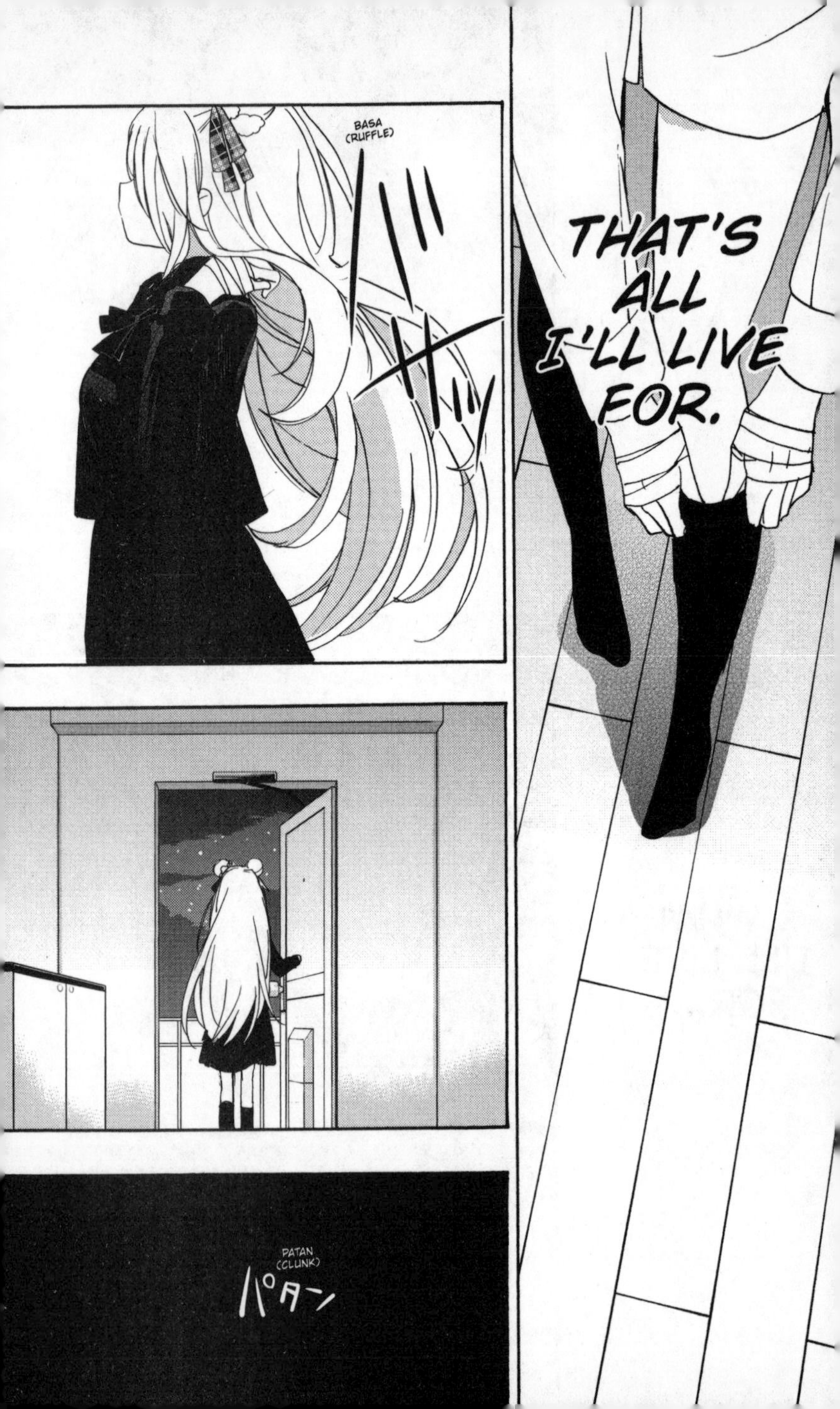
THAT'S ALL I'LL LIVE FOR.
BASA (RUFFLE)
PATAN (CLUNK)

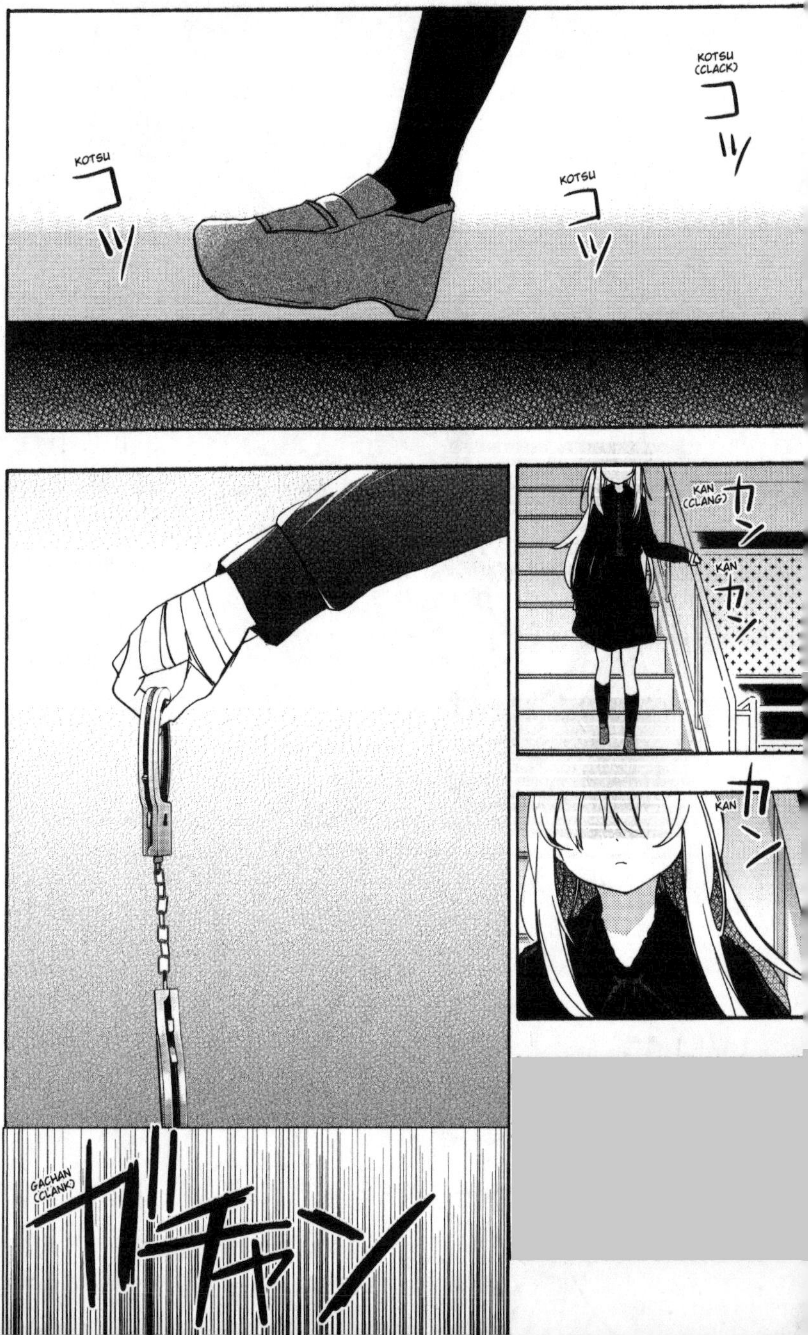
KOTSU (CLACK)
コッ
KOTSU
コッ
KOTSU
コッ
KAN (CLANG)
カン
KAN
カン
KAN
カン
GACHAN (CLANK)
ガチャン

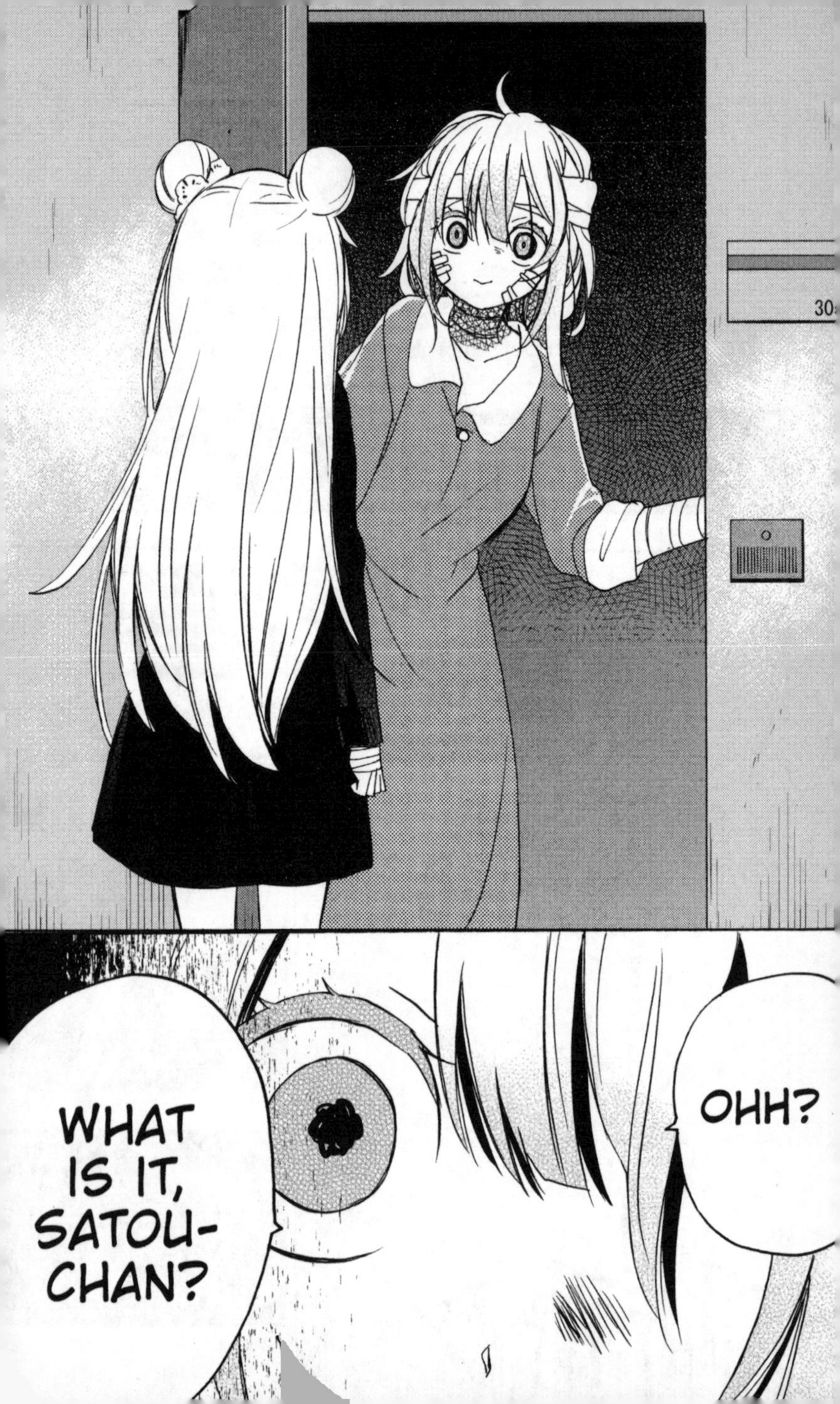
OHH?
WHAT IS IT, SATOU-CHAN?

33RD LIFE: NOISY

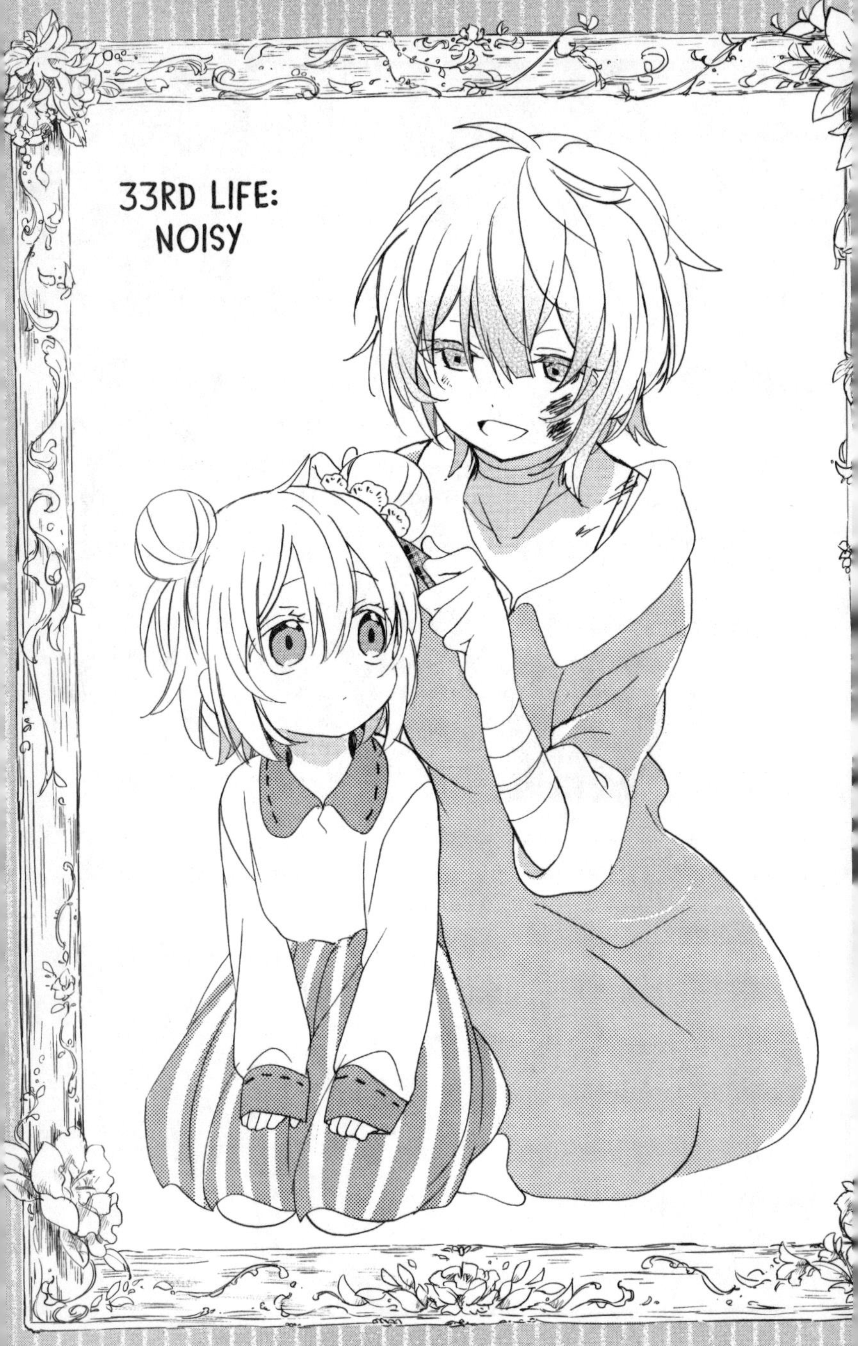

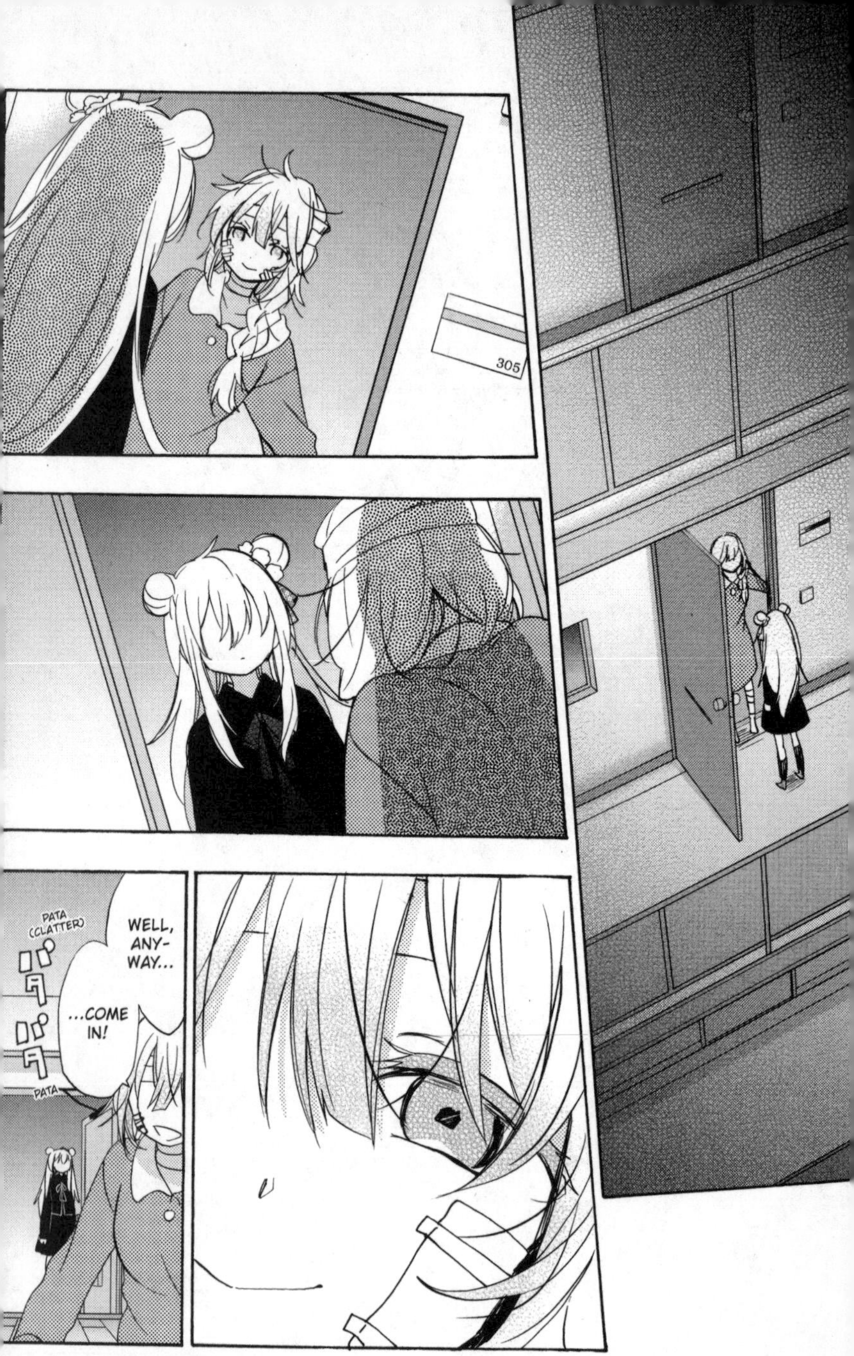
305
WELL, ANY-WAY...
...COME IN!
PATA (CLATTER)
PATA

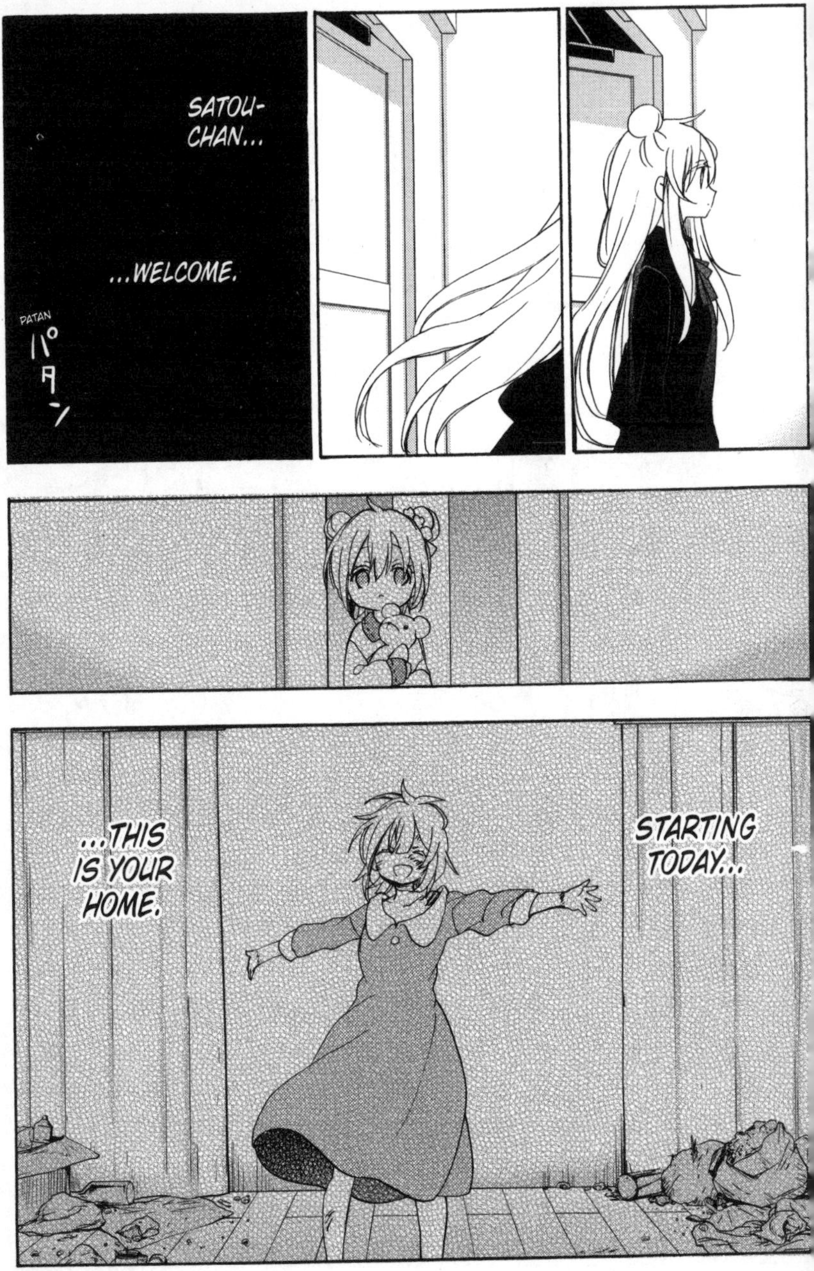
SATOU-CHAN...
...WELCOME.
PATAN
パタン
STARTING TODAY...
...THIS IS YOUR HOME.

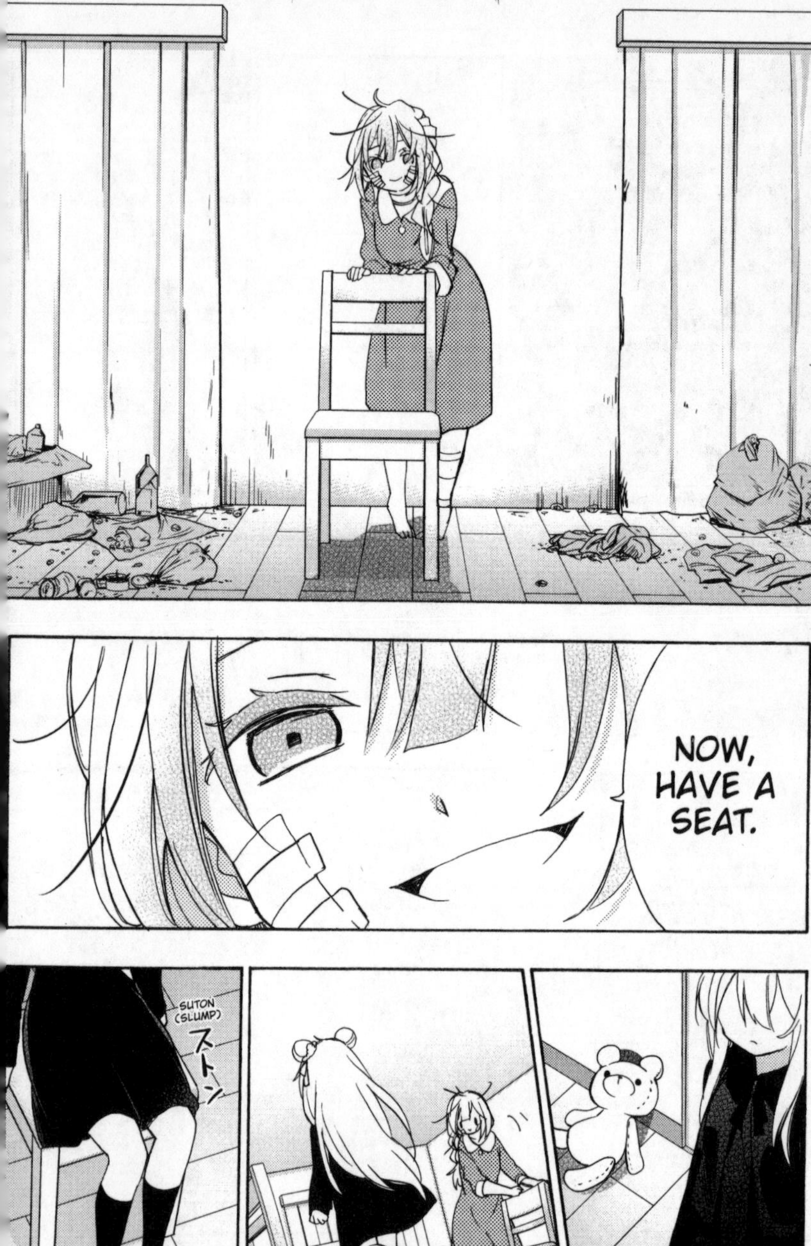
NOW, HAVE A SEAT.
SUTON (SLUMP)
ストン

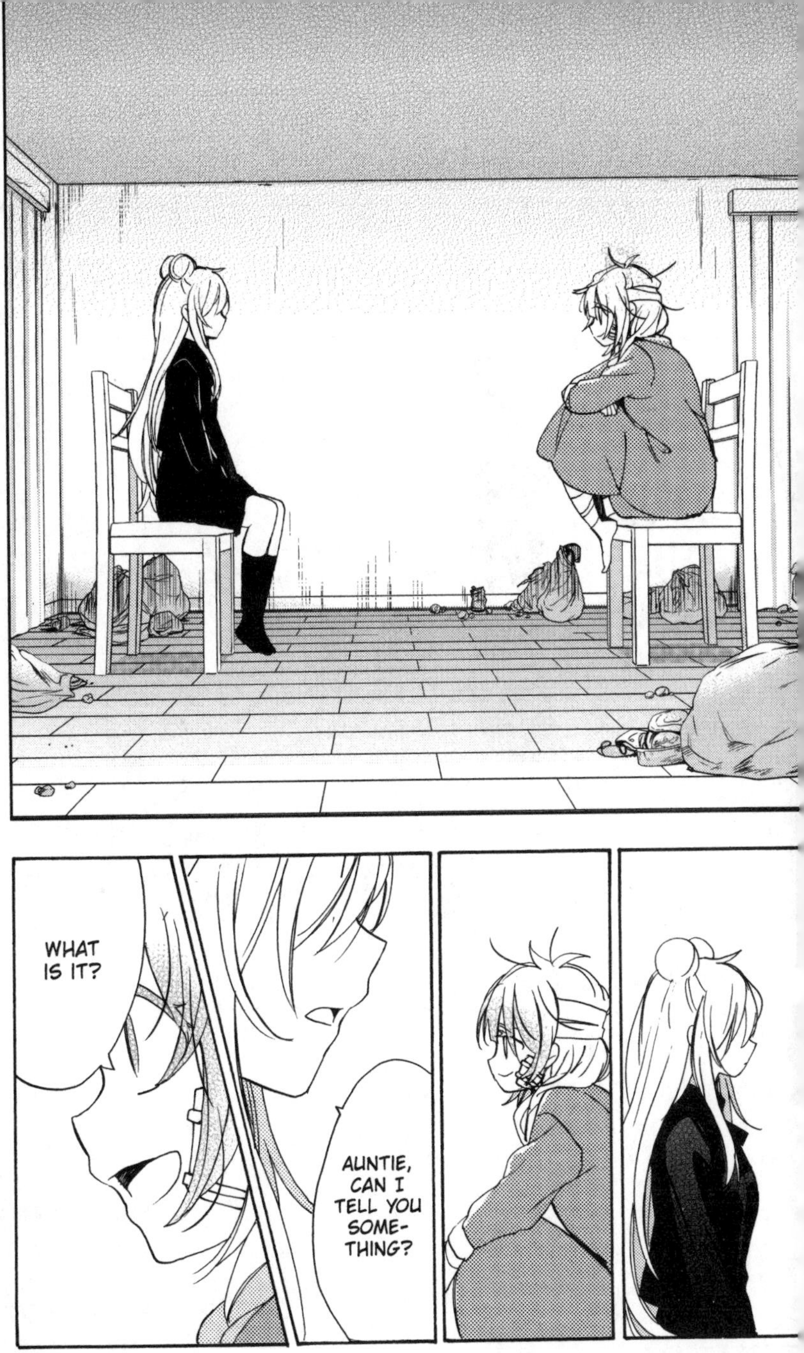
AUNTIE, CAN I TELL YOU SOME-THING?
WHAT IS IT?

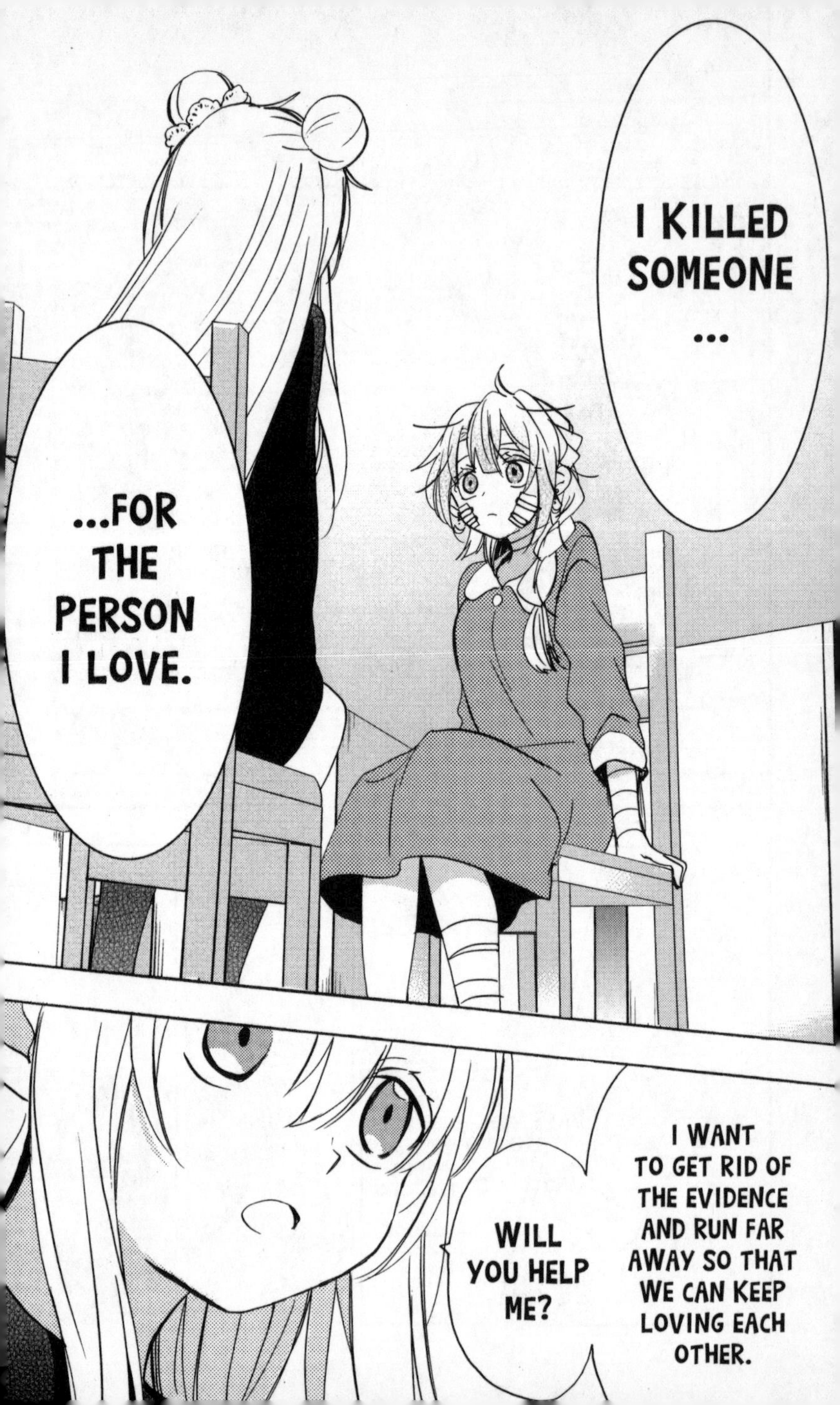
I KILLED SOMEONE ...
...FOR THE PERSON I LOVE.
I WANT TO GET RID OF THE EVIDENCE AND RUN FAR AWAY SO THAT WE CAN KEEP LOVING EACH OTHER.
WILL YOU HELP ME?

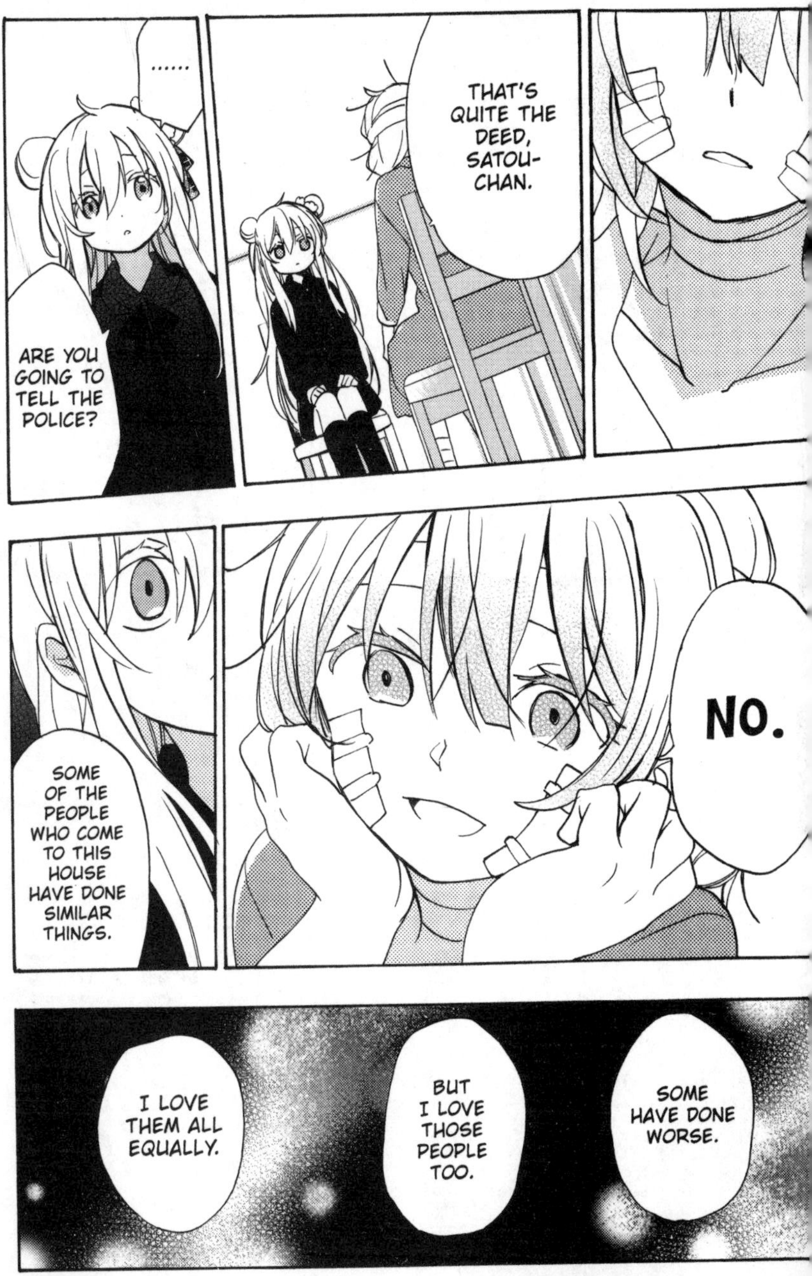
THAT'S QUITE THE DEED, SATOU-CHAN.
......
ARE YOU GOING TO TELL THE POLICE?
NO.
SOME OF THE PEOPLE WHO COME TO THIS HOUSE HAVE DONE SIMILAR THINGS.
SOME HAVE DONE WORSE.
BUT I LOVE THOSE PEOPLE TOO.
I LOVE THEM ALL EQUALLY.

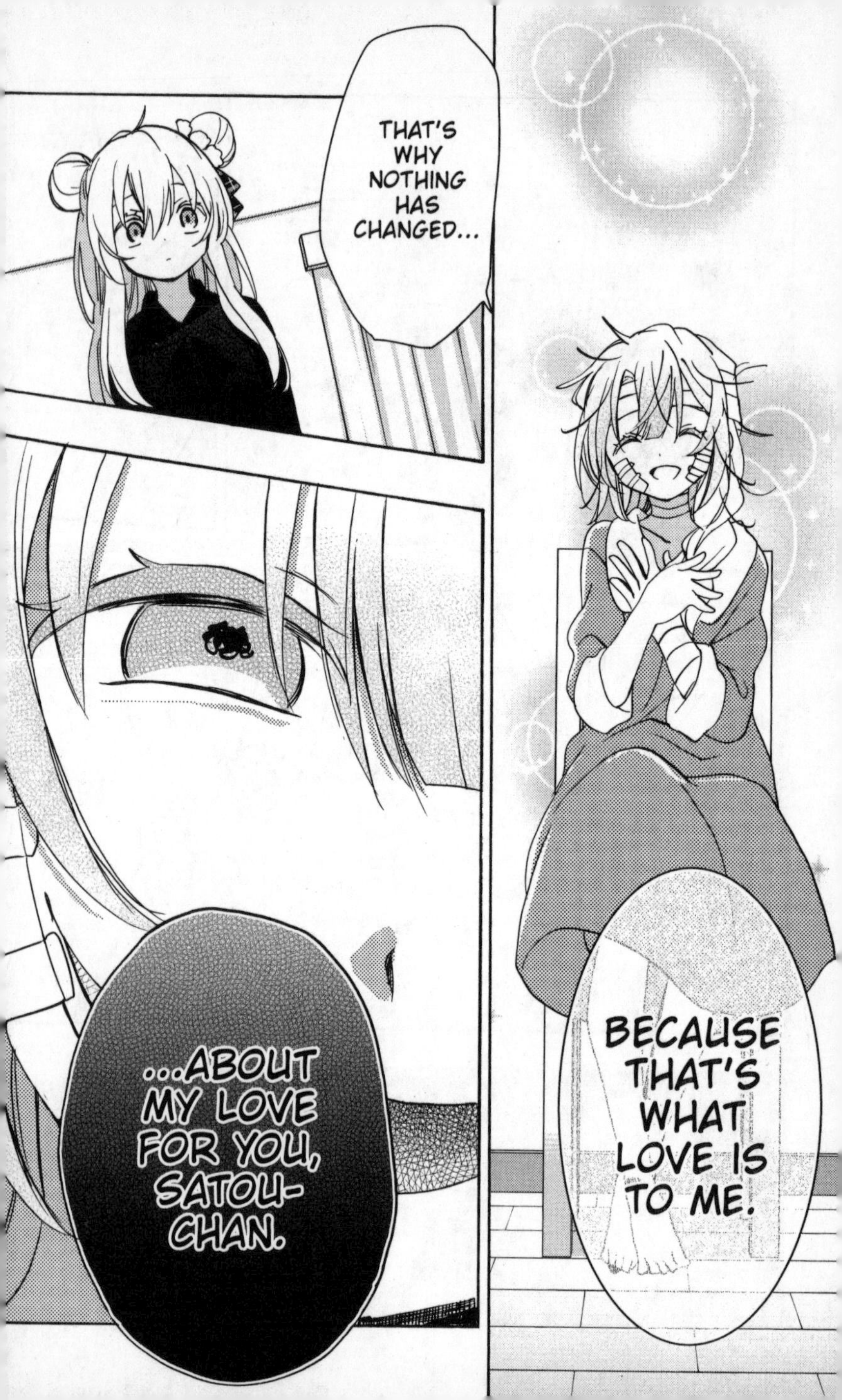
BECAUSE THAT'S WHAT LOVE IS TO ME.
THAT'S WHY NOTHING HAS CHANGED...
...ABOUT MY LOVE FOR YOU, SATOU-CHAN.

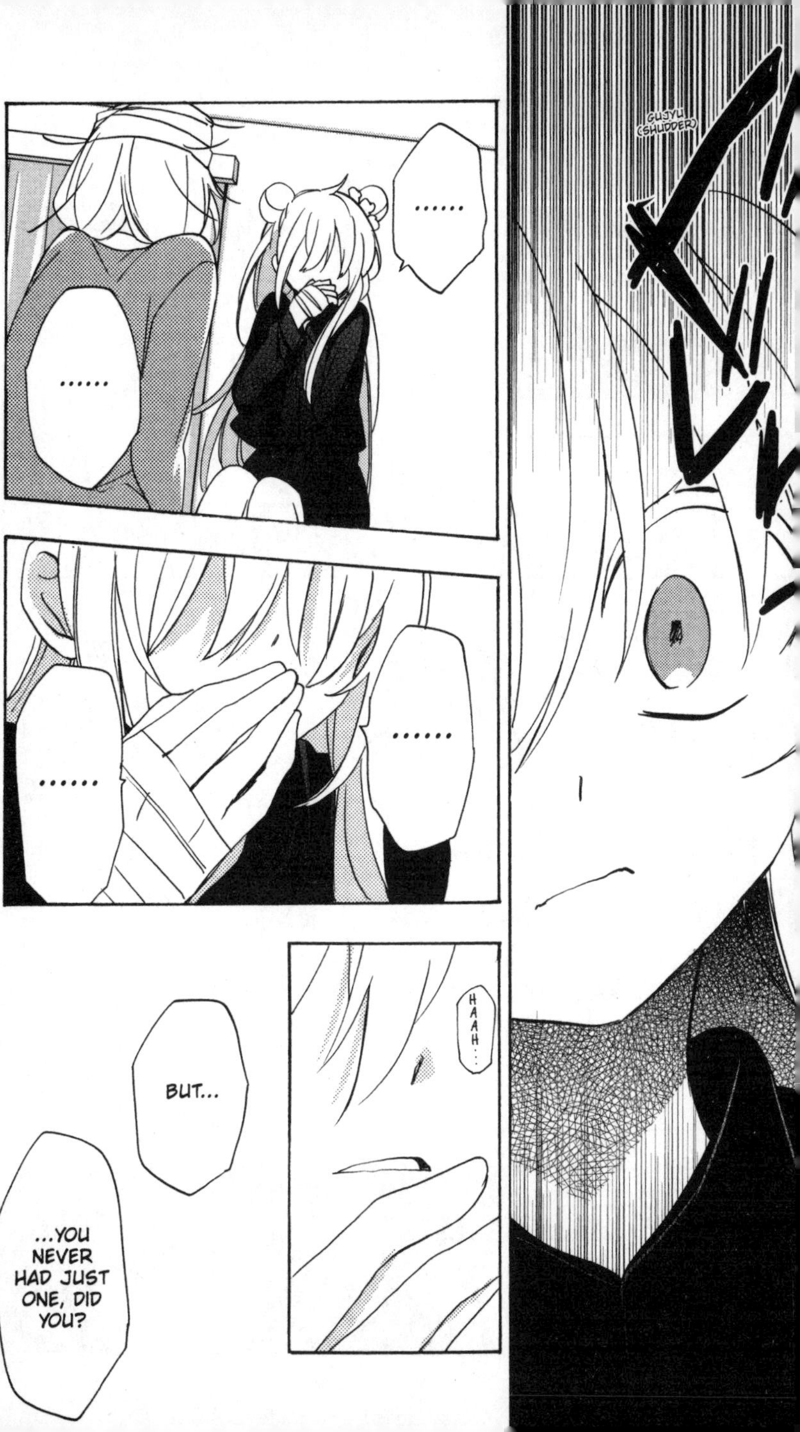
GUJYU (SHUDDER)
......
......
......
......
HAAH...
BUT...
...YOU NEVER HAD JUST ONE, DID YOU?

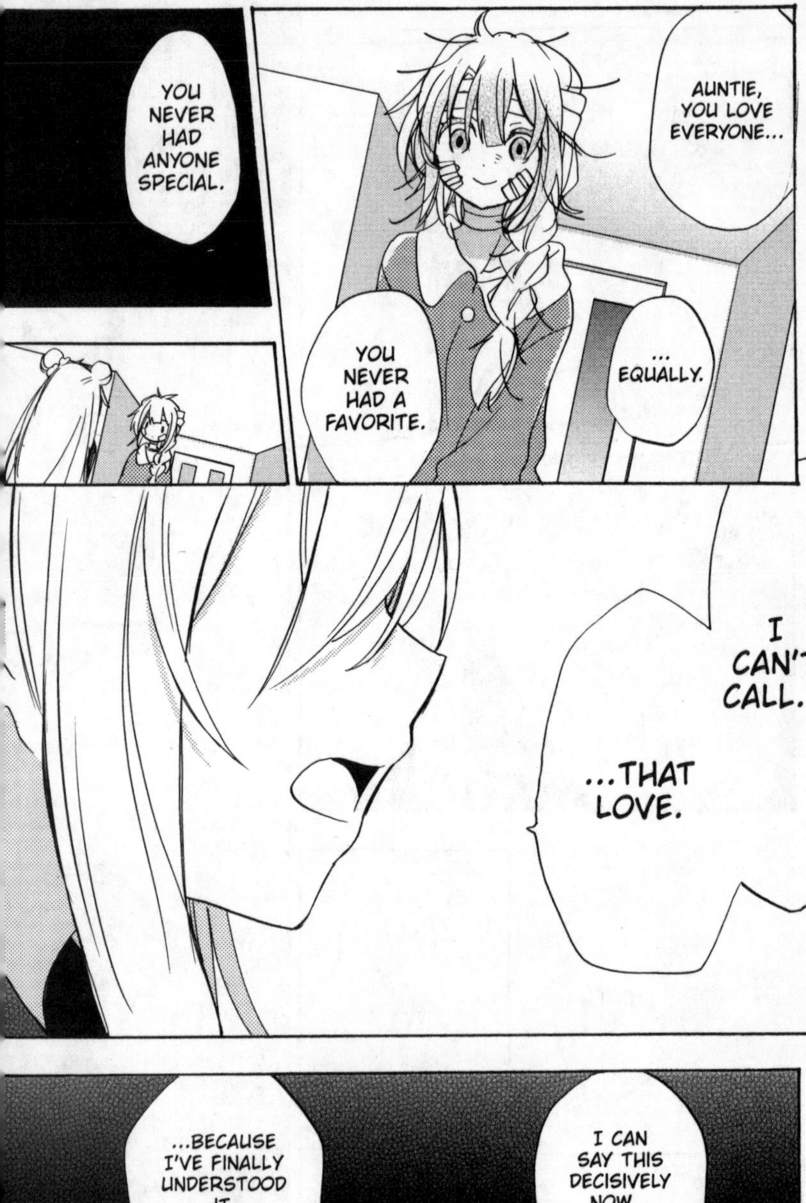
AUNTIE, YOU LOVE EVERYONE...
...EQUALLY.
YOU NEVER HAD A FAVORITE.
YOU NEVER HAD ANYONE SPECIAL.
I CAN'T CALL...
...THAT LOVE.
I CAN SAY THIS DECISIVELY NOW...
...BECAUSE I'VE FINALLY UNDERSTOOD IT.

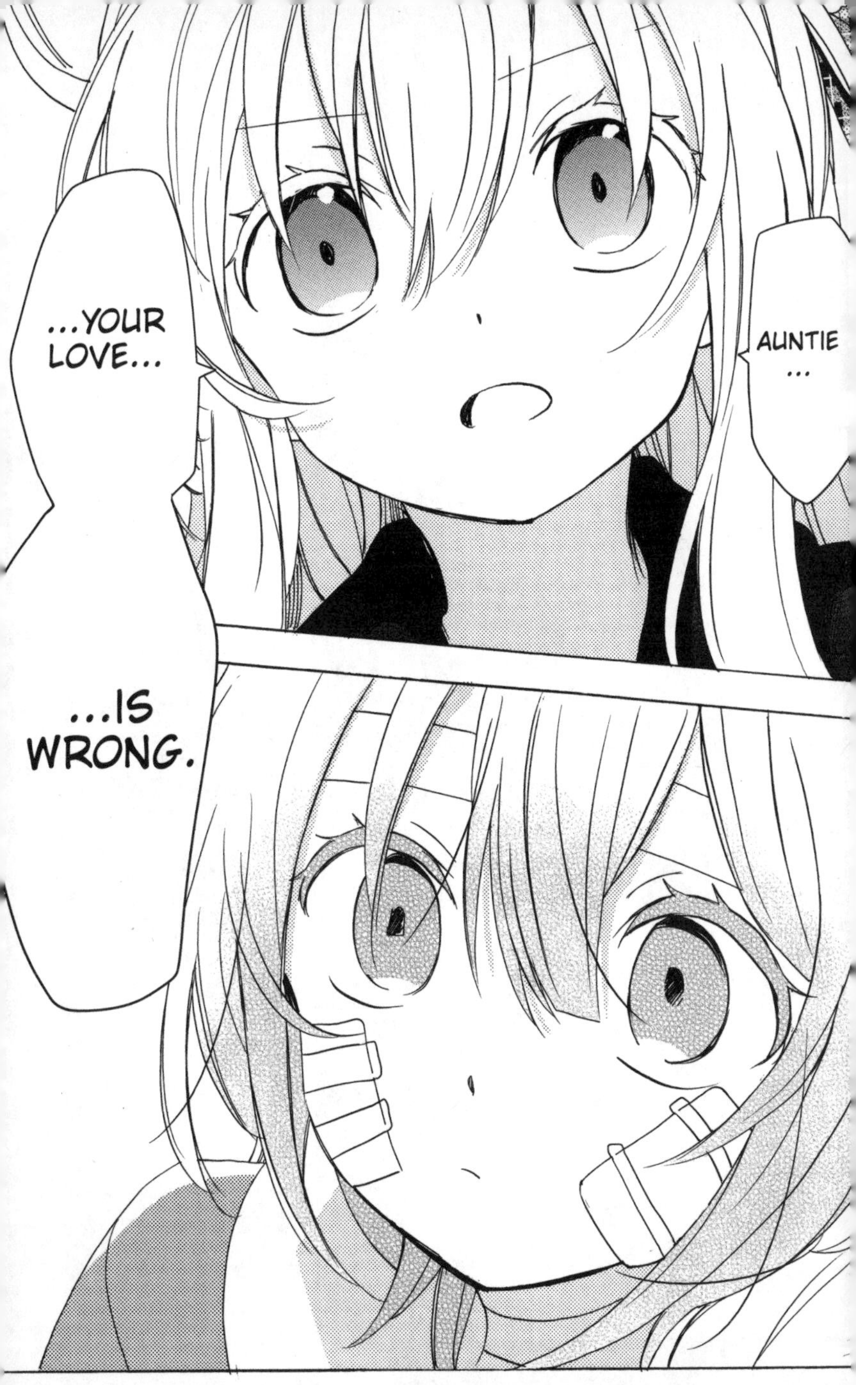
AUNTIE
...
...YOUR LOVE...
...IS WRONG.

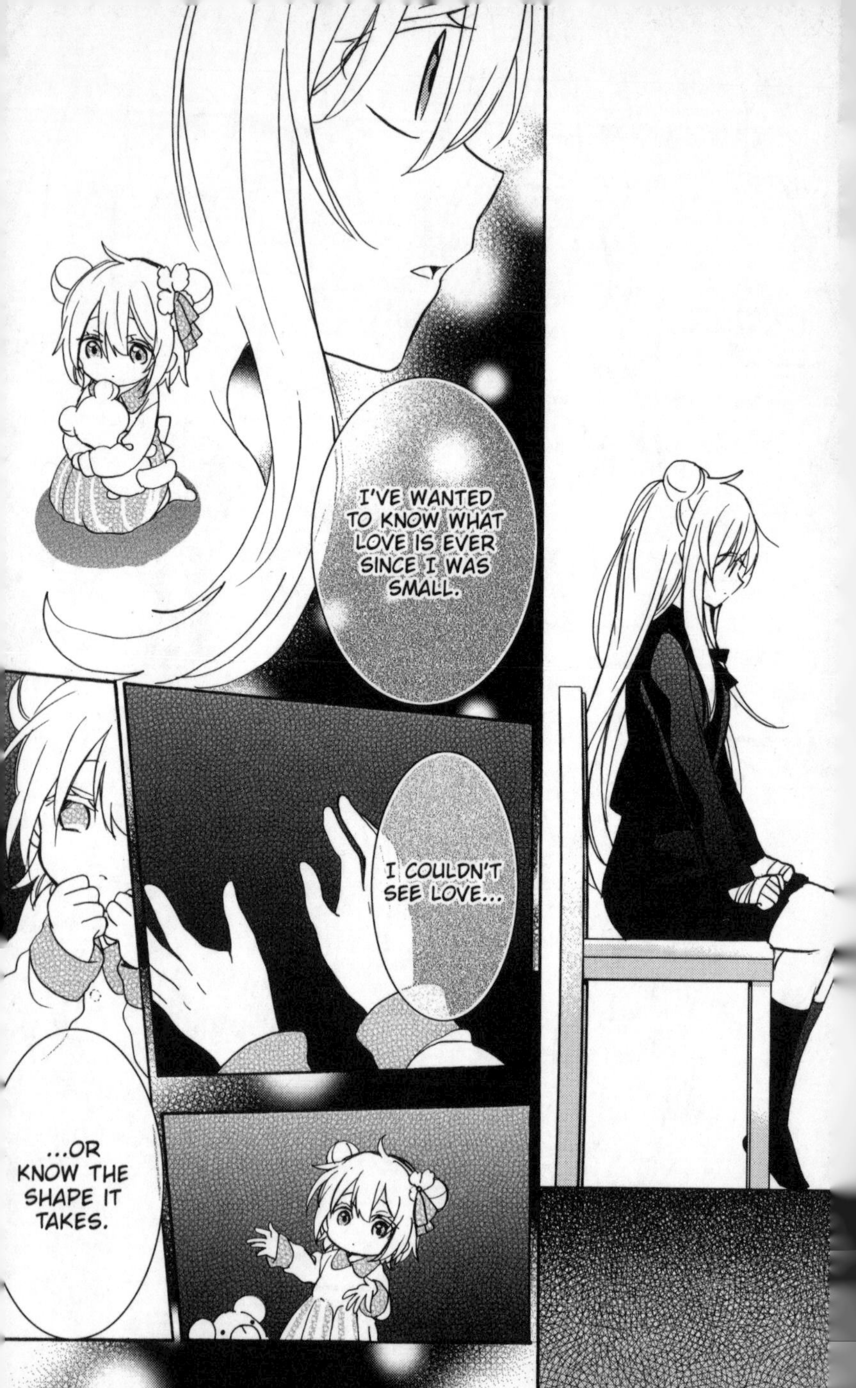
I'VE WANTED TO KNOW WHAT LOVE IS EVER SINCE I WAS SMALL.
I COULDN'T SEE LOVE...
...OR KNOW THE SHAPE IT TAKES.

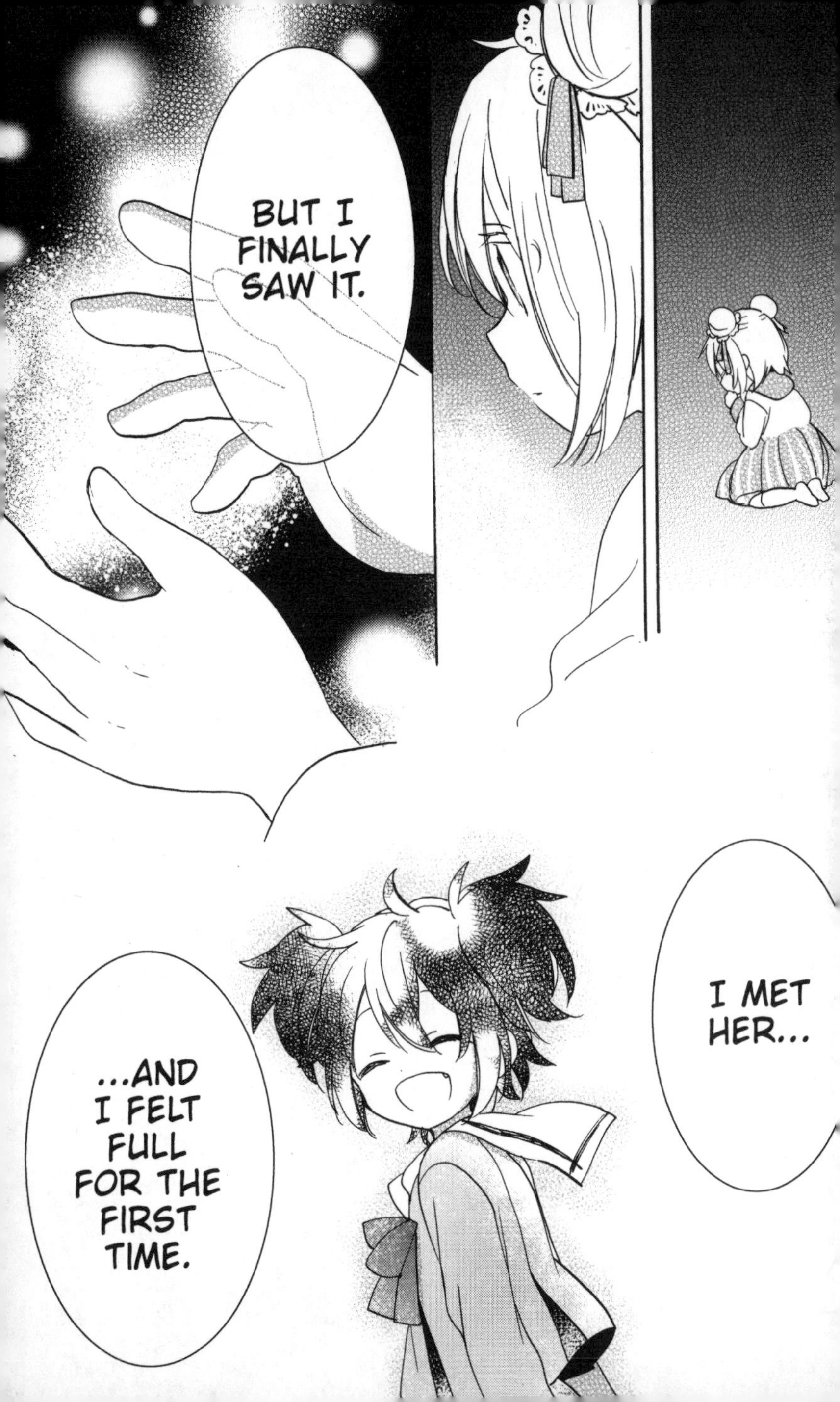
BUT I FINALLY SAW IT.
I MET HER...
...AND I FELT FULL FOR THE FIRST TIME.

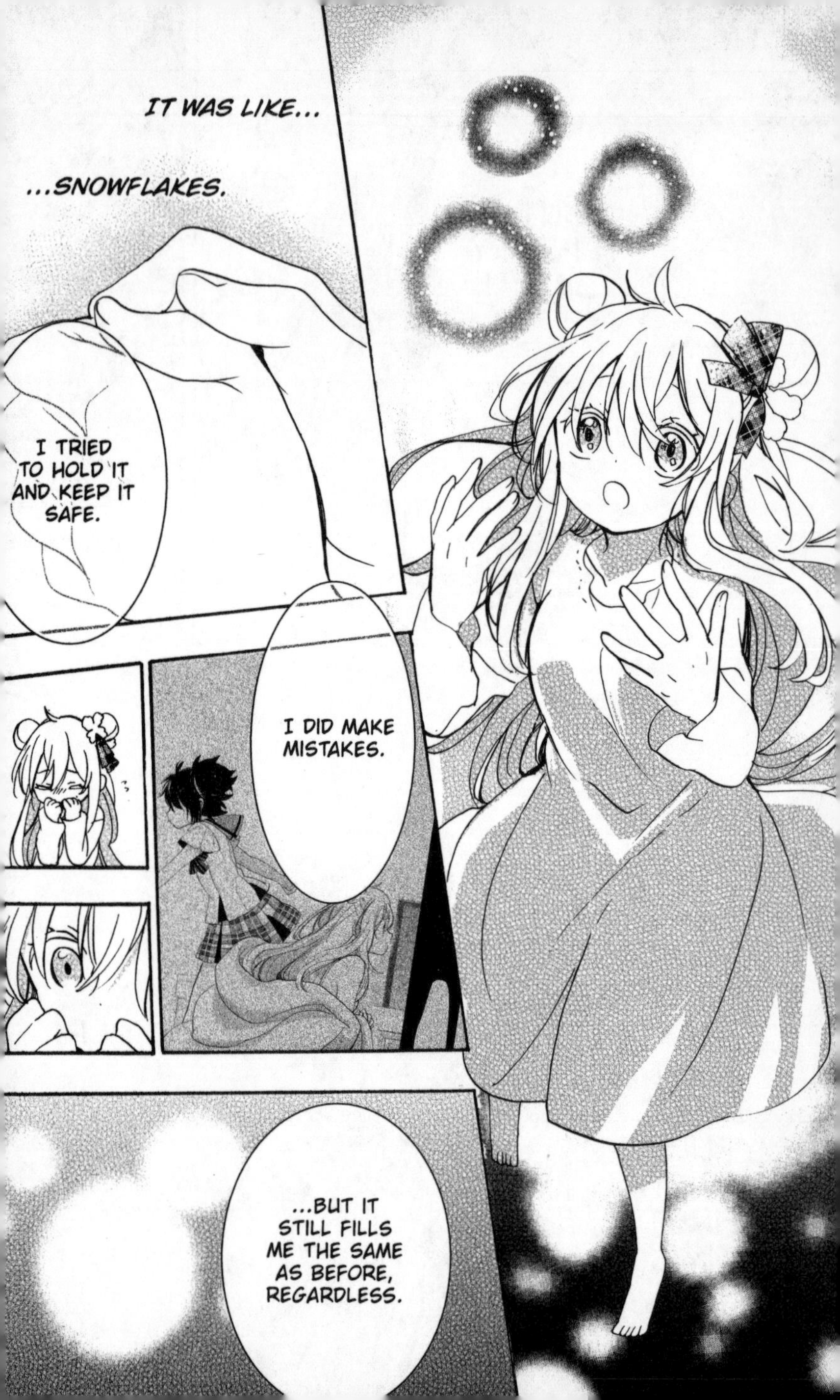
IT WAS LIKE...
...SNOWFLAKES.
I TRIED TO HOLD IT AND KEEP IT SAFE.
I DID MAKE MISTAKES.
...BUT IT STILL FILLS ME THE SAME AS BEFORE, REGARDLESS.

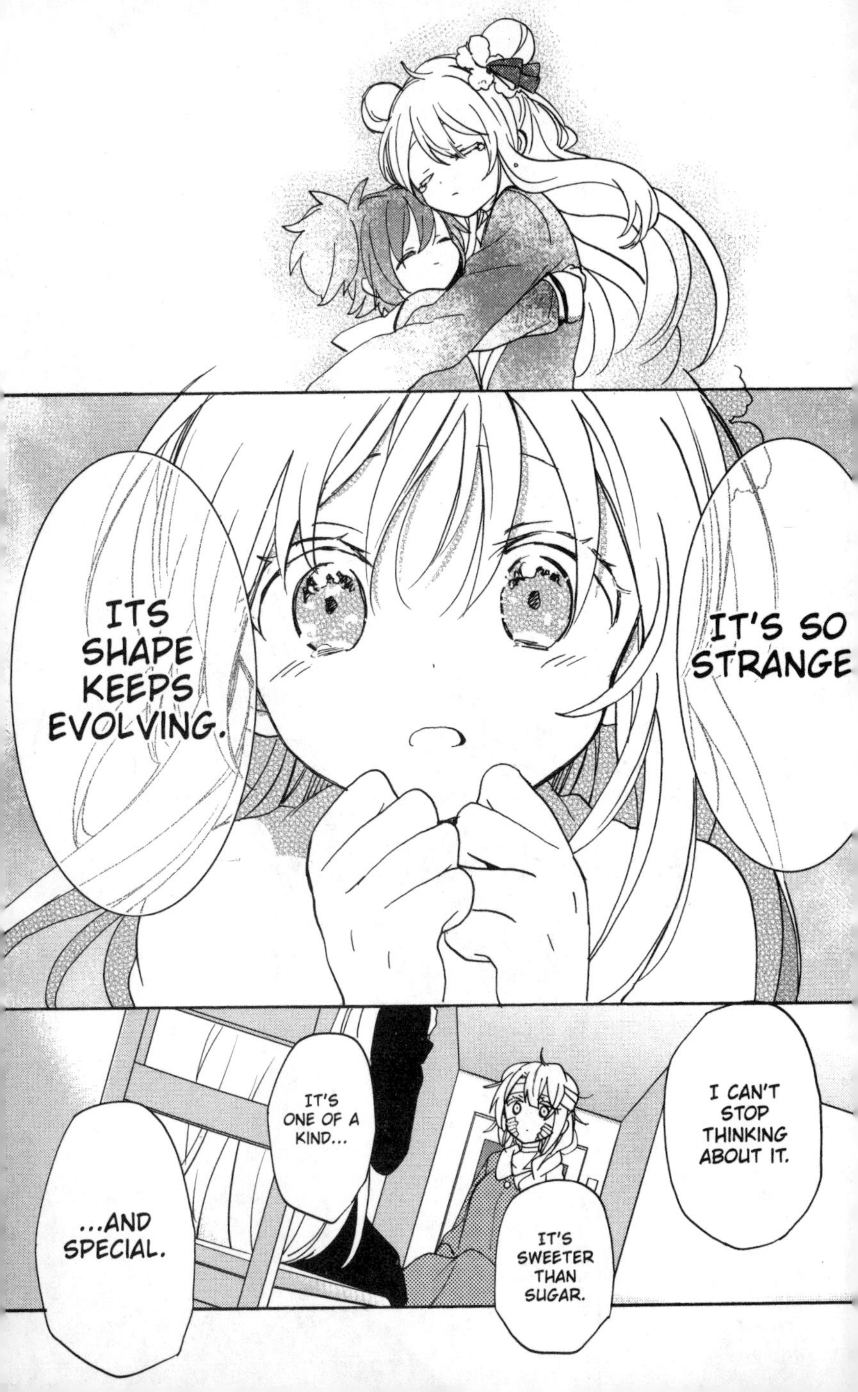
IT'S SO STRANGE
ITS SHAPE KEEPS EVOLVING.
I CAN'T STOP THINKING ABOUT IT.
IT'S ONE OF A KIND...
IT'S SWEETER THAN SUGAR.
...AND SPECIAL.

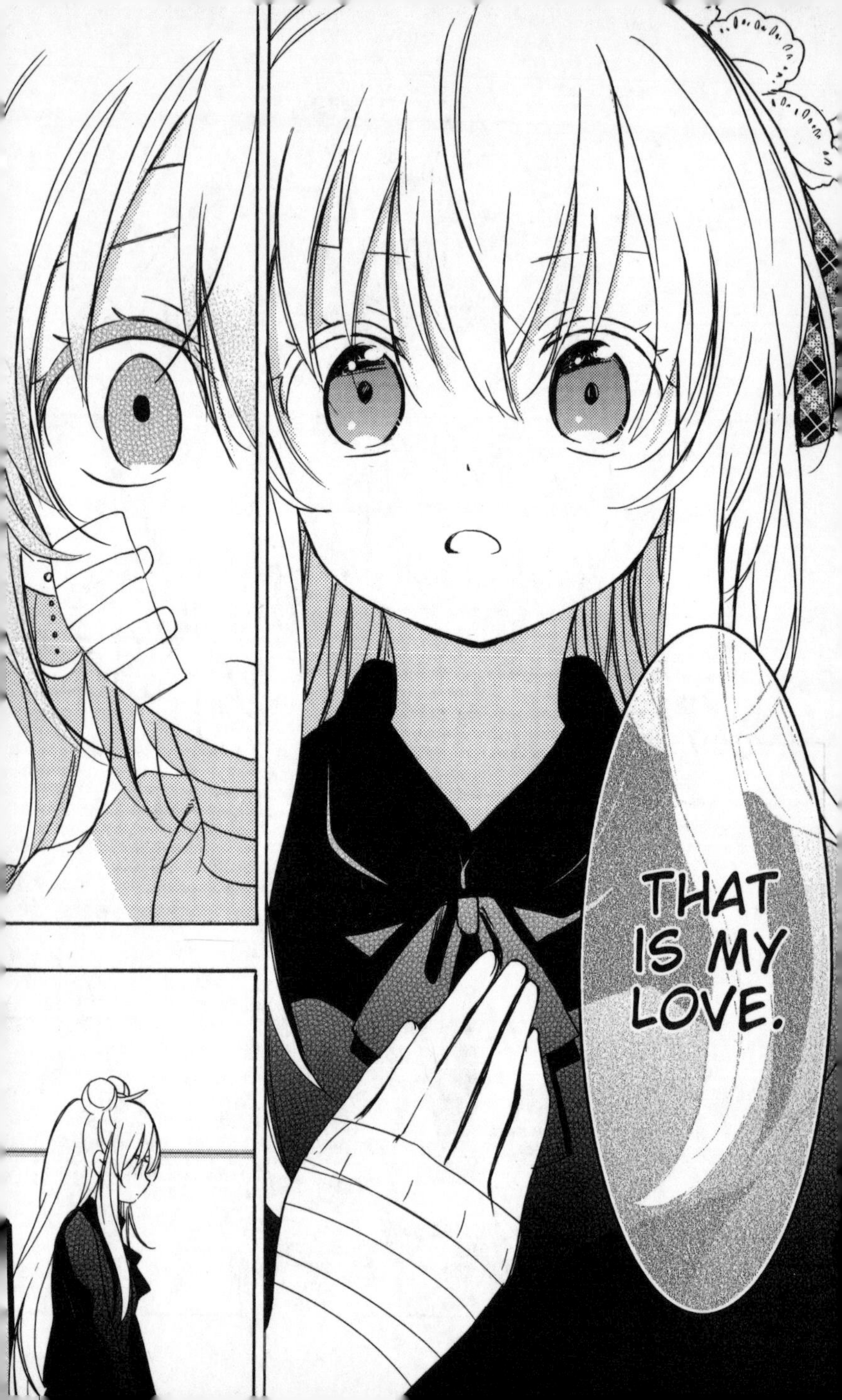
THAT IS MY LOVE.

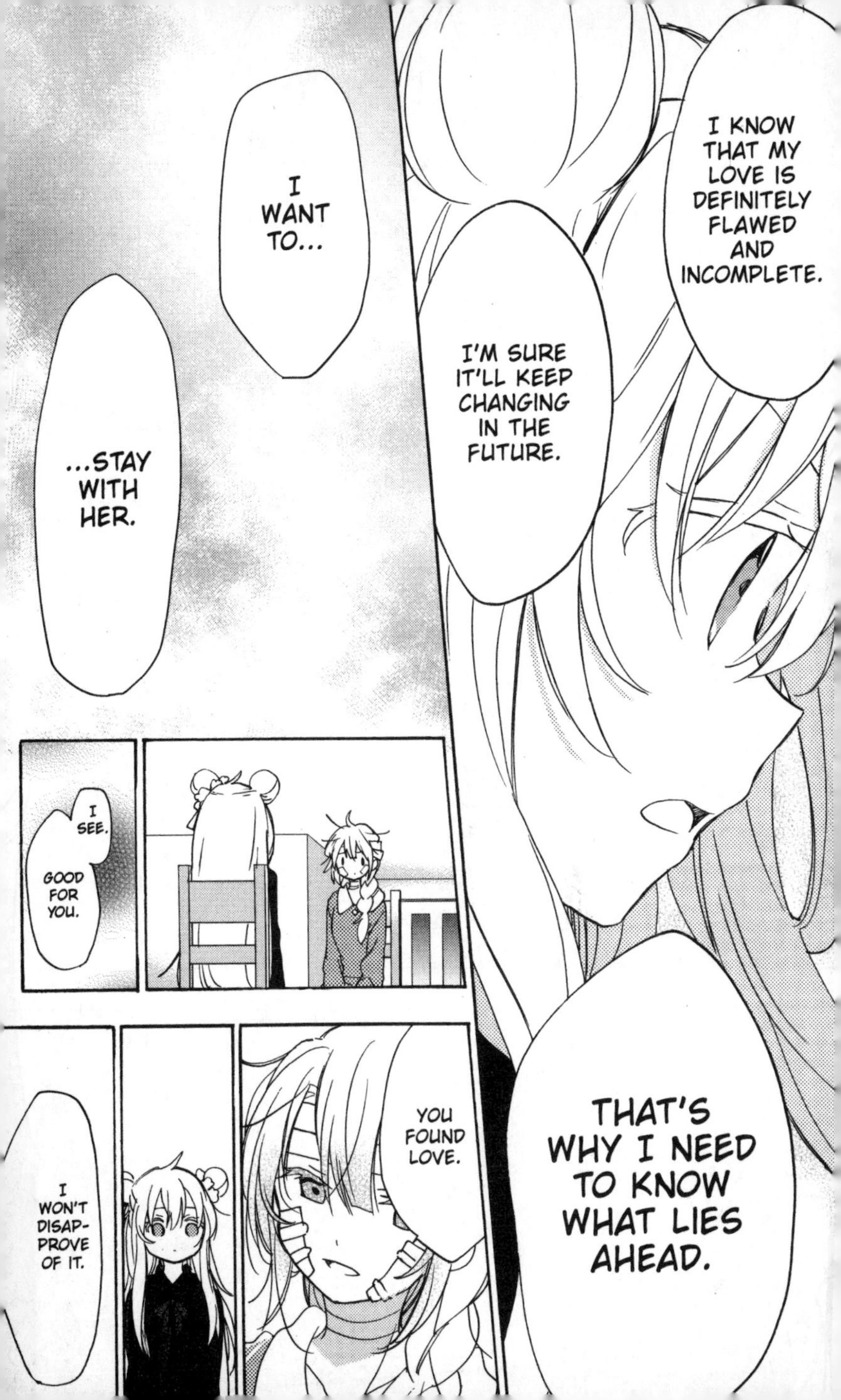
I KNOW THAT MY LOVE IS DEFINITELY FLAWED AND INCOMPLETE.
I'M SURE IT'LL KEEP CHANGING IN THE FUTURE.
THAT'S WHY I NEED TO KNOW WHAT LIES AHEAD.
I WANT TO...
...STAY WITH HER.
I SEE.
GOOD FOR YOU.
YOU FOUND LOVE.
I WON'T DISAPPROVE OF IT.

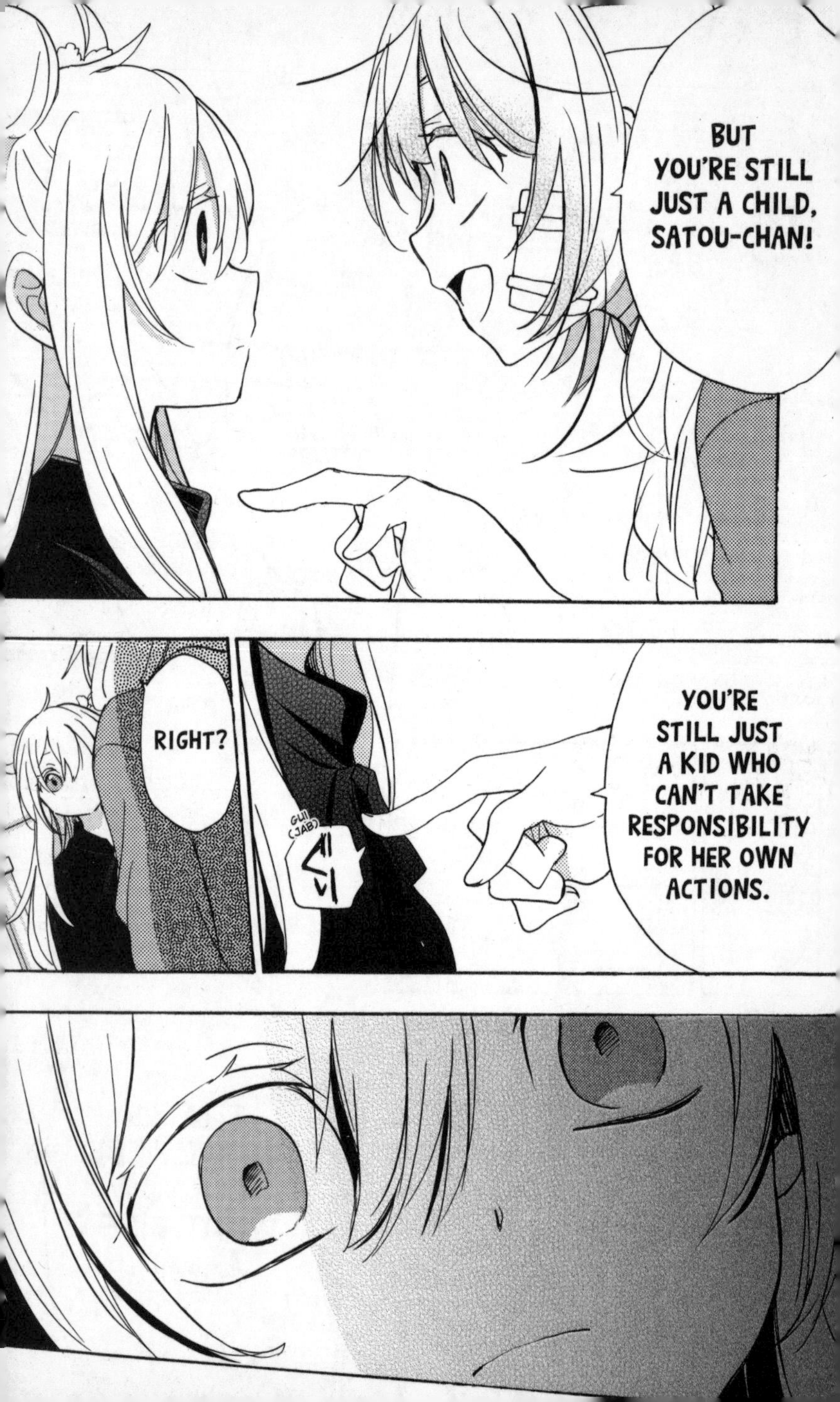
BUT YOU'RE STILL JUST A CHILD, SATOU-CHAN!
YOU'RE STILL JUST A KID WHO CAN'T TAKE RESPONSIBILITY FOR HER OWN ACTIONS.
GUI (JAB)
RIGHT?

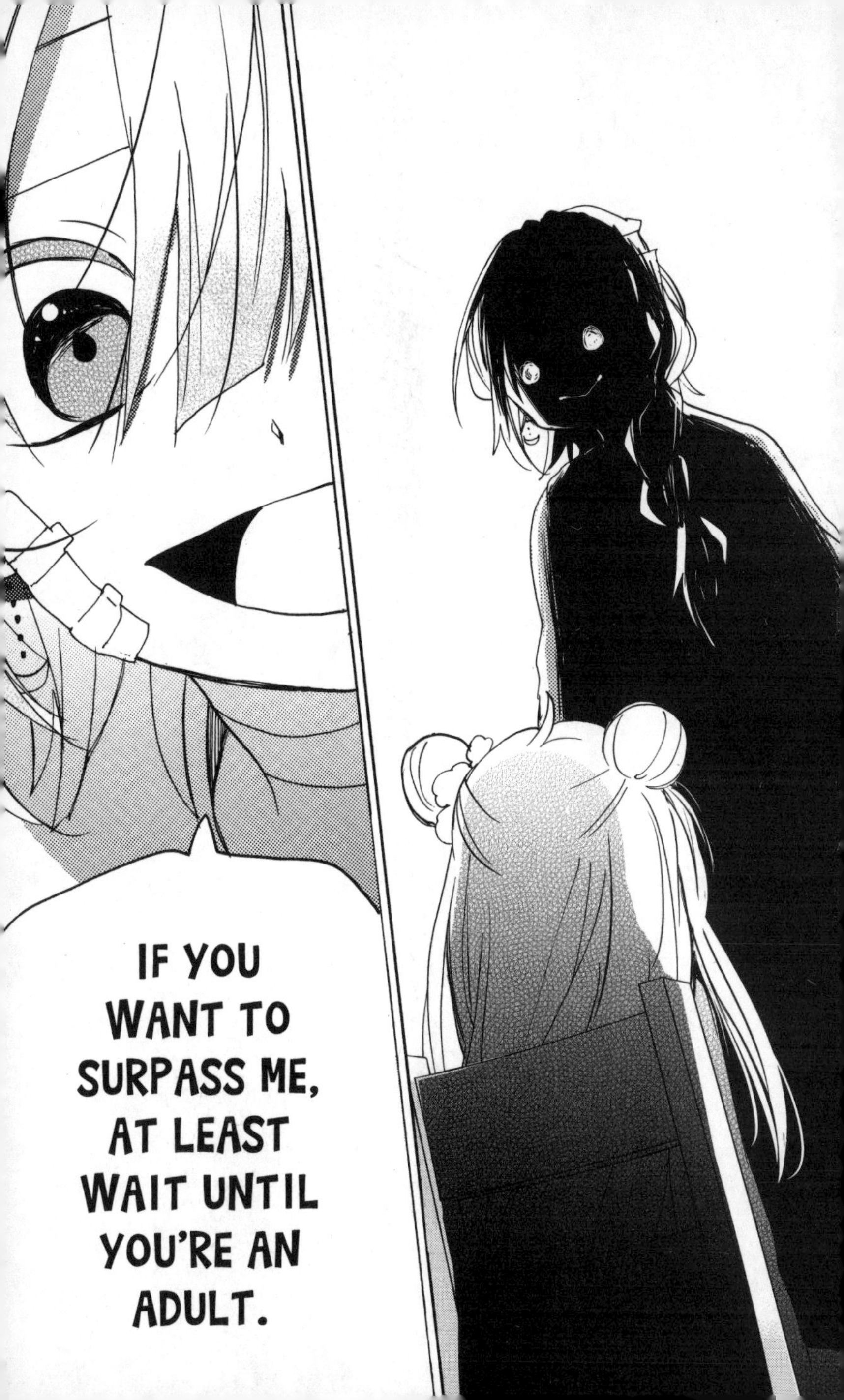
IF YOU WANT TO SURPASS ME, AT LEAST WAIT UNTIL YOU'RE AN ADULT.

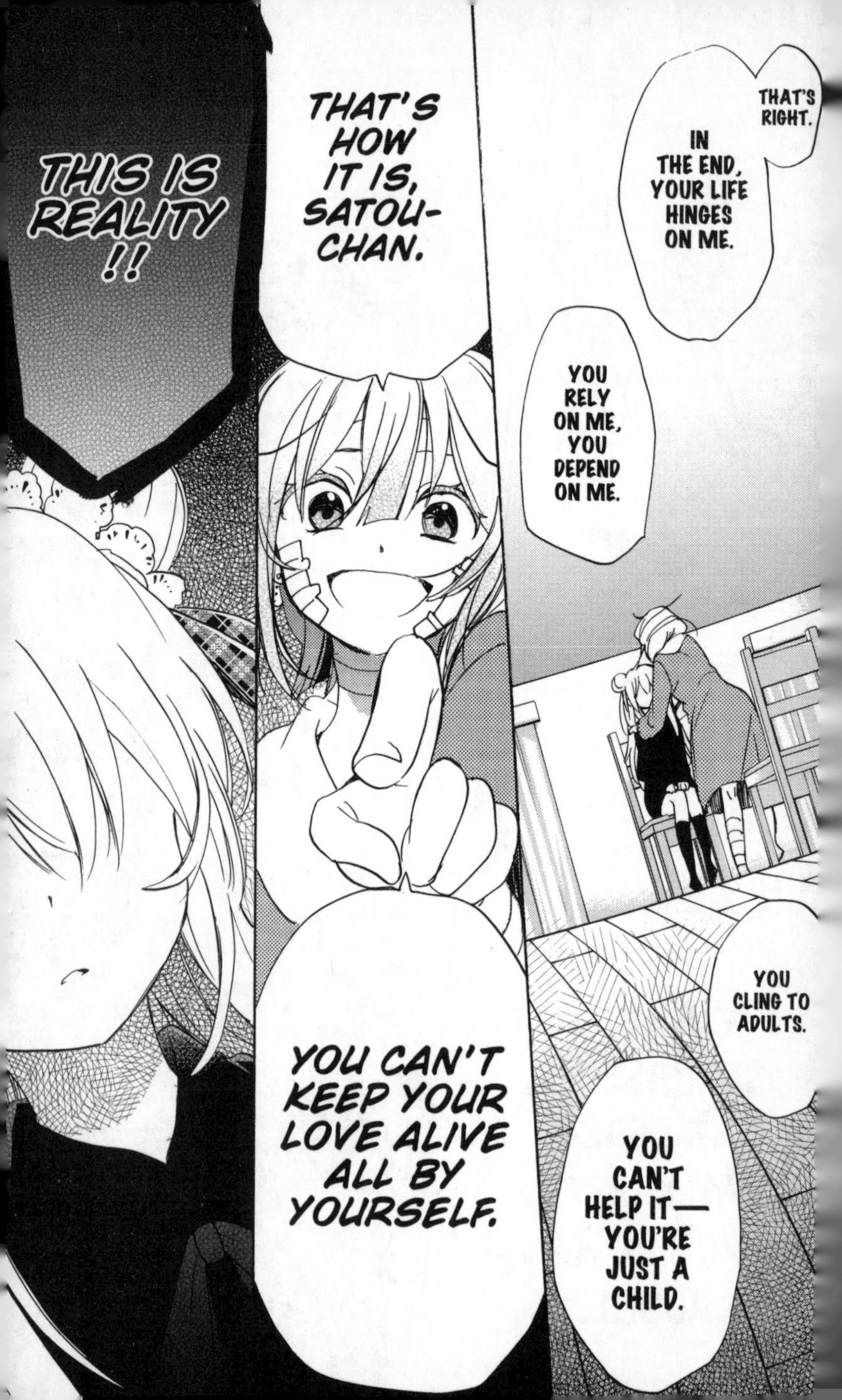
THAT'S RIGHT.
IN THE END, YOUR LIFE HINGES ON ME.
YOU RELY ON ME, YOU DEPEND ON ME.
YOU CLING TO ADULTS.
YOU CAN'T HELP IT—YOU'RE JUST A CHILD.
THAT'S HOW IT IS, SATOU-CHAN.
YOU CAN'T KEEP YOUR LOVE ALIVE ALL BY YOURSELF.
THIS IS REALITY !!

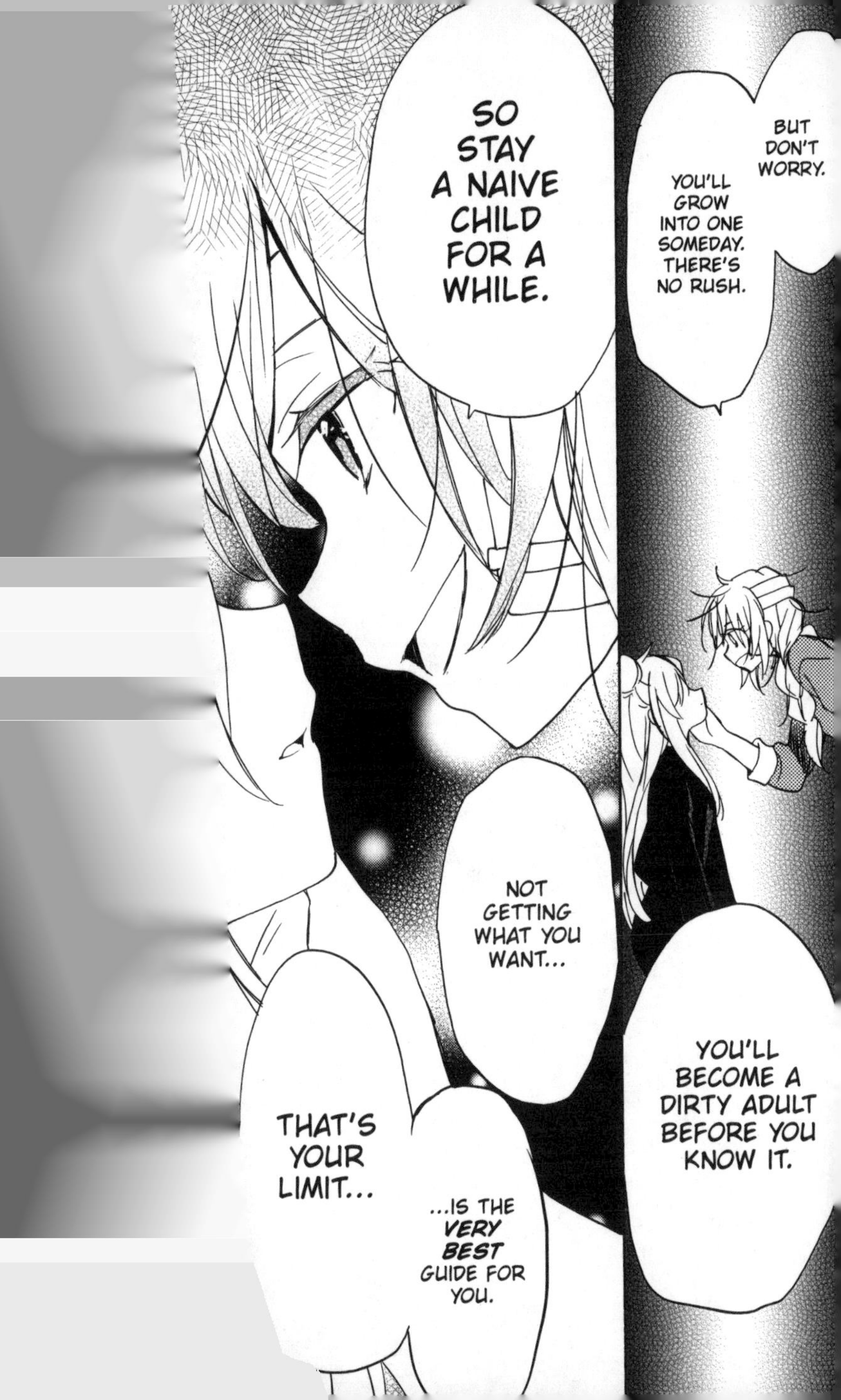
BUT DON'T WORRY.
YOU'LL GROW INTO ONE SOMEDAY. THERE'S NO RUSH.
YOU'LL BECOME A DIRTY ADULT BEFORE YOU KNOW IT.
SO STAY A NAIVE CHILD FOR A WHILE.
NOT GETTING WHAT YOU WANT...
THAT'S YOUR LIMIT...
...IS THE *VERY BEST* GUIDE FOR YOU.

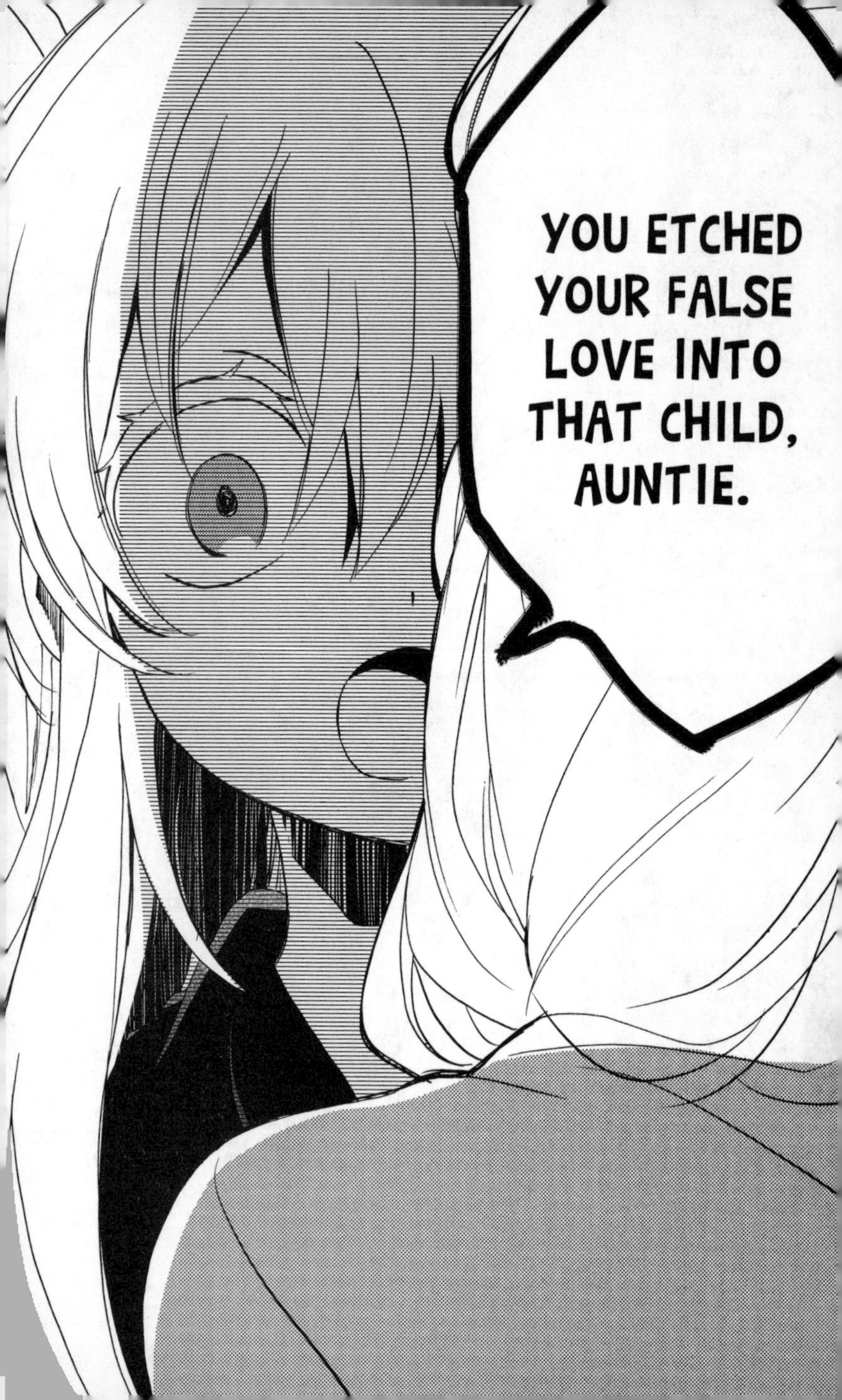
YOU ETCHED YOUR FALSE LOVE INTO THAT CHILD, AUNTIE.

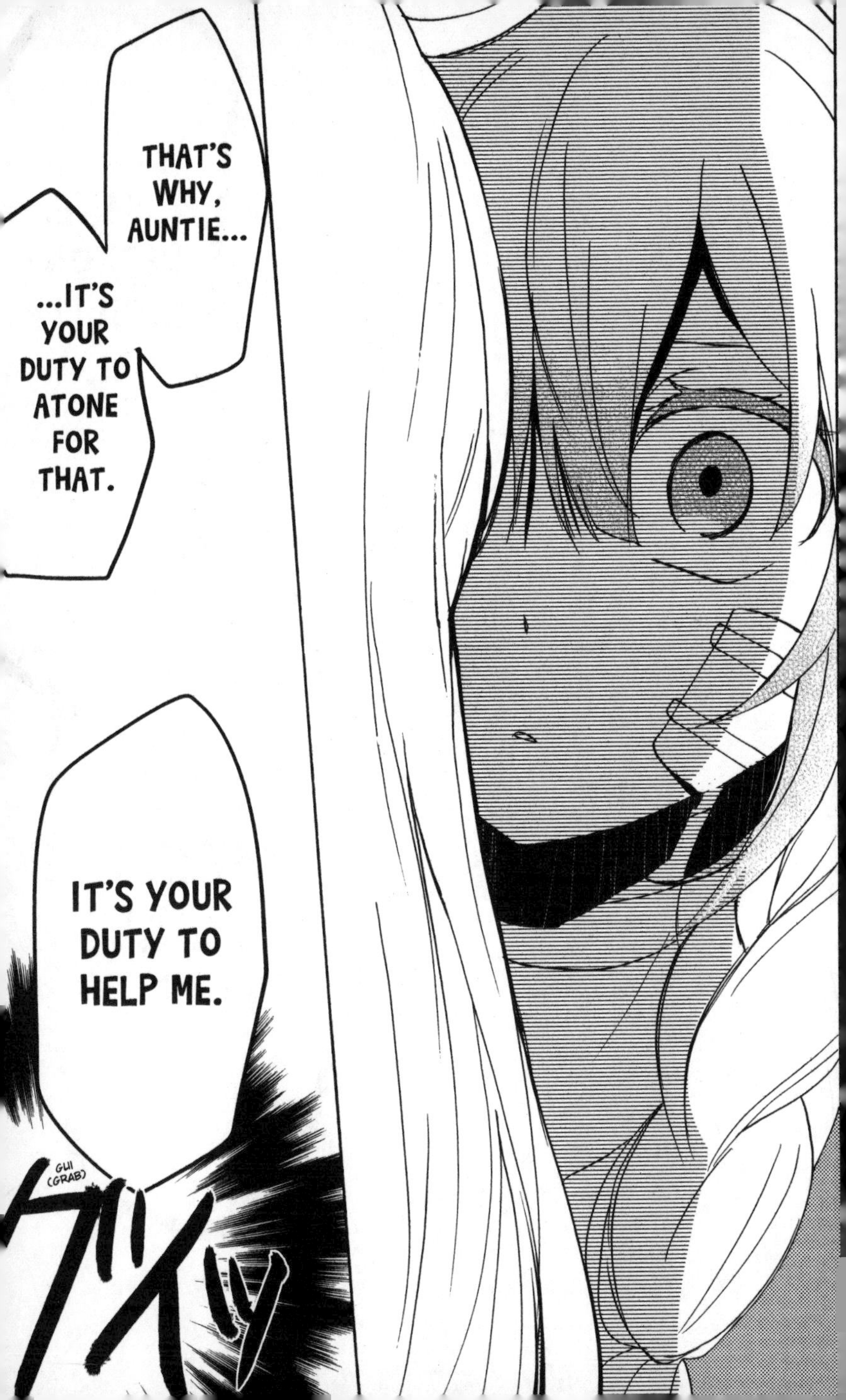
THAT'S WHY, AUNTIE...
...IT'S YOUR DUTY TO ATONE FOR THAT.
IT'S YOUR DUTY TO HELP ME.
GUI (GRAB)

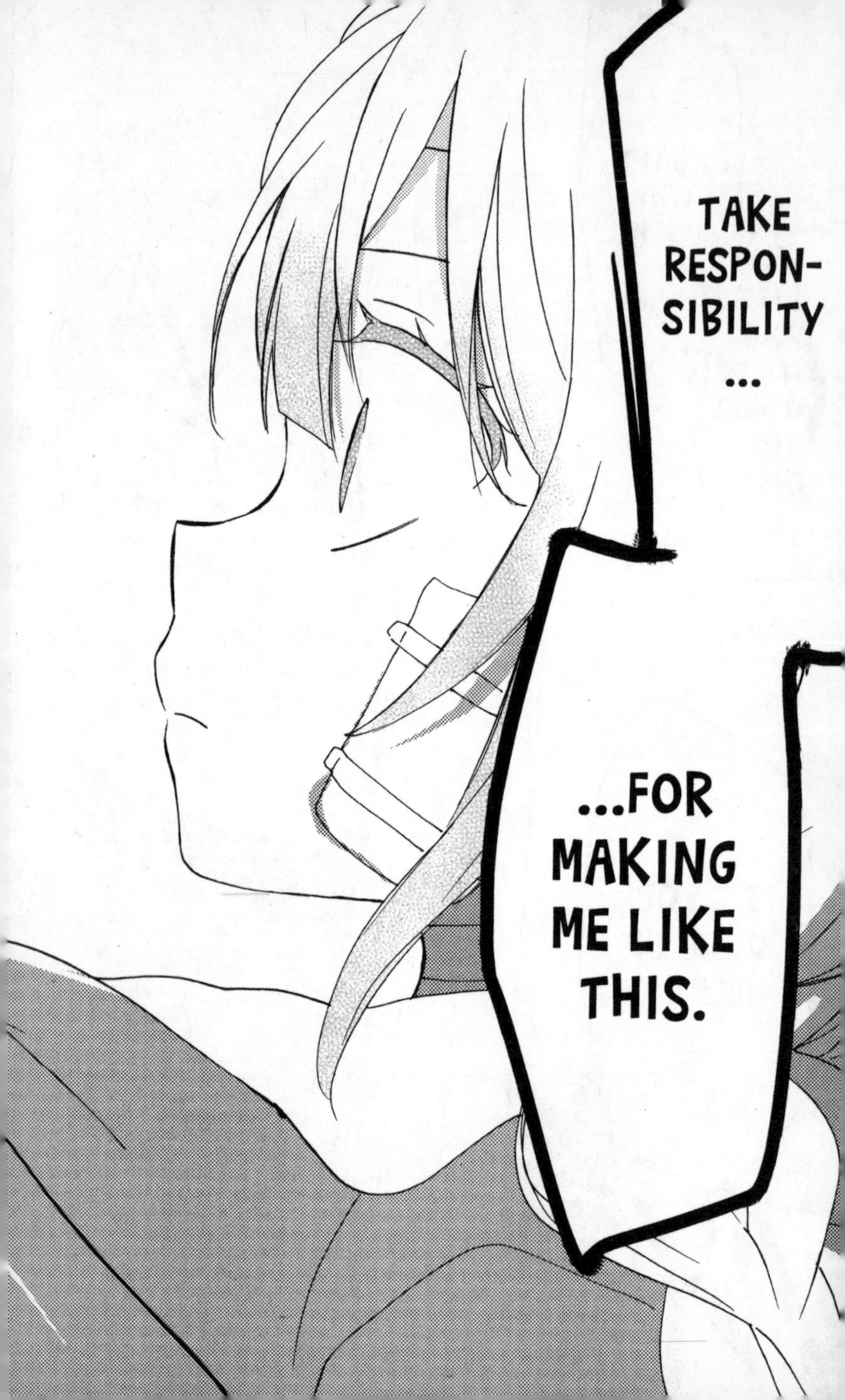
TAKE RESPON-SIBILITY ...
...FOR MAKING ME LIKE THIS.

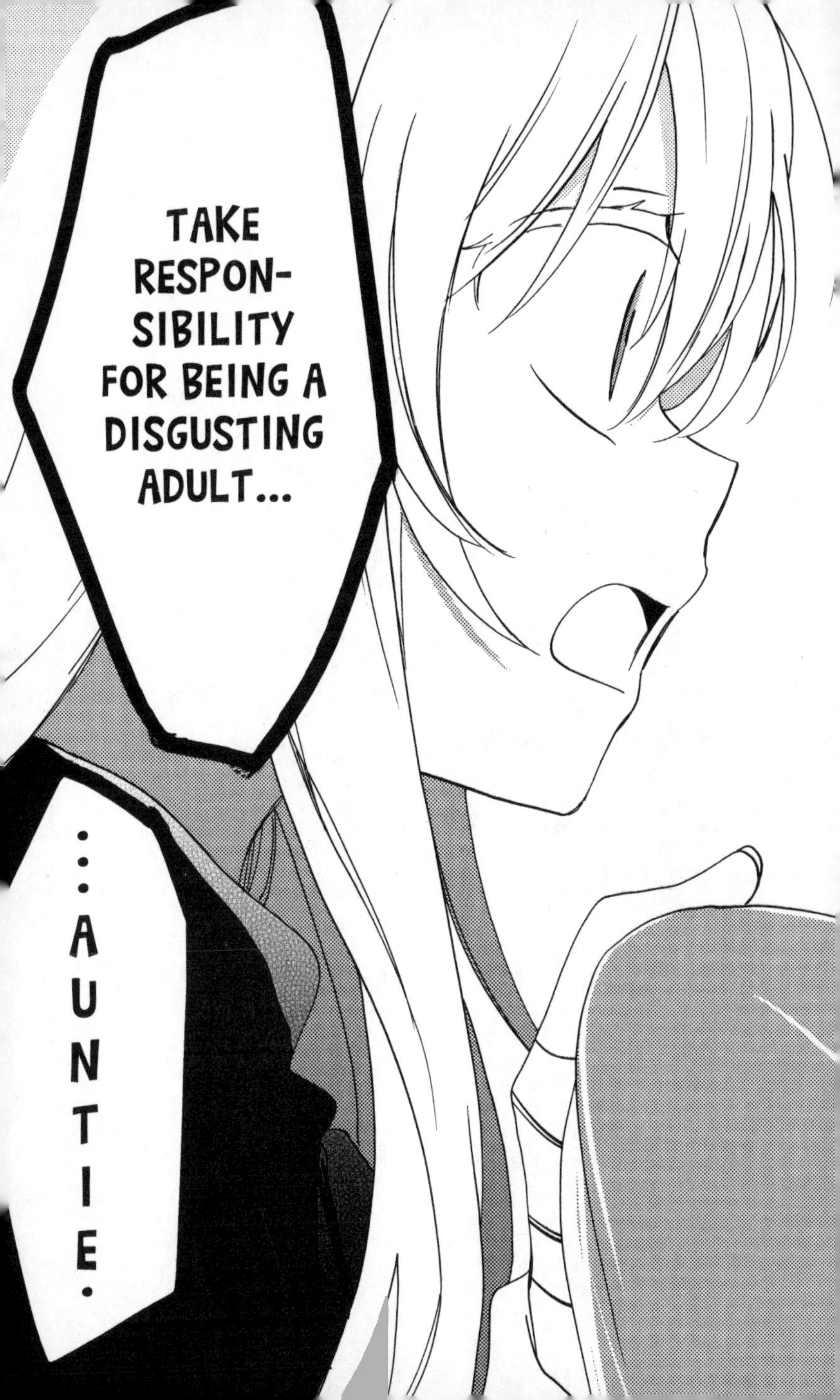
TAKE RESPON-SIBILITY FOR BEING A DISGUSTING ADULT...
...AUNTIE.

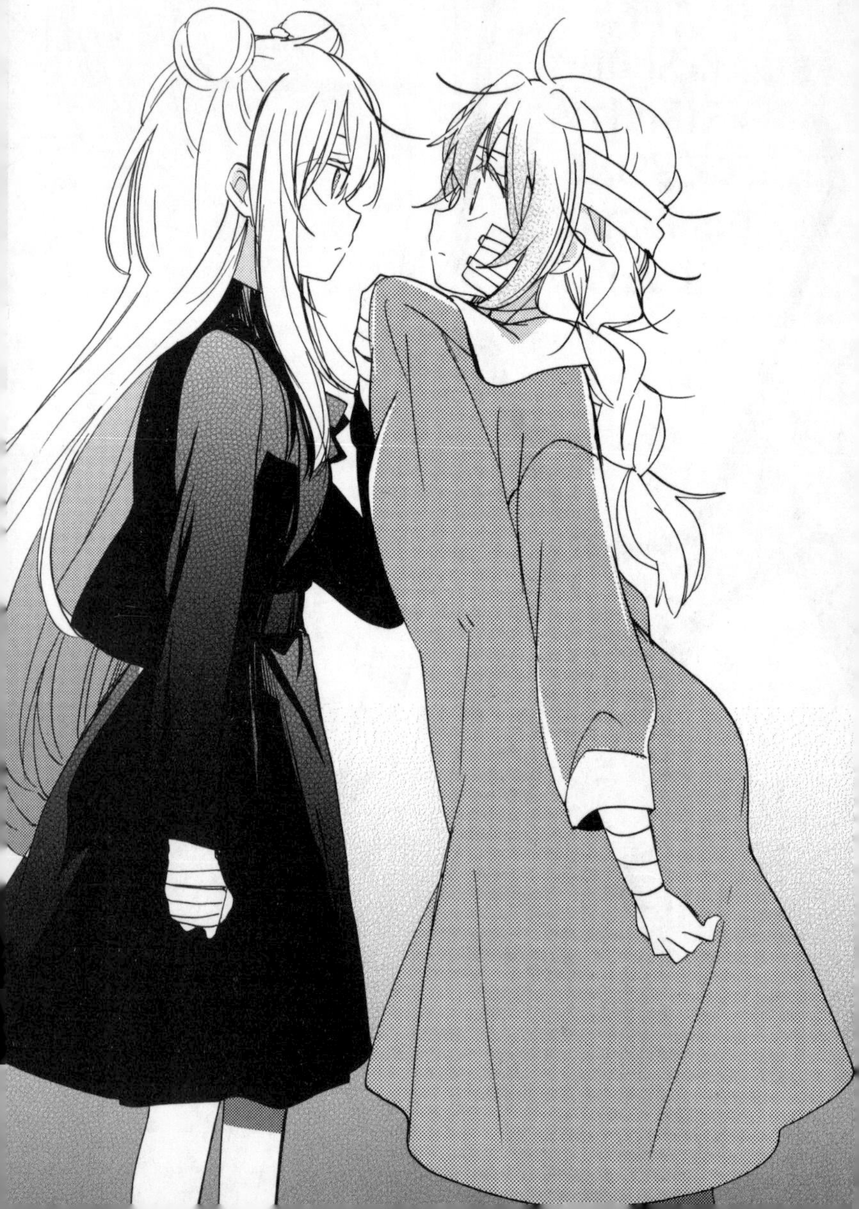

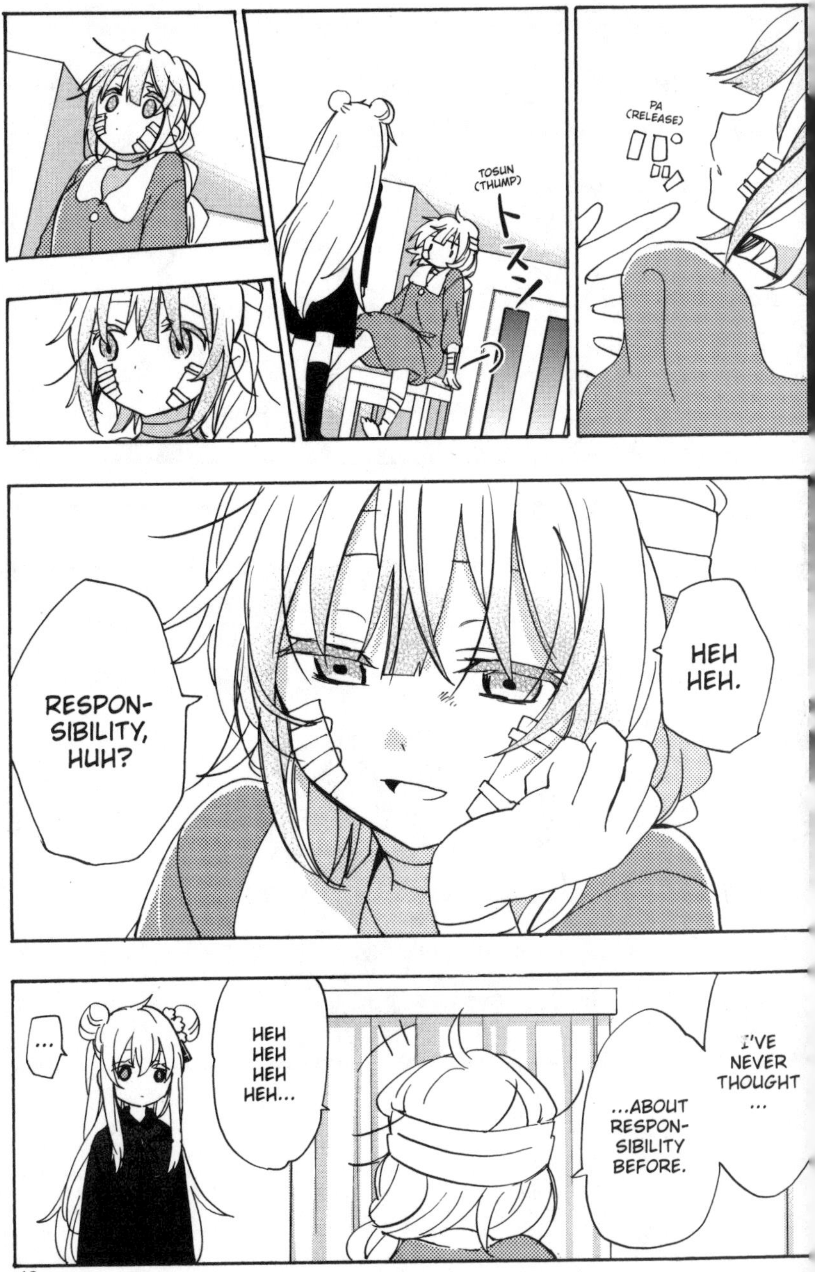
PA (RELEASE)
TOSUN (THUMP)
トスン
HEH HEH.
RESPON-SIBILITY, HUH?
I'VE NEVER THOUGHT ...
...ABOUT RESPON-SIBILITY BEFORE.
HEH HEH HEH HEH...
...

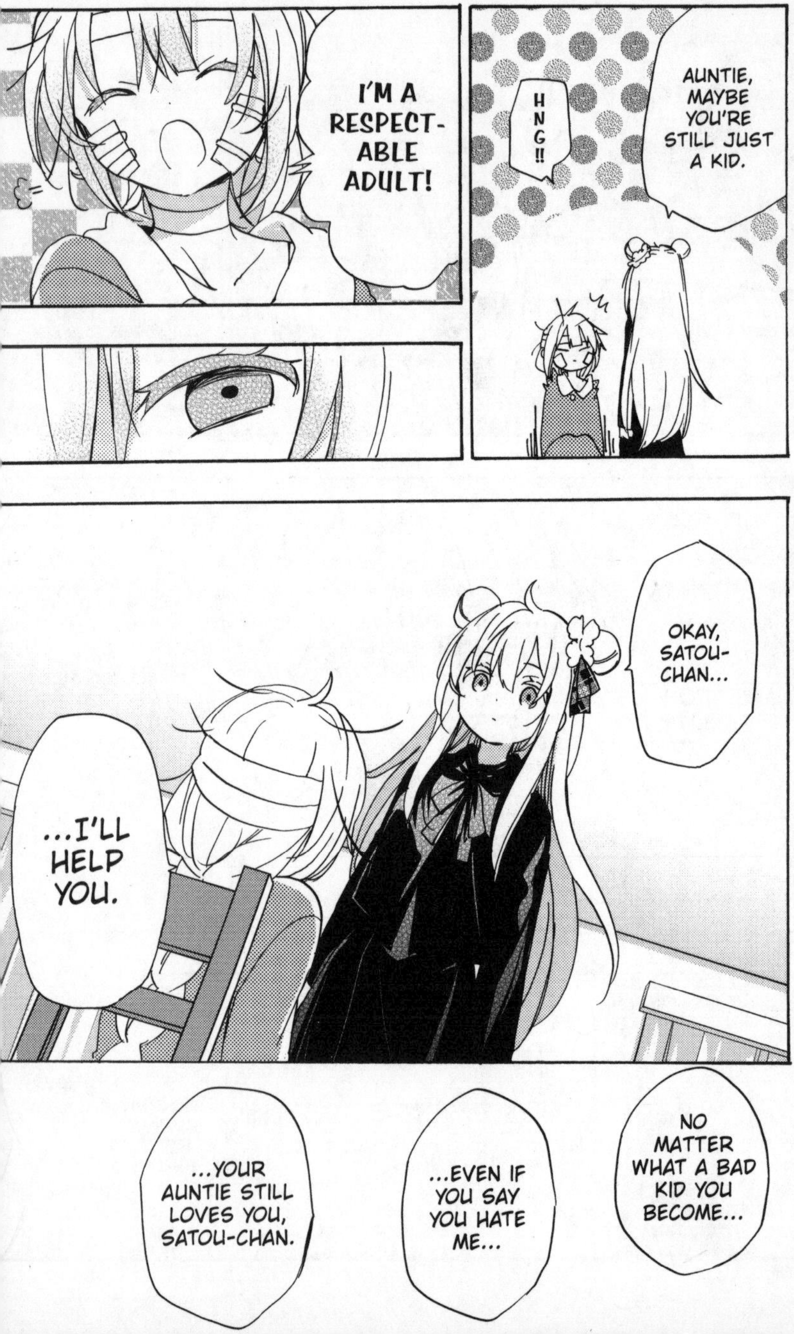
AUNTIE, MAYBE YOU'RE STILL JUST A KID.
HNG!!
I'M A RESPECTABLE ADULT!
OKAY, SATOU-CHAN...
...I'LL HELP YOU.
NO MATTER WHAT A BAD KID YOU BECOME...
...EVEN IF YOU SAY YOU HATE ME...
...YOUR AUNTIE STILL LOVES YOU, SATOU-CHAN.

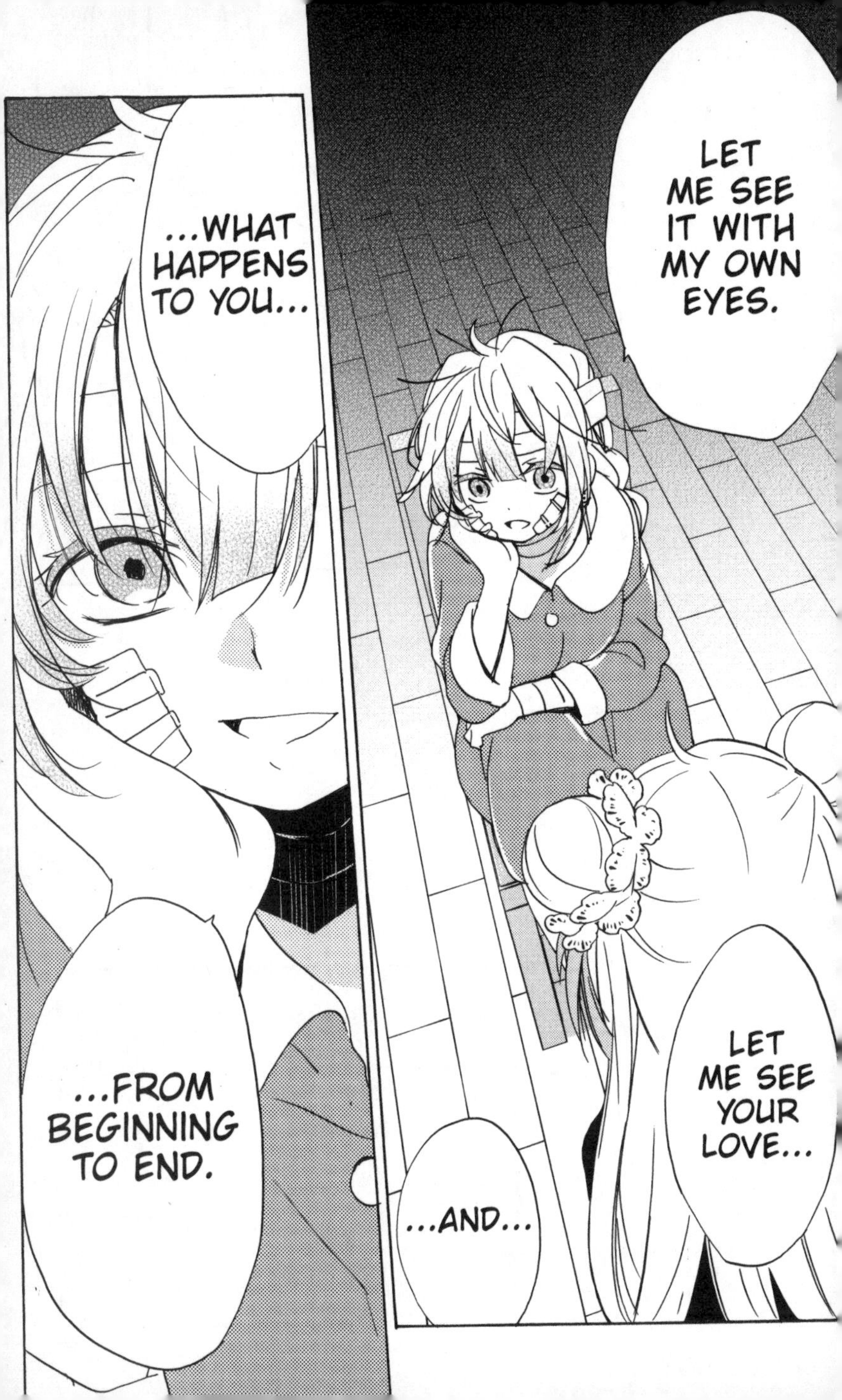
LET ME SEE IT WITH MY OWN EYES.
LET ME SEE YOUR LOVE...
...AND...
...WHAT HAPPENS TO YOU...
...FROM BEGINNING TO END.

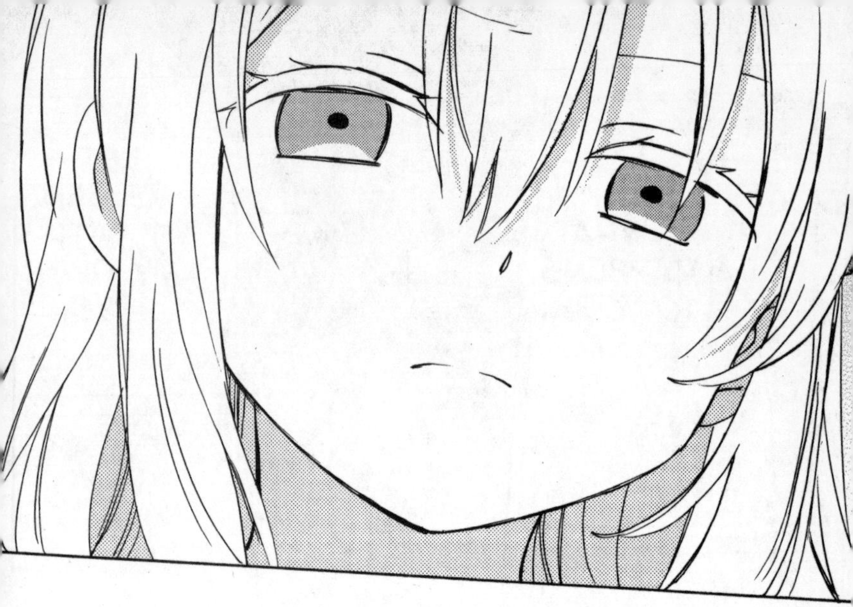

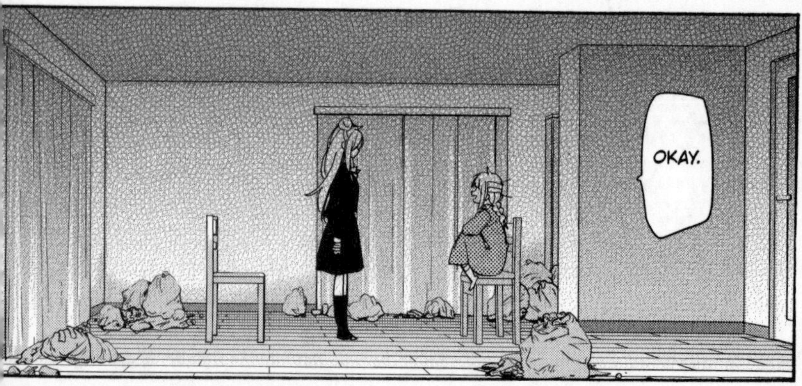
OKAY.

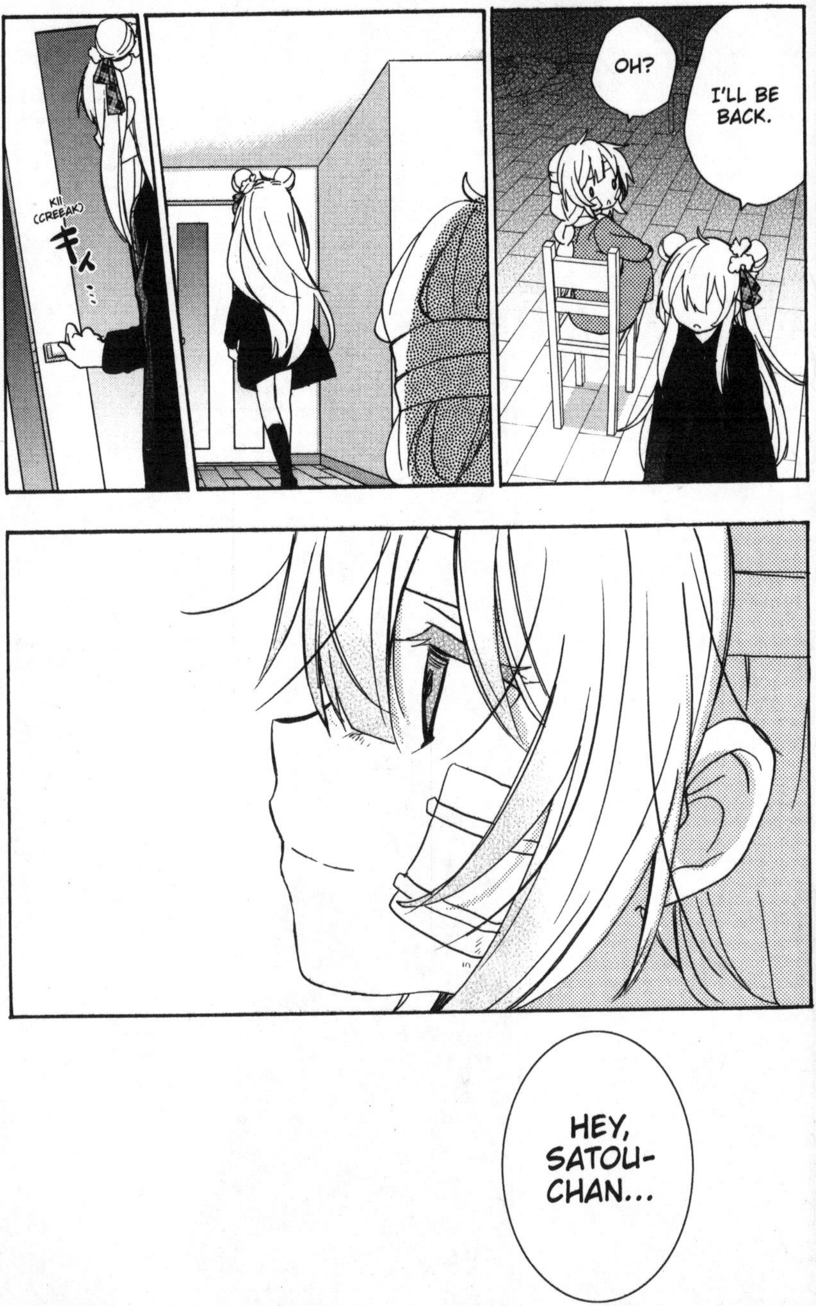
I'LL BE BACK.
OH?
KII (CREEAK)
キィ…
HEY, SATOU-CHAN...

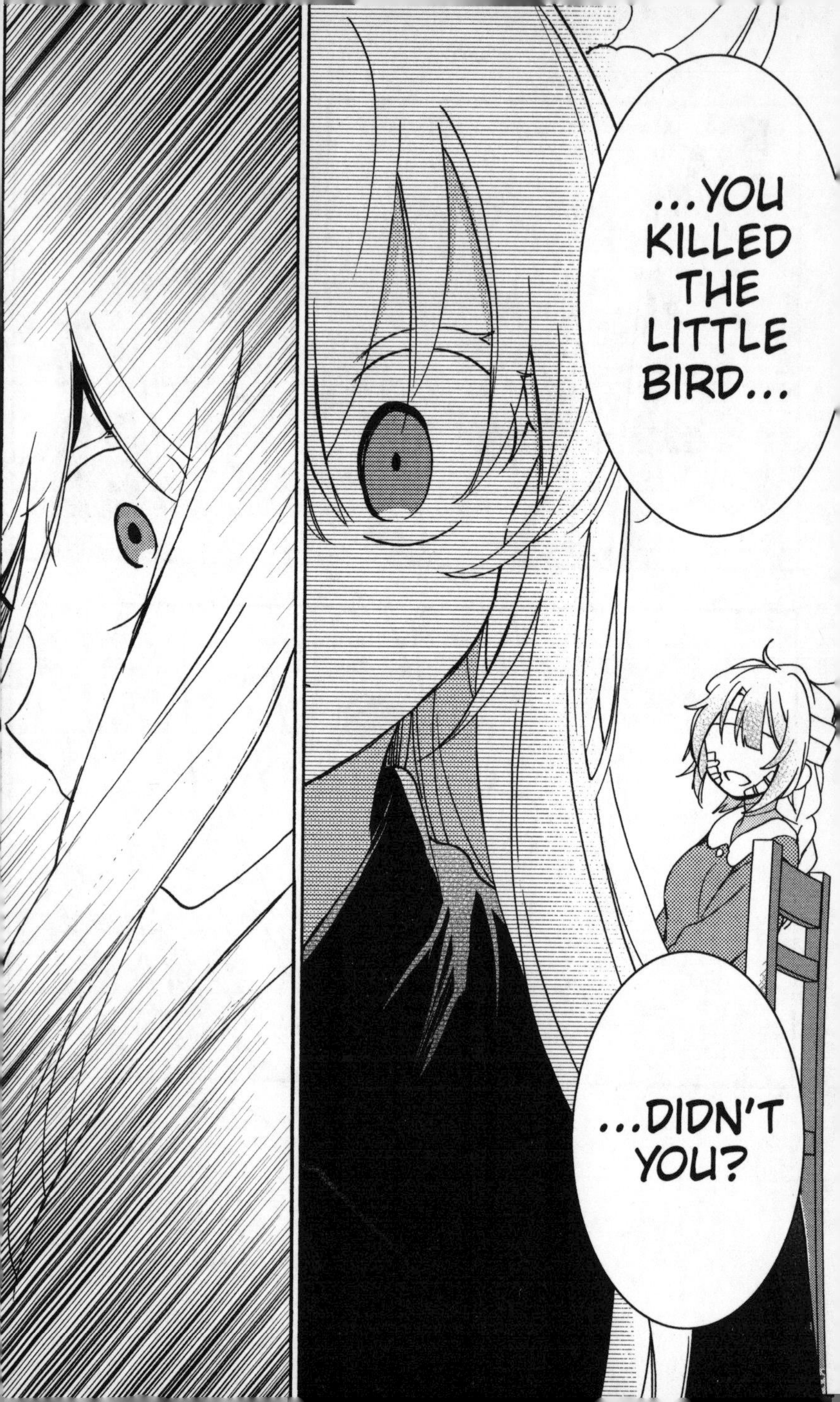
...YOU KILLED THE LITTLE BIRD...
...DIDN'T YOU?

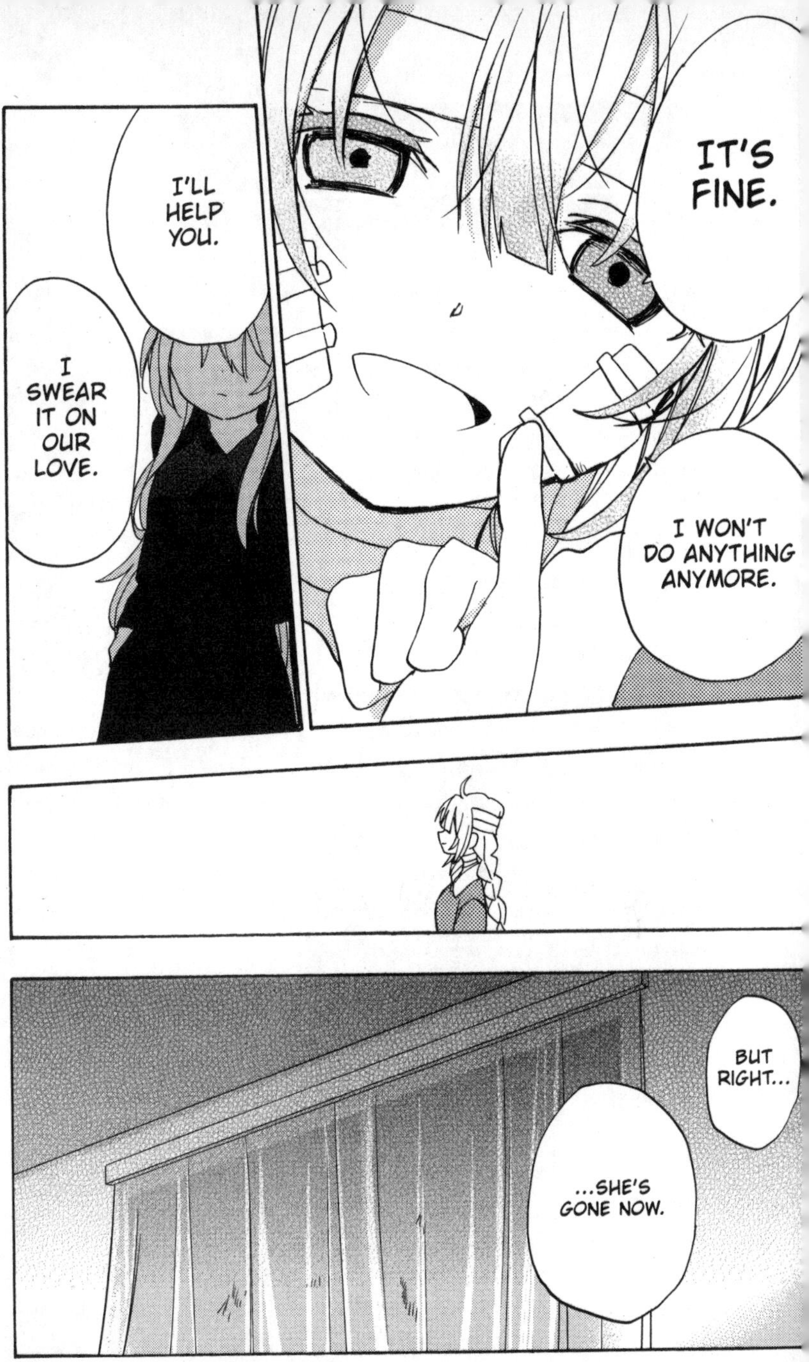
IT'S FINE.
I WON'T DO ANYTHING ANYMORE.
I'LL HELP YOU.
I SWEAR IT ON OUR LOVE.
BUT RIGHT...
...SHE'S GONE NOW.

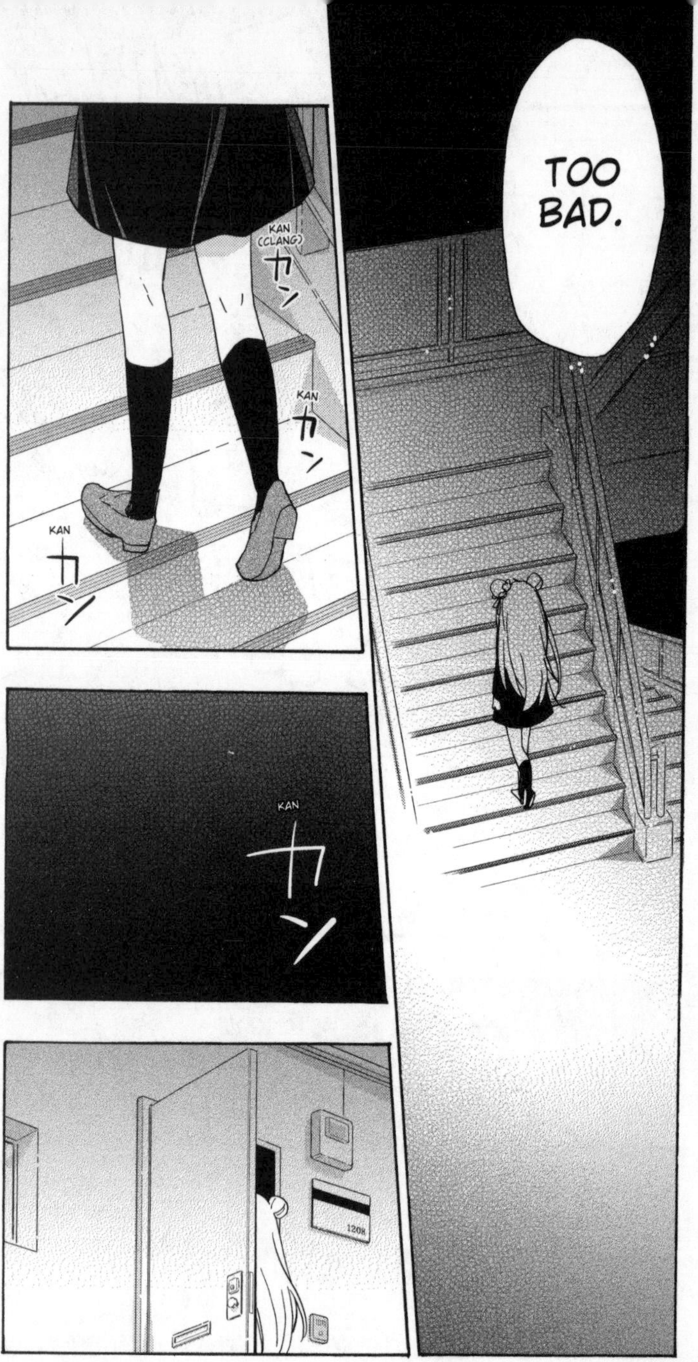
TOO BAD.
KAN (CLANG)
カン
KAN
カン
KAN
カン
KAN
カン
1208

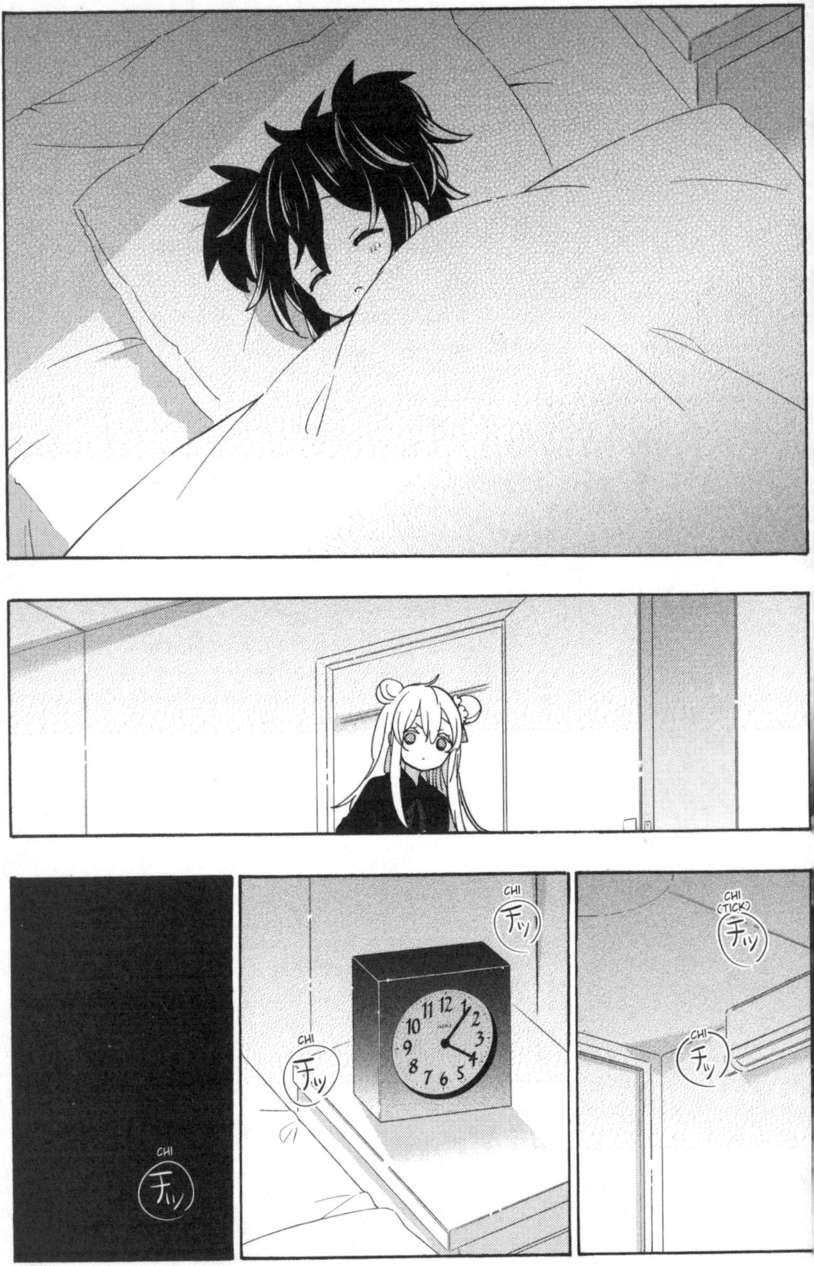
CHI (TICK)
チッ
CHI
チッ
CHI
チッ
CHI
チッ
CHI
チッ

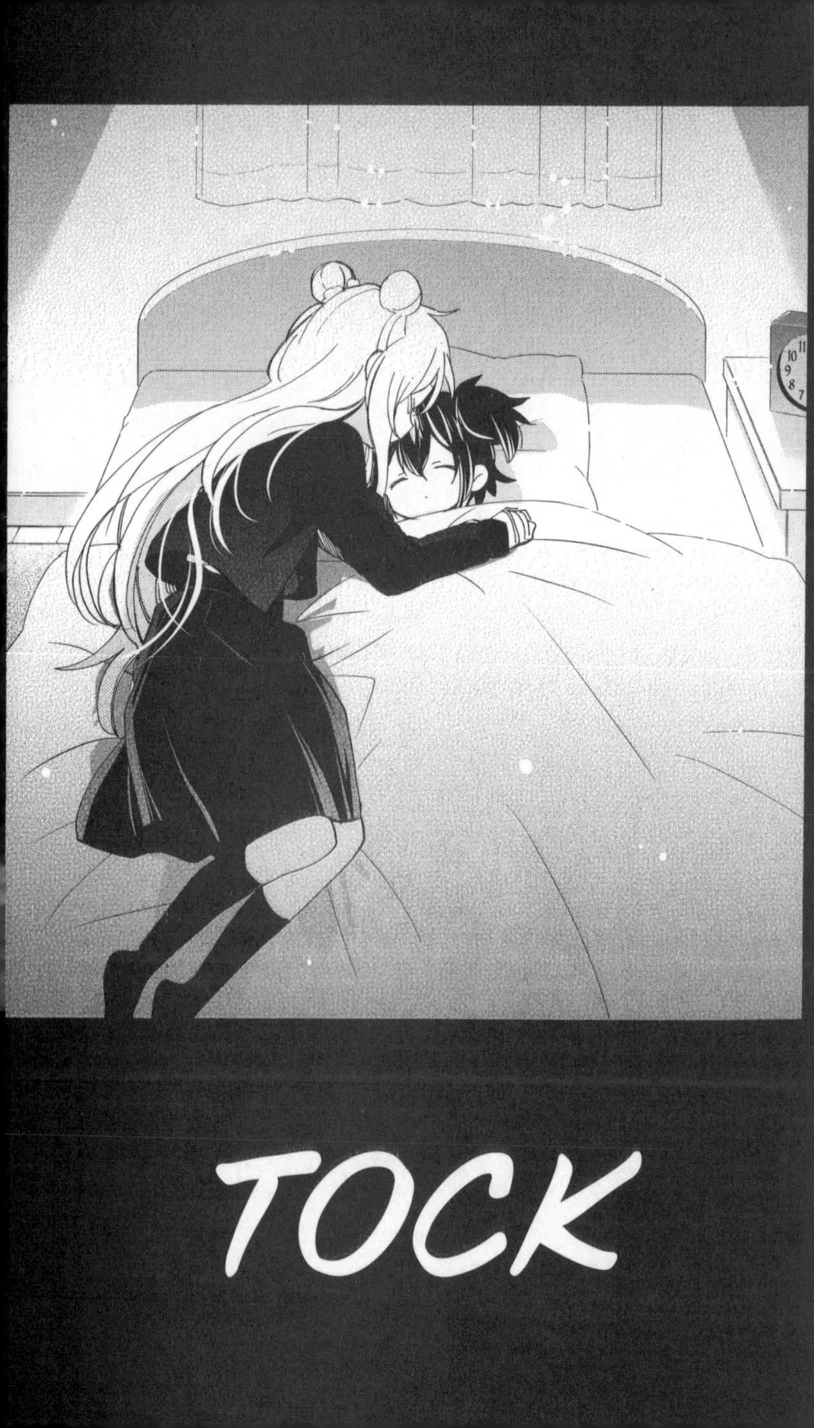
TOCK

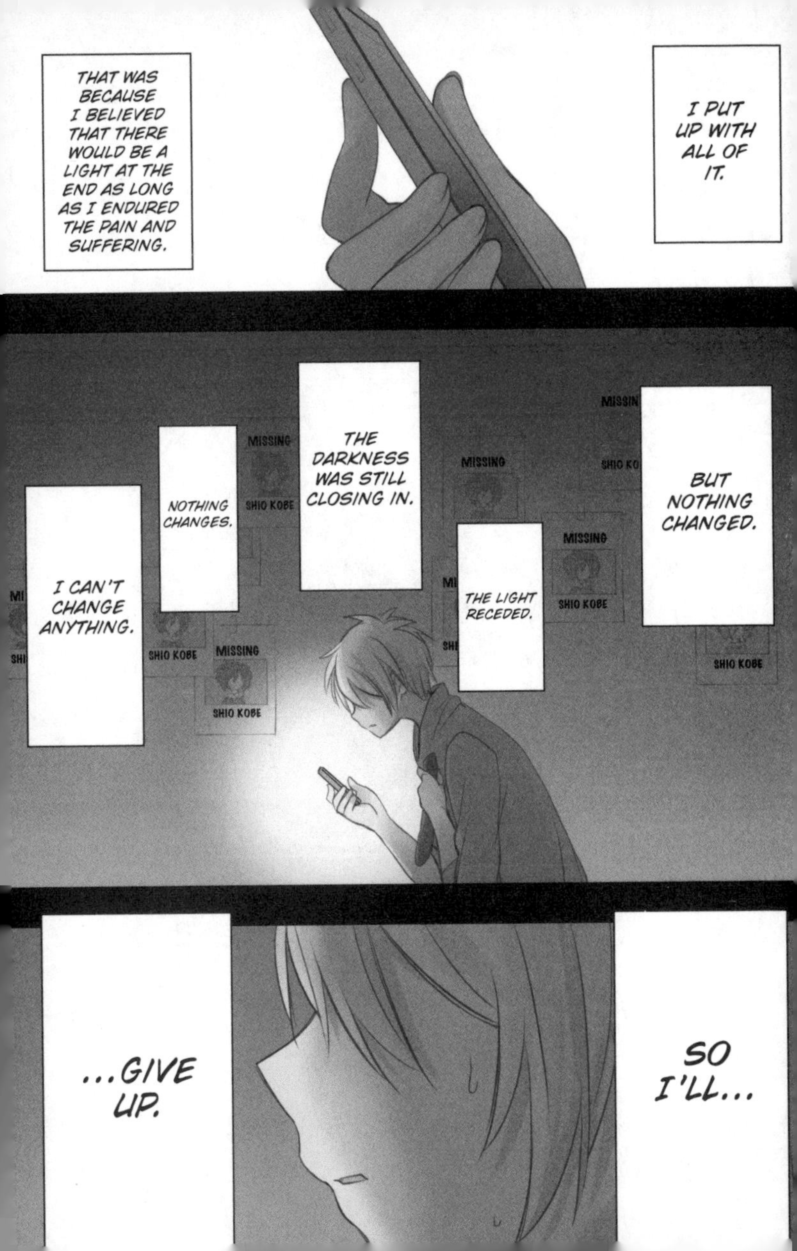
I PUT UP WITH ALL OF IT.
THAT WAS BECAUSE I BELIEVED THAT THERE WOULD BE A LIGHT AT THE END AS LONG AS I ENDURED THE PAIN AND SUFFERING.
BUT NOTHING CHANGED.
THE DARKNESS WAS STILL CLOSING IN.
MISSING
SHIO KOBE
THE LIGHT RECEDED.
NOTHING CHANGES.
I CAN'T CHANGE ANYTHING.
SO I'LL...
...GIVE UP.

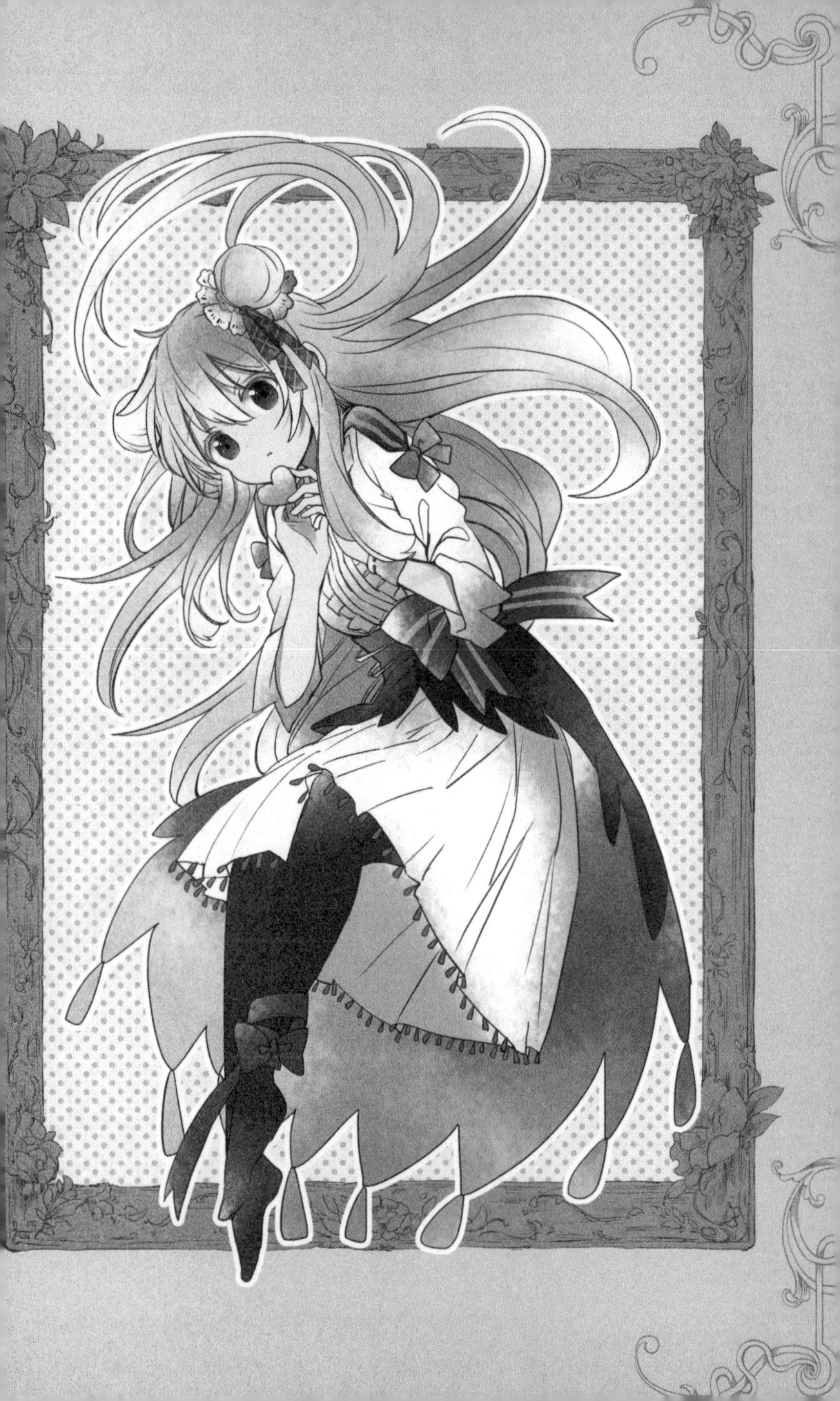

34TH LIFE: DAYBREAK AND THE BOY

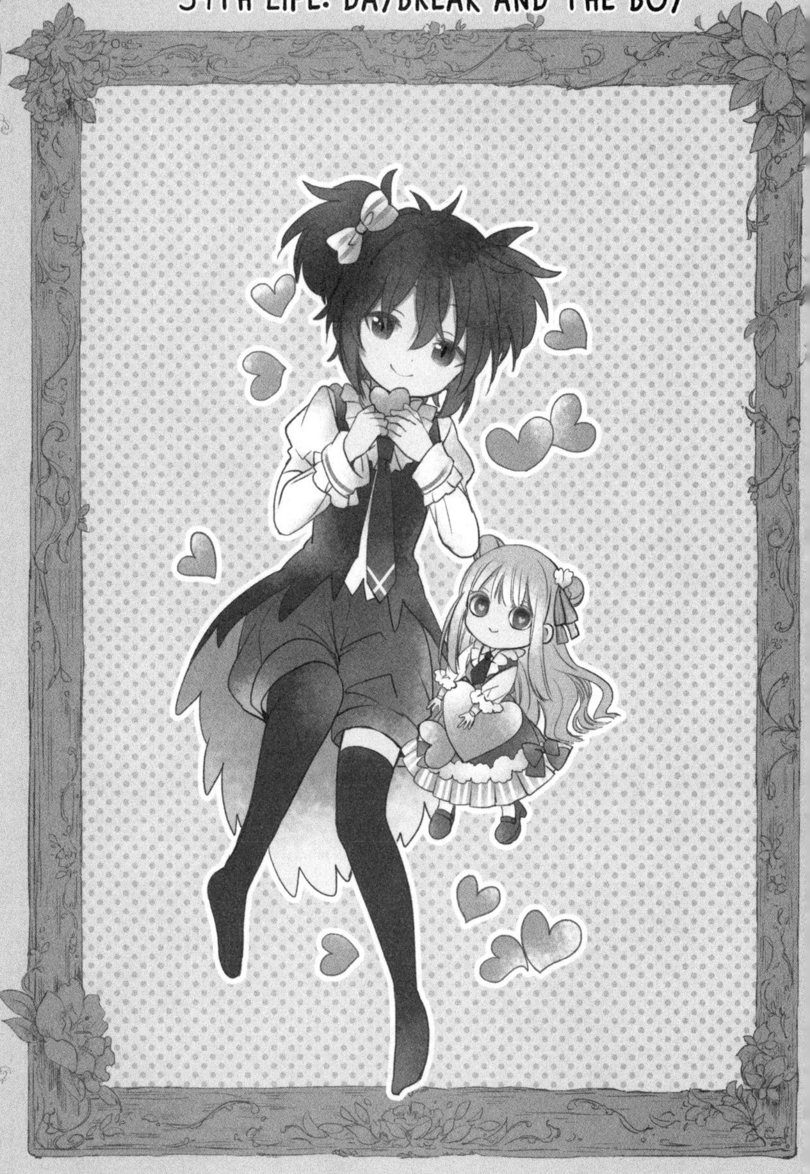

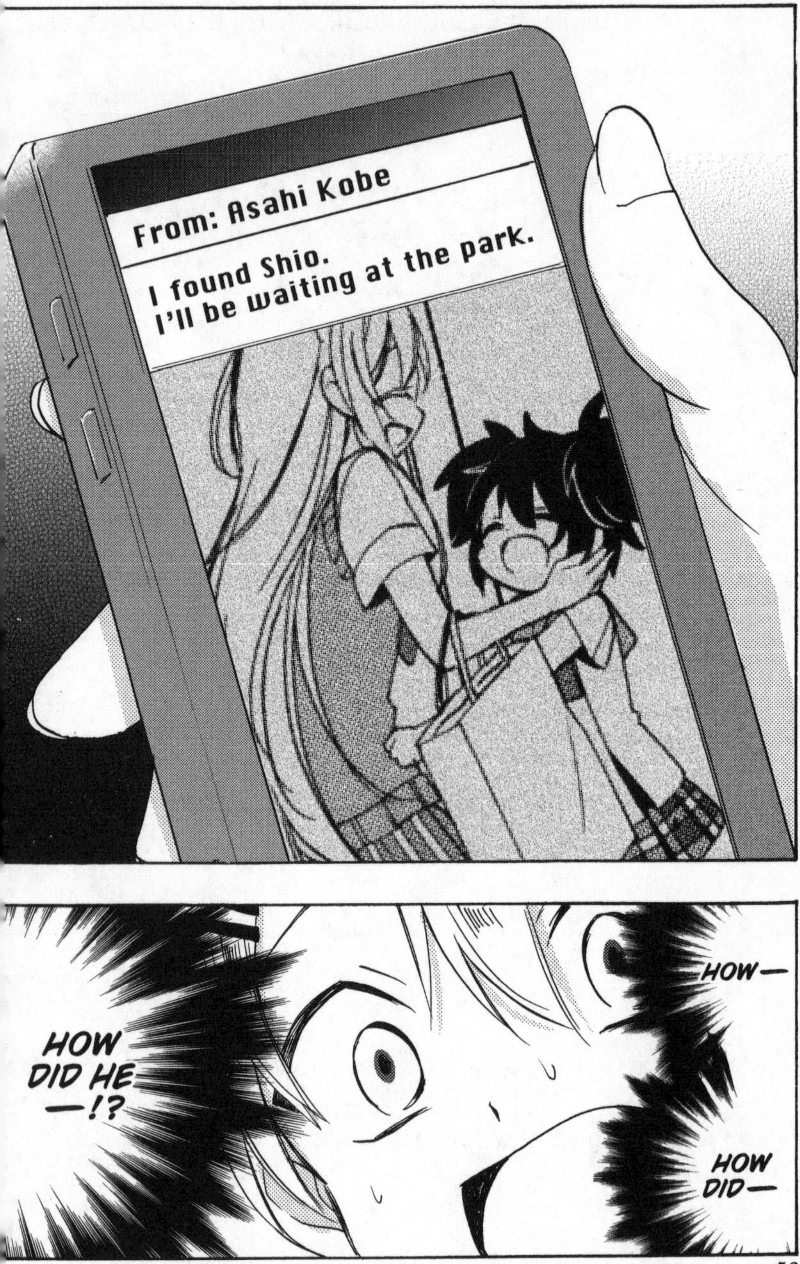
From: Asahi Kobe
I found Shio.
I'll be waiting at the park.
HOW—
HOW DID—
HOW DID HE —!?

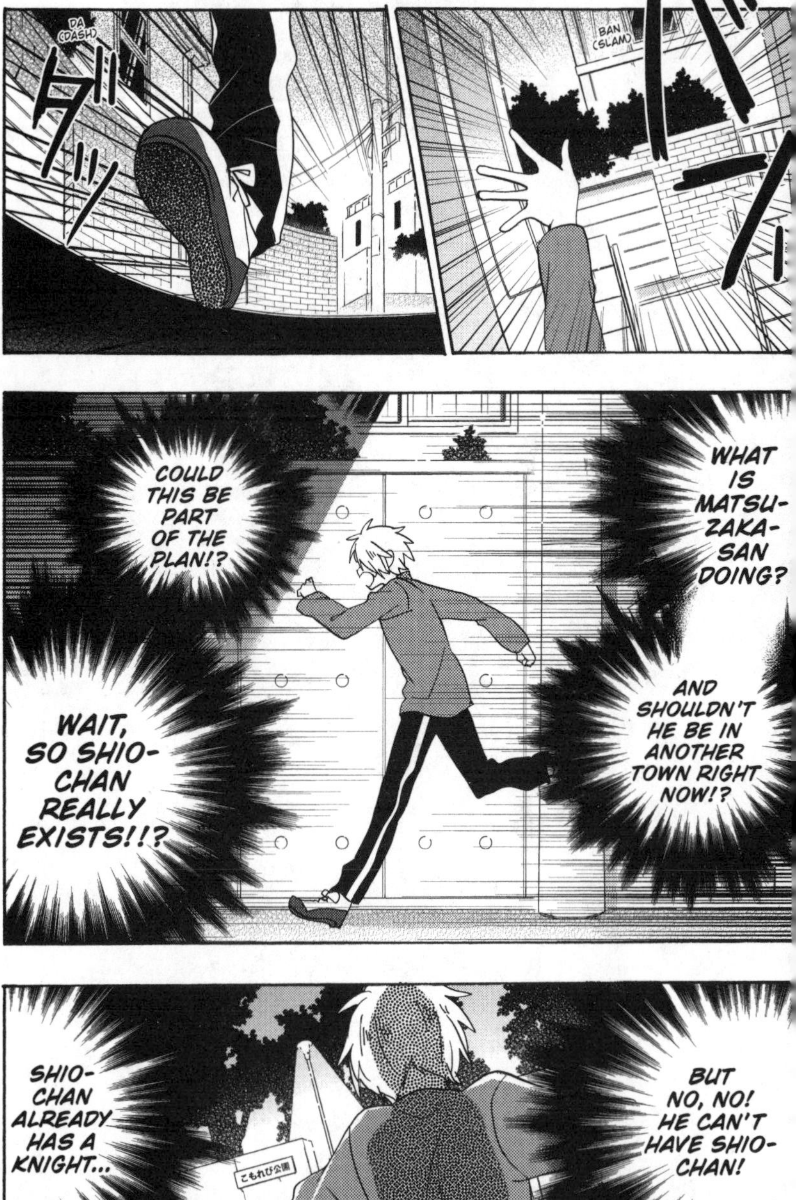
BAN (SLAM)
DA (DASH)
WHAT IS MATSU-ZAKA-SAN DOING?
AND SHOULDN'T HE BE IN ANOTHER TOWN RIGHT NOW!?
COULD THIS BE PART OF THE PLAN!?
WAIT, SO SHIO-CHAN REALLY EXISTS!!?
BUT NO, NO! HE CAN'T HAVE SHIO-CHAN!
こもれび公園
SHIO-CHAN ALREADY HAS A KNIGHT...

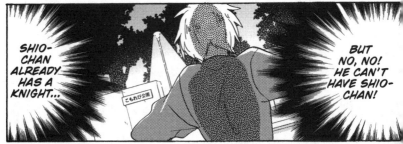

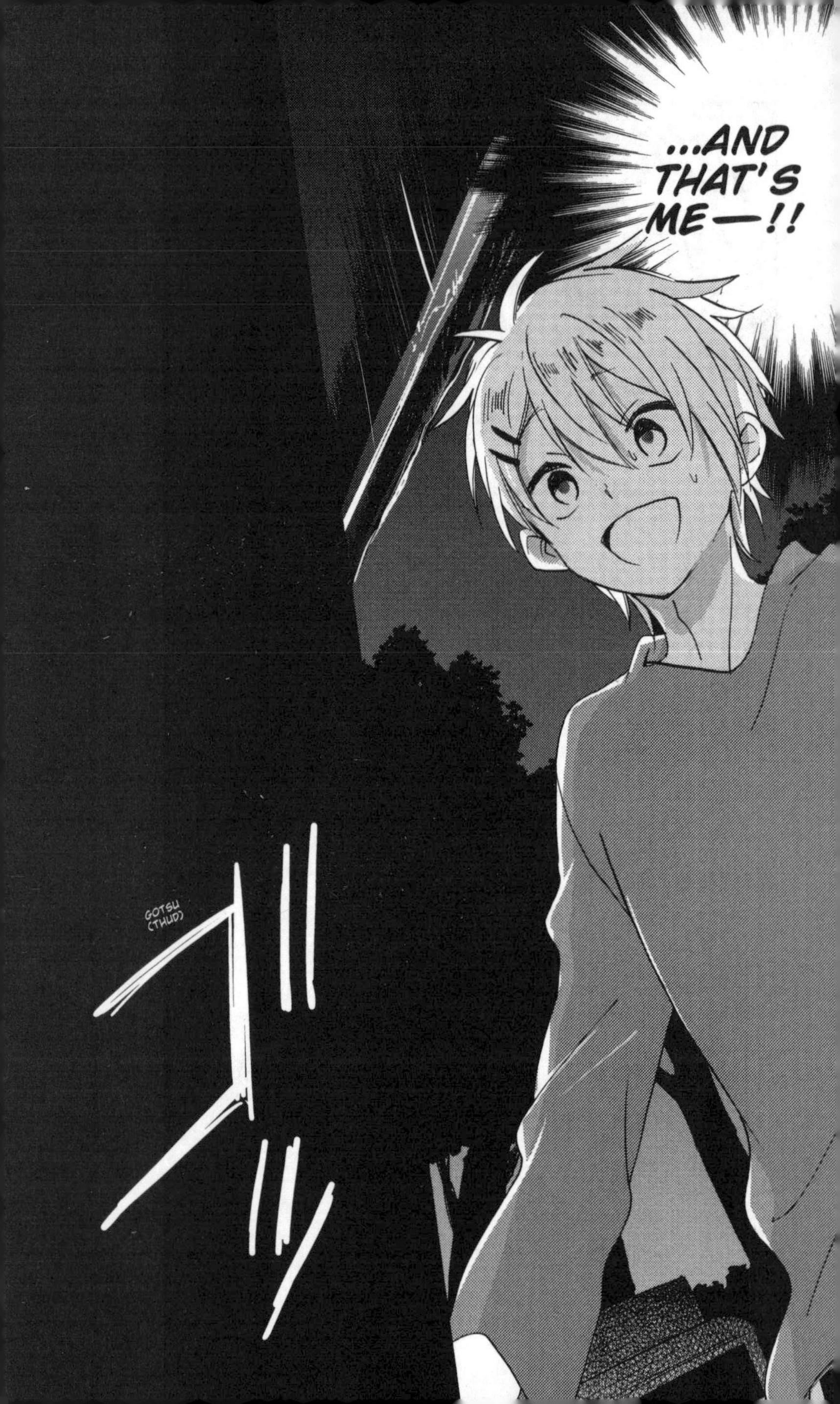
...AND THAT'S ME—!!
GOTSU (THUD)

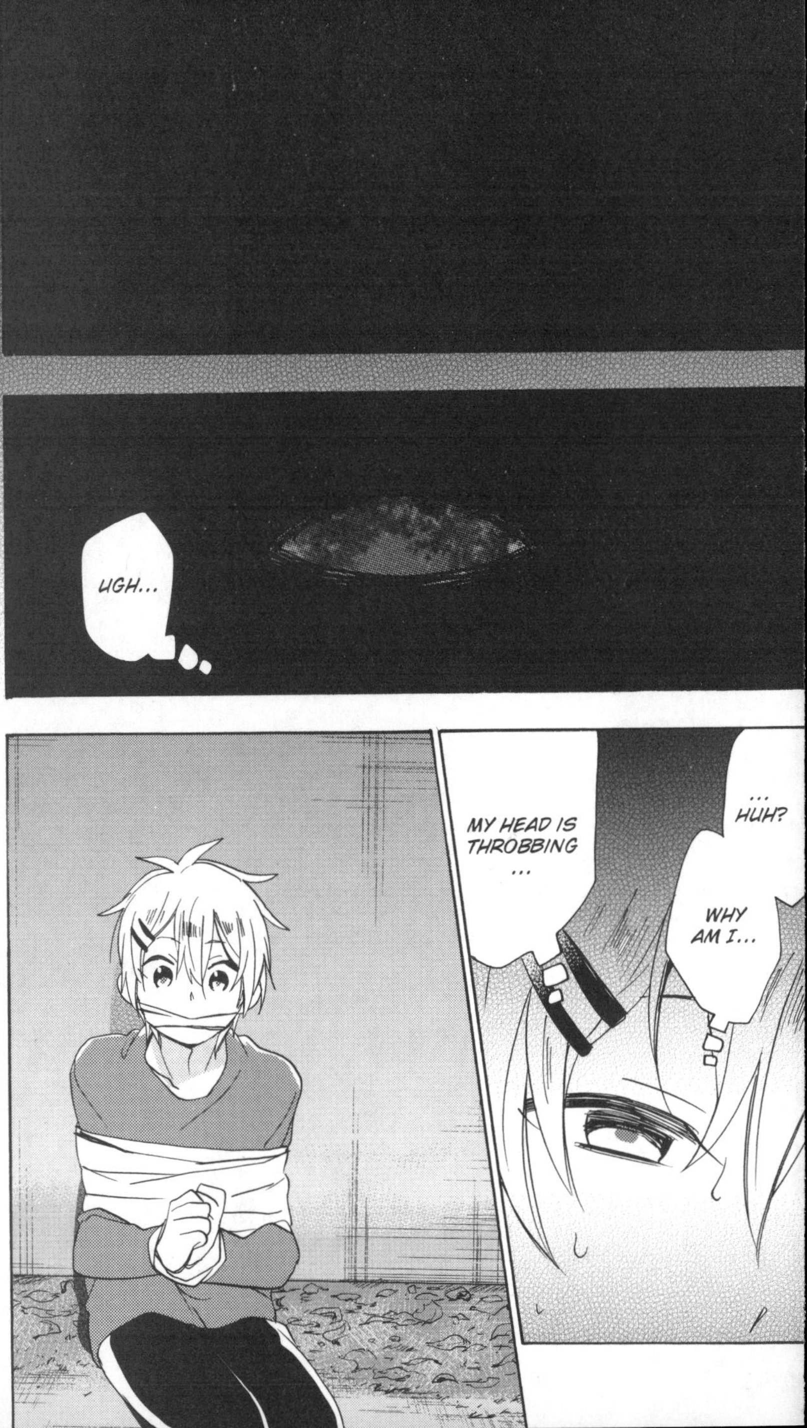
UGH...
... HUH?
WHY AM I...
MY HEAD IS THROBBING ...

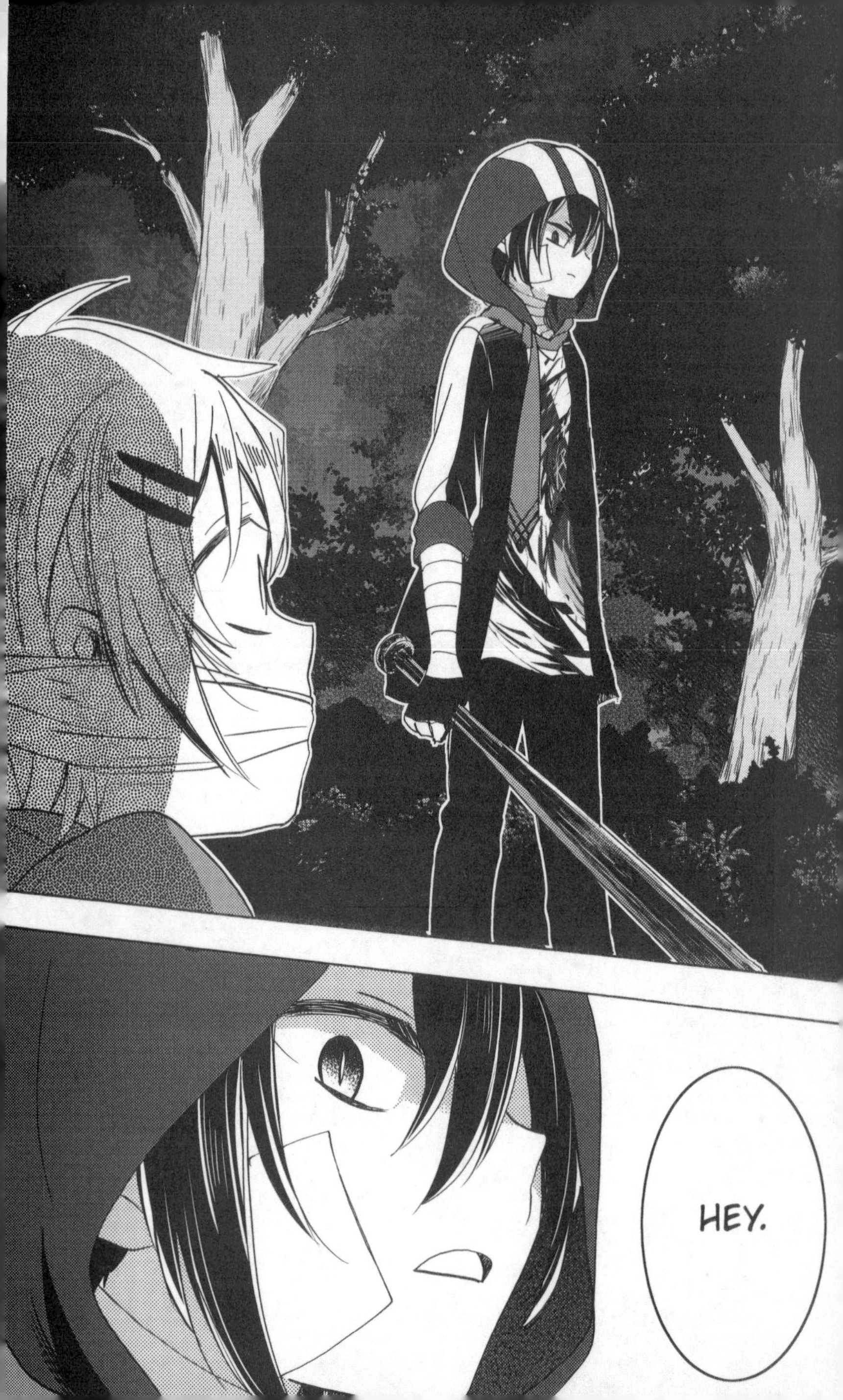
HEY.

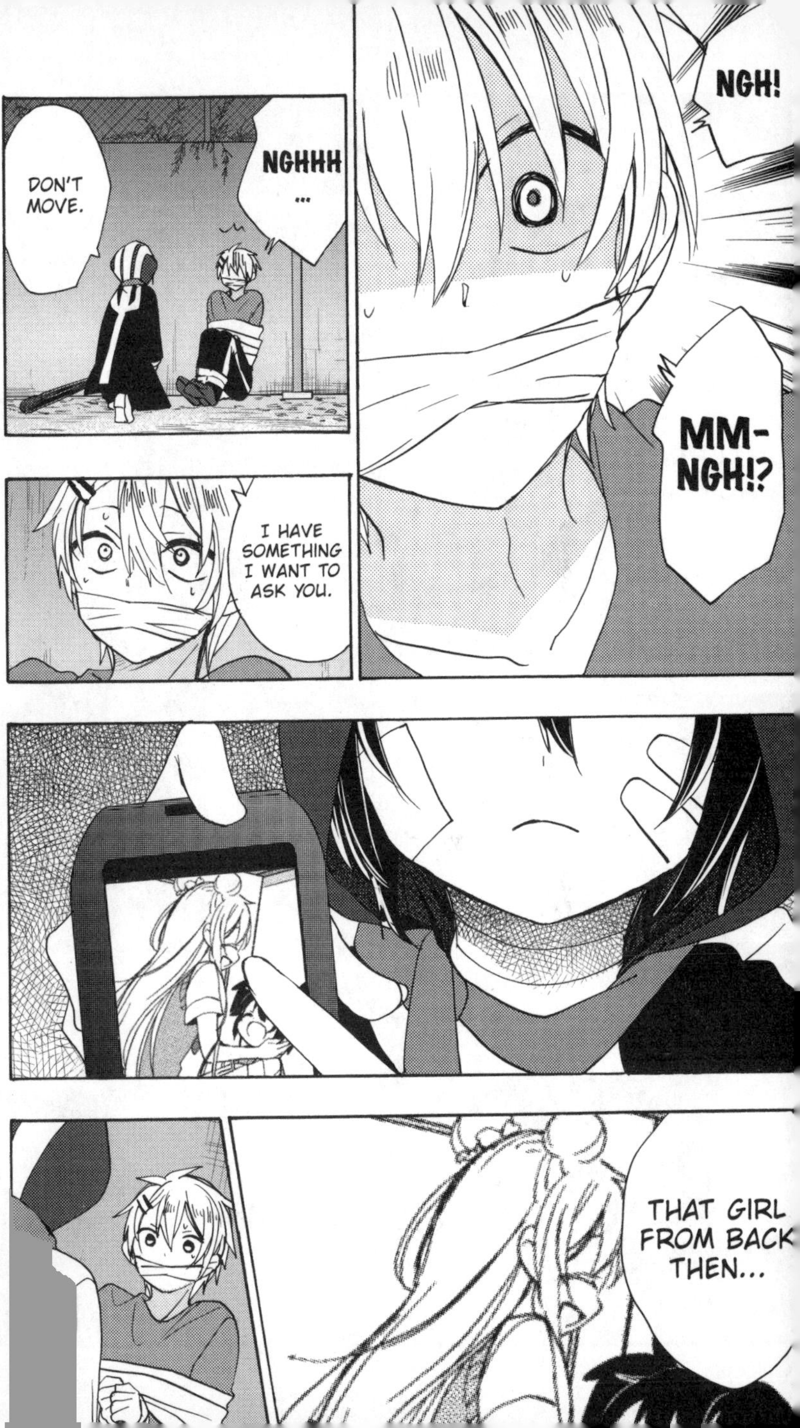
NGH!
MM-NGH!?
DON'T MOVE.
NGHHH ...
I HAVE SOMETHING I WANT TO ASK YOU.
THAT GIRL FROM BACK THEN...

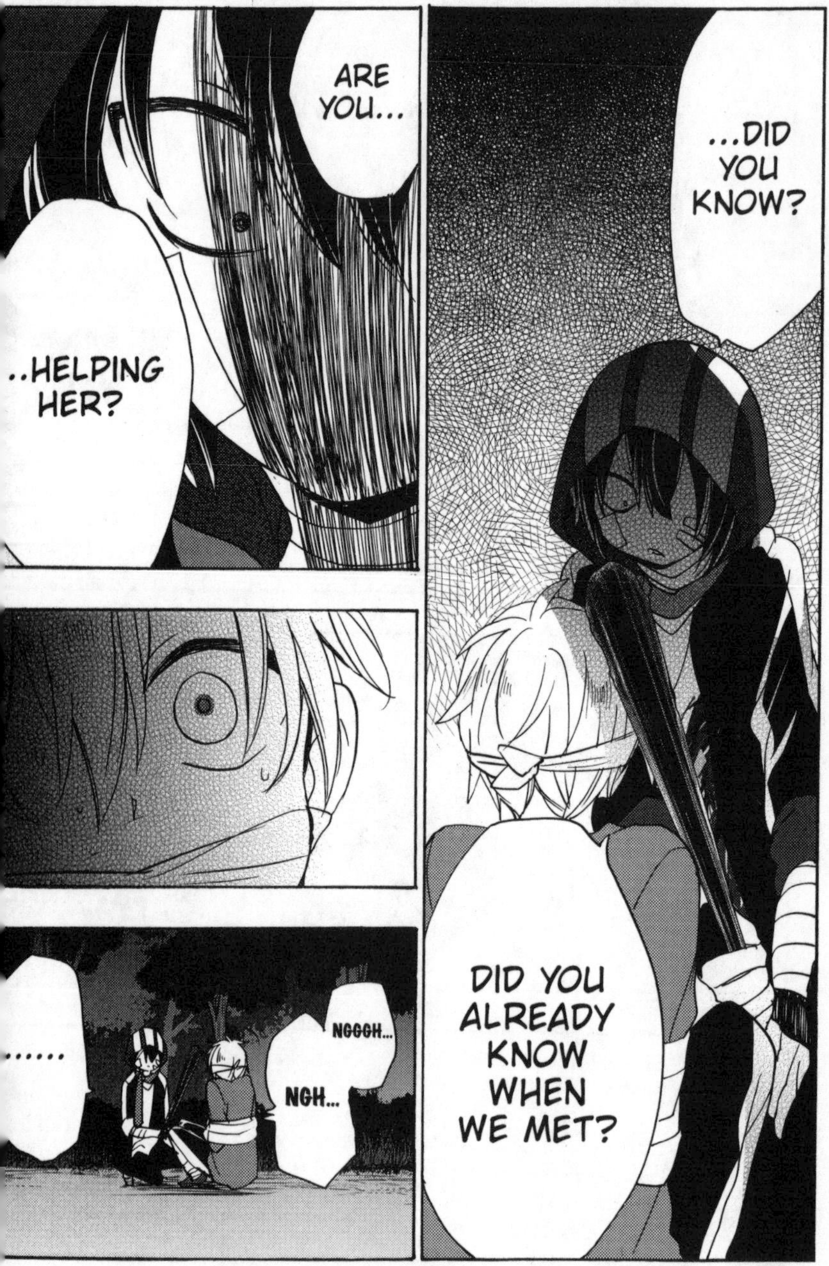
...DID YOU KNOW?
DID YOU ALREADY KNOW WHEN WE MET?
ARE YOU...
..HELPING HER?
NGGGH...
NGH...
......

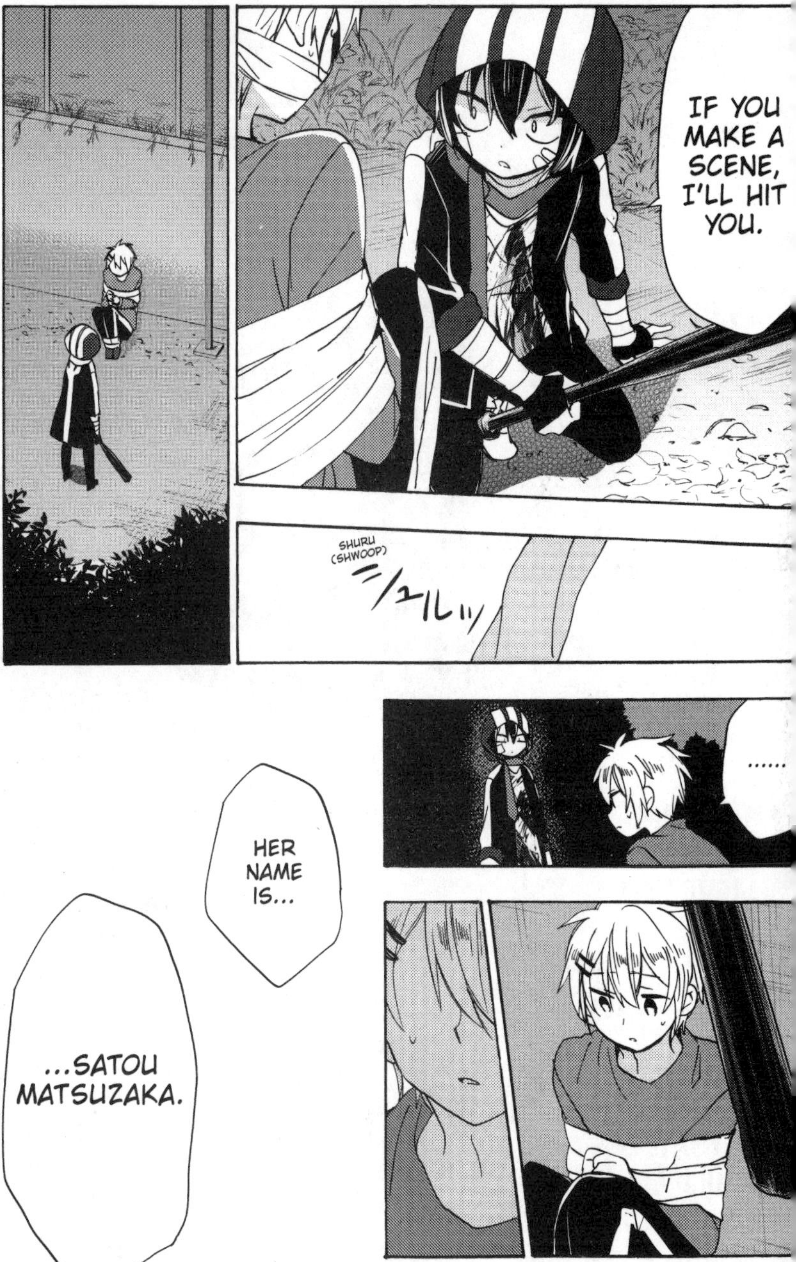
IF YOU MAKE A SCENE, I'LL HIT YOU.
SHURU (SHWOOP)
シュルッ
......
HER NAME IS...
...SATOU MATSUZAKA.

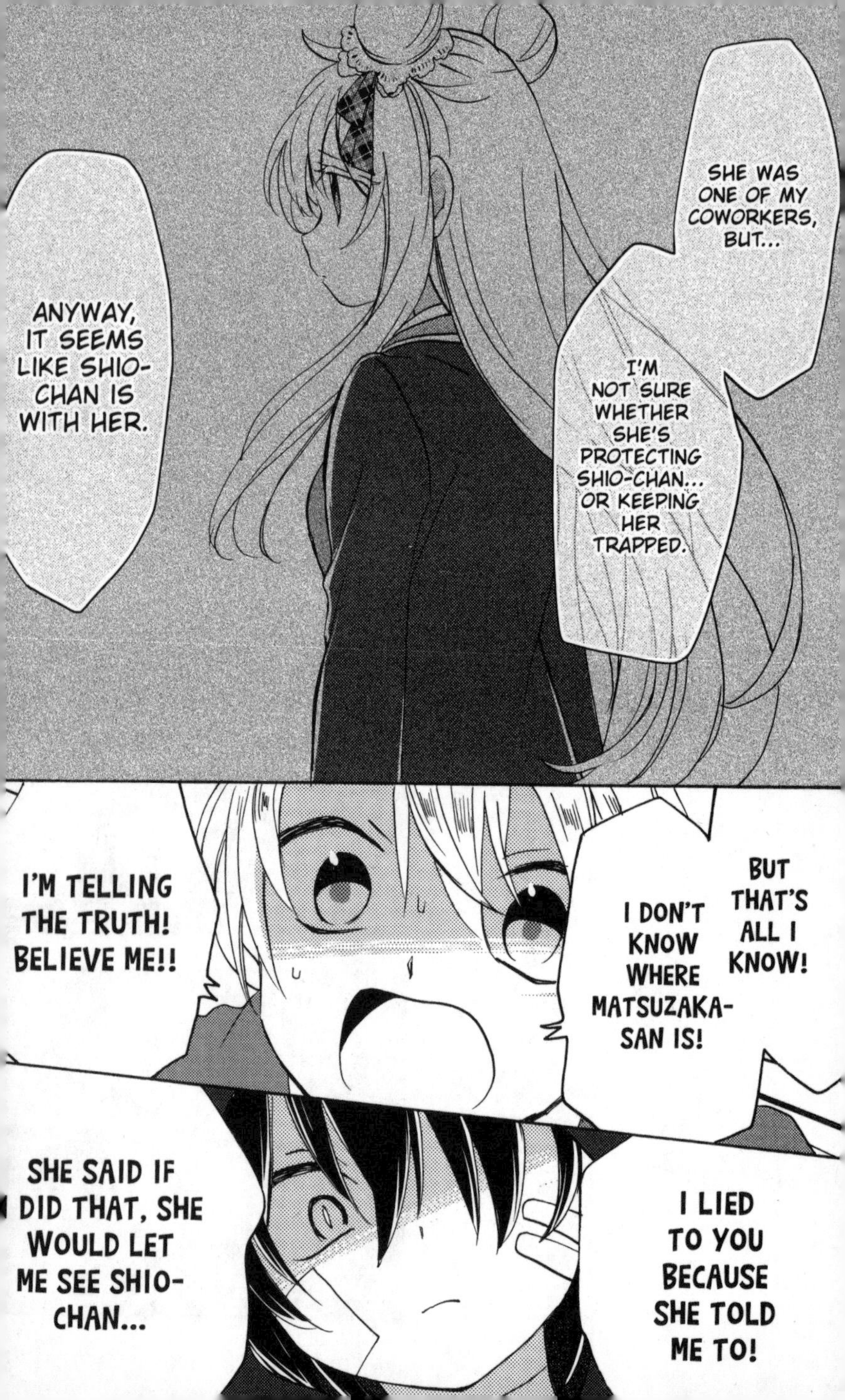
SHE WAS ONE OF MY COWORKERS, BUT...
I'M NOT SURE WHETHER SHE'S PROTECTING SHIO-CHAN... OR KEEPING HER TRAPPED.
ANYWAY, IT SEEMS LIKE SHIO-CHAN IS WITH HER.
BUT THAT'S ALL I KNOW!
I DON'T KNOW WHERE MATSUZAKA-SAN IS!
I'M TELLING THE TRUTH! BELIEVE ME!!
I LIED TO YOU BECAUSE SHE TOLD ME TO!
SHE SAID IF DID THAT, SHE WOULD LET ME SEE SHIO-CHAN...

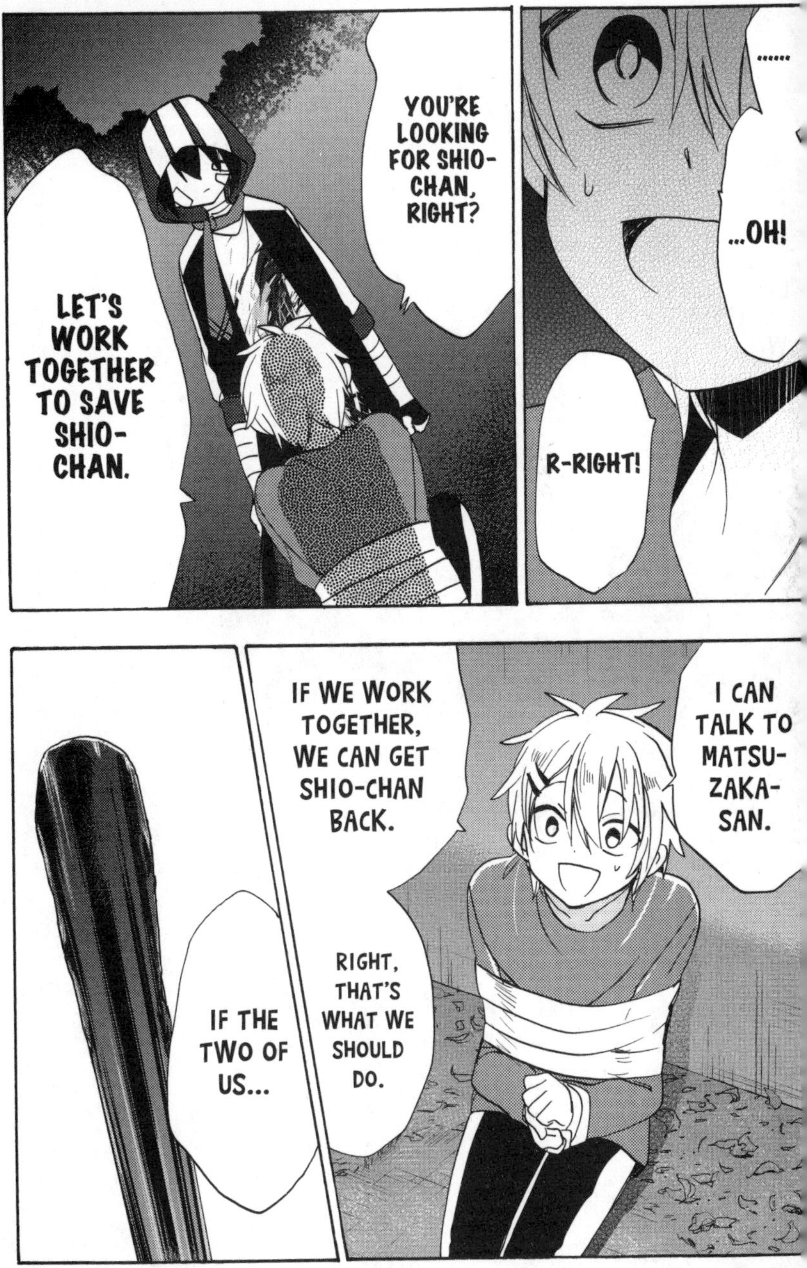
......
...OH!
R-RIGHT!
YOU'RE LOOKING FOR SHIO-CHAN, RIGHT?
LET'S WORK TOGETHER TO SAVE SHIO-CHAN.
I CAN TALK TO MATSU-ZAKA-SAN.
IF WE WORK TOGETHER, WE CAN GET SHIO-CHAN BACK.
RIGHT, THAT'S WHAT WE SHOULD DO.
IF THE TWO OF US...

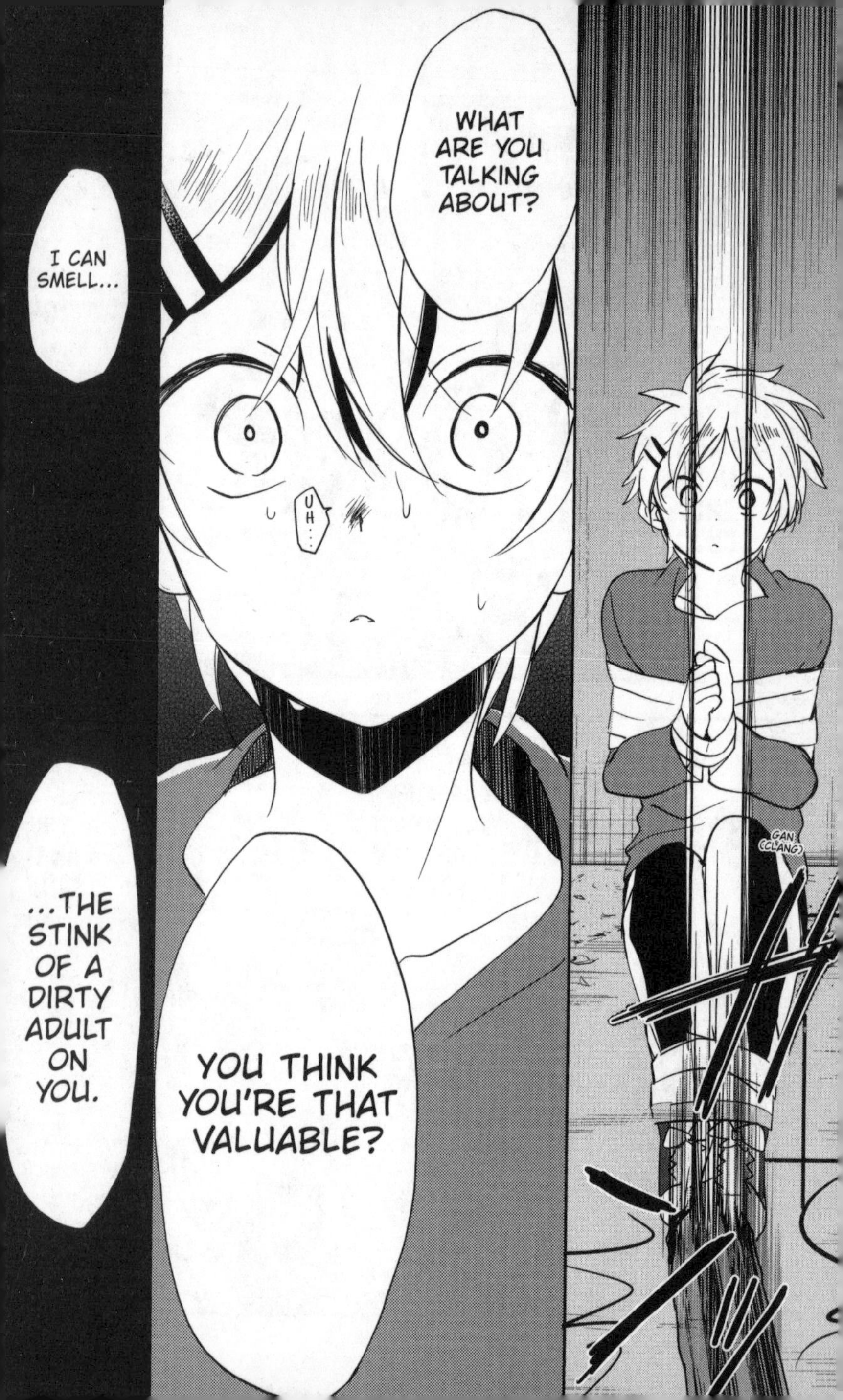
GAN (CLANG)
WHAT ARE YOU TALKING ABOUT?
UH...
YOU THINK YOU'RE THAT VALUABLE?
I CAN SMELL...
...THE STINK OF A DIRTY ADULT ON YOU.

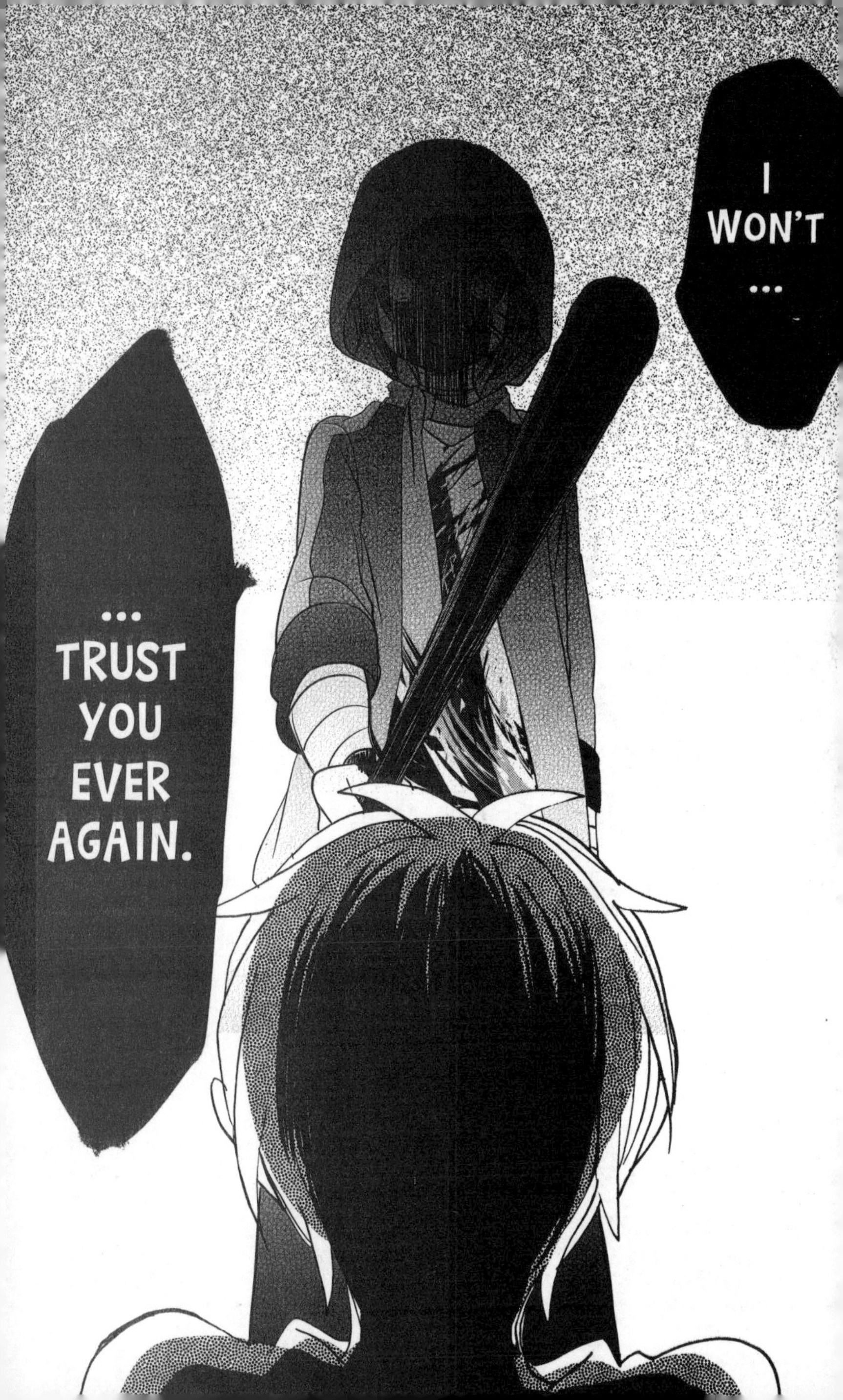
I WON'T ...
... TRUST YOU EVER AGAIN.

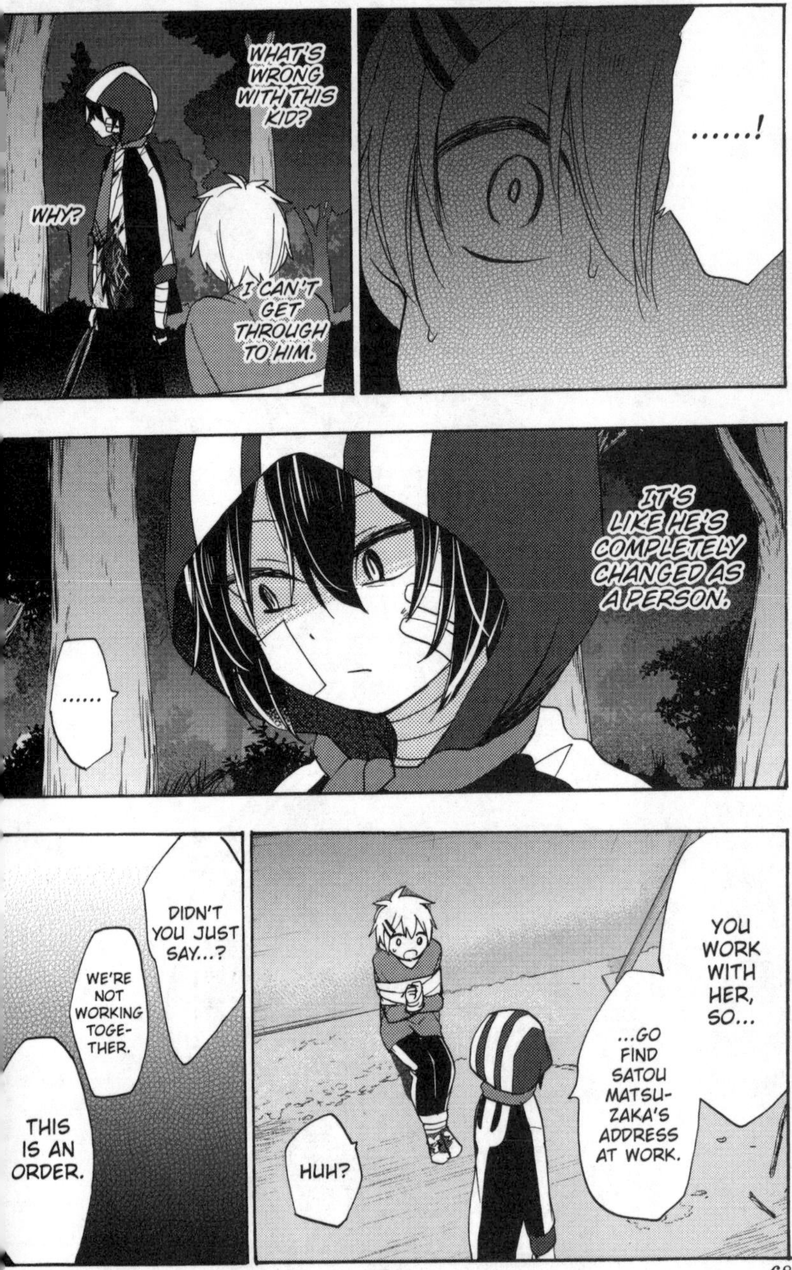
......!
WHAT'S WRONG WITH THIS KID?
WHY?
I CAN'T GET THROUGH TO HIM.
IT'S LIKE HE'S COMPLETELY CHANGED AS A PERSON.
......
YOU WORK WITH HER, SO...
...GO FIND SATOU MATSU-ZAKA'S ADDRESS AT WORK.
HUH?
DIDN'T YOU JUST SAY...?
WE'RE NOT WORKING TOGE-THER.
THIS IS AN ORDER.

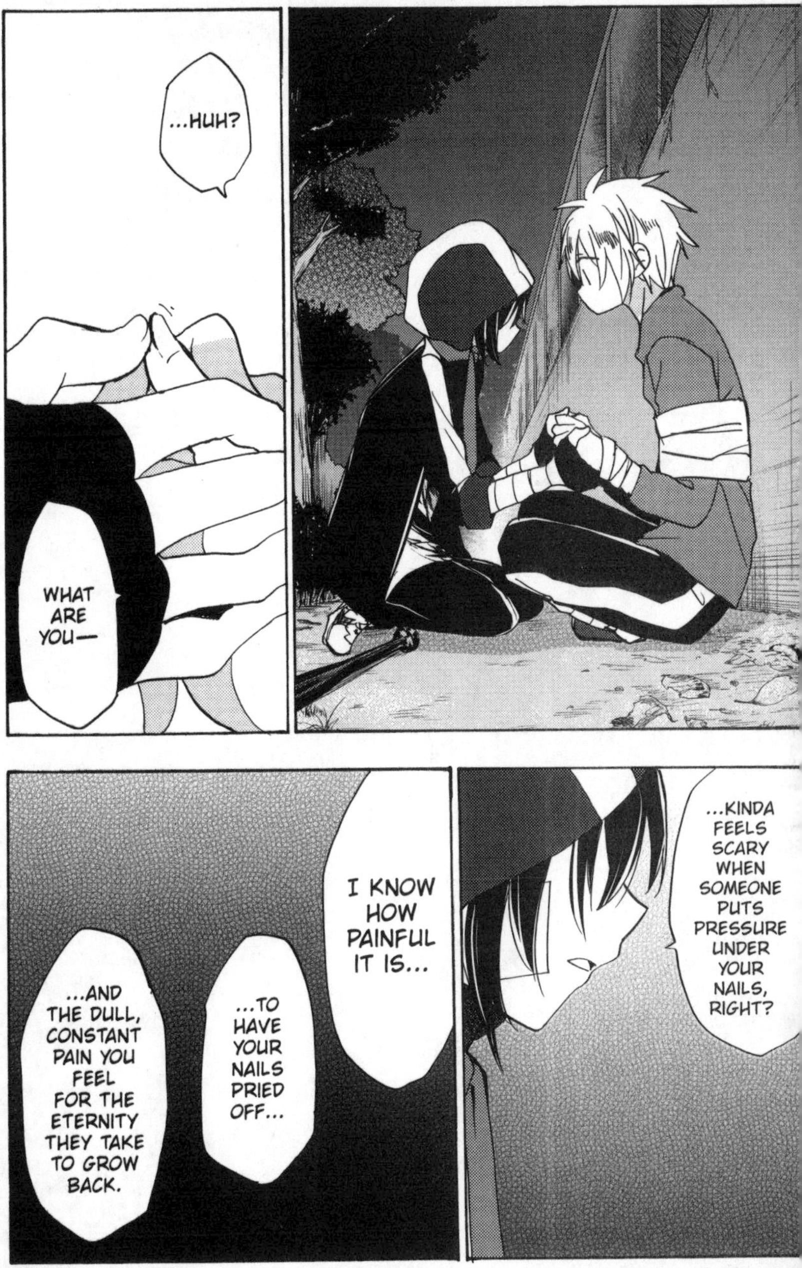
...HUH?
WHAT ARE YOU—
...KINDA FEELS SCARY WHEN SOMEONE PUTS PRESSURE UNDER YOUR NAILS, RIGHT?
I KNOW HOW PAINFUL IT IS...
...TO HAVE YOUR NAILS PRIED OFF...
...AND THE DULL, CONSTANT PAIN YOU FEEL FOR THE ETERNITY THEY TAKE TO GROW BACK.

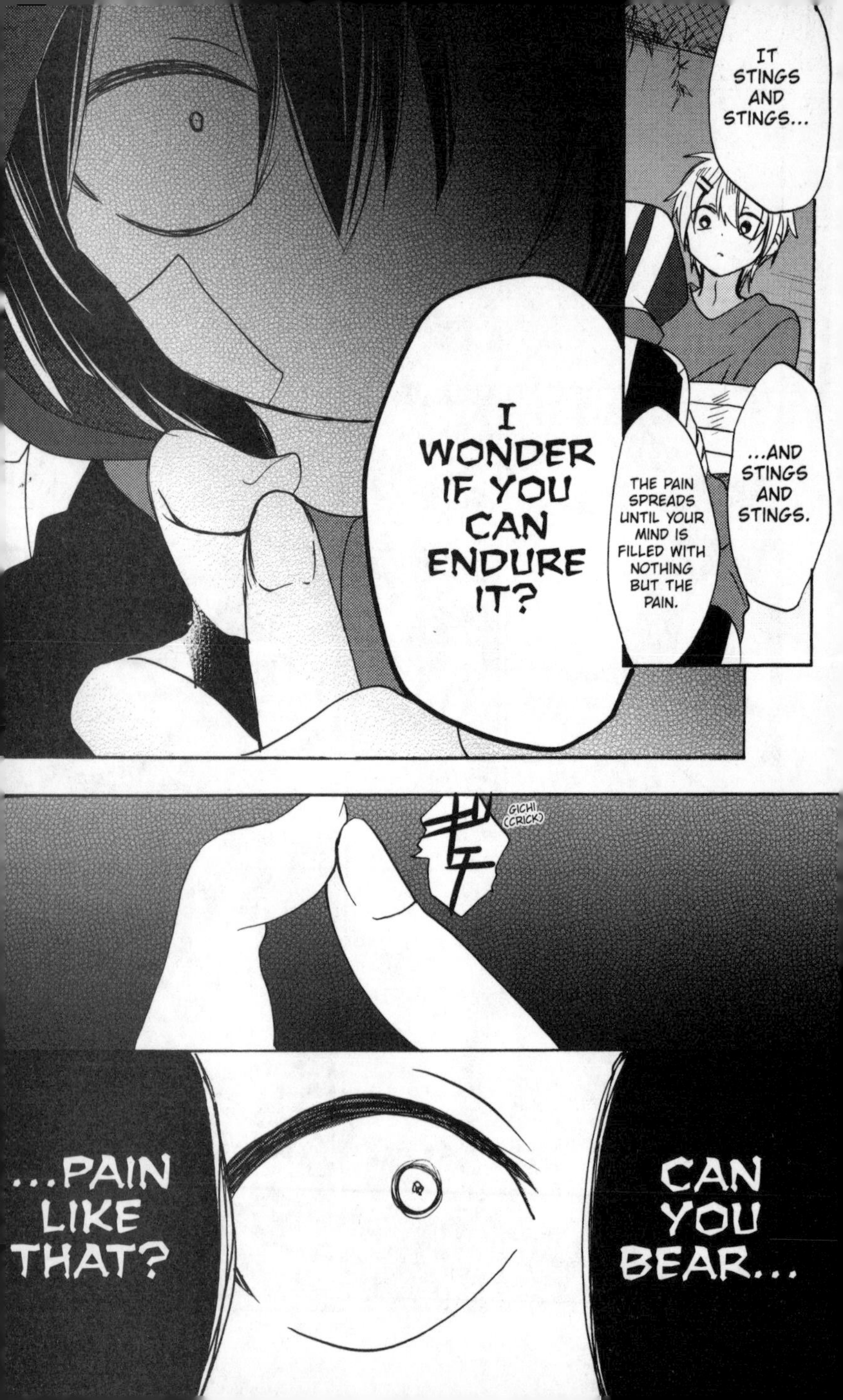
IT STINGS AND STINGS...
...AND STINGS AND STINGS.
THE PAIN SPREADS UNTIL YOUR MIND IS FILLED WITH NOTHING BUT THE PAIN.
I WONDER IF YOU CAN ENDURE IT?
GICHI (CRICK)
CAN YOU BEAR...
...PAIN LIKE THAT?

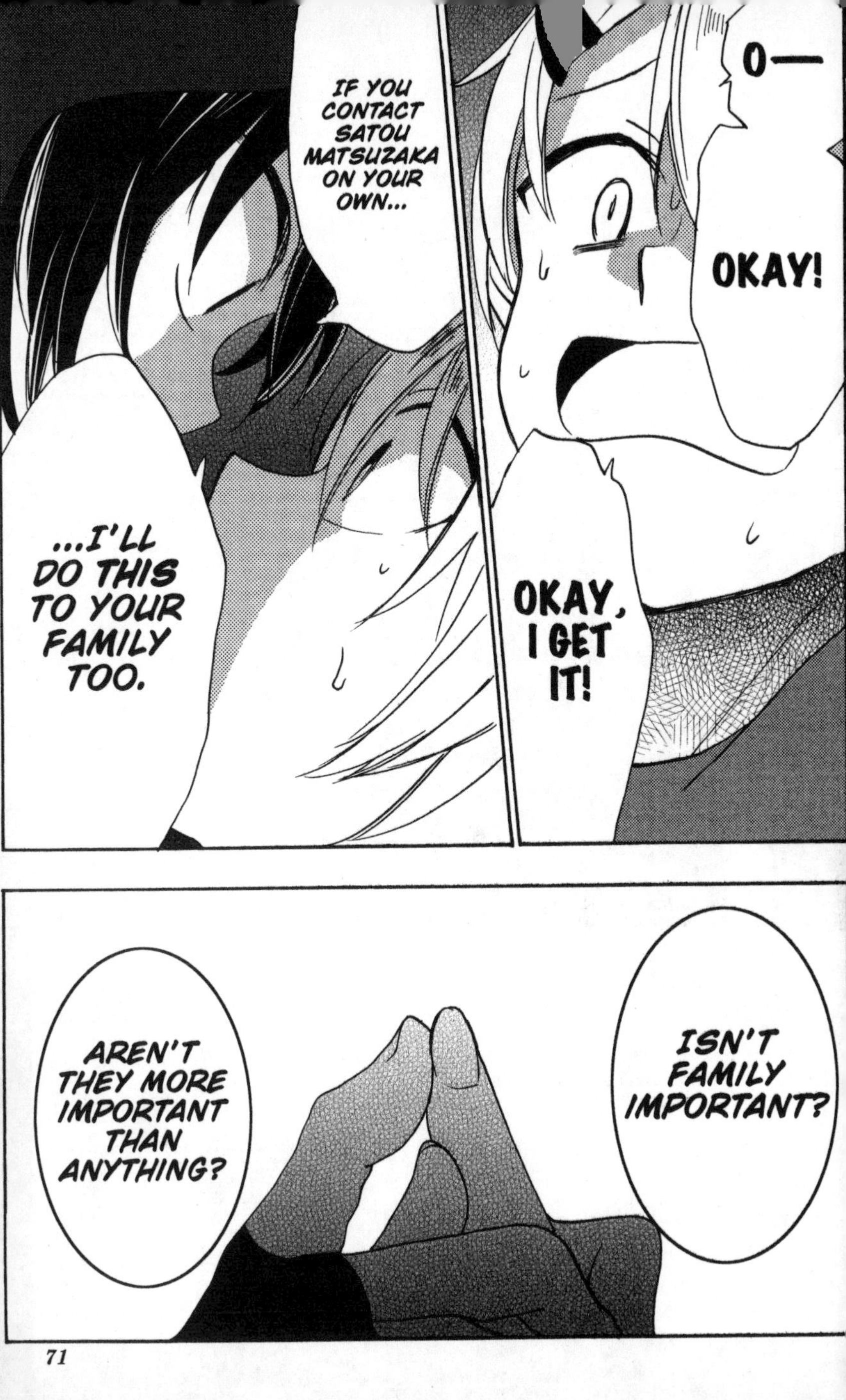
O—
OKAY!
OKAY, I GET IT!
IF YOU CONTACT SATOU MATSUZAKA ON YOUR OWN...
...I'LL DO THIS TO YOUR FAMILY TOO.
ISN'T FAMILY IMPORTANT?
AREN'T THEY MORE IMPORTANT THAN ANYTHING?

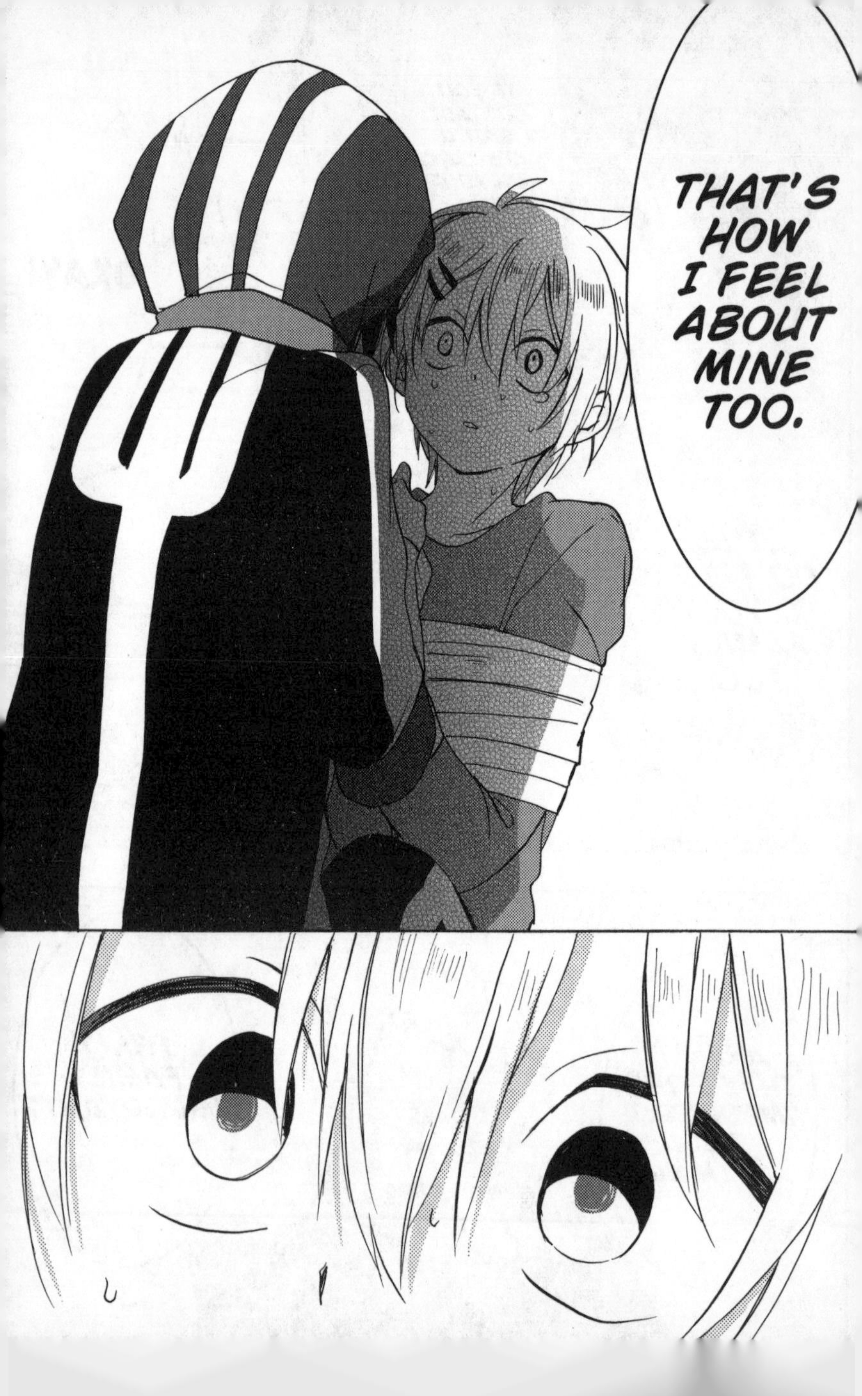
THAT'S HOW I FEEL ABOUT MINE TOO.

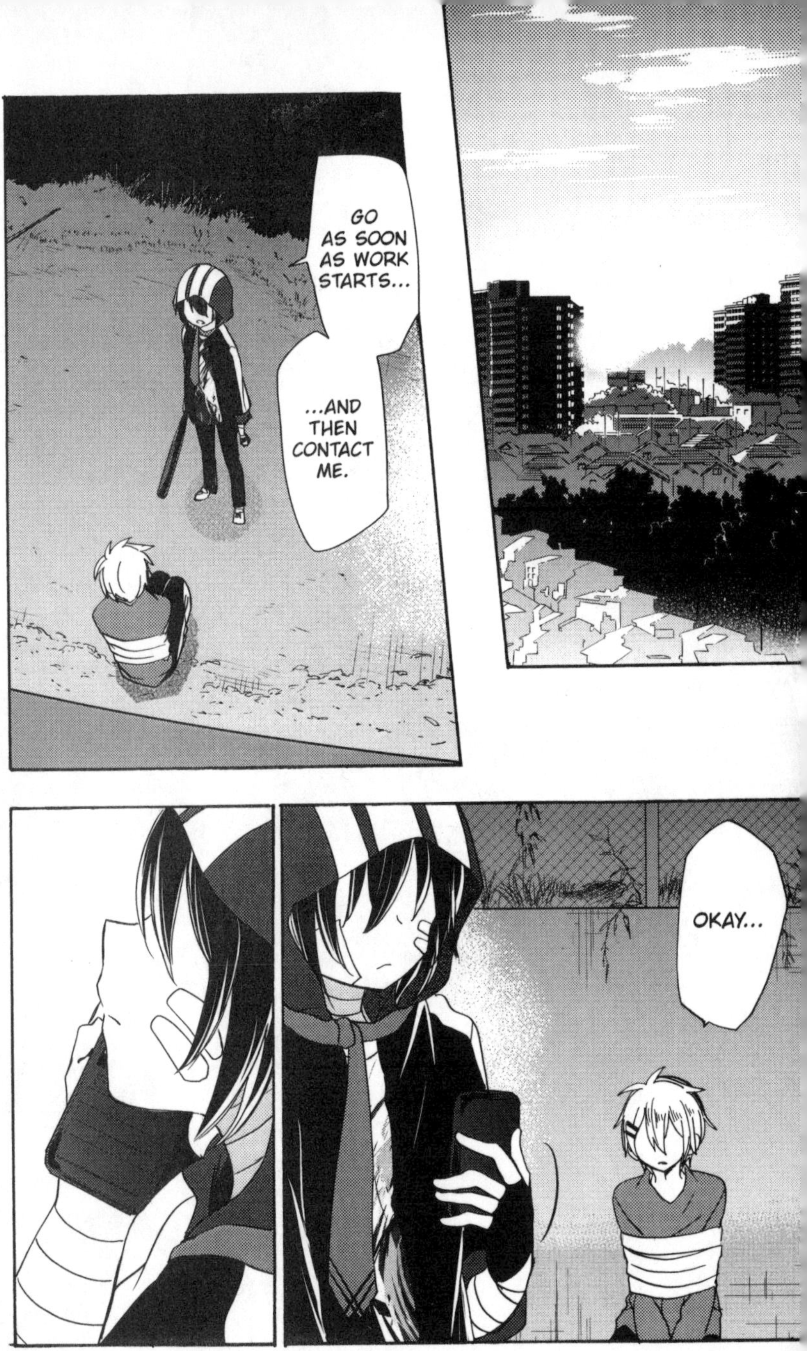
GO AS SOON AS WORK STARTS...
...AND THEN CONTACT ME.
OKAY...

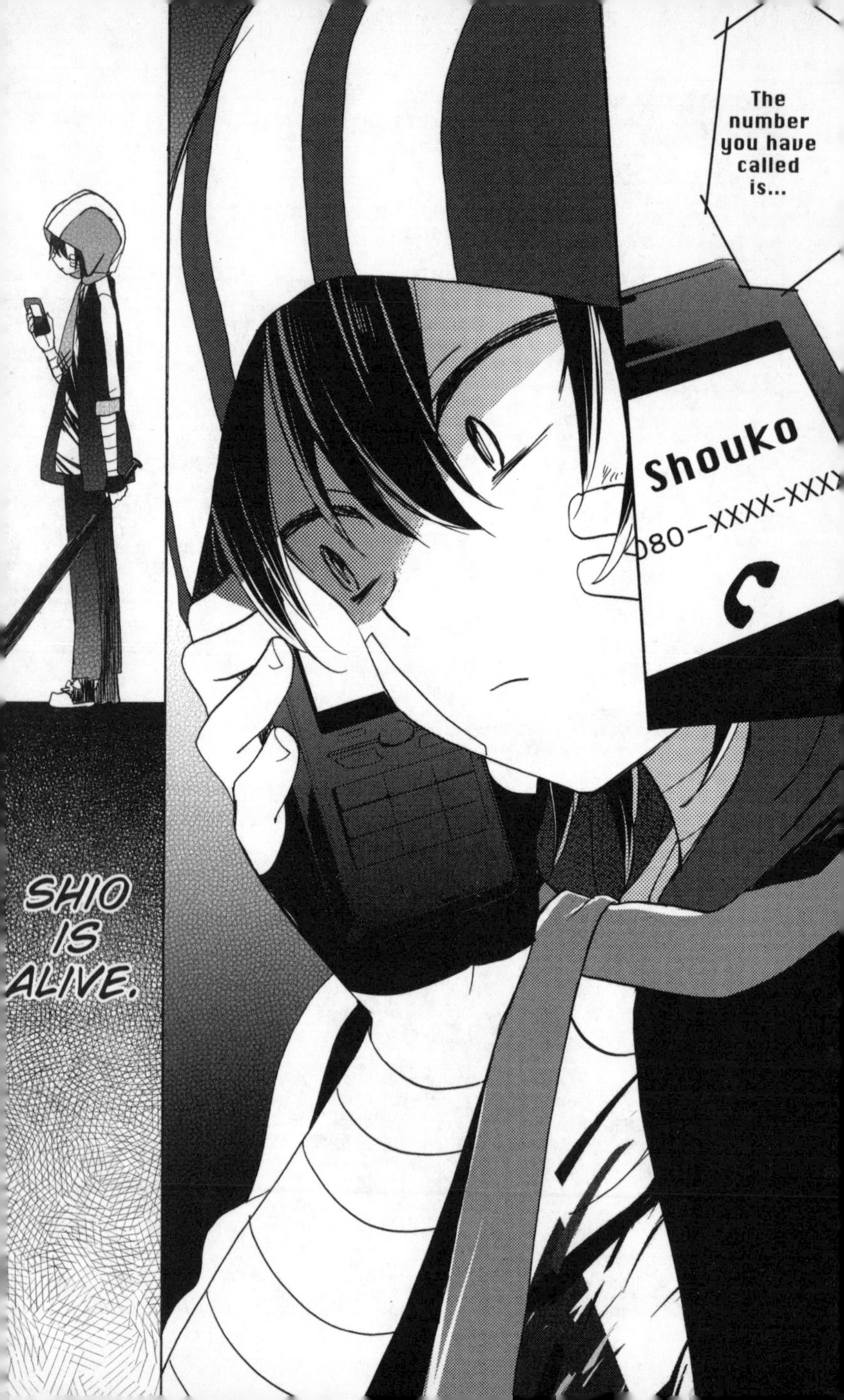
The number you have called is...
Shouko
080–XXXX–XXX
SHIO IS ALIVE.

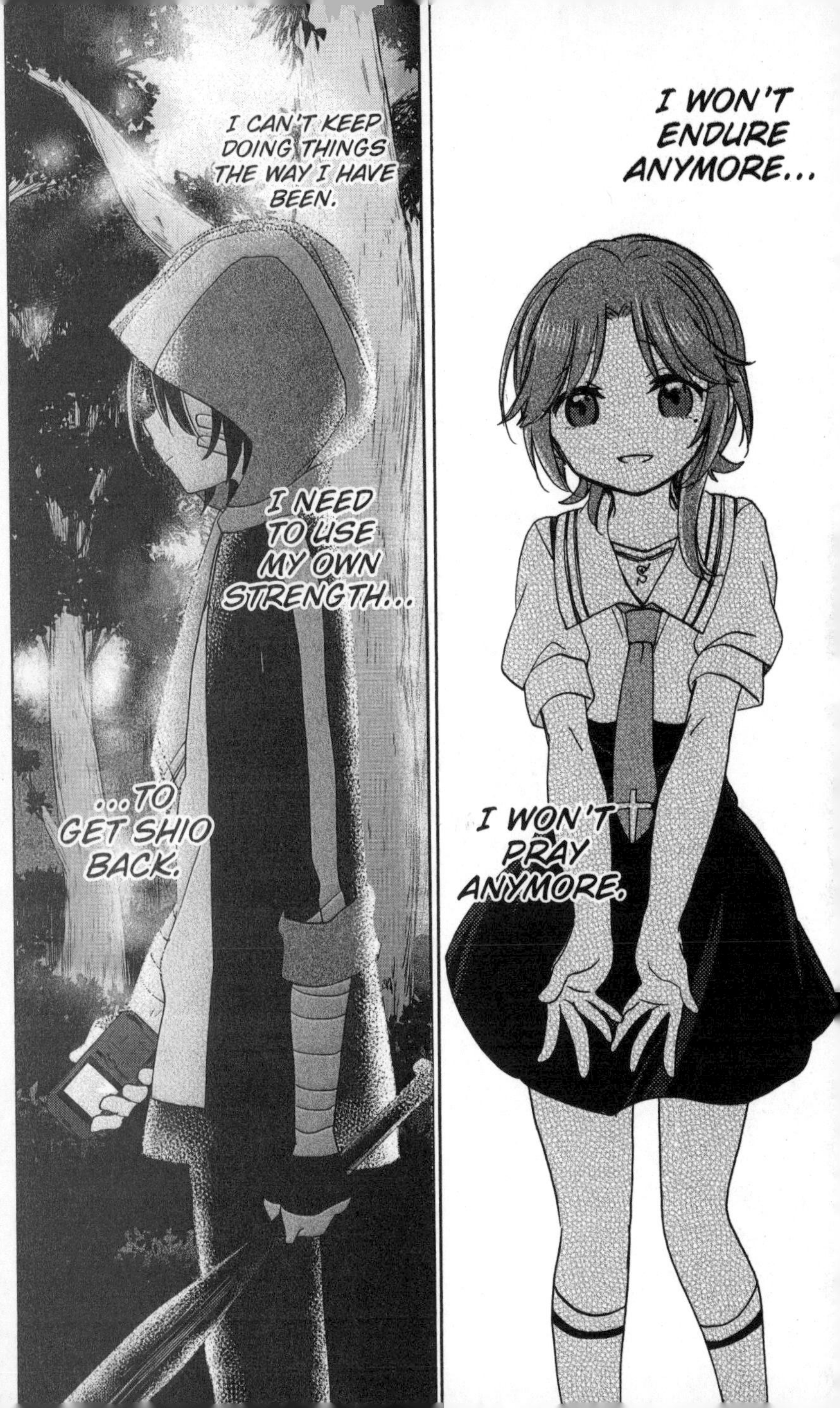
I WON'T ENDURE ANYMORE...
I WON'T PRAY ANYMORE.
I CAN'T KEEP DOING THINGS THE WAY I HAVE BEEN.
I NEED TO USE MY OWN STRENGTH...
...TO GET SHIO BACK.

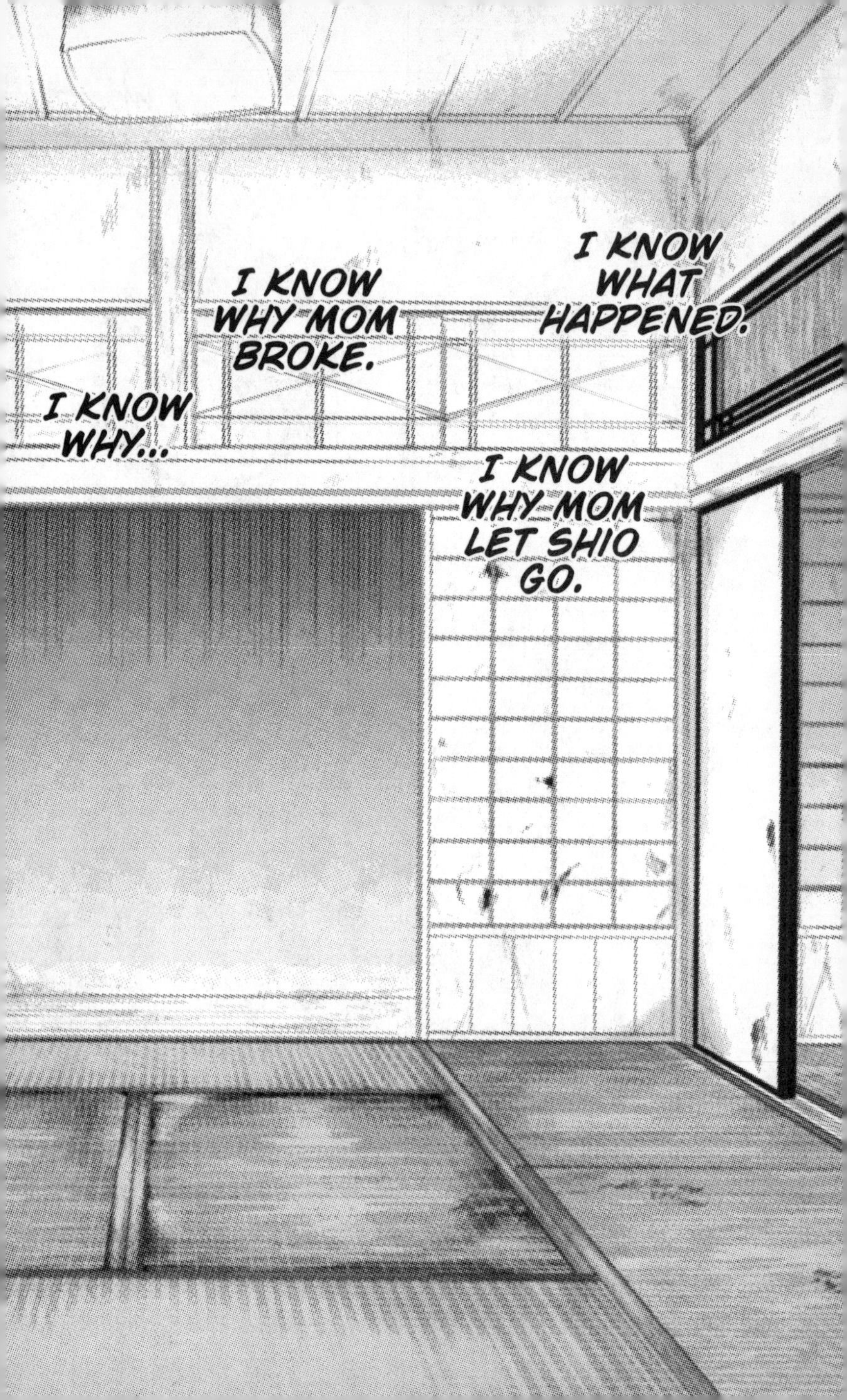
I KNOW WHAT HAPPENED.
I KNOW WHY MOM BROKE.
I KNOW WHY MOM LET SHIO GO.
I KNOW WHY...

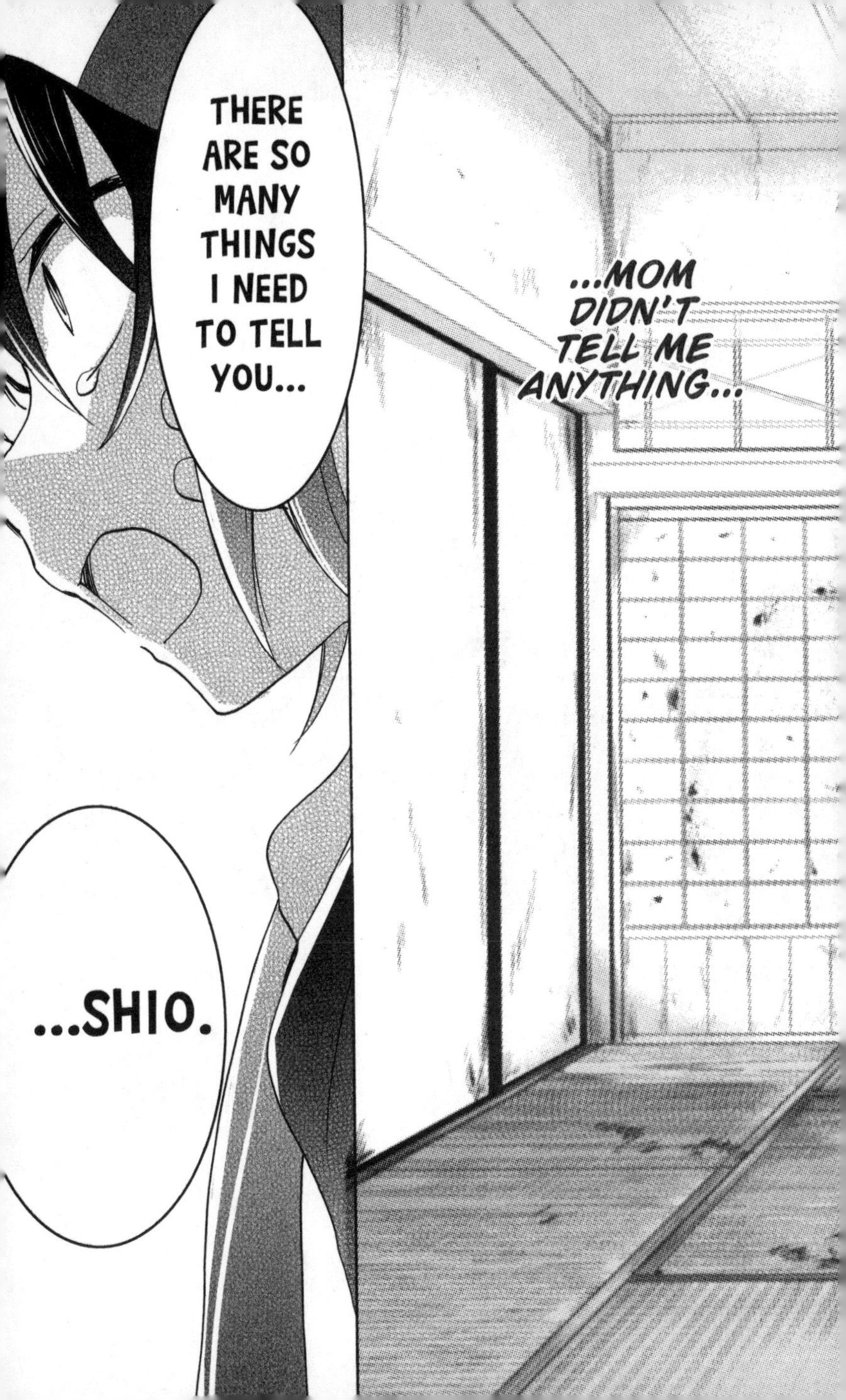
...MOM DIDN'T TELL ME ANYTHING...
THERE ARE SO MANY THINGS I NEED TO TELL YOU...
...SHIO.

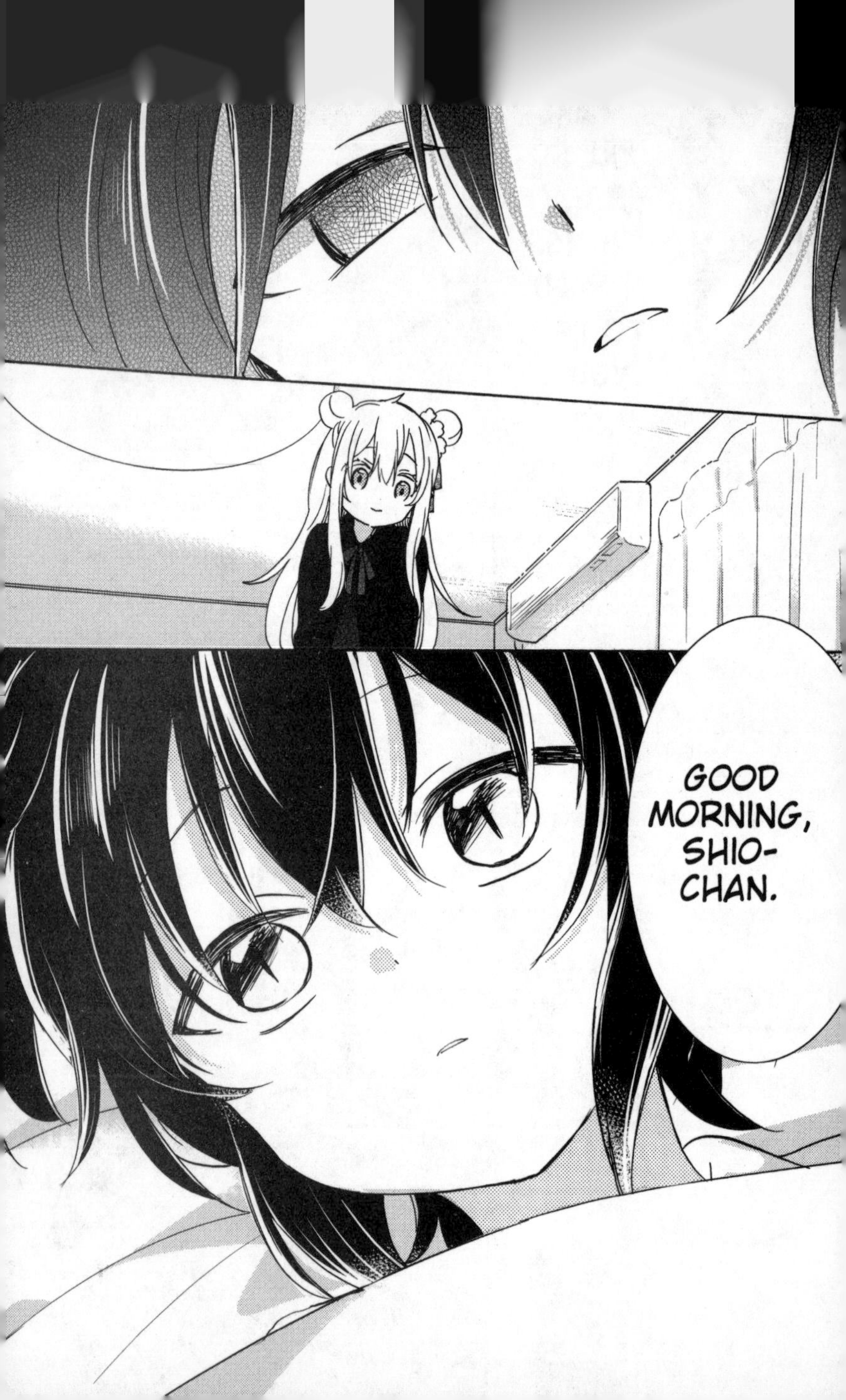
GOOD MORNING, SHIO-CHAN.

Happy
Sugar
Life

Happy
Sugar
Life

35TH LIFE: PANDORA'S BOX

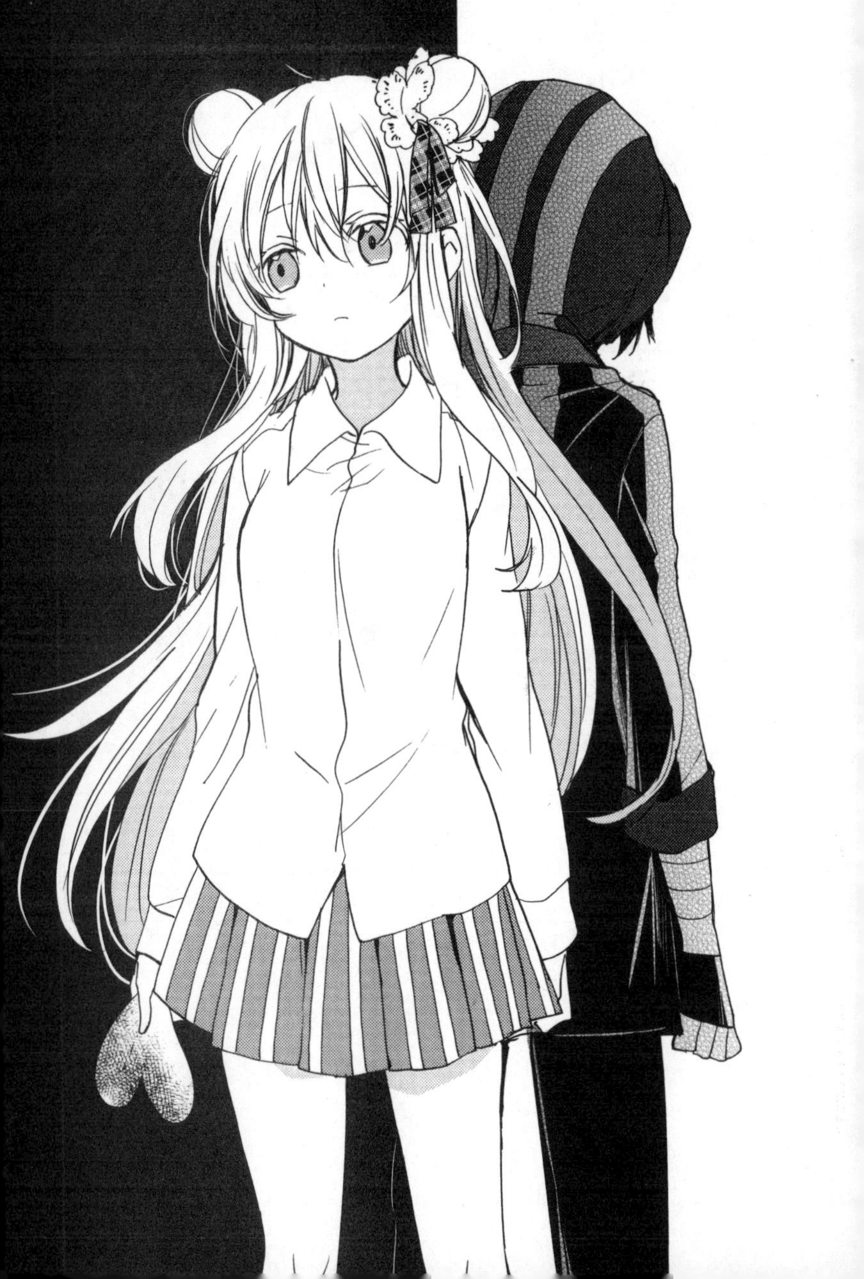

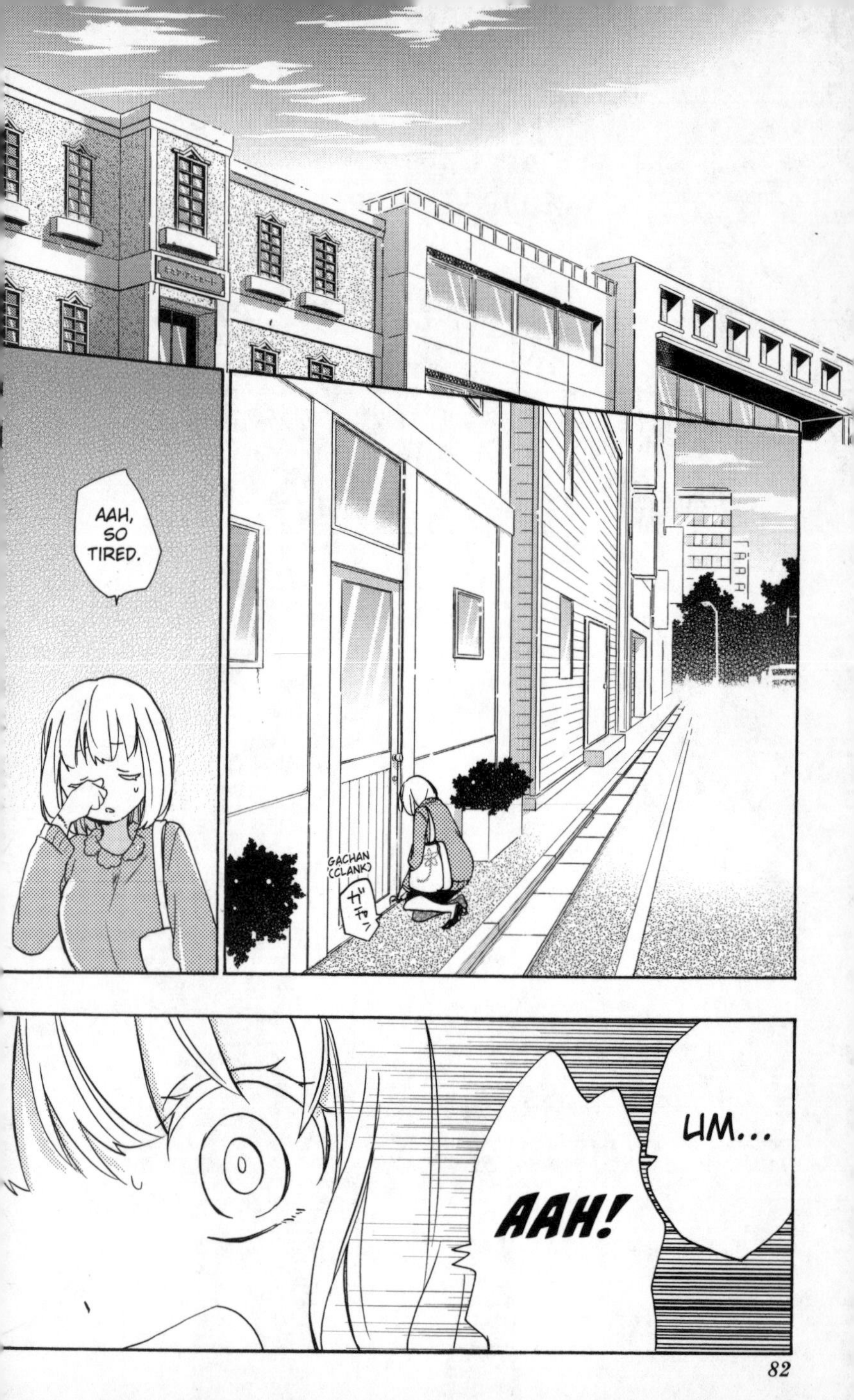

GACHAN (CLANK)
AAH, SO TIRED.
UM...
AAH!

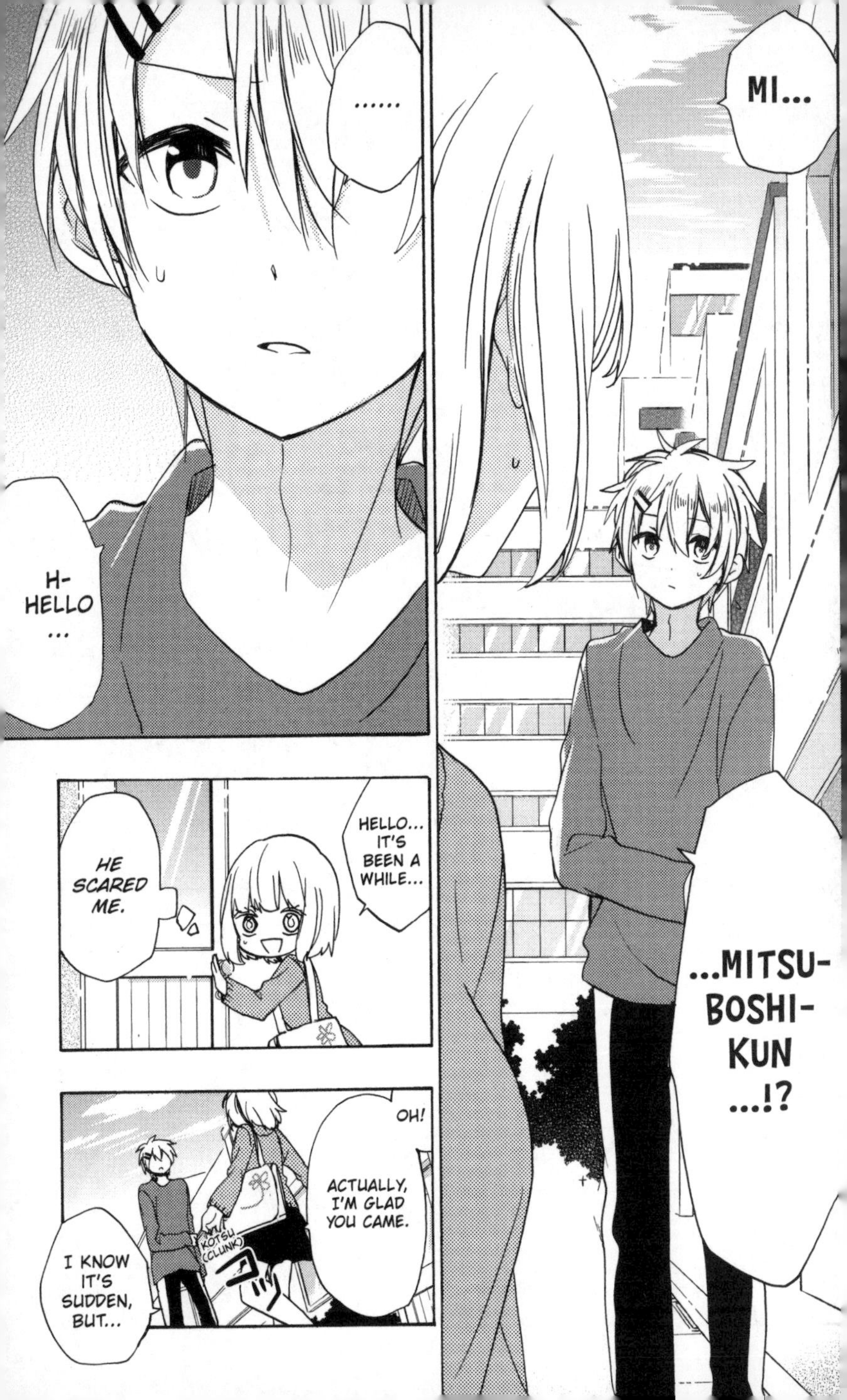
MI...
...MITSU-BOSHI-KUN...!?
......
H-HELLO...
HELLO... IT'S BEEN A WHILE...
HE SCARED ME.
OH!
ACTUALLY, I'M GLAD YOU CAME.
KOTSU (CLUNK)
I KNOW IT'S SUDDEN, BUT...

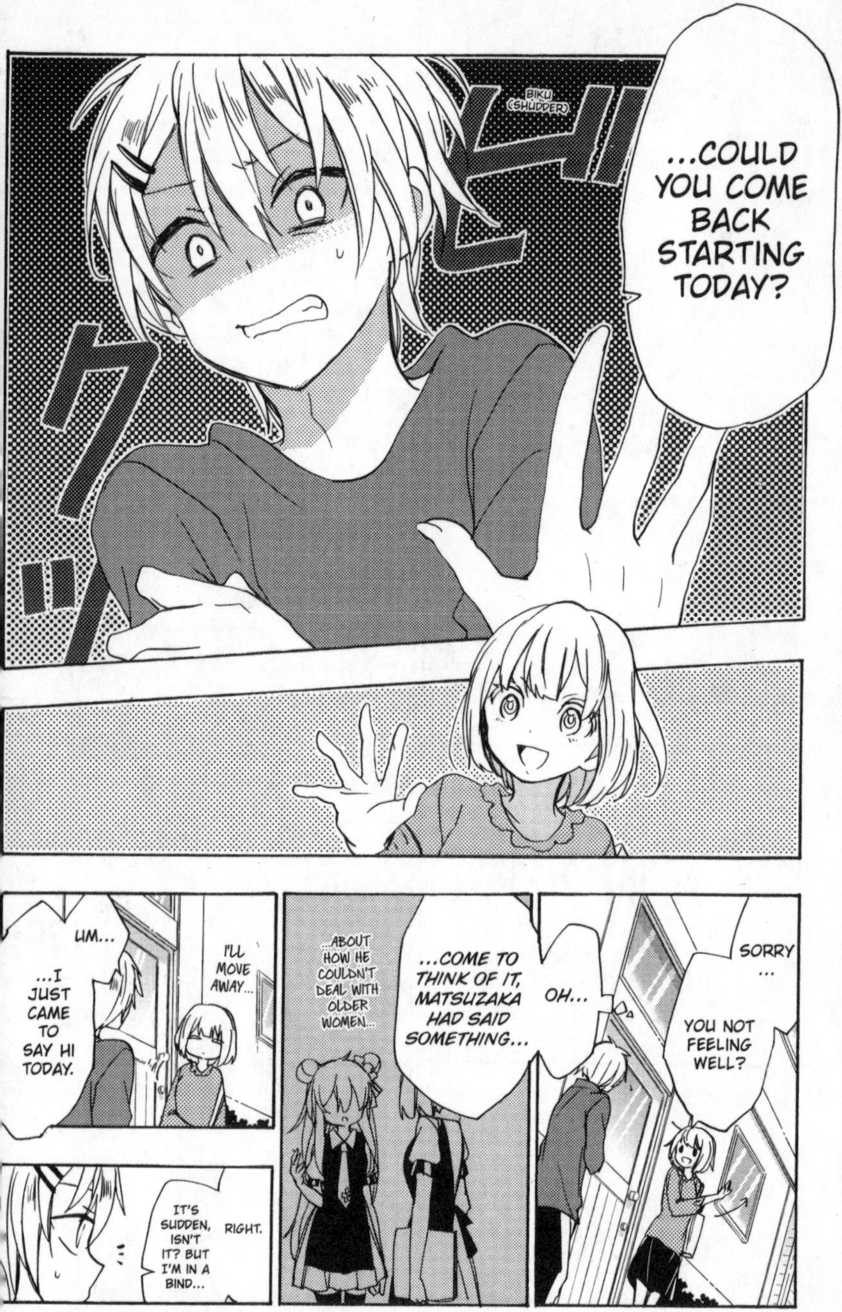
BIKU (SHUDDER)
...COULD YOU COME BACK STARTING TODAY?
SORRY ...
YOU NOT FEELING WELL?
OH...
...COME TO THINK OF IT, MATSUZAKA HAD SAID SOMETHING...
...ABOUT HOW HE COULDN'T DEAL WITH OLDER WOMEN...
UM...
...I JUST CAME TO SAY HI TODAY.
I'LL MOVE AWAY...
RIGHT.
IT'S SUDDEN, ISN'T IT? BUT I'M IN A BIND...

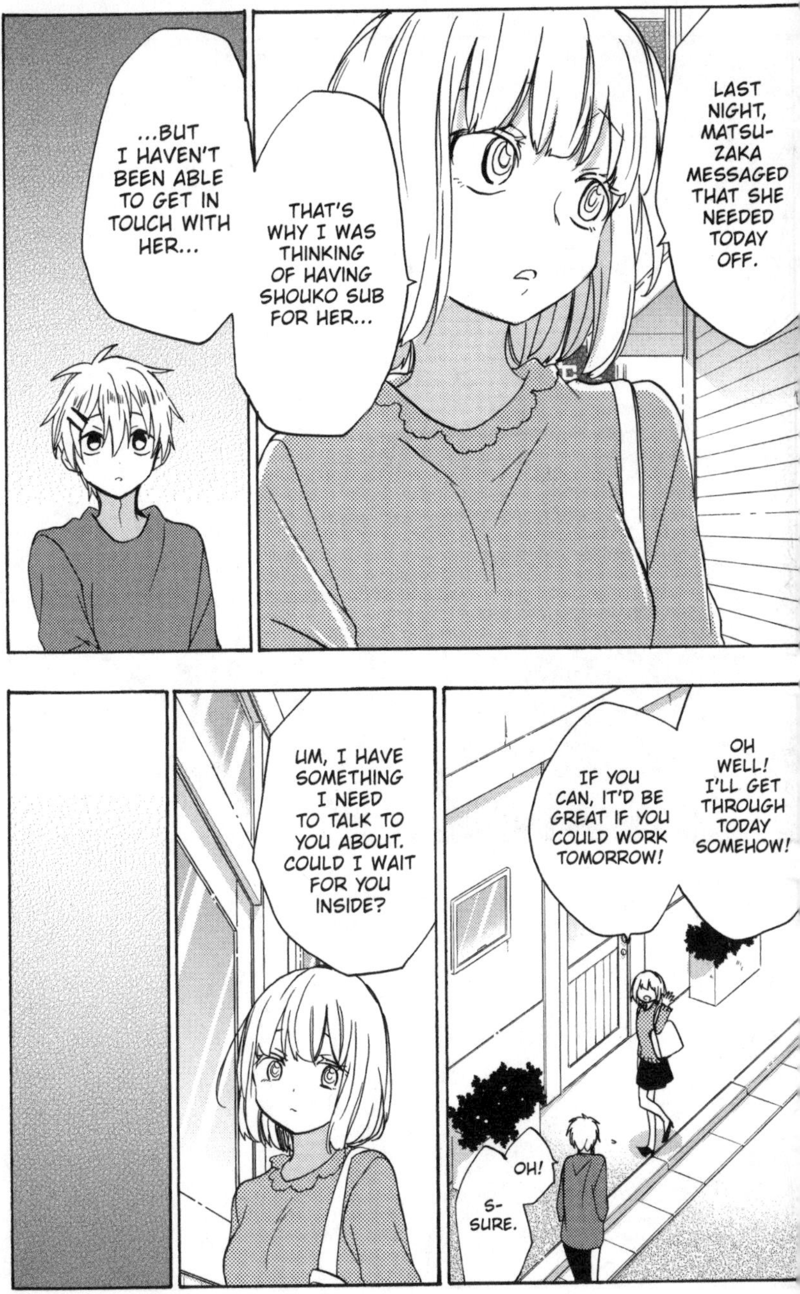
LAST NIGHT, MATSU-ZAKA MESSAGED THAT SHE NEEDED TODAY OFF.
THAT'S WHY I WAS THINKING OF HAVING SHOUKO SUB FOR HER...
...BUT I HAVEN'T BEEN ABLE TO GET IN TOUCH WITH HER...
OH WELL! I'LL GET THROUGH TODAY SOMEHOW!
IF YOU CAN, IT'D BE GREAT IF YOU COULD WORK TOMORROW!
OH!
S-SURE.
UM, I HAVE SOMETHING I NEED TO TALK TO YOU ABOUT. COULD I WAIT FOR YOU INSIDE?

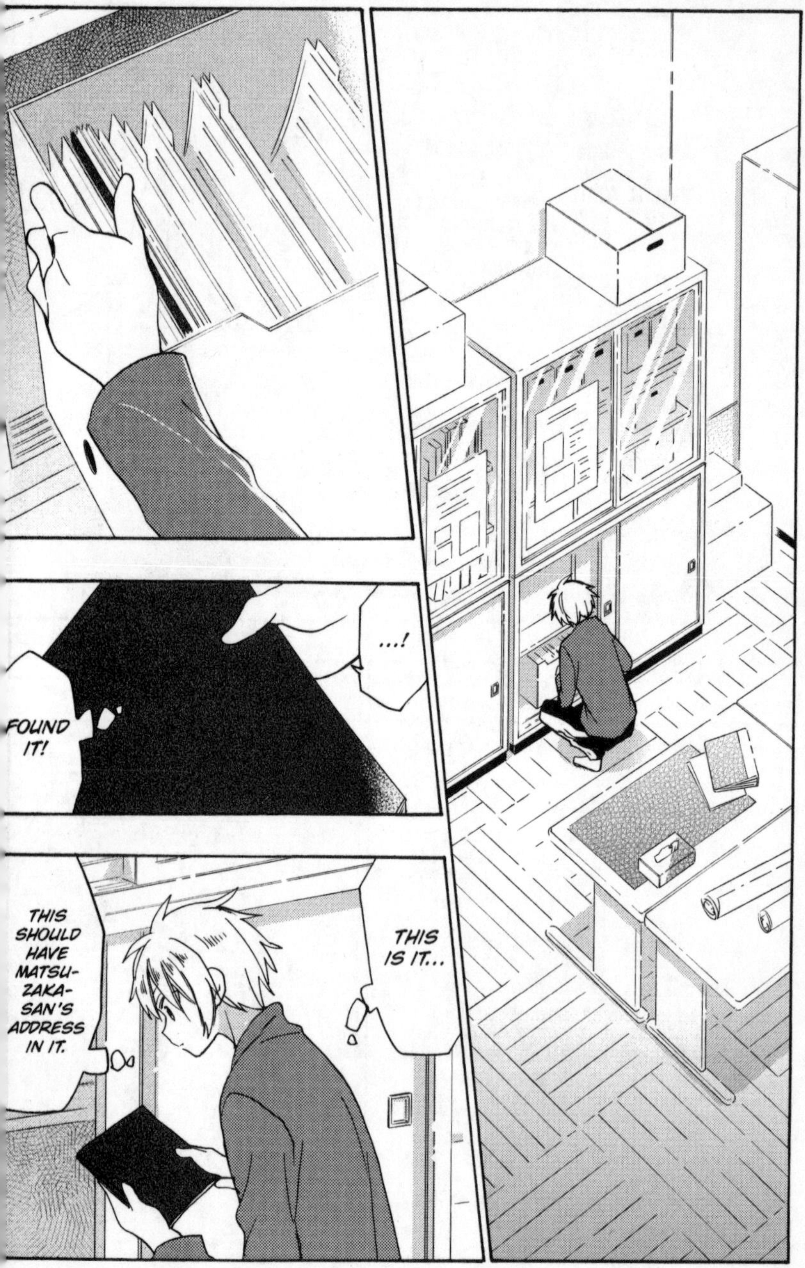
...!
FOUND IT!
THIS IS IT...
THIS SHOULD HAVE MATSU-ZAKA-SAN'S ADDRESS IN IT.

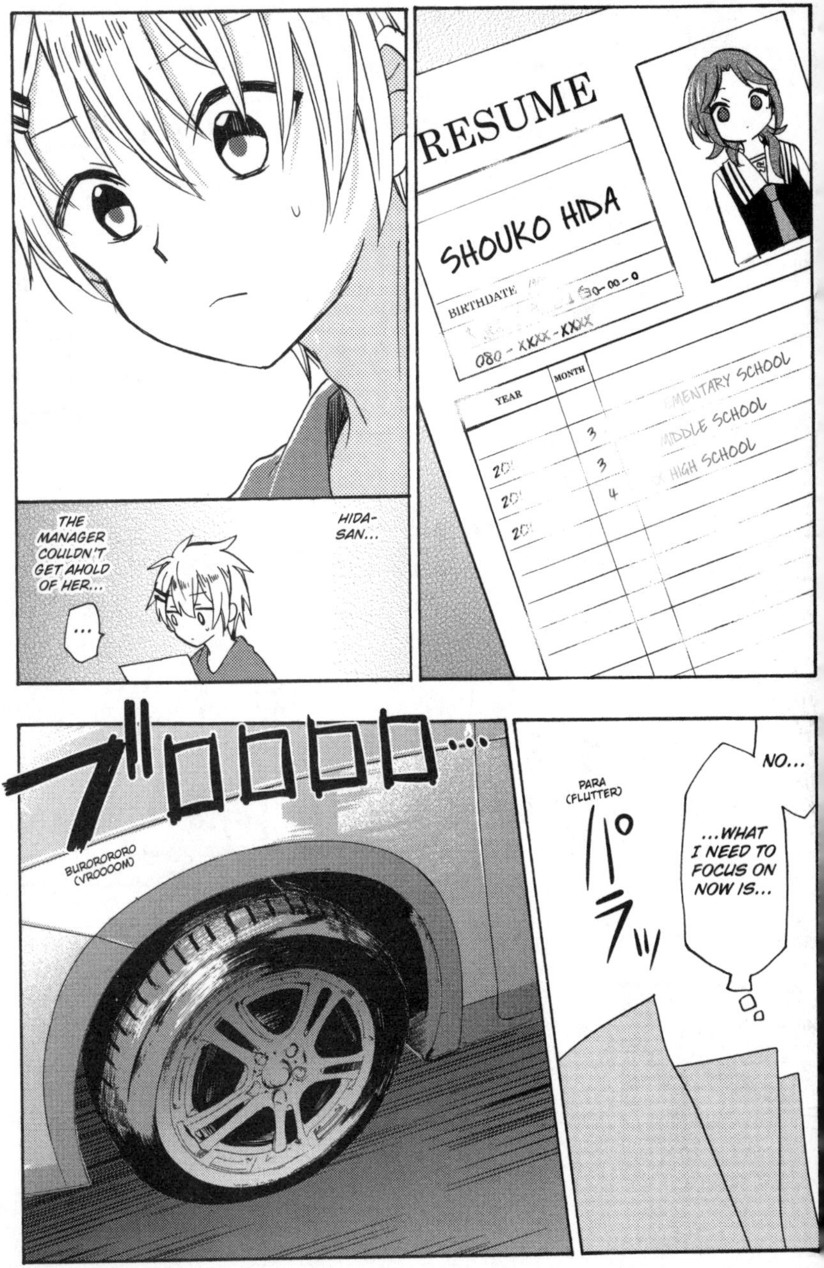
RESUME
SHOUKO HIDA
BIRTHDATE
080 - XXXX - XXXX
YEAR
MONTH
MIDDLE SCHOOL
HIGH SCHOOL
HIDA-SAN...
THE MANAGER COULDN'T GET AHOLD OF HER...
...
NO...
...WHAT I NEED TO FOCUS ON NOW IS...
PARA (FLUTTER)
BURORORORO (VROOOOM)

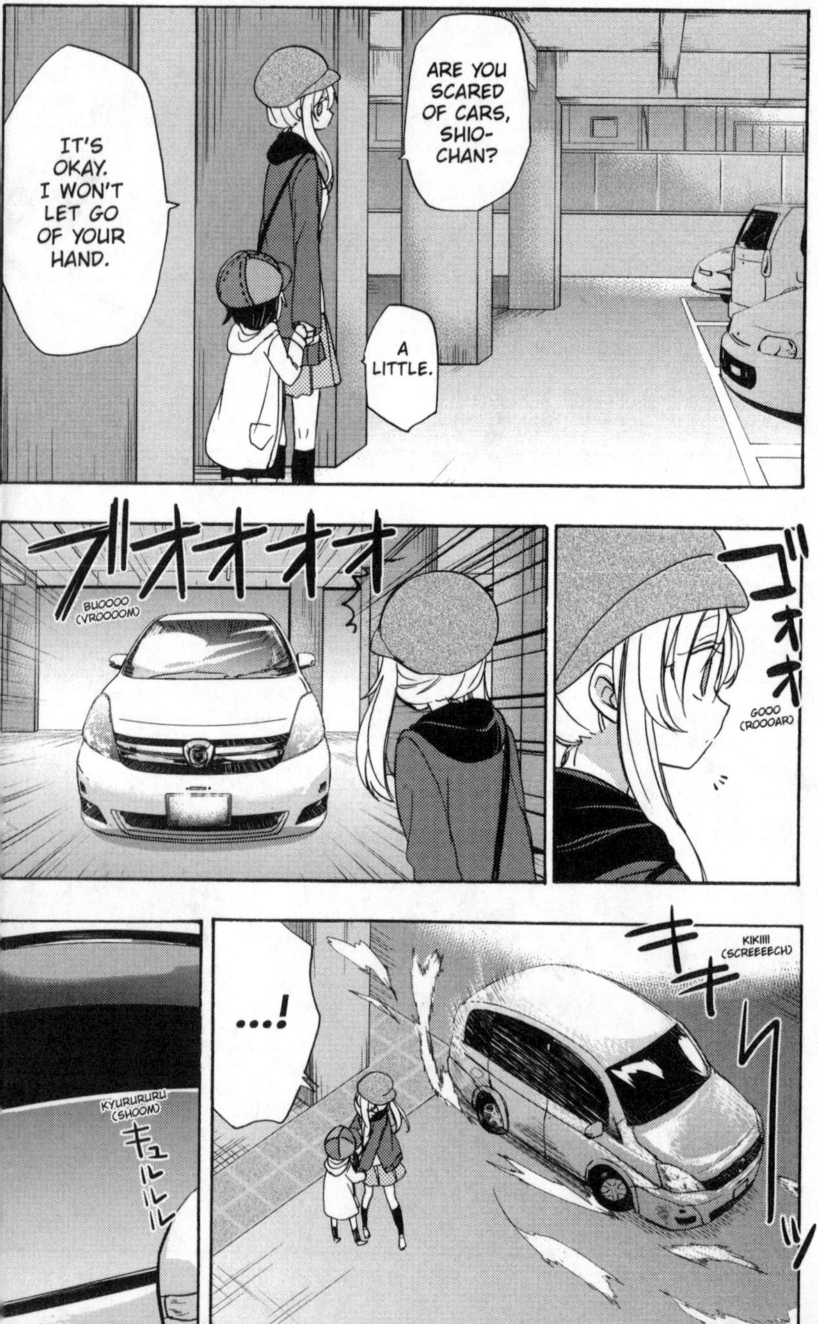
ARE YOU SCARED OF CARS, SHIO-CHAN?
A LITTLE.
IT'S OKAY. I WON'T LET GO OF YOUR HAND.
ゴォォ
GOOO (ROOOAR)
ブオオオオ
BUOOOO (VROOOOM)
KIKIIII (SCREEEECH)
...!
KYURURURU (SHOOM)
キュルルル

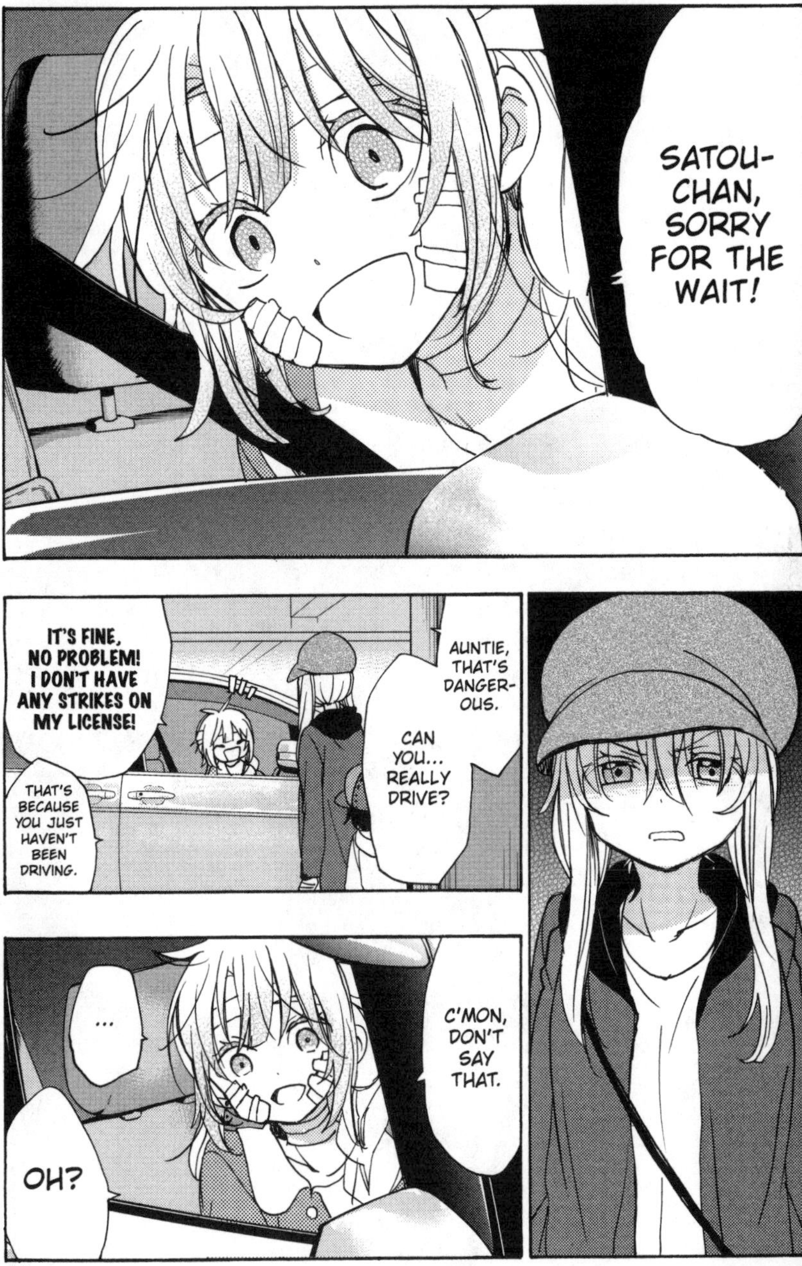

SATOU-CHAN, SORRY FOR THE WAIT!
AUNTIE, THAT'S DANGER-OUS.
CAN YOU... REALLY DRIVE?
IT'S FINE, NO PROBLEM! I DON'T HAVE ANY STRIKES ON MY LICENSE!
THAT'S BECAUSE YOU JUST HAVEN'T BEEN DRIVING.
C'MON, DON'T SAY THAT.
...
OH?

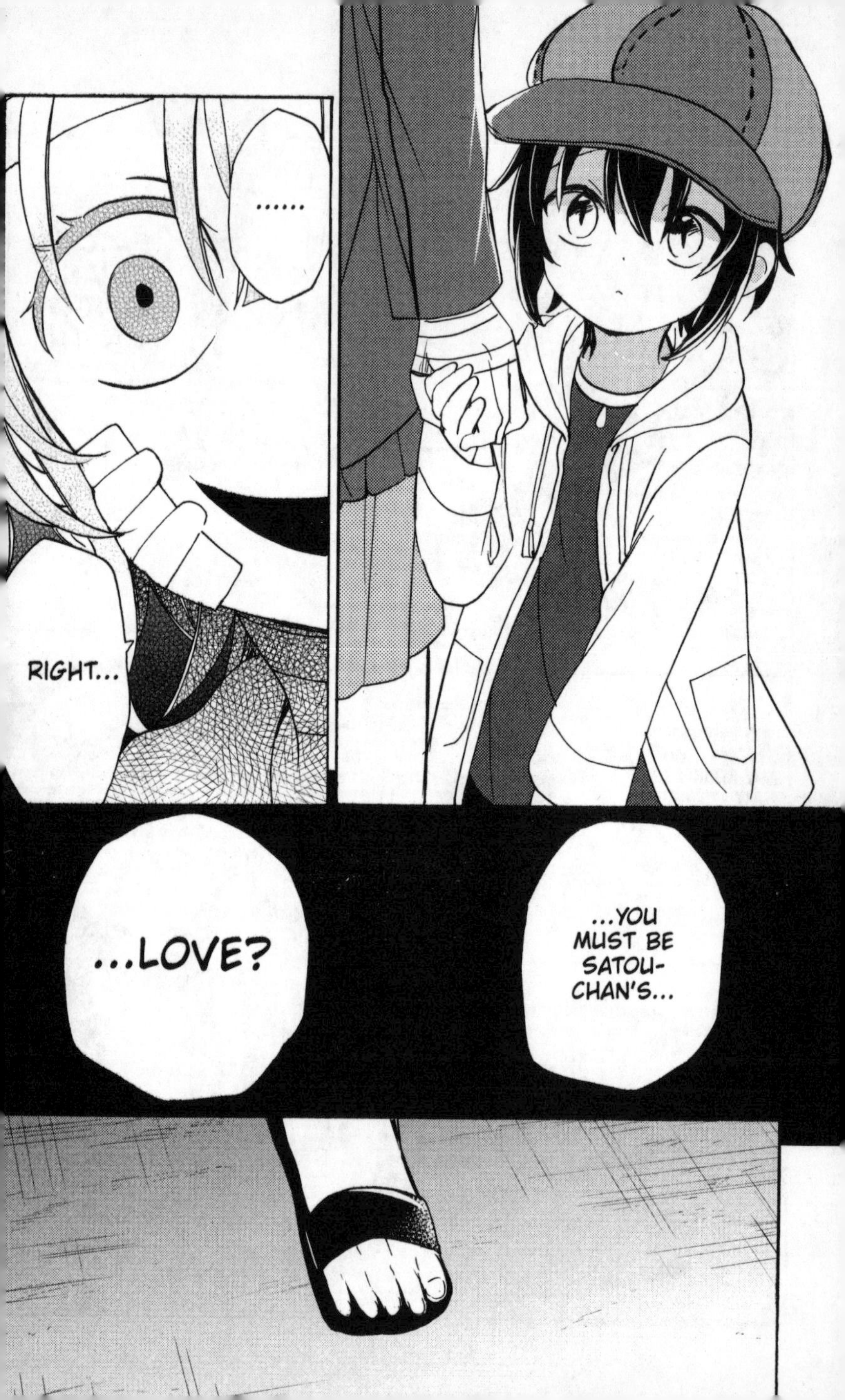
......
RIGHT...
...YOU MUST BE SATOU-CHAN'S...
...LOVE?

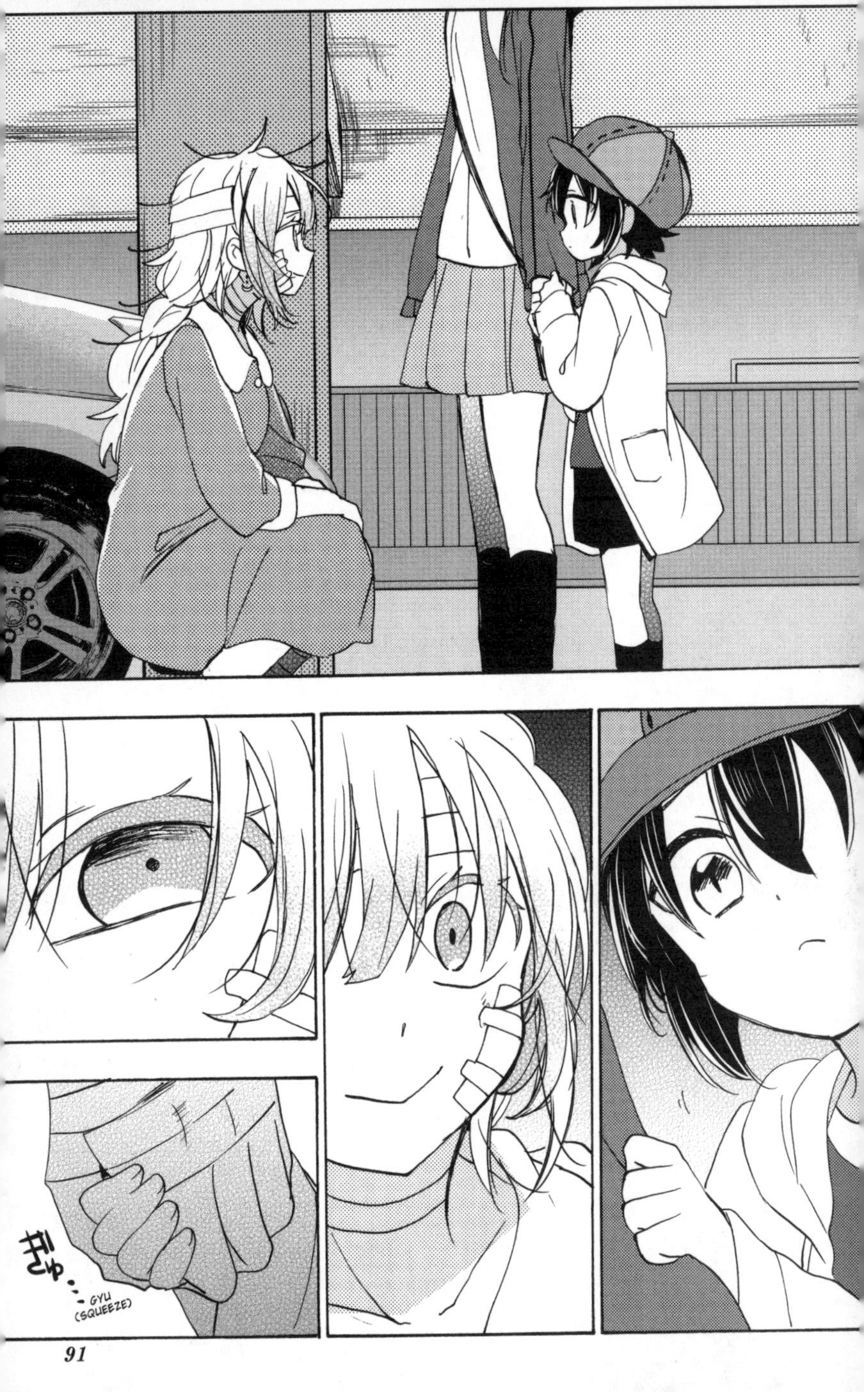
ぎゅ…
GYU (SQUEEZE)

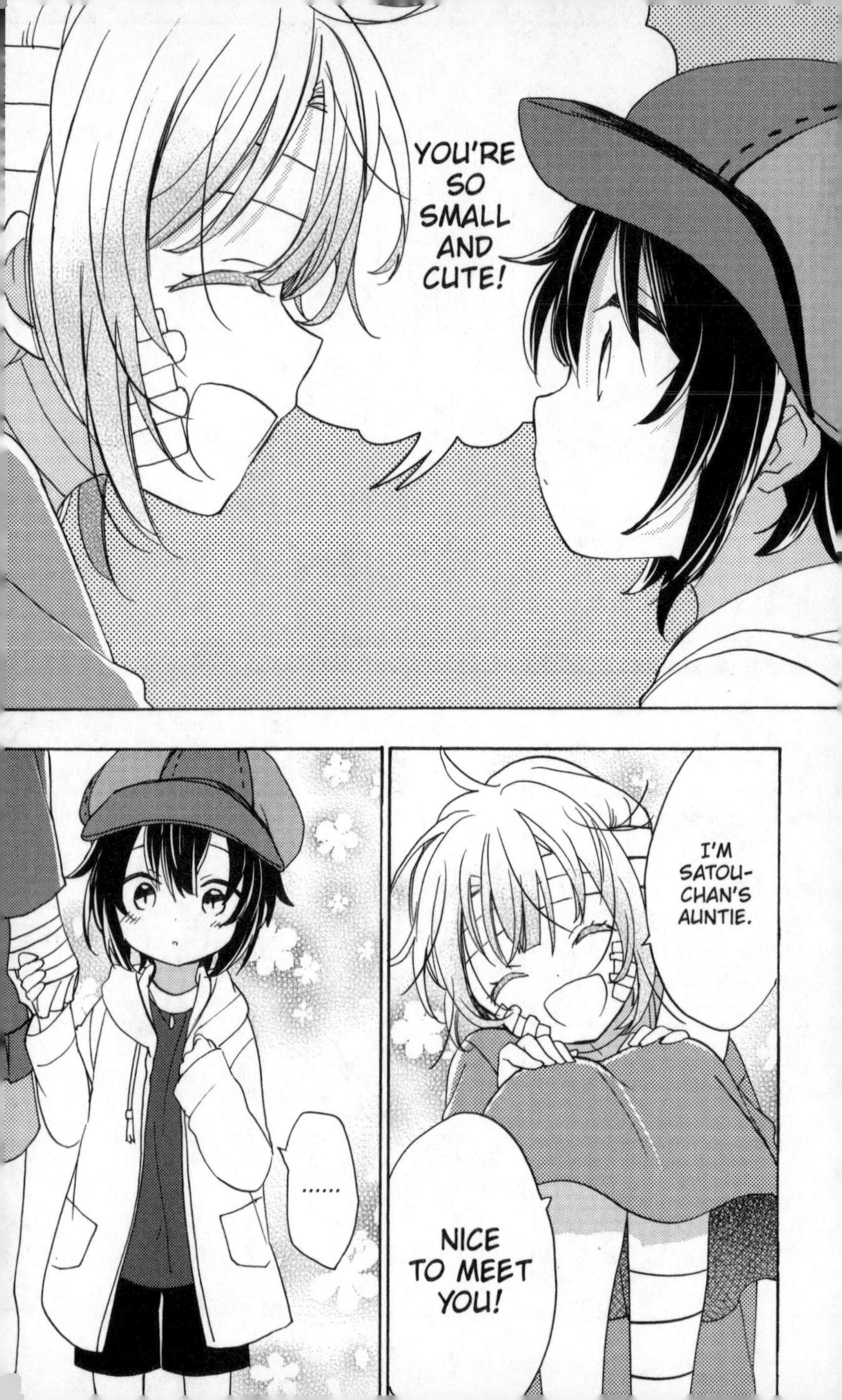
YOU'RE SO SMALL AND CUTE!
I'M SATOU-CHAN'S AUNTIE.
NICE TO MEET YOU!
......

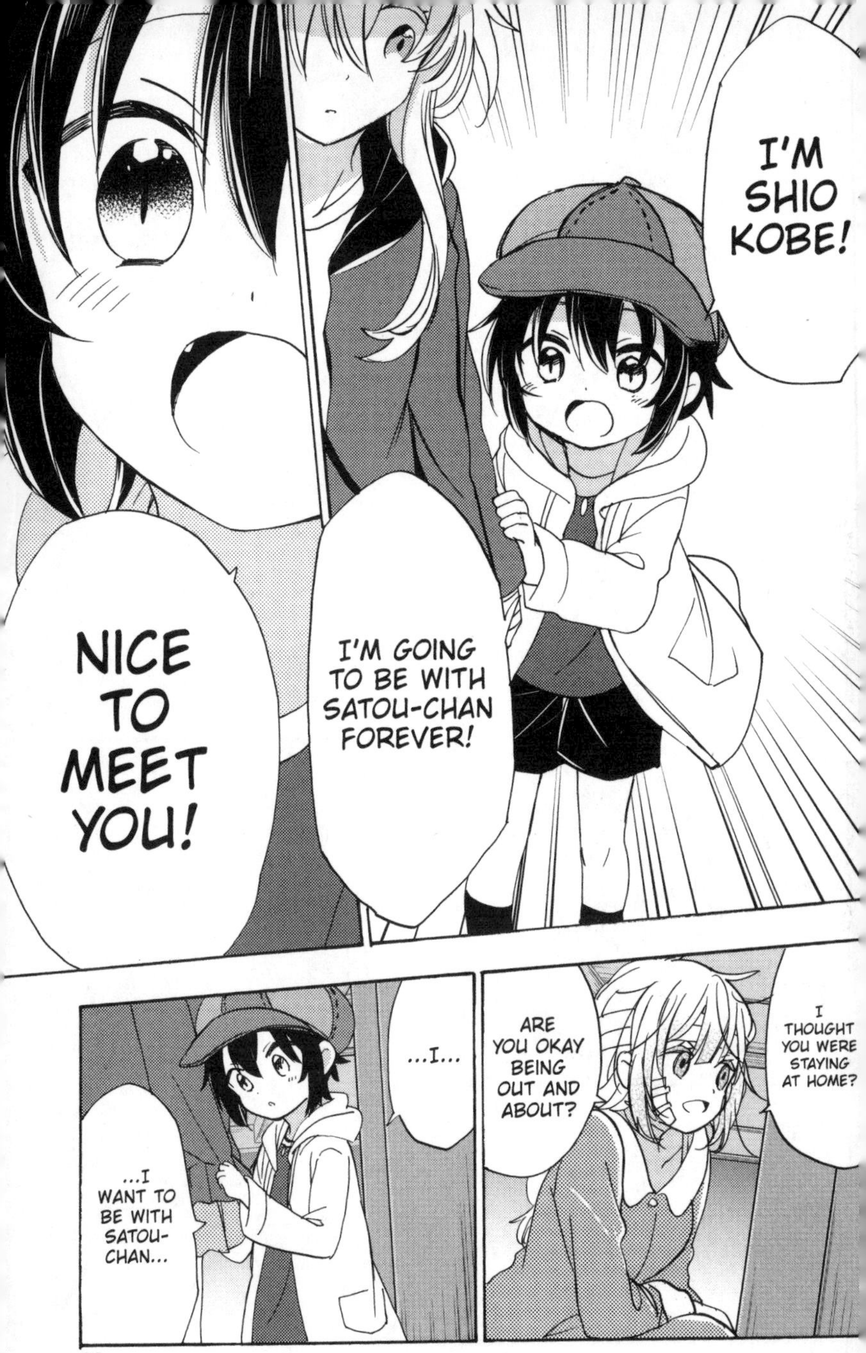
I'M SHIO KOBE!
I'M GOING TO BE WITH SATOU-CHAN FOREVER!
NICE TO MEET YOU!
I THOUGHT YOU WERE STAYING AT HOME?
ARE YOU OKAY BEING OUT AND ABOUT?
...I...
...I WANT TO BE WITH SATOU-CHAN...

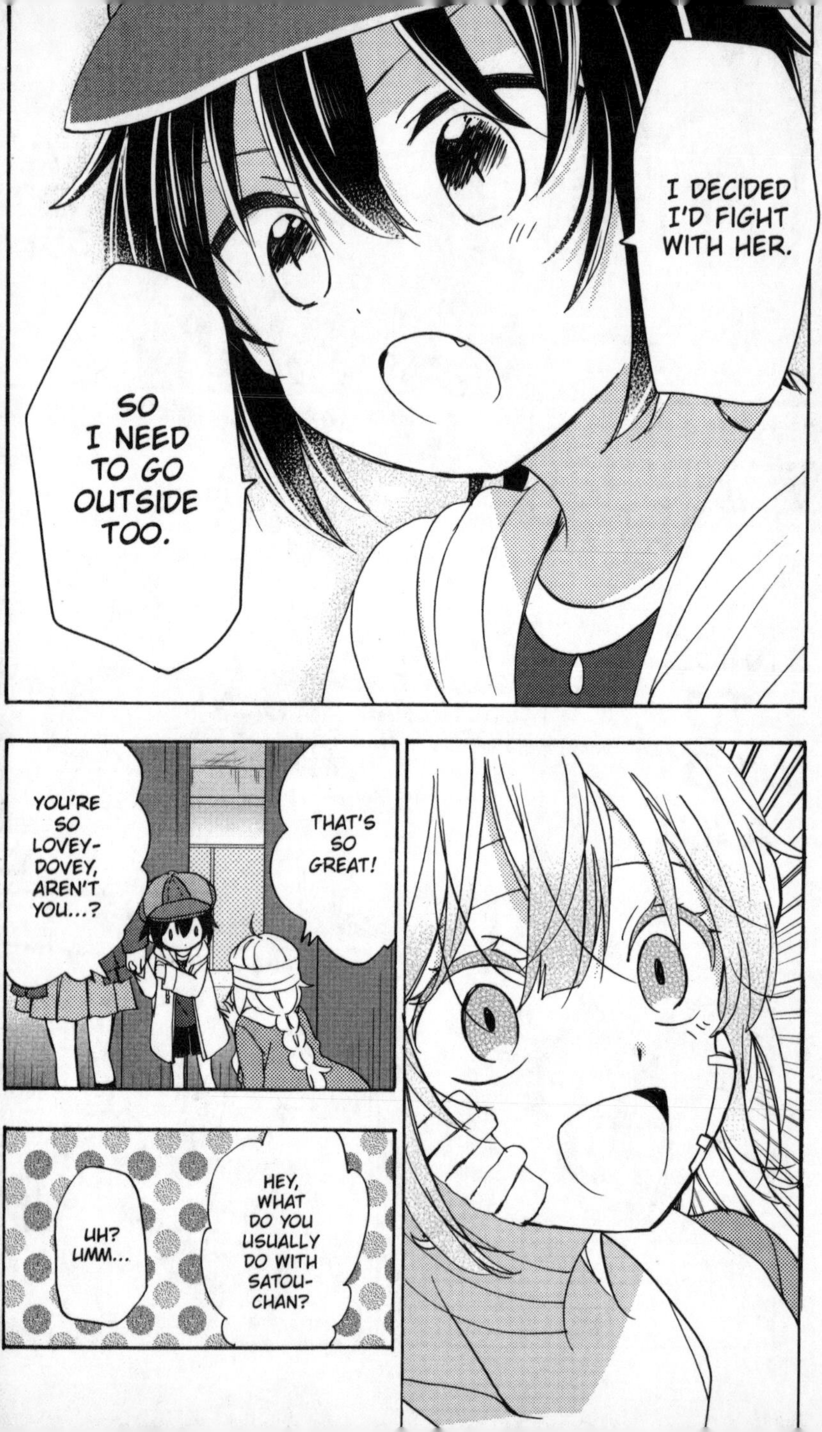
I DECIDED I'D FIGHT WITH HER.
SO I NEED TO GO OUTSIDE TOO.
THAT'S SO GREAT!
YOU'RE SO LOVEY-DOVEY, AREN'T YOU...?
HEY, WHAT DO YOU USUALLY DO WITH SATOU-CHAN?
UH? UMM...

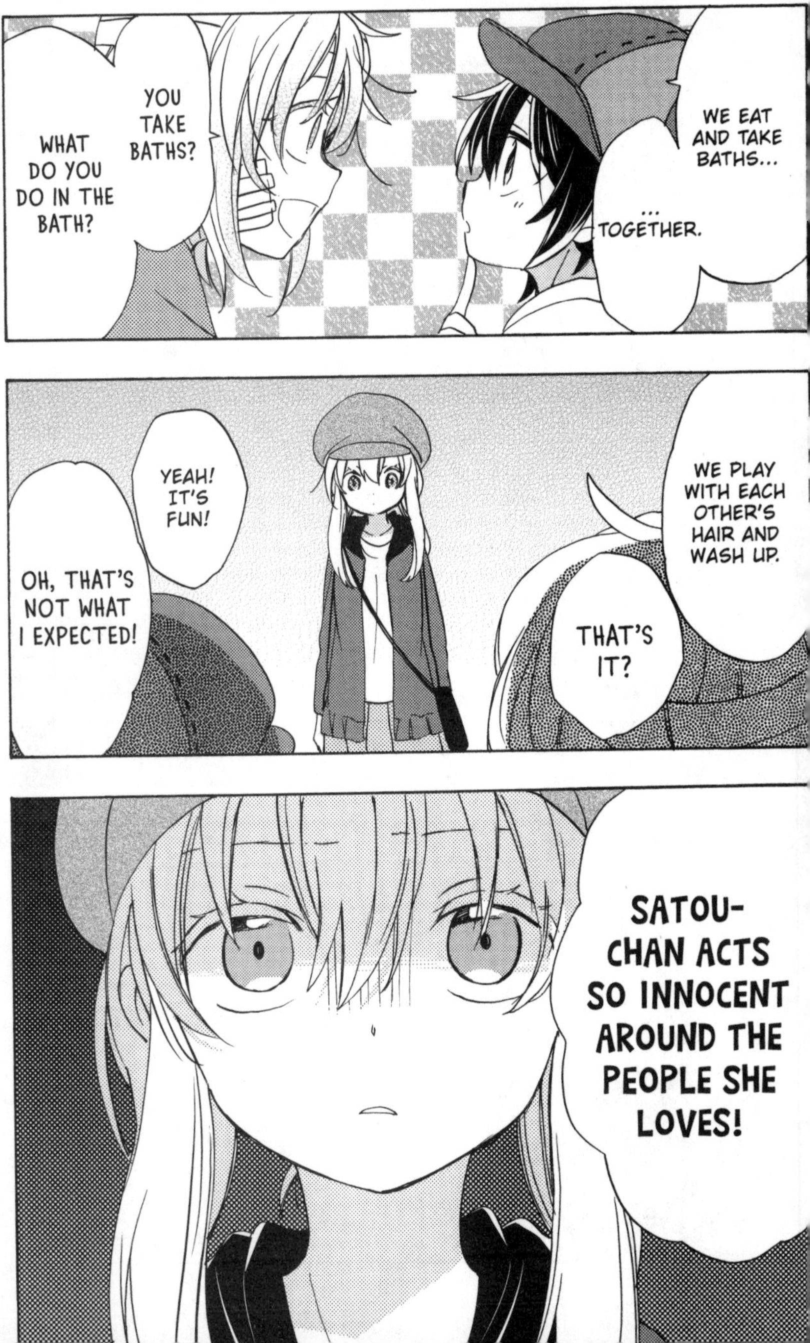
WE EAT AND TAKE BATHS...
...TOGETHER.
YOU TAKE BATHS?
WHAT DO YOU DO IN THE BATH?
WE PLAY WITH EACH OTHER'S HAIR AND WASH UP.
THAT'S IT?
YEAH! IT'S FUN!
OH, THAT'S NOT WHAT I EXPECTED!
SATOU-CHAN ACTS SO INNOCENT AROUND THE PEOPLE SHE LOVES!

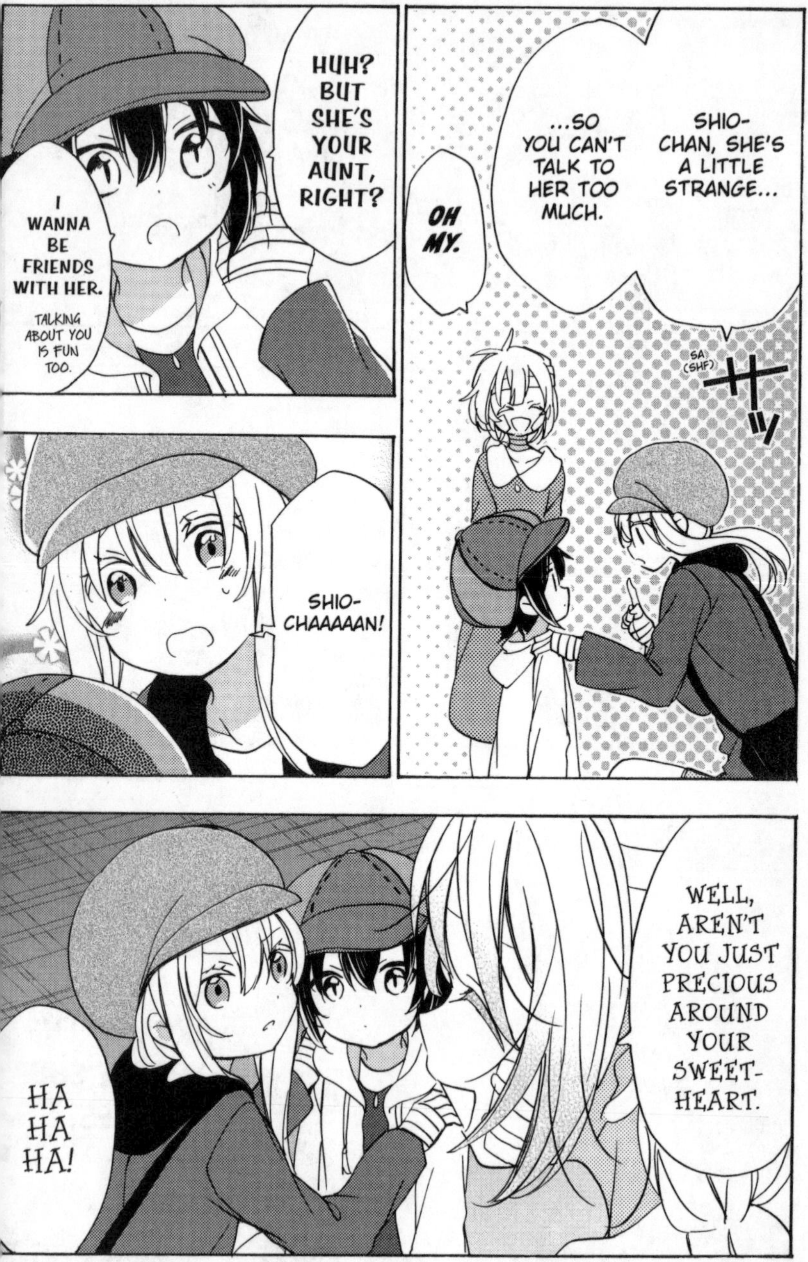
SHIO-CHAN, SHE'S A LITTLE STRANGE...
...SO YOU CAN'T TALK TO HER TOO MUCH.
OH MY.
SA (SHF)
HUH? BUT SHE'S YOUR AUNT, RIGHT?
I WANNA BE FRIENDS WITH HER.
TALKING ABOUT YOU IS FUN TOO.
SHIO-CHAAAAAN!
WELL, AREN'T YOU JUST PRECIOUS AROUND YOUR SWEET-HEART.
HA HA HA HA!

NOW,
GET IN.

BURORORORORO
(VROOOOOM)

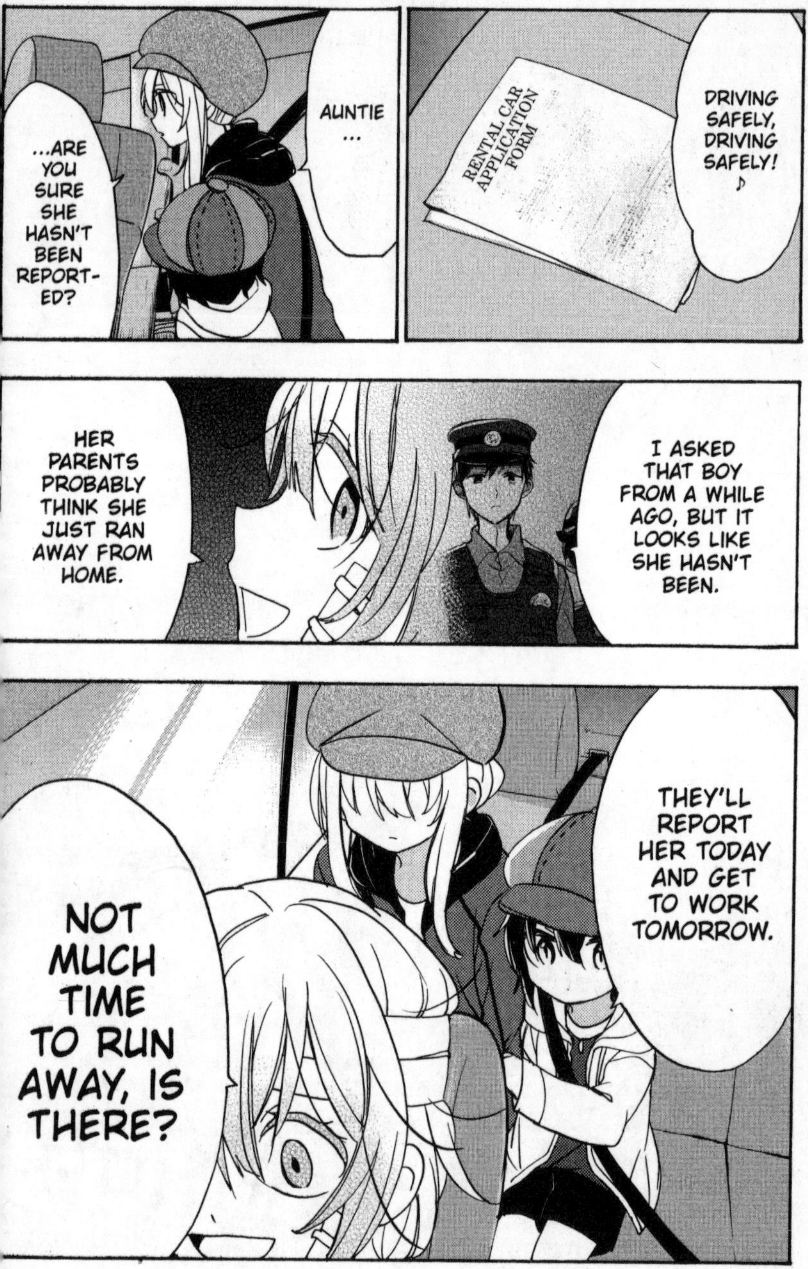
DRIVING SAFELY, DRIVING SAFELY! ♪
RENTAL CAR APPLICATION FORM
AUNTIE ...
...ARE YOU SURE SHE HASN'T BEEN REPORTED?
I ASKED THAT BOY FROM A WHILE AGO, BUT IT LOOKS LIKE SHE HASN'T BEEN.
HER PARENTS PROBABLY THINK SHE JUST RAN AWAY FROM HOME.
THEY'LL REPORT HER TODAY AND GET TO WORK TOMORROW.
NOT MUCH TIME TO RUN AWAY, IS THERE?

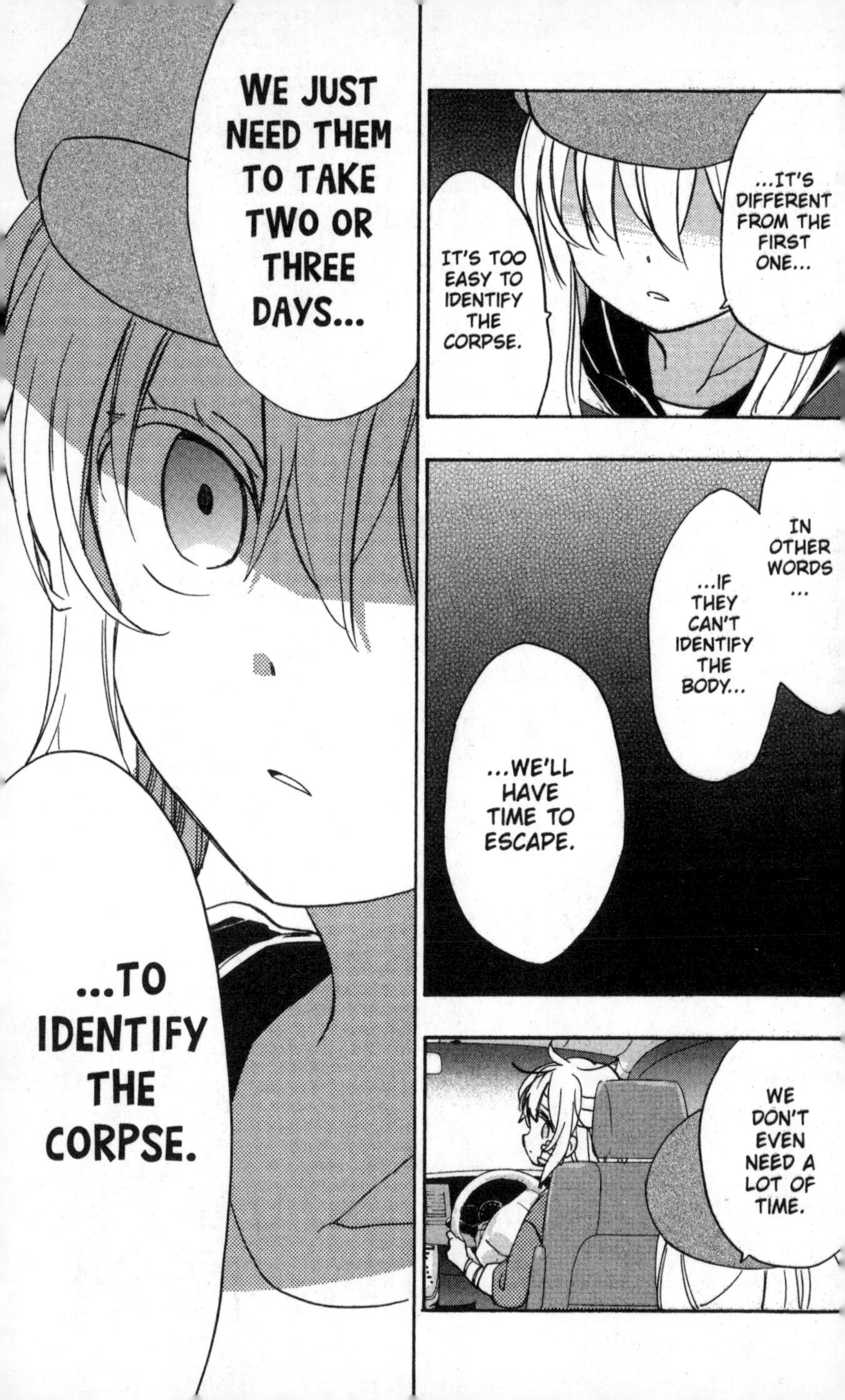
...IT'S DIFFERENT FROM THE FIRST ONE...
IT'S TOO EASY TO IDENTIFY THE CORPSE.
IN OTHER WORDS...
...IF THEY CAN'T IDENTIFY THE BODY...
...WE'LL HAVE TIME TO ESCAPE.
WE DON'T EVEN NEED A LOT OF TIME.
WE JUST NEED THEM TO TAKE TWO OR THREE DAYS...
...TO IDENTIFY THE CORPSE.

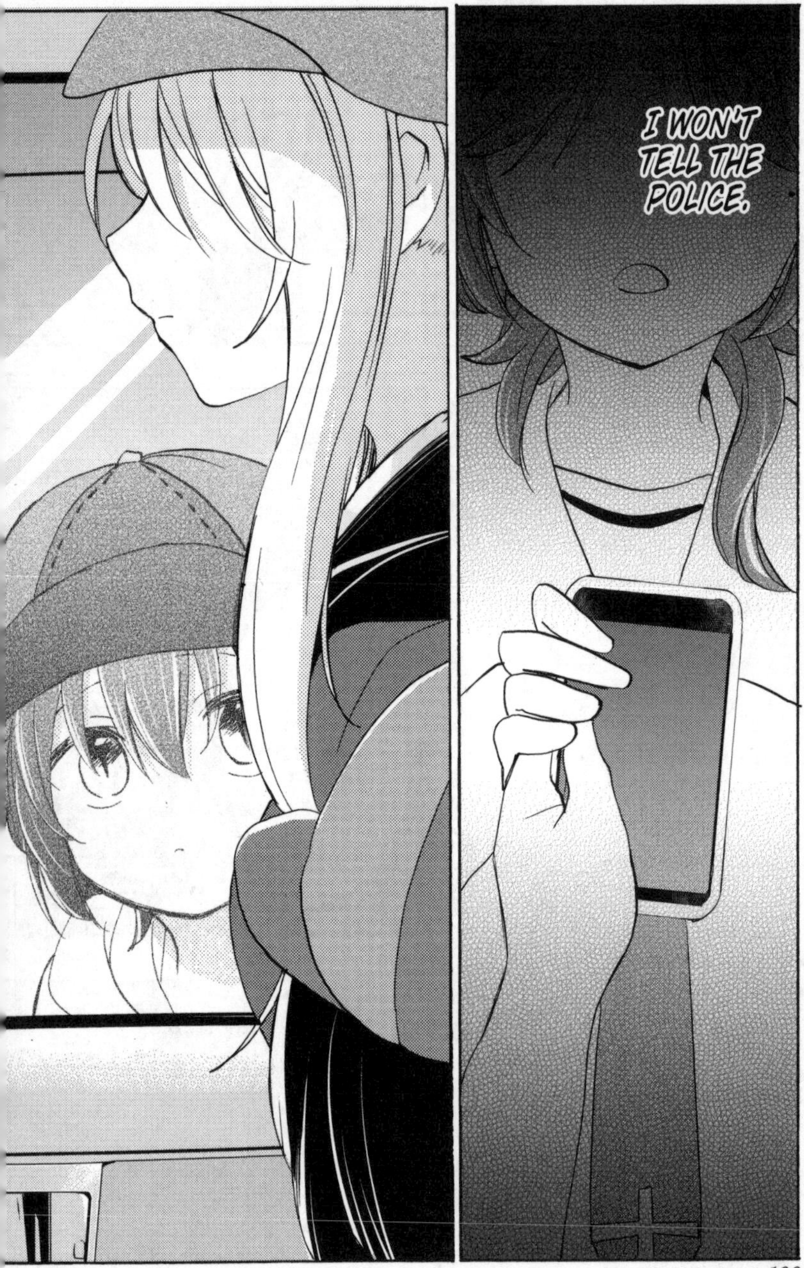
I WON'T
TELL THE
POLICE.

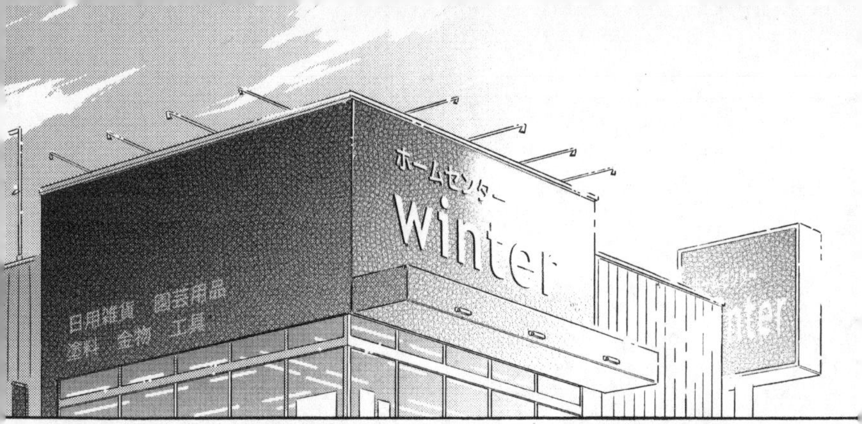
ホームセンター
winter
日用雑貨 園芸用品
塗料 金物 工具

SIGN: DAILY NECESSITIES / GARDENING SUPPLIES / PAINT / METAL / TOOLS

SIGN: HOME CENTER WINTER

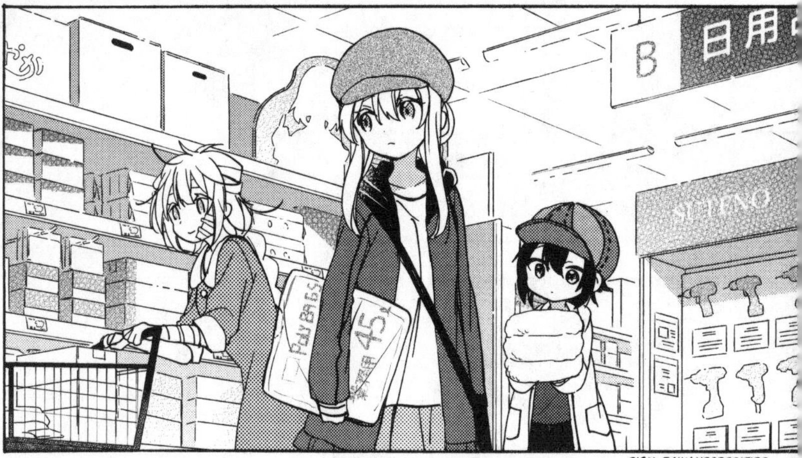
B
日用

SIGN: DAILY NECESSITIES

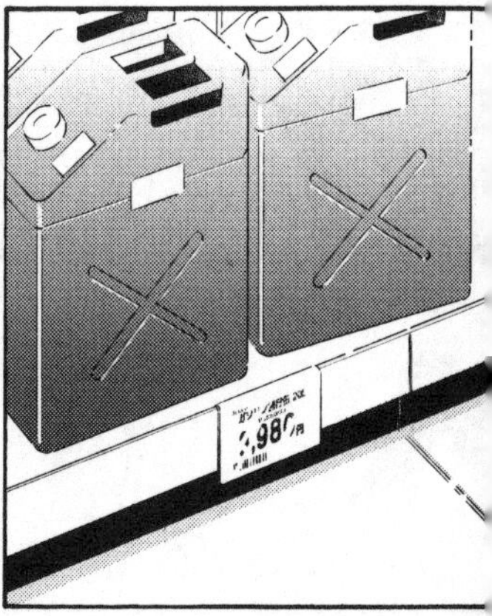

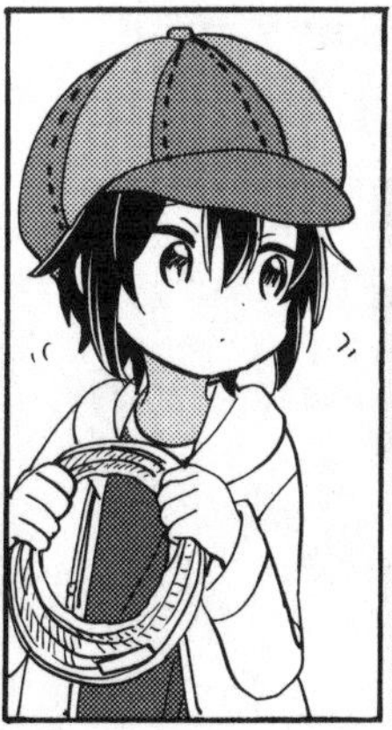

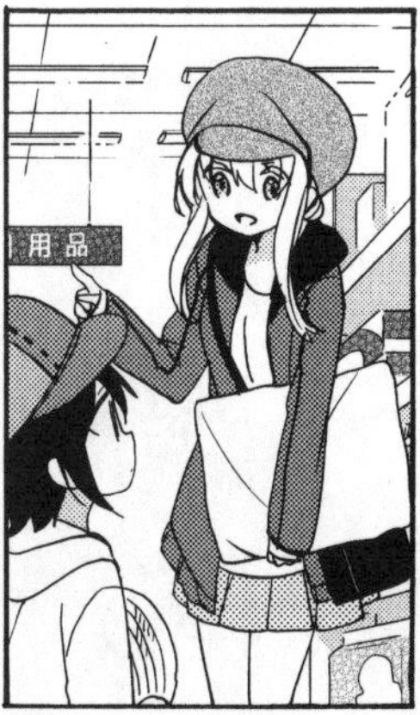

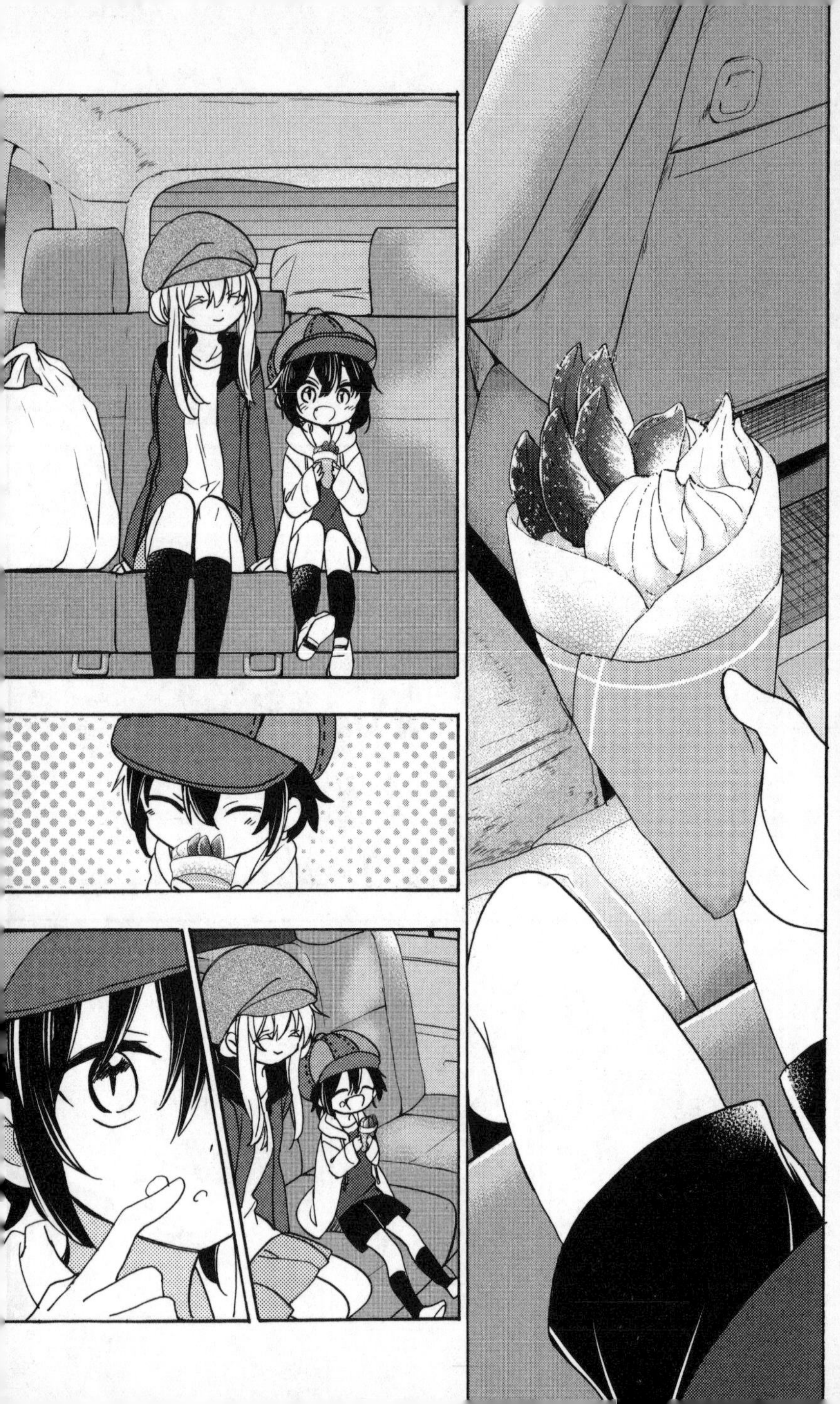

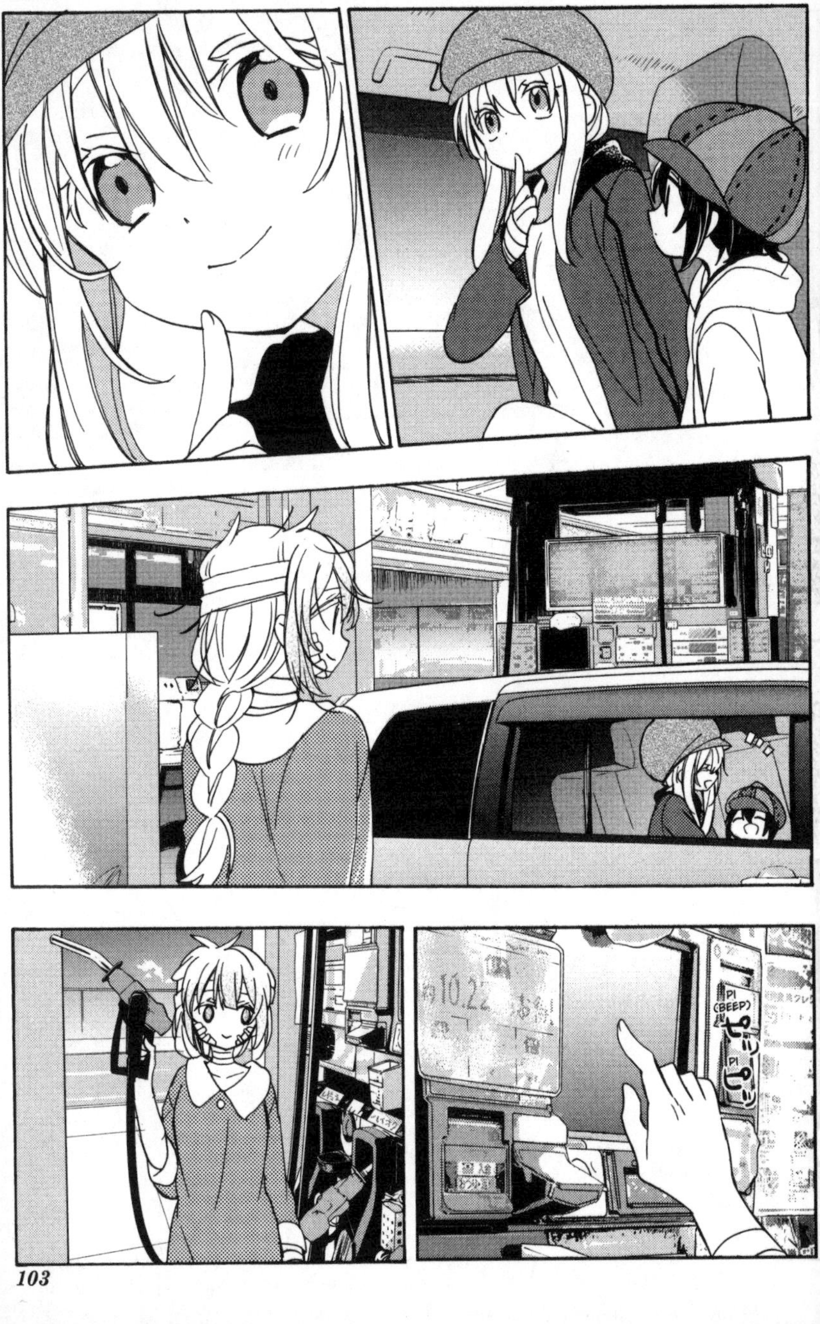
PI (BEEP)
ピッ
PI
ピッ

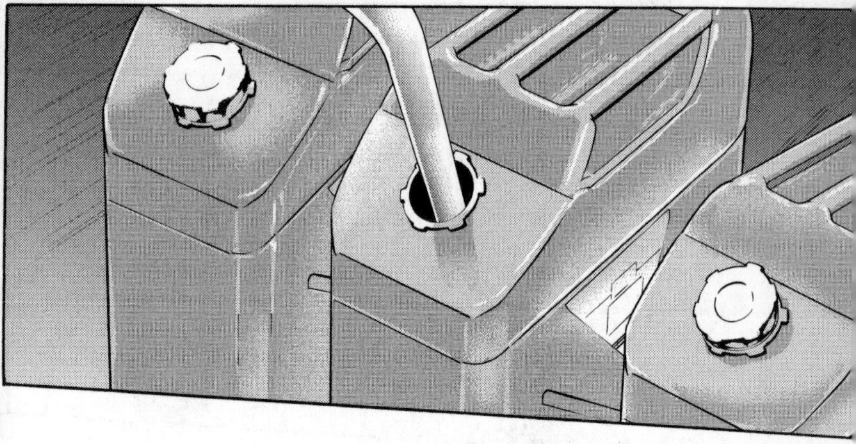

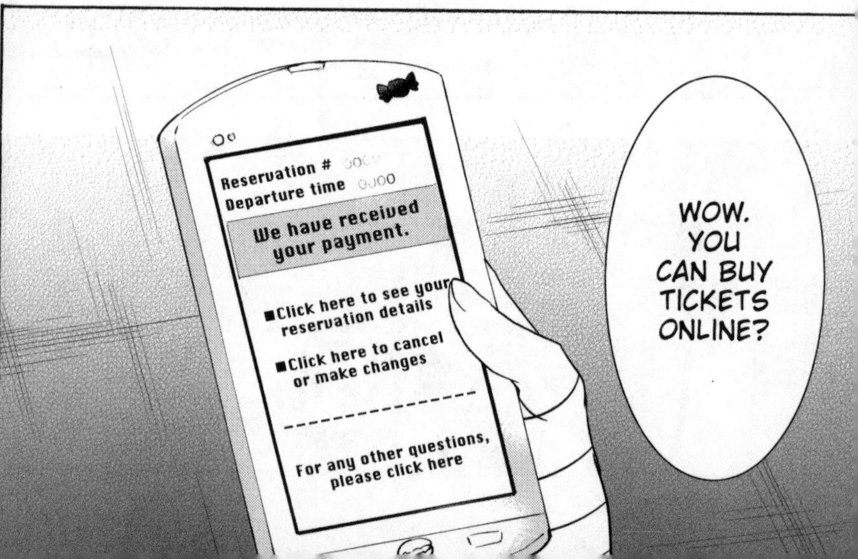
Reservation #
Departure time
We have received your payment.
■Click here to see your reservation details
■Click here to cancel or make changes
For any other questions, please click here
WOW. YOU CAN BUY TICKETS ONLINE?

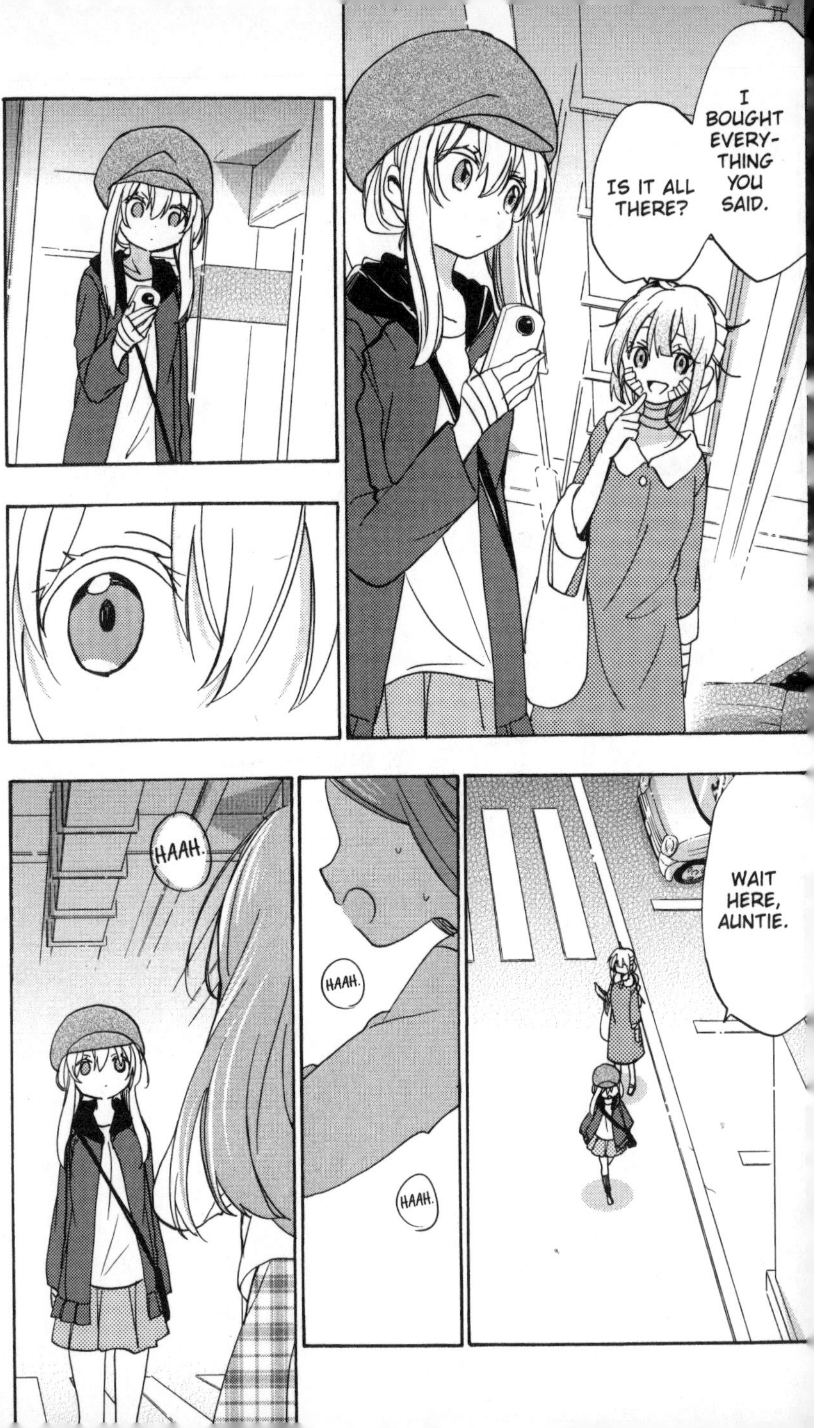
I BOUGHT EVERY-THING YOU SAID.
IS IT ALL THERE?
WAIT HERE, AUNTIE.
HAAH.
HAAH.
HAAH.

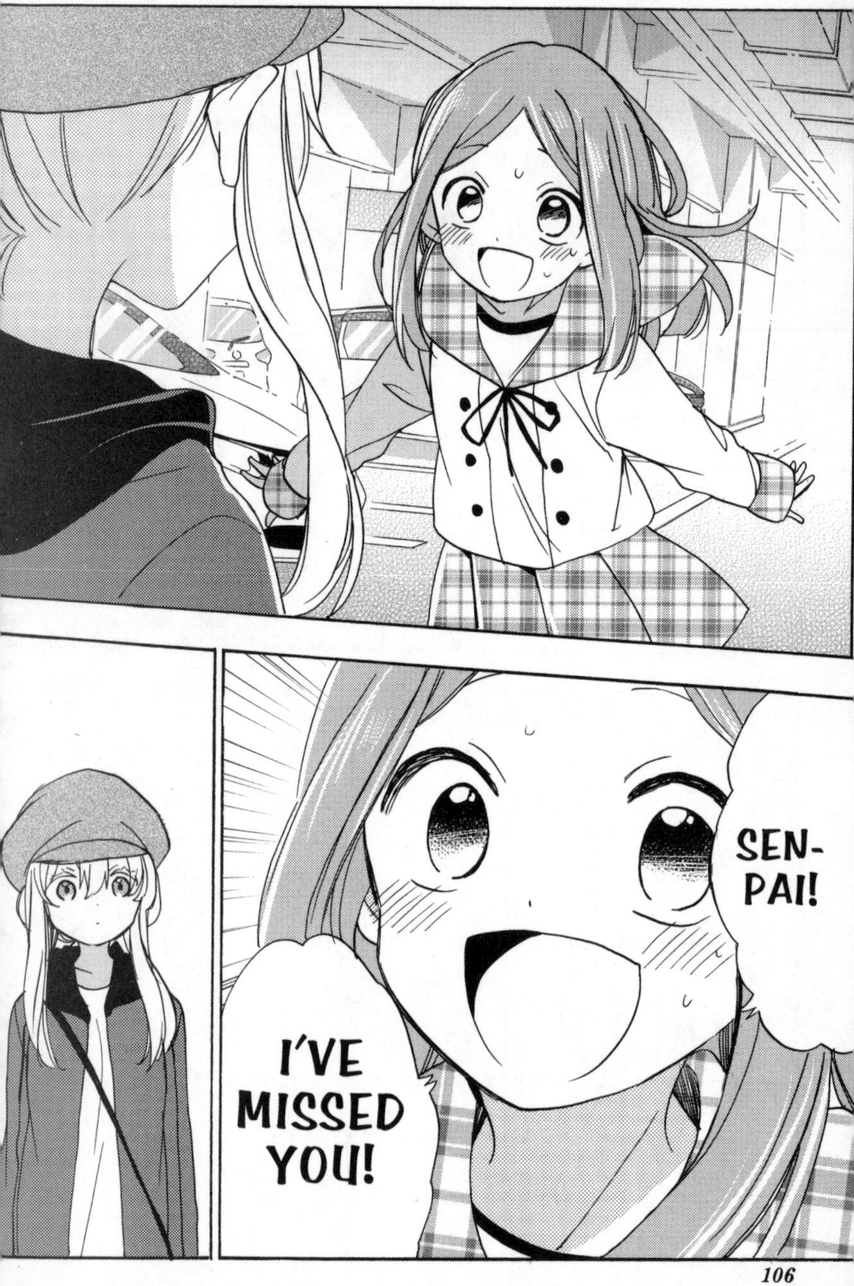
SEN-PAI!
I'VE MISSED YOU!

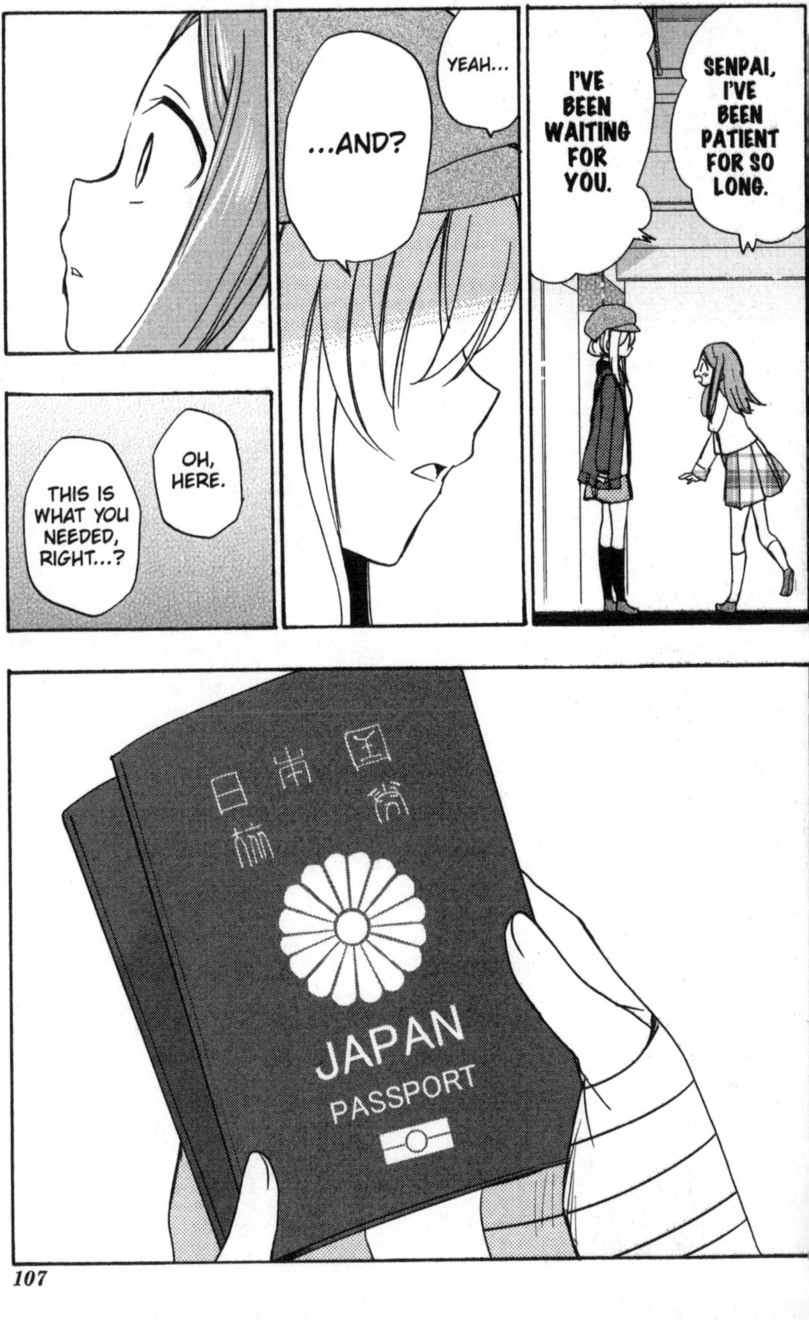
SENPAI, I'VE BEEN PATIENT FOR SO LONG.
I'VE BEEN WAITING FOR YOU.
YEAH...
...AND?
OH, HERE.
THIS IS WHAT YOU NEEDED, RIGHT...?
JAPAN
PASSPORT

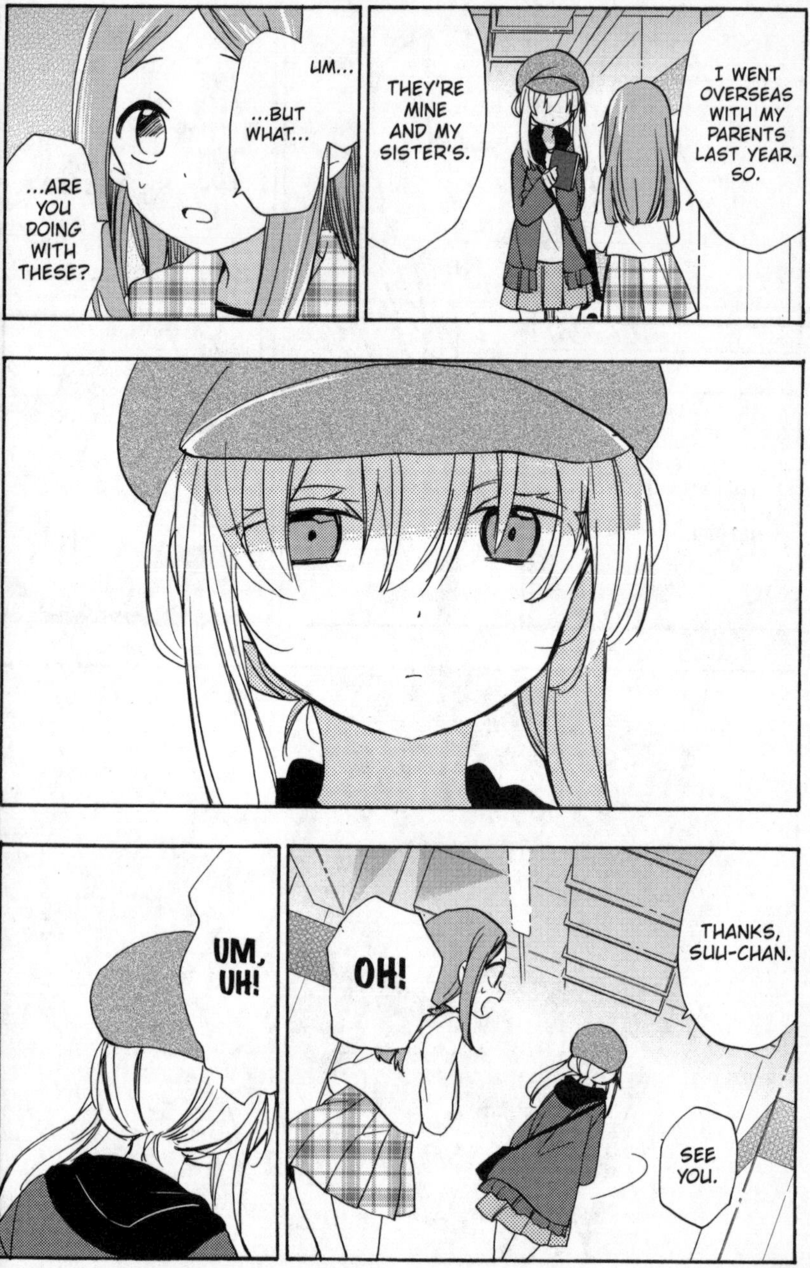
I WENT OVERSEAS WITH MY PARENTS LAST YEAR, SO.
THEY'RE MINE AND MY SISTER'S.
UM...
...BUT WHAT...
...ARE YOU DOING WITH THESE?
THANKS, SUU-CHAN.
OH!
SEE YOU.
UM, UH!

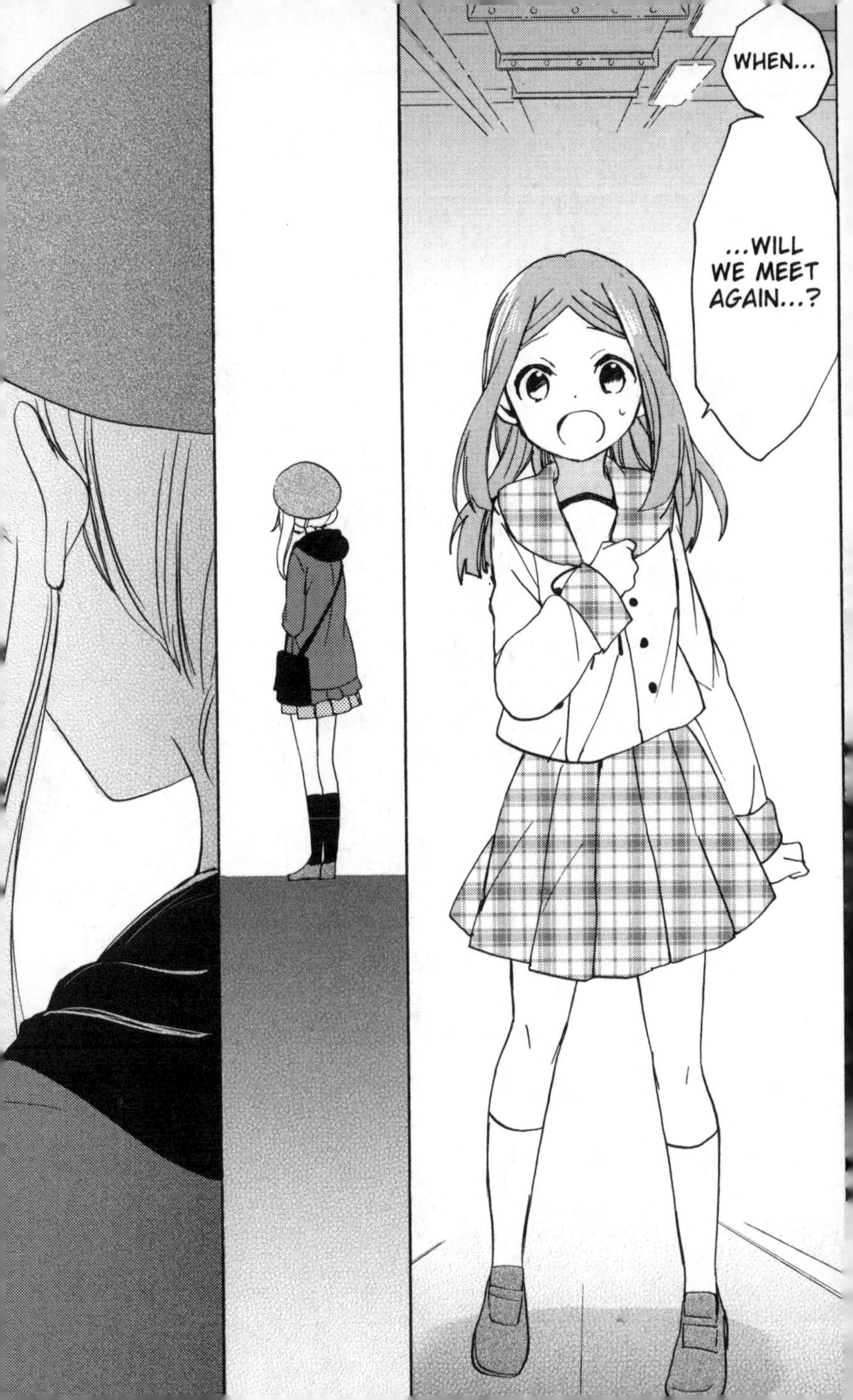
WHEN...
...WILL WE MEET AGAIN...?

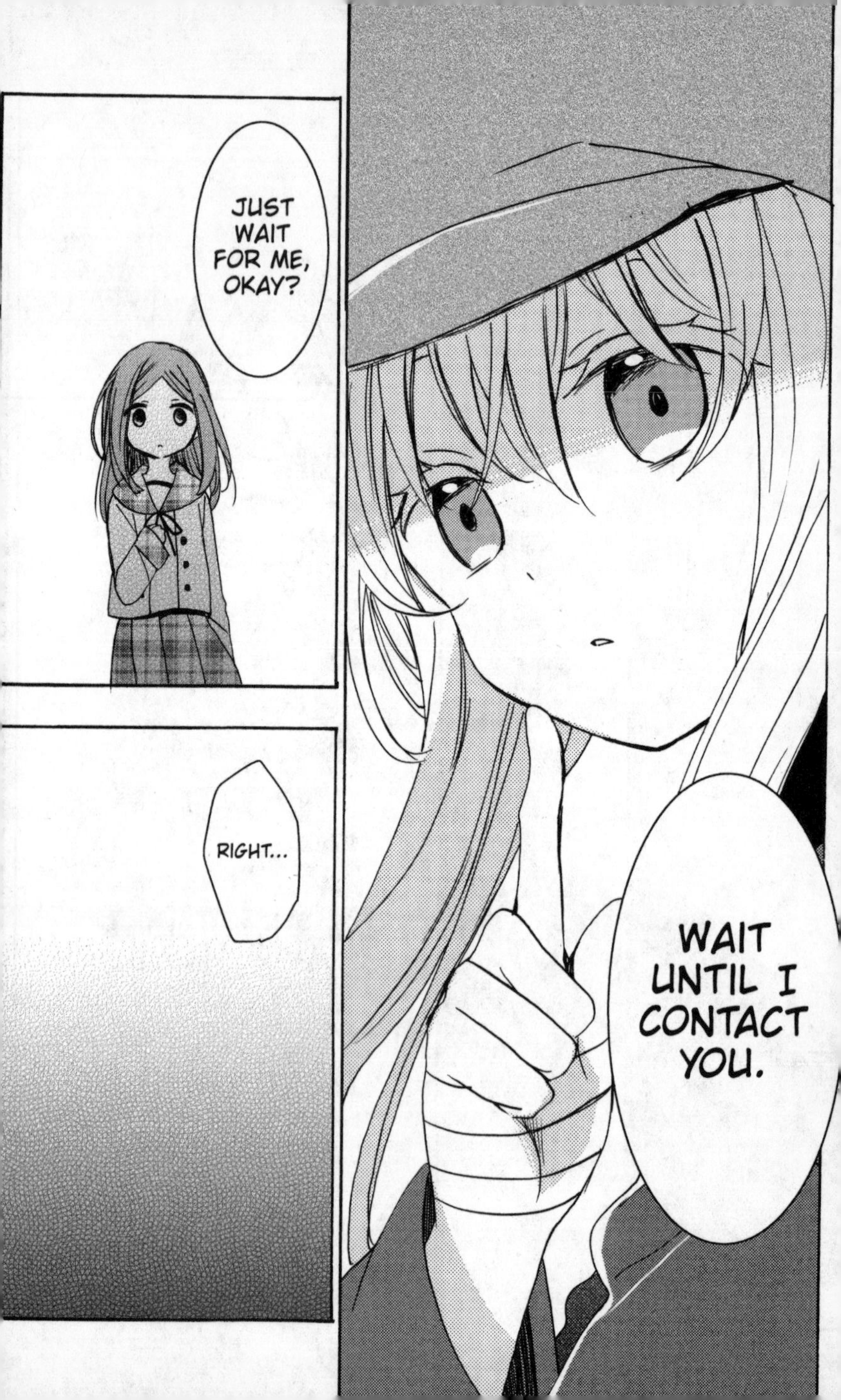
WAIT UNTIL I CONTACT YOU.
JUST WAIT FOR ME, OKAY?
RIGHT...

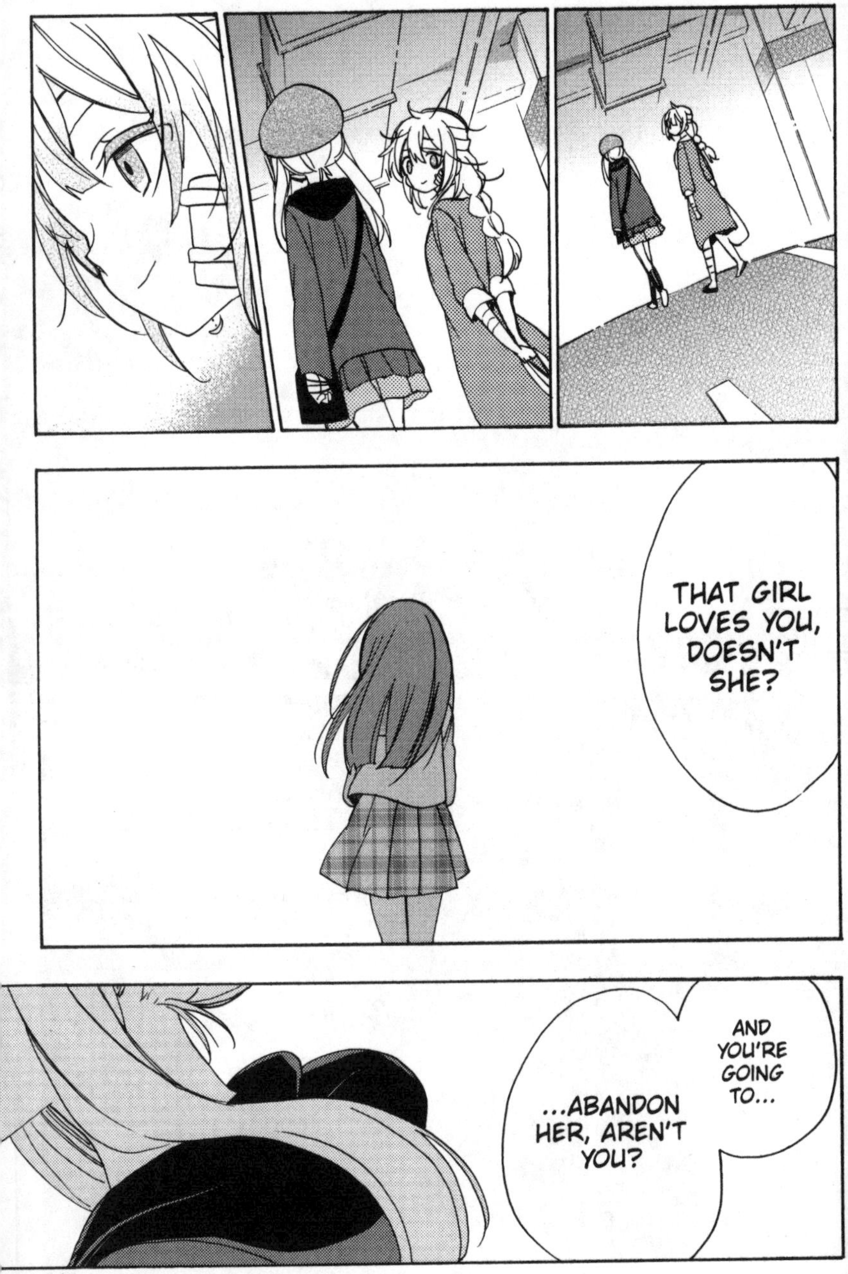
THAT GIRL LOVES YOU, DOESN'T SHE?
AND YOU'RE GOING TO...
...ABANDON HER, AREN'T YOU?

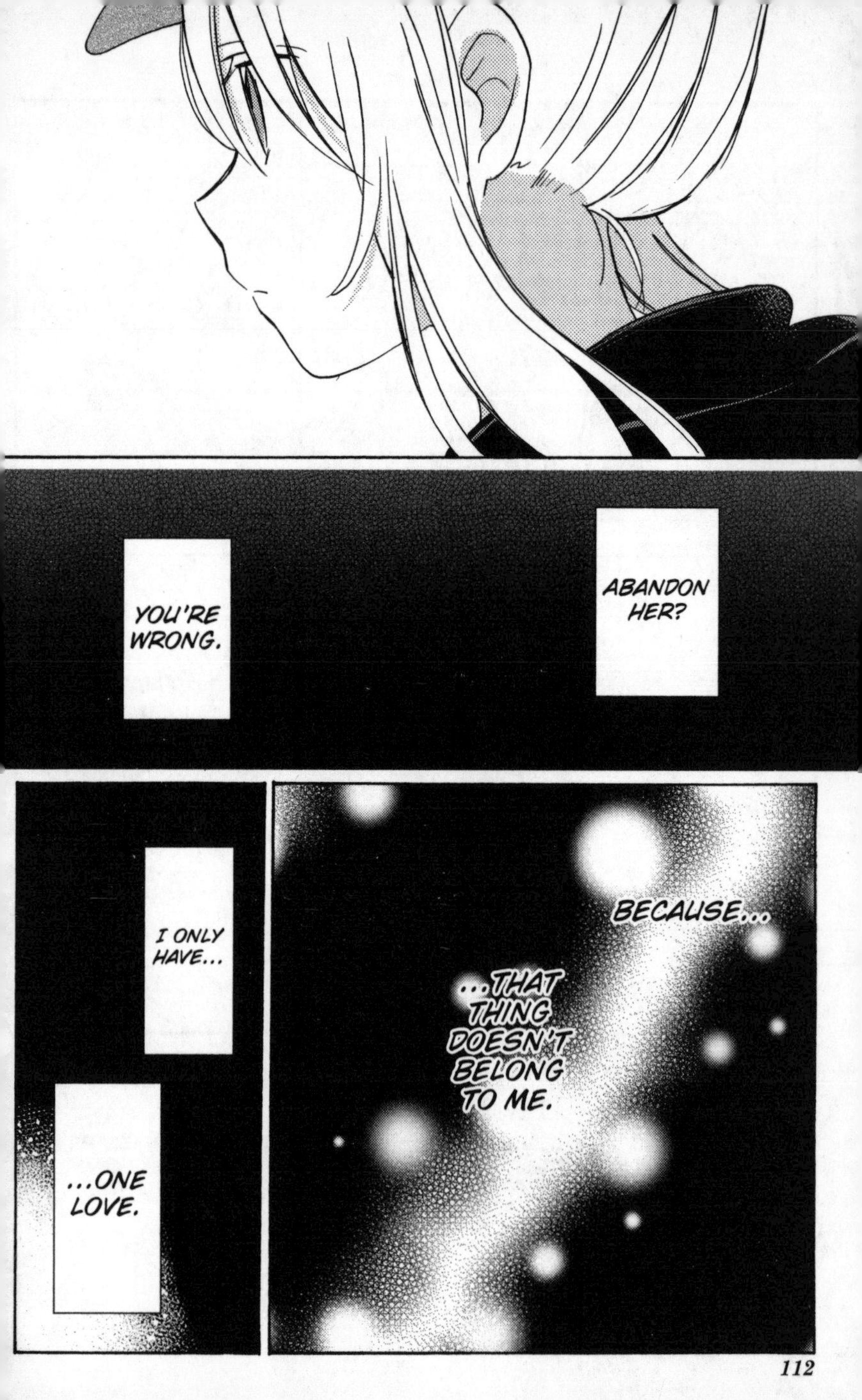
ABANDON HER?
YOU'RE WRONG.
BECAUSE...
...THAT THING DOESN'T BELONG TO ME.
I ONLY HAVE...
...ONE LOVE.

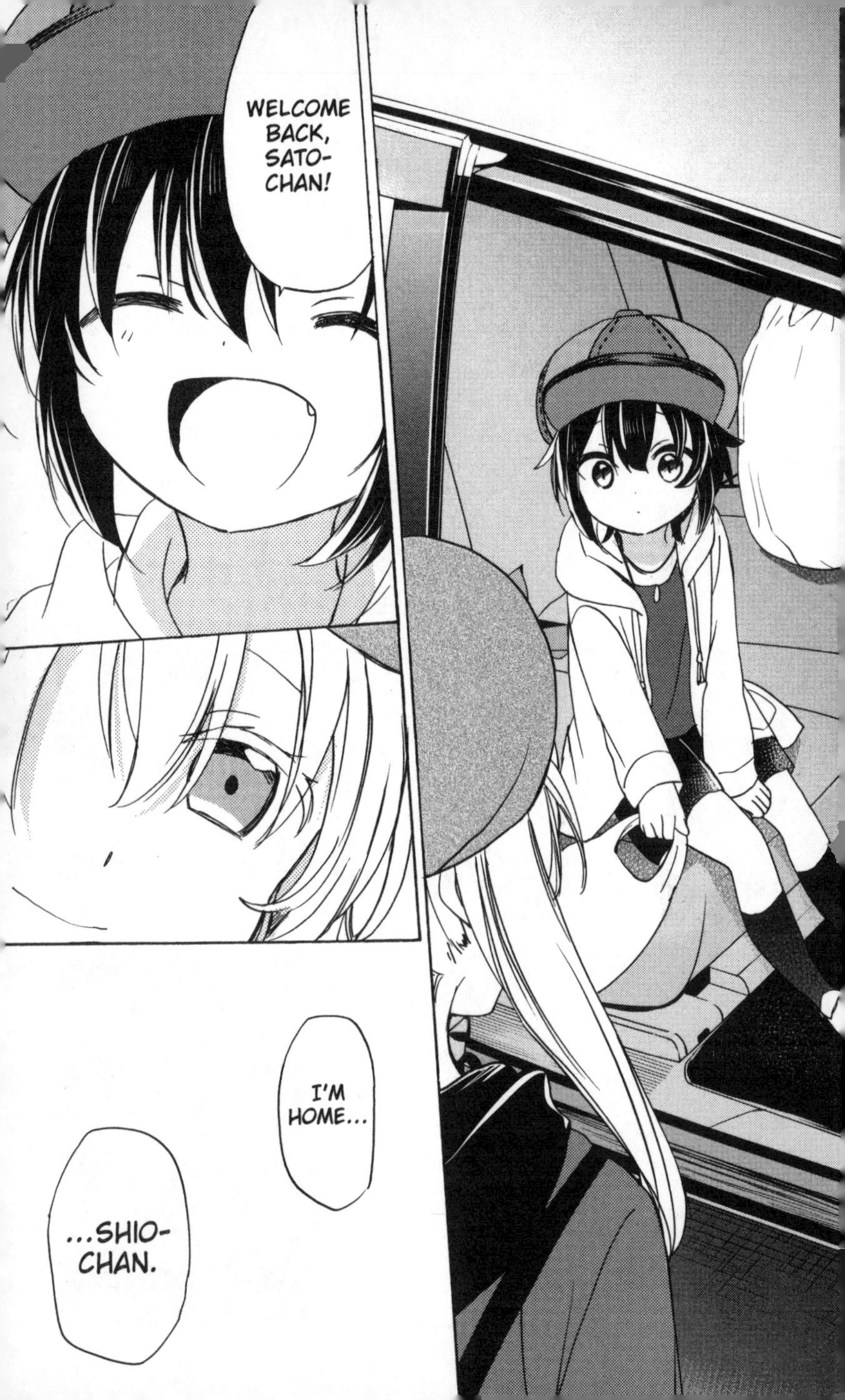
WELCOME BACK, SATO-CHAN!
I'M HOME...
...SHIO-CHAN.

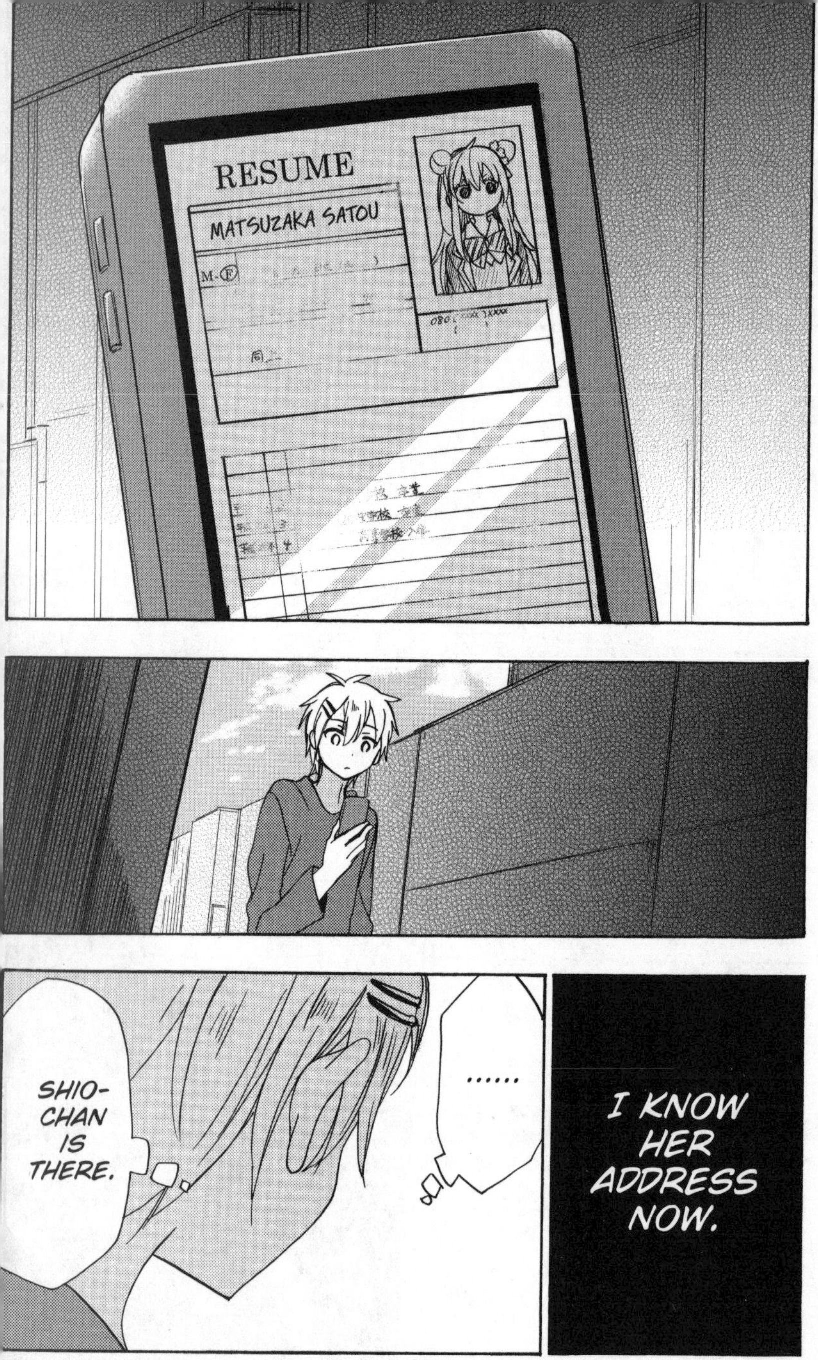
RESUME
MATSUZAKA SATOU
I KNOW HER ADDRESS NOW.
......
SHIO-CHAN IS THERE.

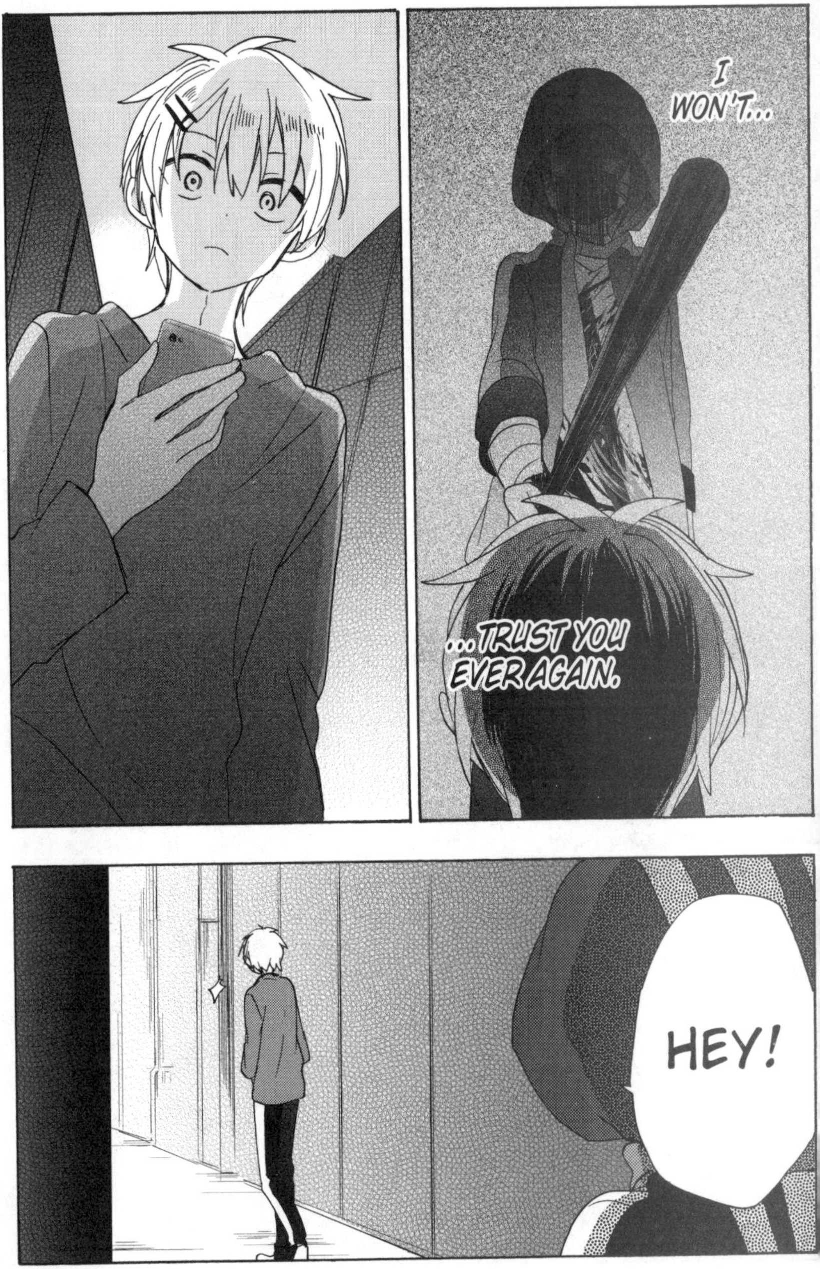
I WON'T...
...TRUST YOU EVER AGAIN.
HEY!

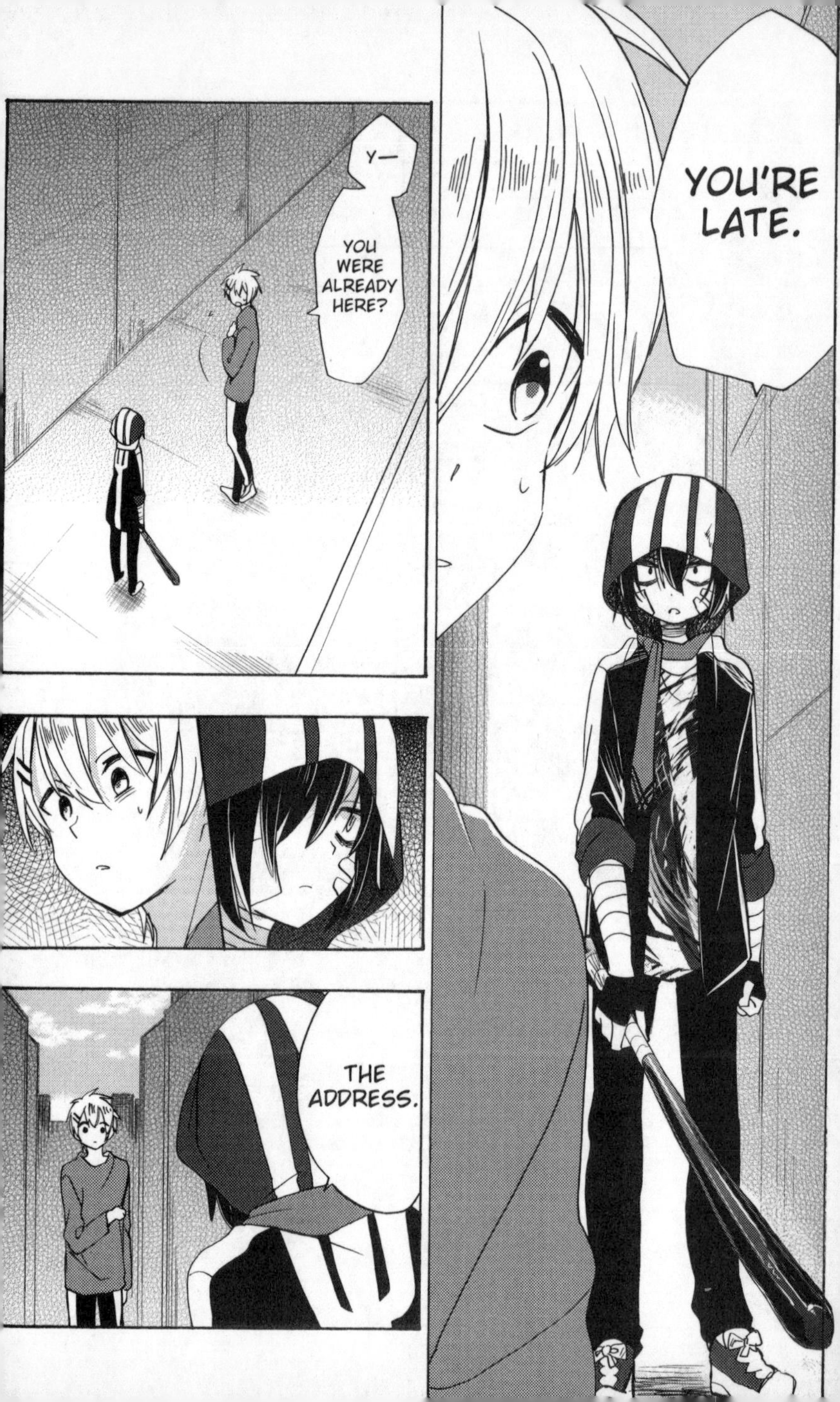
YOU'RE LATE.
Y—
YOU WERE ALREADY HERE?
THE ADDRESS.

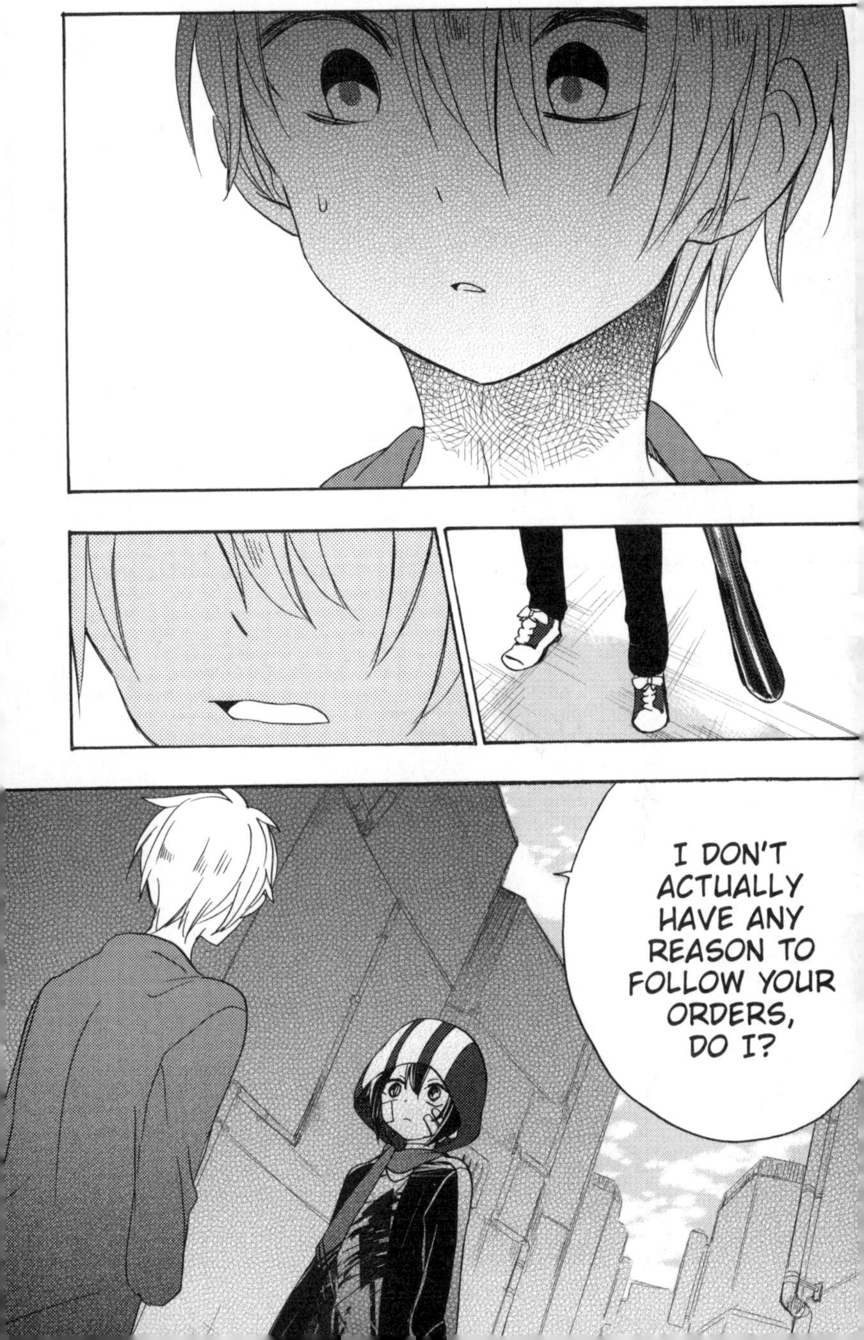
I DON'T ACTUALLY HAVE ANY REASON TO FOLLOW YOUR ORDERS, DO I?

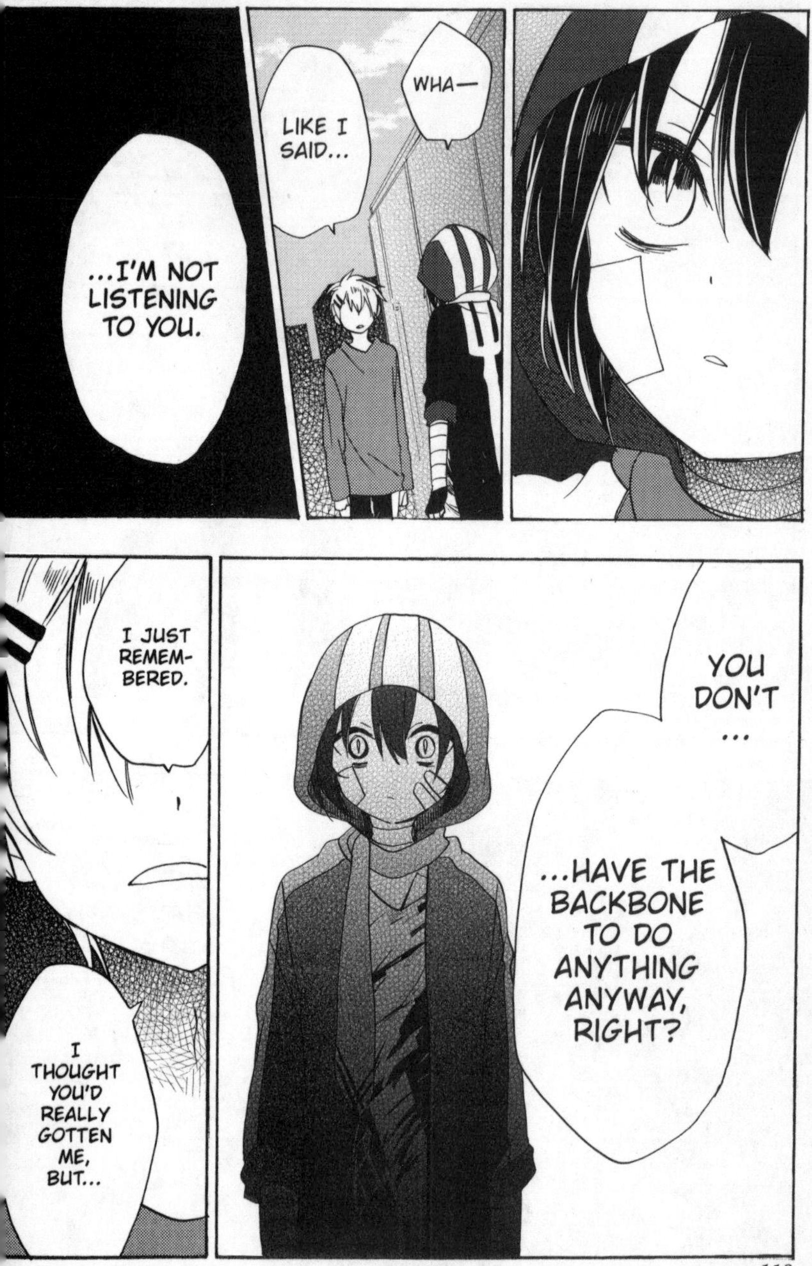
WHA—
LIKE I SAID...
...I'M NOT LISTENING TO YOU.
YOU DON'T ...
...HAVE THE BACKBONE TO DO ANYTHING ANYWAY, RIGHT?
I JUST REMEMBERED.
I THOUGHT YOU'D REALLY GOTTEN ME, BUT...

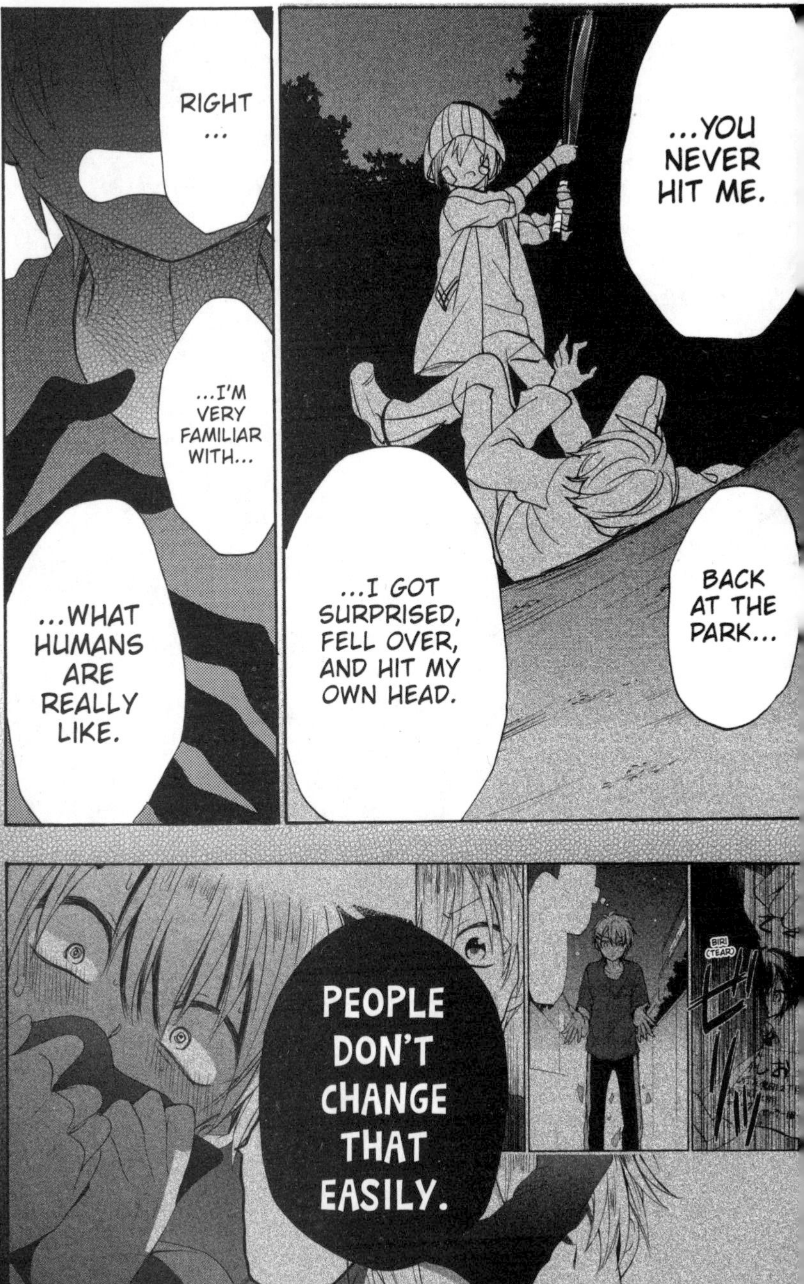
...YOU NEVER HIT ME.
BACK AT THE PARK...
...I GOT SURPRISED, FELL OVER, AND HIT MY OWN HEAD.
RIGHT...
...I'M VERY FAMILIAR WITH...
...WHAT HUMANS ARE REALLY LIKE.
BIRI (TEAR)
PEOPLE DON'T CHANGE THAT EASILY.

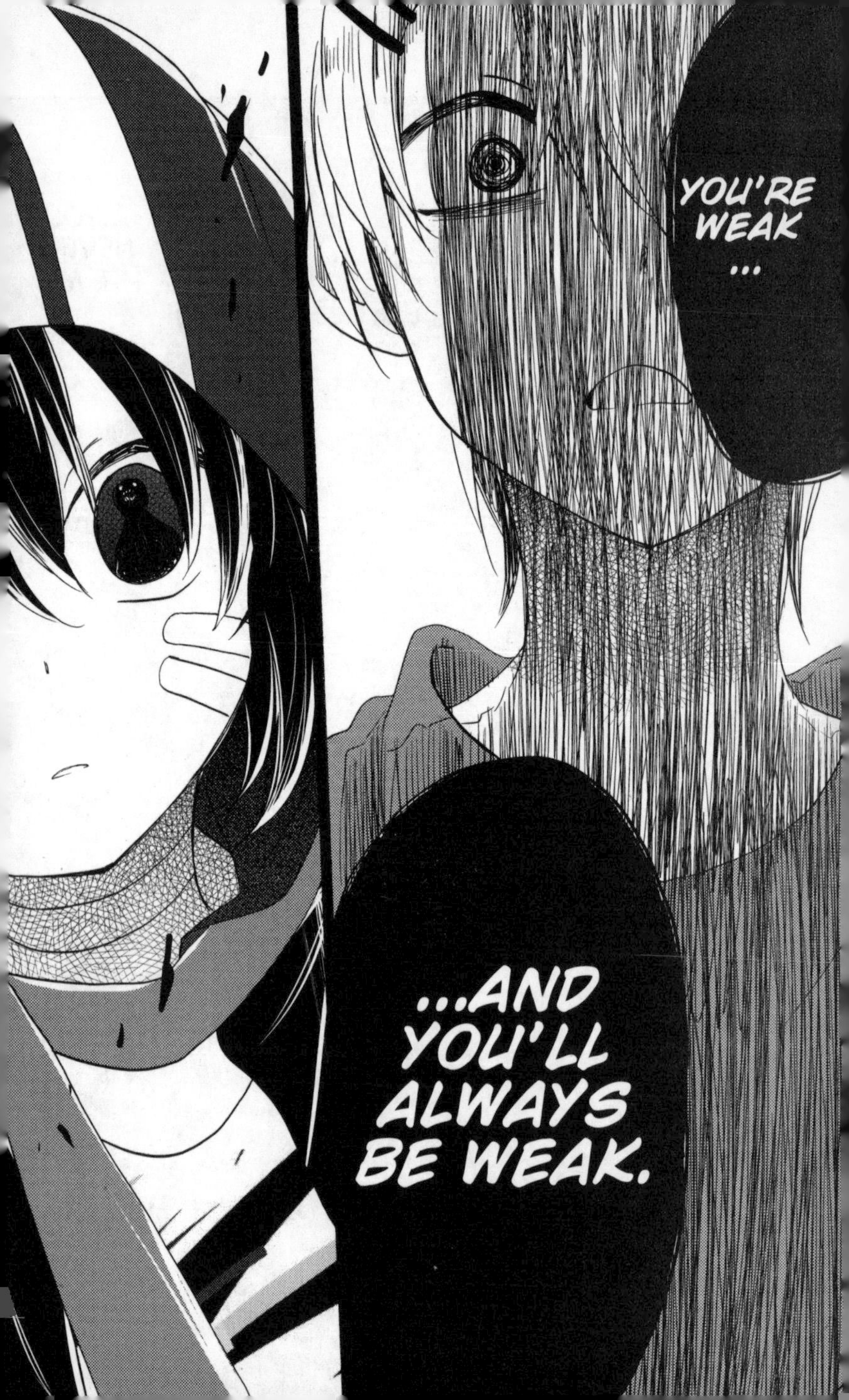
YOU'RE WEAK ...
...AND YOU'LL ALWAYS BE WEAK.

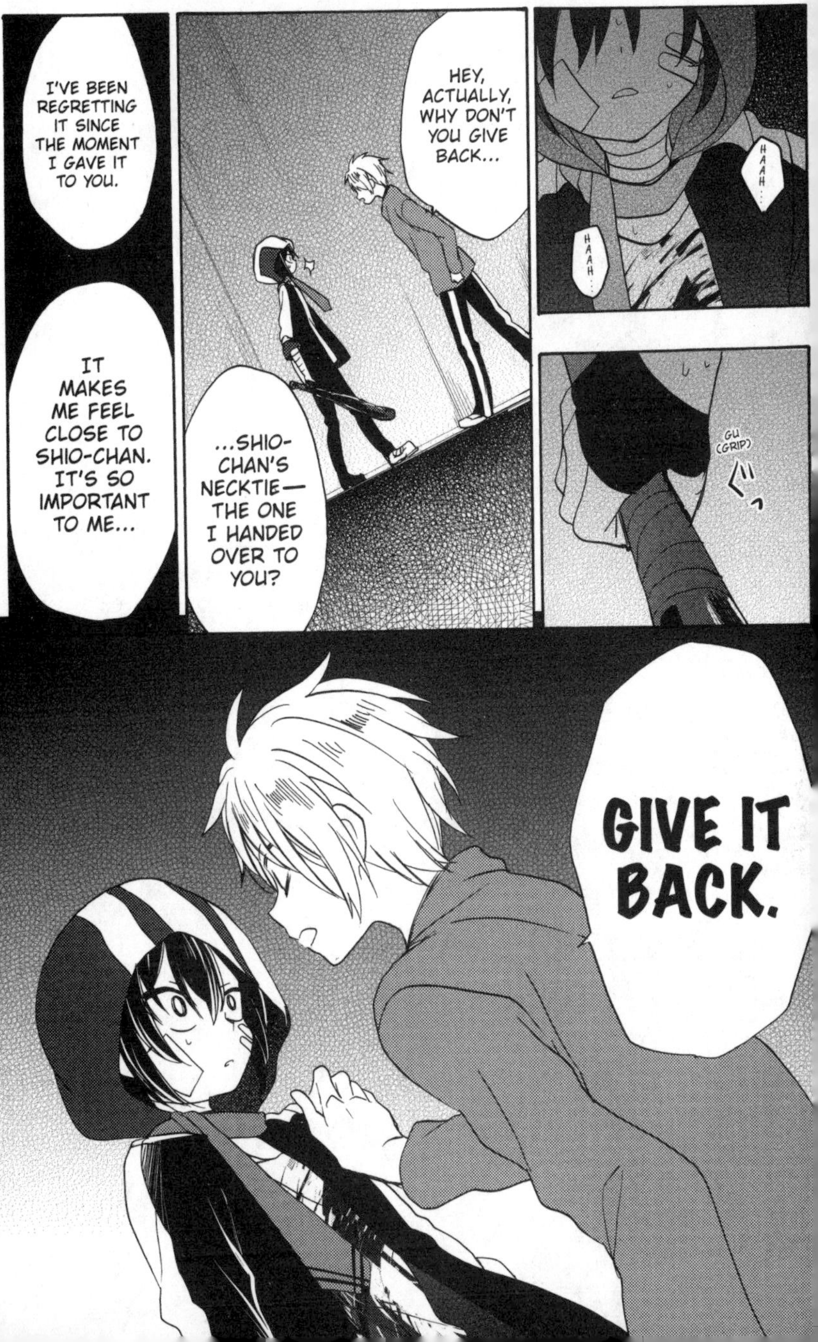
HAAH...
HAAH...
GU (GRIP)
HEY, ACTUALLY, WHY DON'T YOU GIVE BACK...
...SHIO-CHAN'S NECKTIE—THE ONE I HANDED OVER TO YOU?
I'VE BEEN REGRETTING IT SINCE THE MOMENT I GAVE IT TO YOU.
IT MAKES ME FEEL CLOSE TO SHIO-CHAN. IT'S SO IMPORTANT TO ME...
GIVE IT BACK.

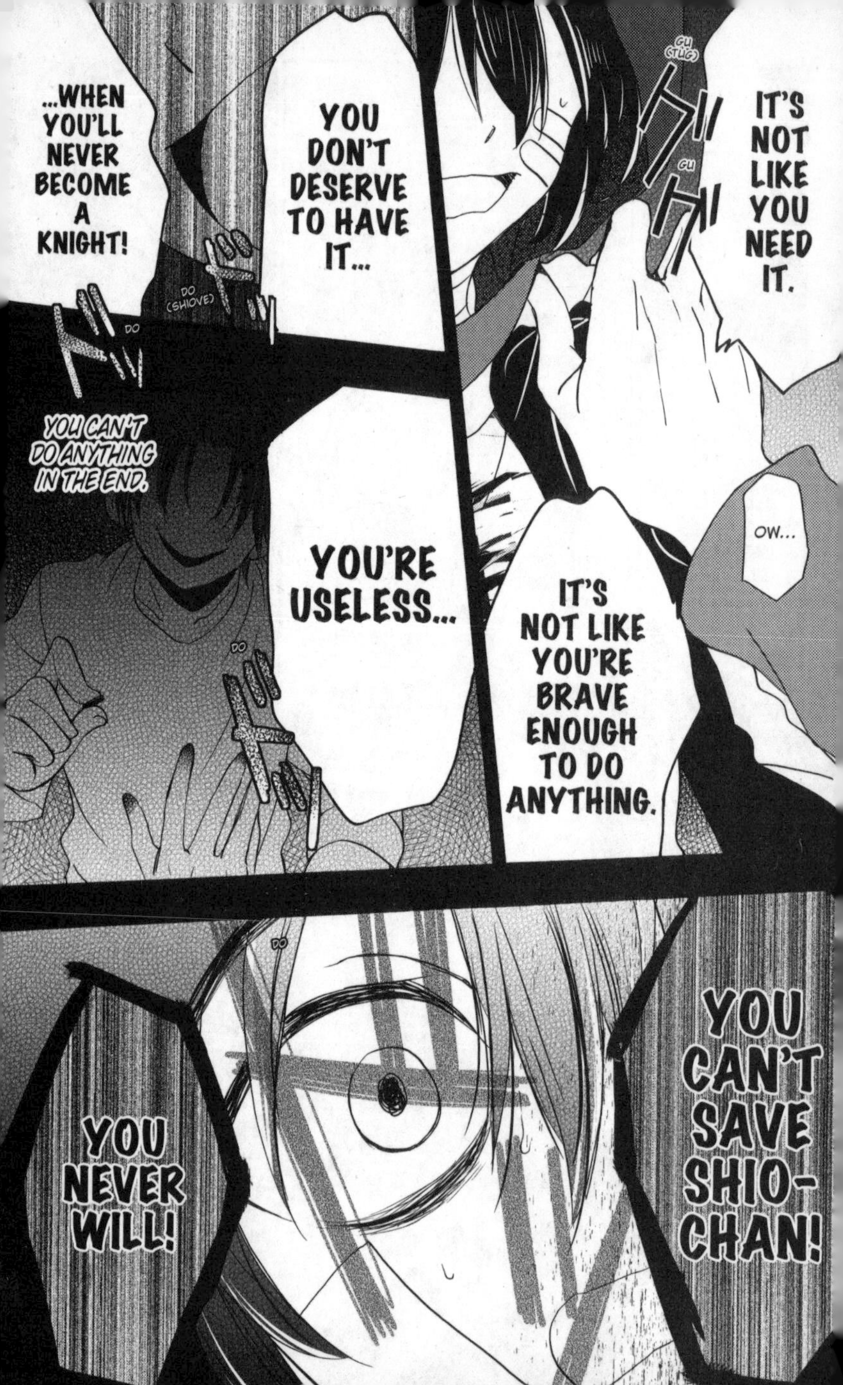
GU (TUG)
GU
IT'S NOT LIKE YOU NEED IT.
OW...
IT'S NOT LIKE YOU'RE BRAVE ENOUGH TO DO ANYTHING.
YOU DON'T DESERVE TO HAVE IT...
...WHEN YOU'LL NEVER BECOME A KNIGHT!
DO (SHOVE)
DO
YOU'RE USELESS...
YOU CAN'T DO ANYTHING IN THE END.
DO
DO
YOU CAN'T SAVE SHIO-CHAN!
YOU NEVER WILL!

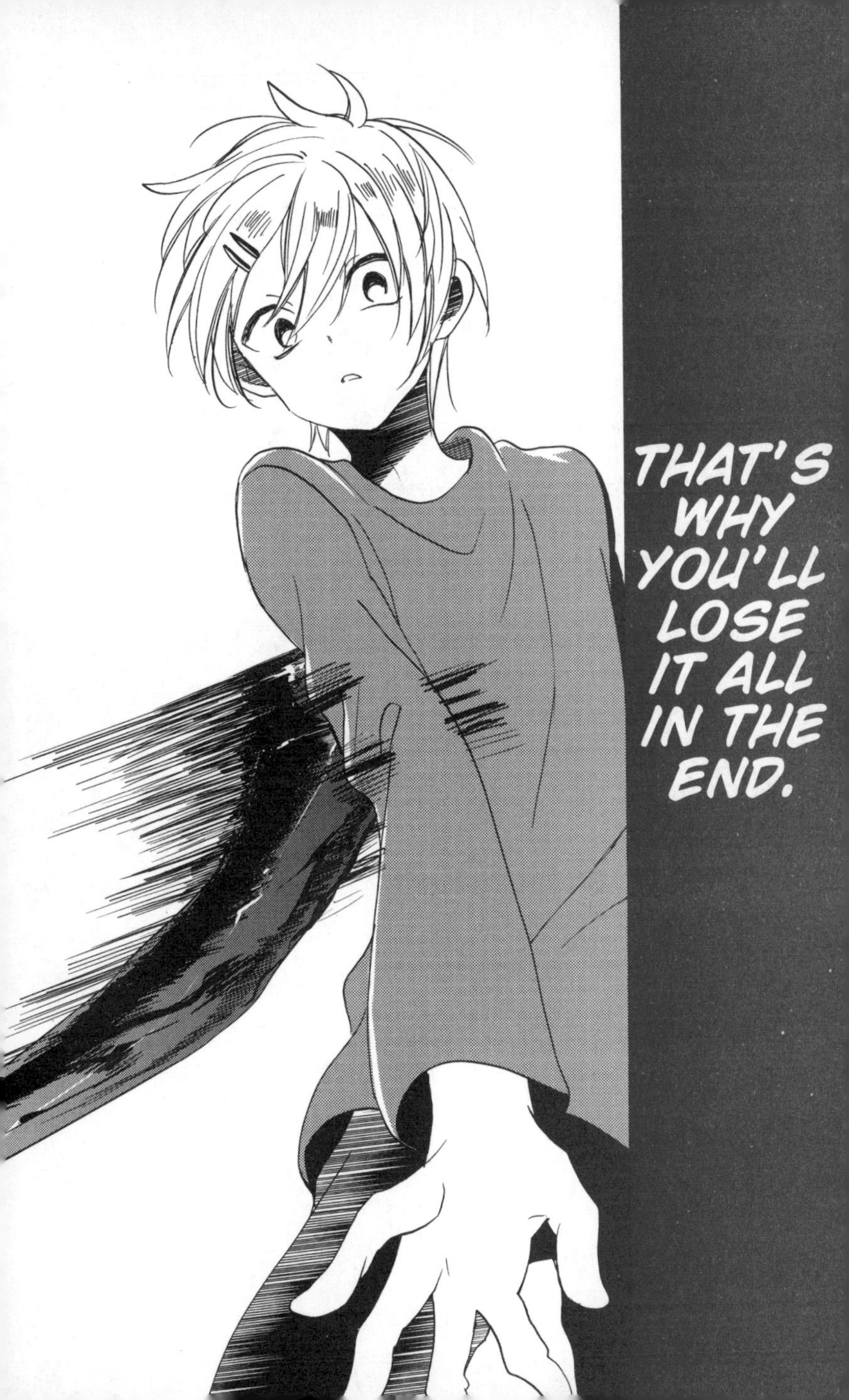
THAT'S WHY YOU'LL LOSE IT ALL IN THE END.

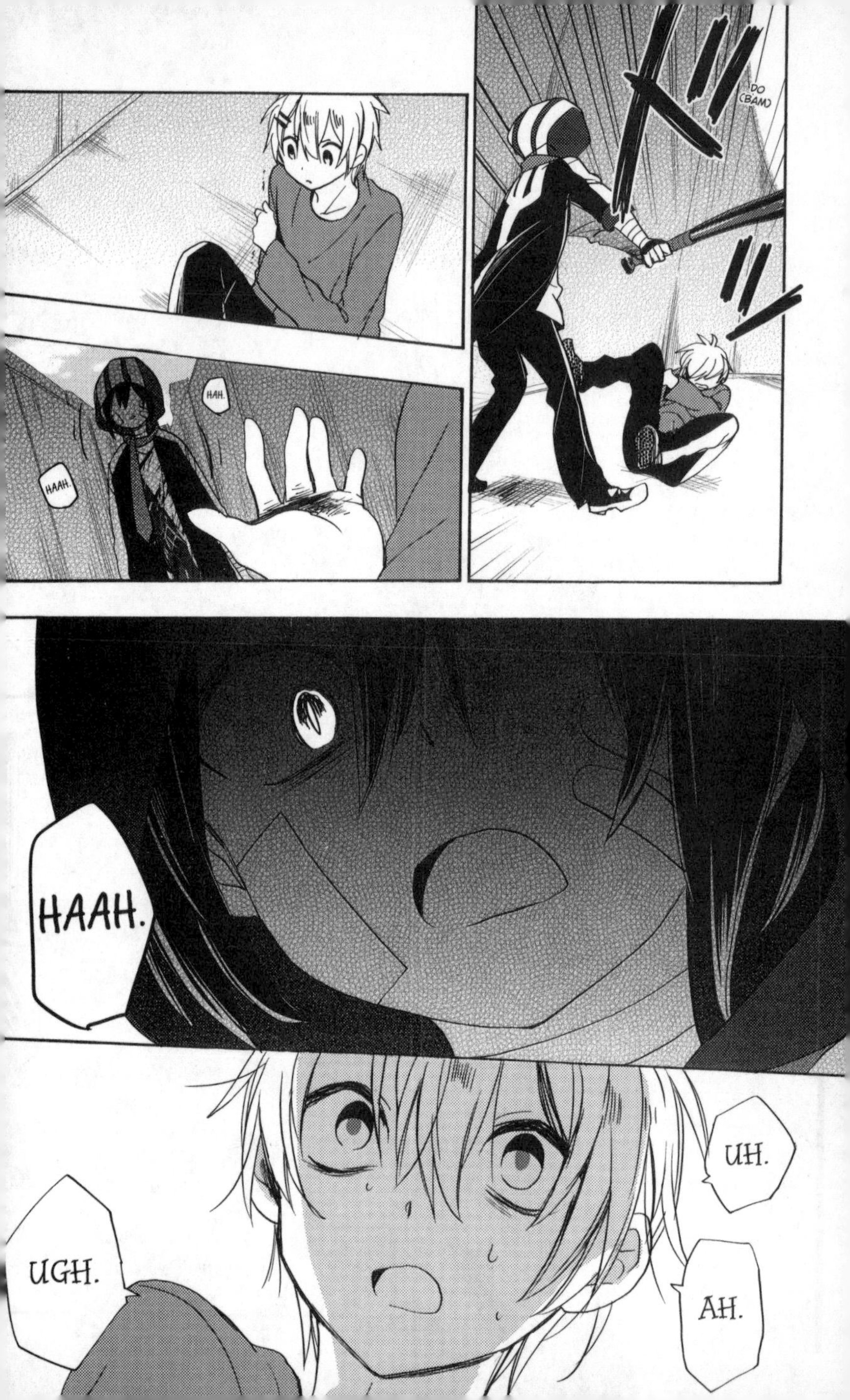
DO
(BAM)
HAH.
HAAH.
HAAH.
UH.
AH.
UGH.

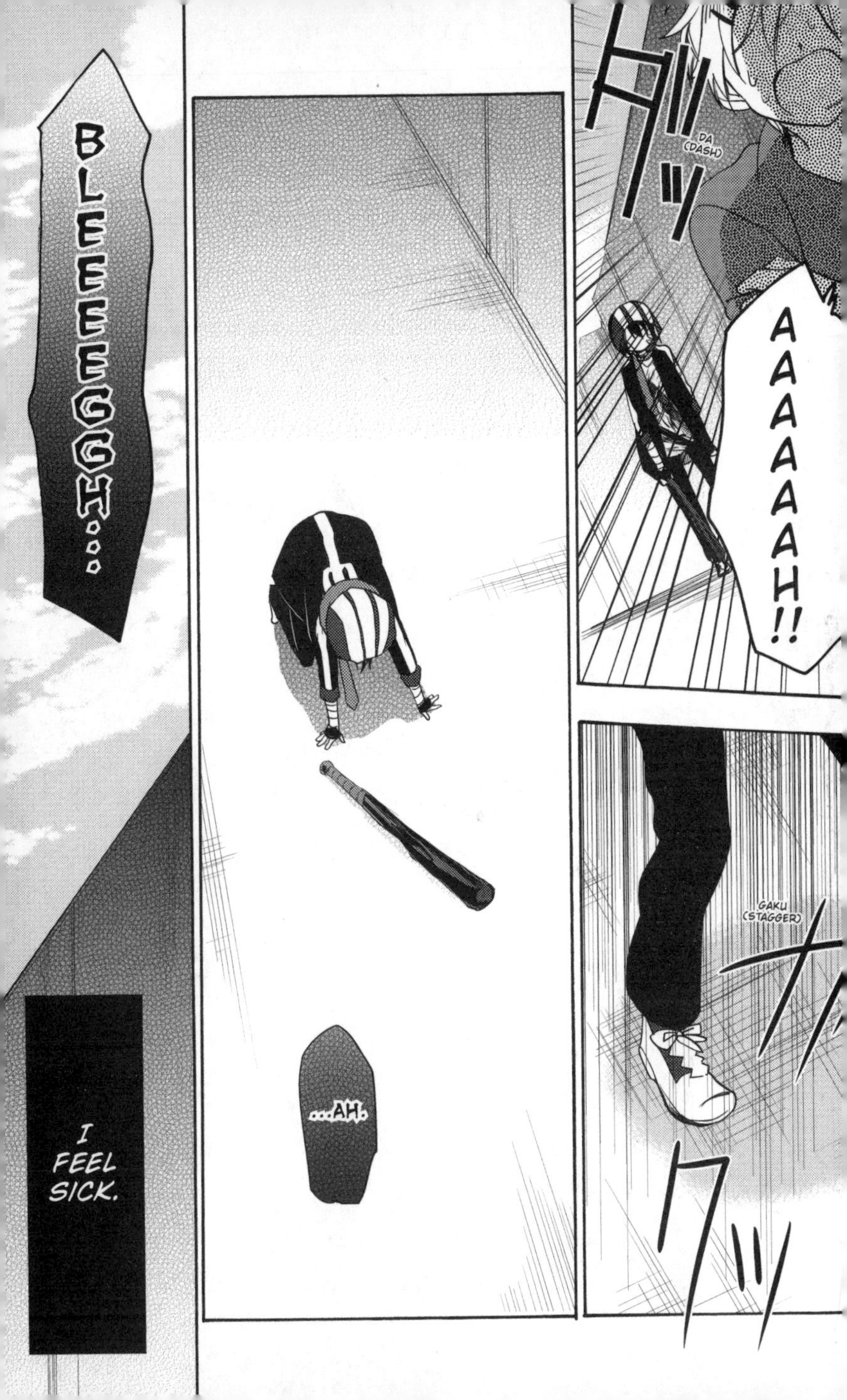
DA (DASH)
AAAAAAAH!!
GAKU (STAGGER)
...AH.
BLEEEEGGH...
I FEEL SICK.

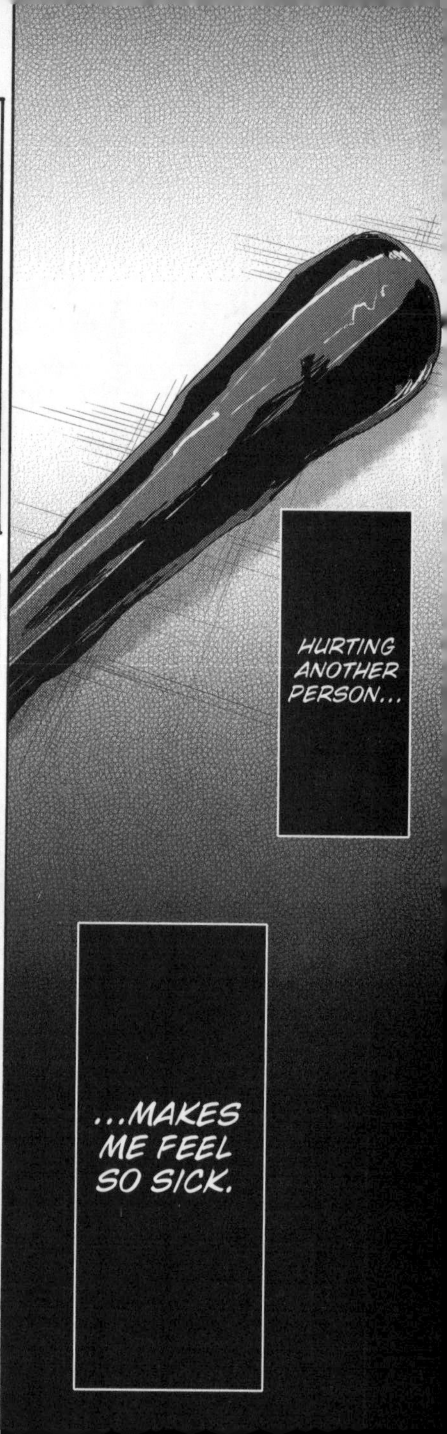
HURTING ANOTHER PERSON...
...MAKES ME FEEL SO SICK.

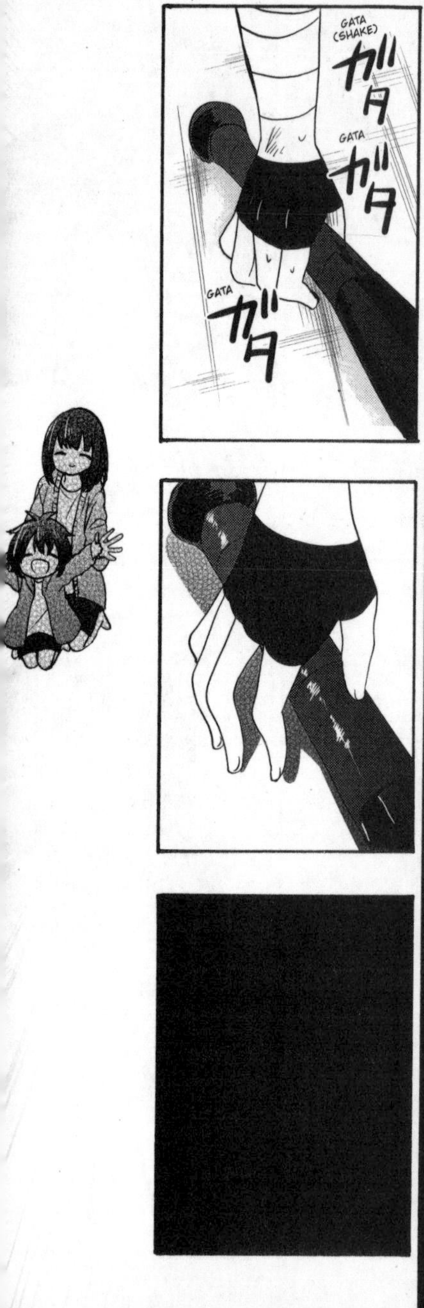
GATA (SHAKE)
ガタ
GATA
ガタ
GATA
ガタ

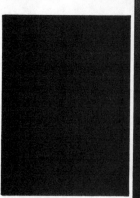

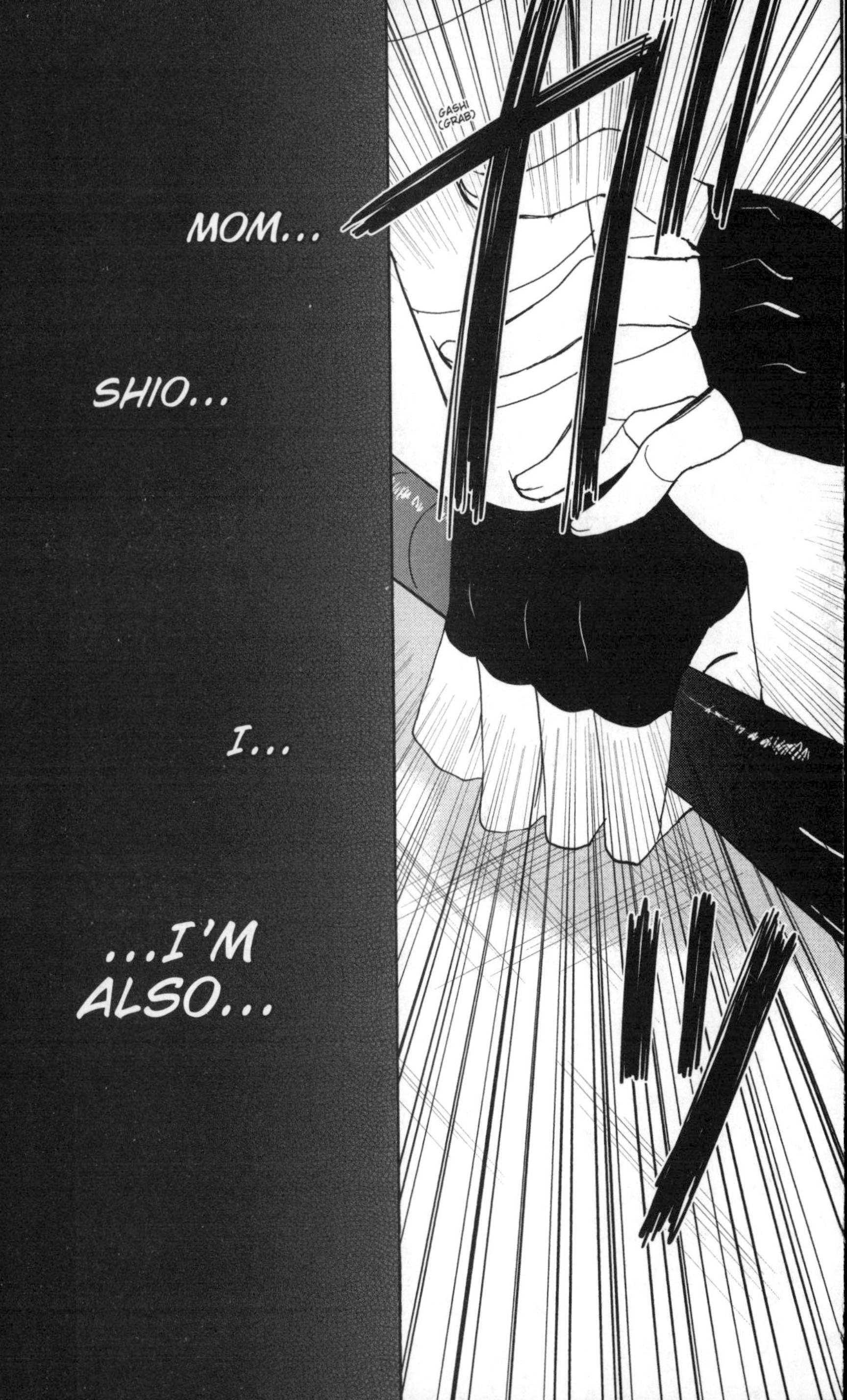
GASHI (GRAB)
MOM...
SHIO...
I...
...I'M ALSO...

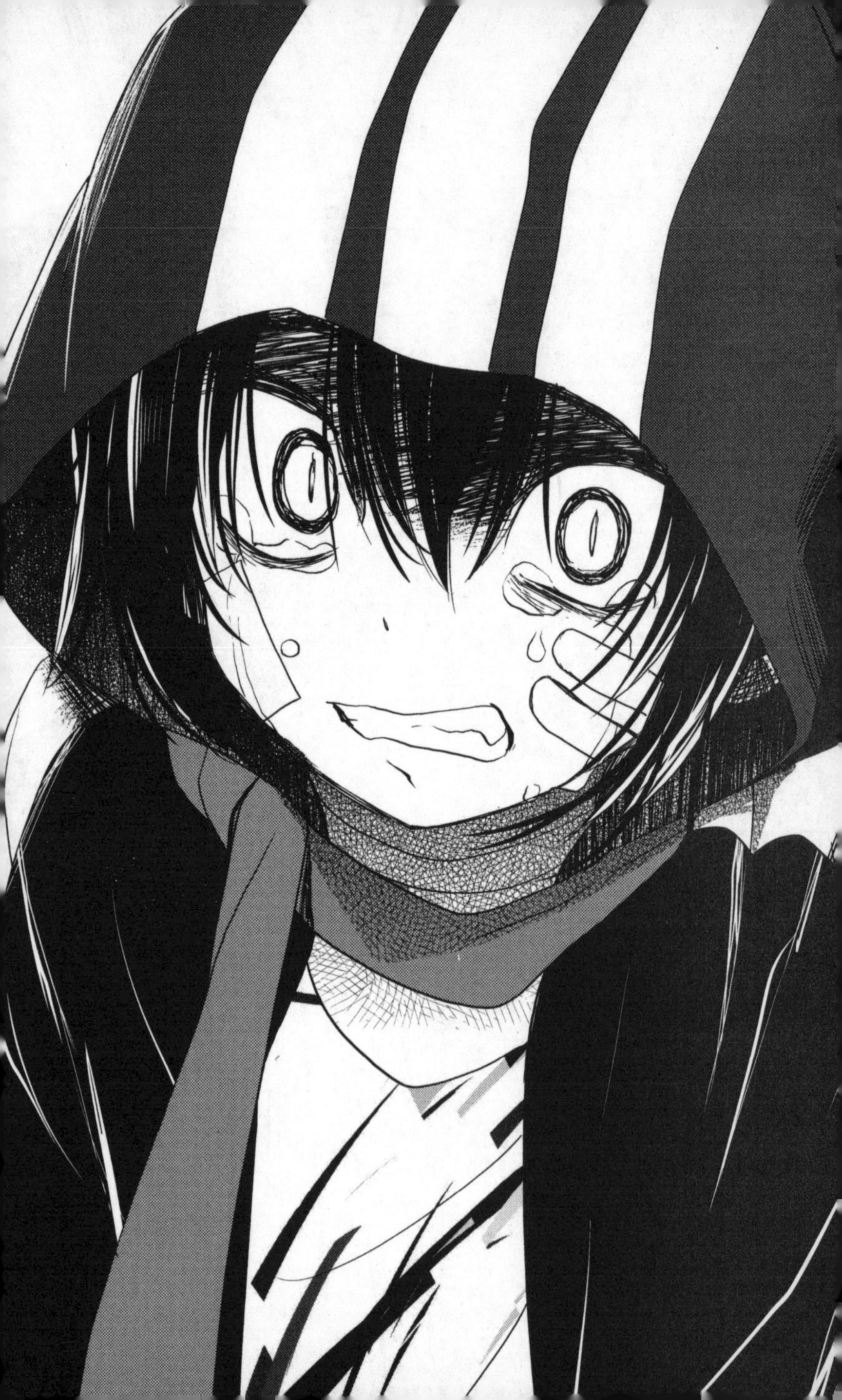

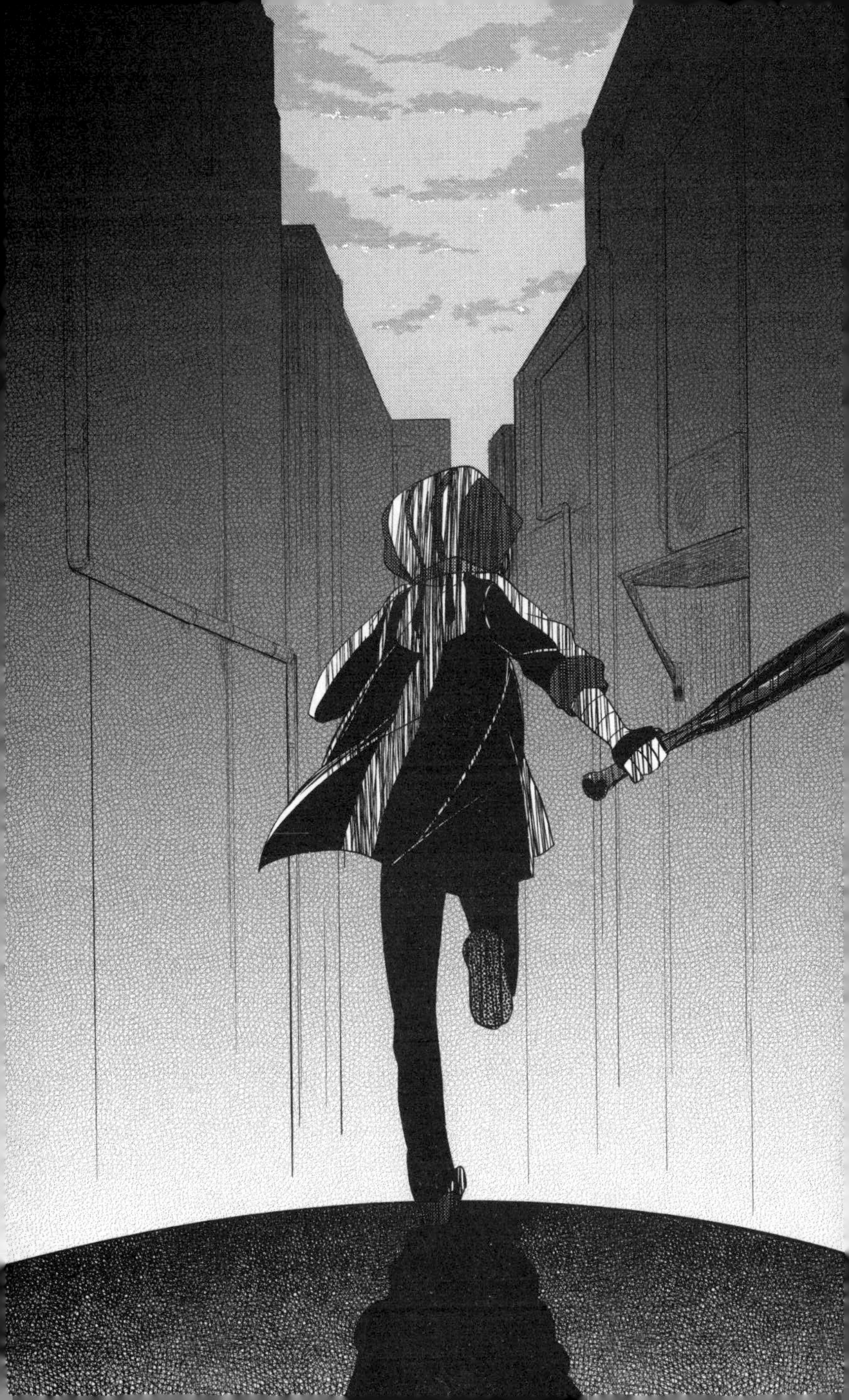

Happy
Sugar
Life

ヒュッ
HYU
(FWISH)

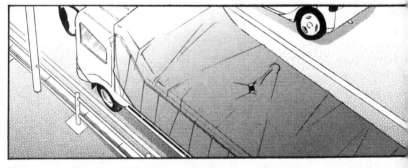

ブロロロロ
BURORORORO
(VROOOM)

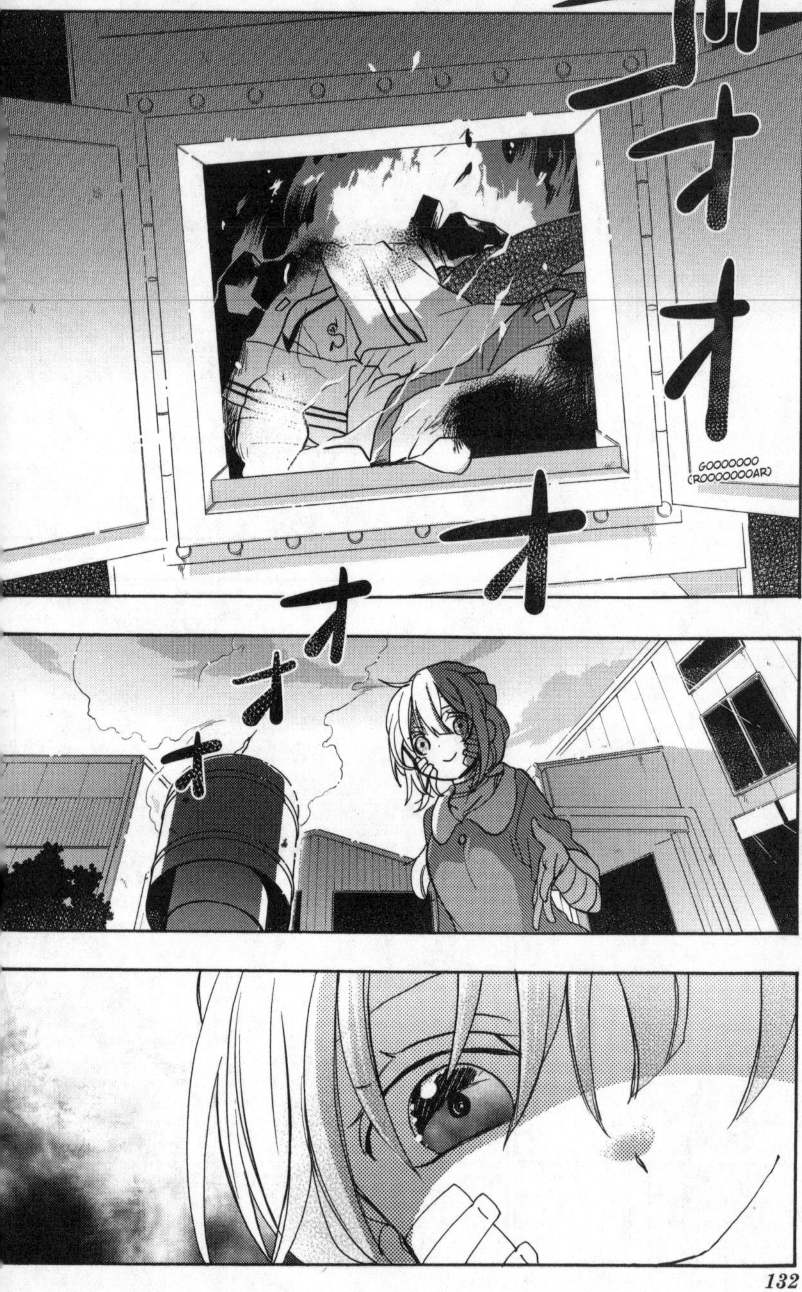
ゴオオオオオ
GOOOOOOO
(ROOOOOOOOAR)

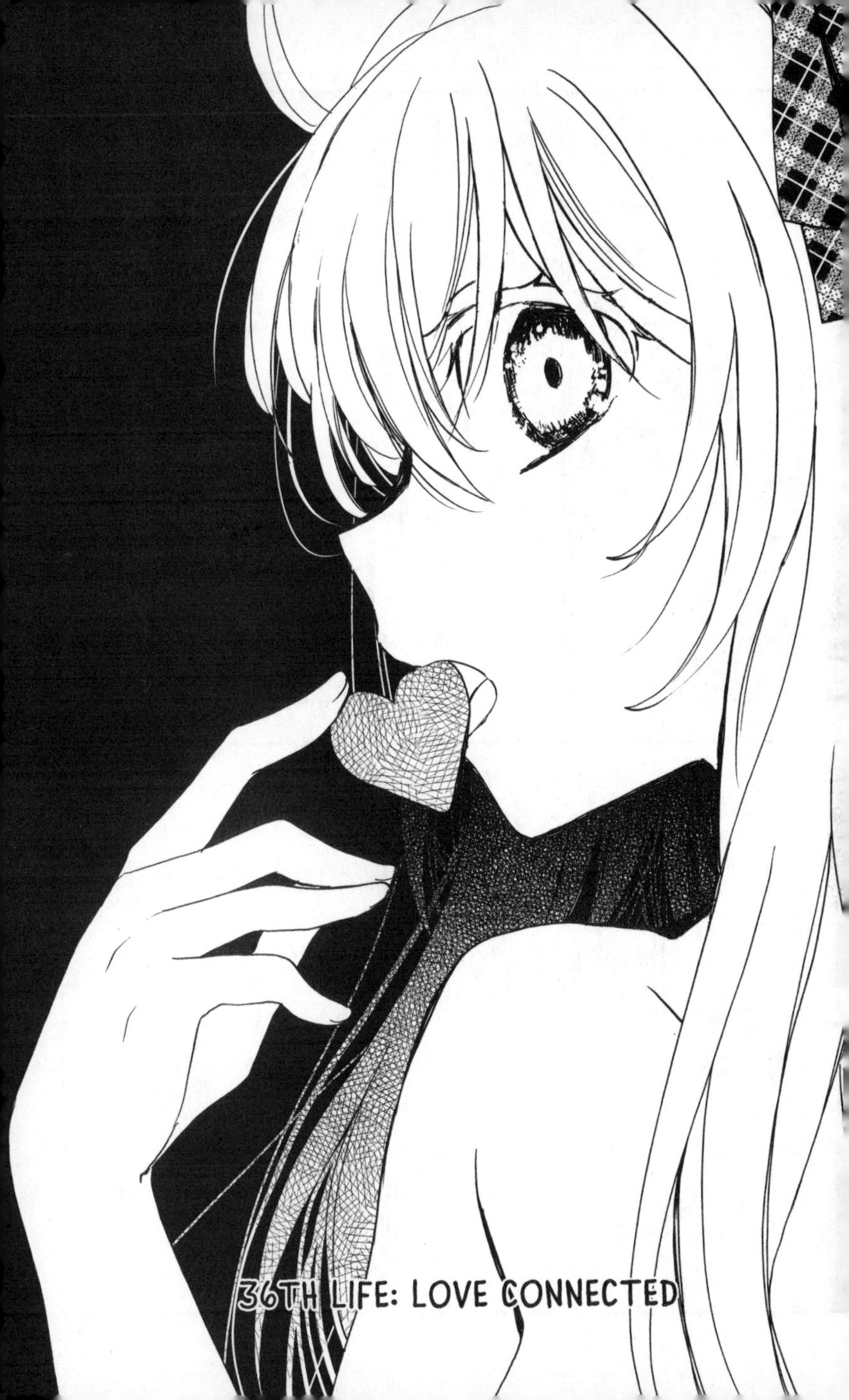
36TH LIFE: LOVE CONNECTED

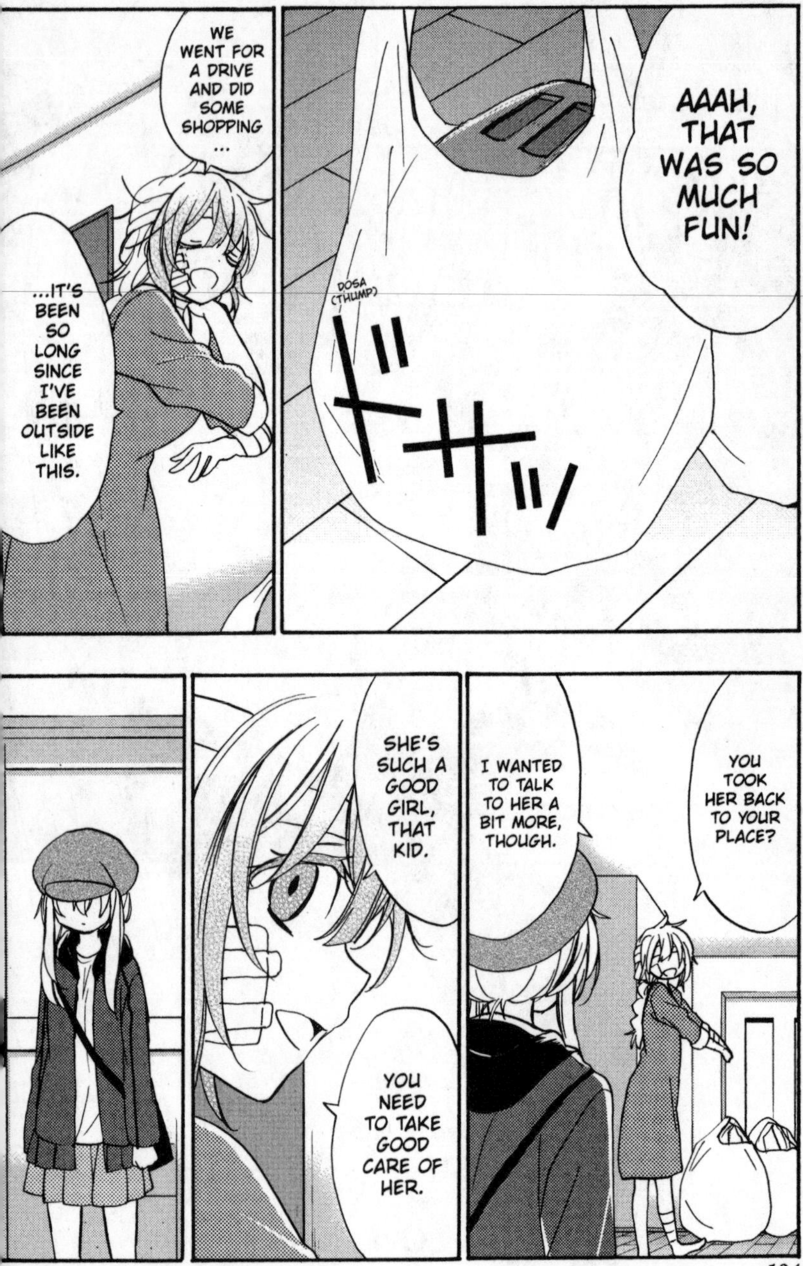
AAAH, THAT WAS SO MUCH FUN!
DOSA (THUMP)
ドサッ
WE WENT FOR A DRIVE AND DID SOME SHOPPING ...
...IT'S BEEN SO LONG SINCE I'VE BEEN OUTSIDE LIKE THIS.
YOU TOOK HER BACK TO YOUR PLACE?
I WANTED TO TALK TO HER A BIT MORE, THOUGH.
SHE'S SUCH A GOOD GIRL, THAT KID.
YOU NEED TO TAKE GOOD CARE OF HER.

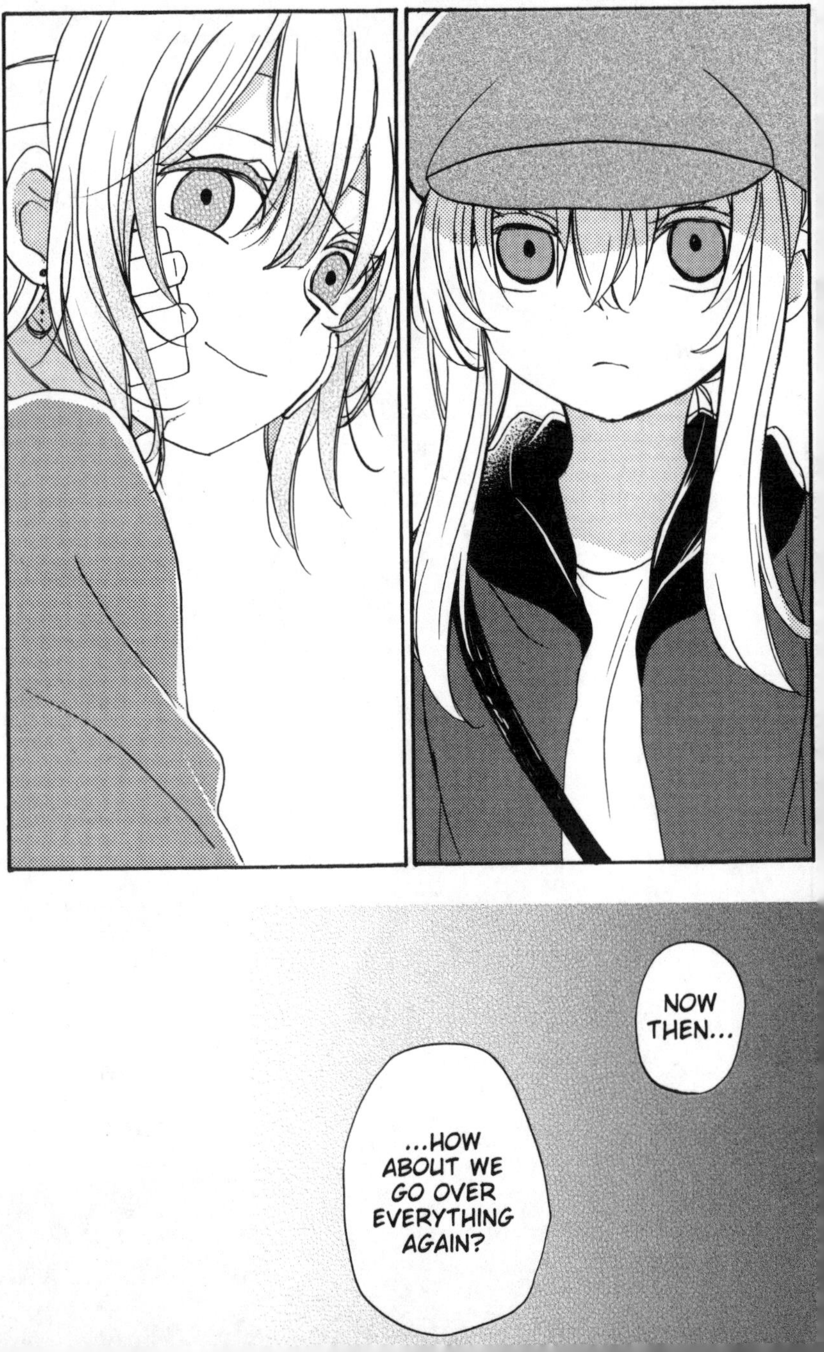
NOW THEN...
...HOW ABOUT WE GO OVER EVERYTHING AGAIN?

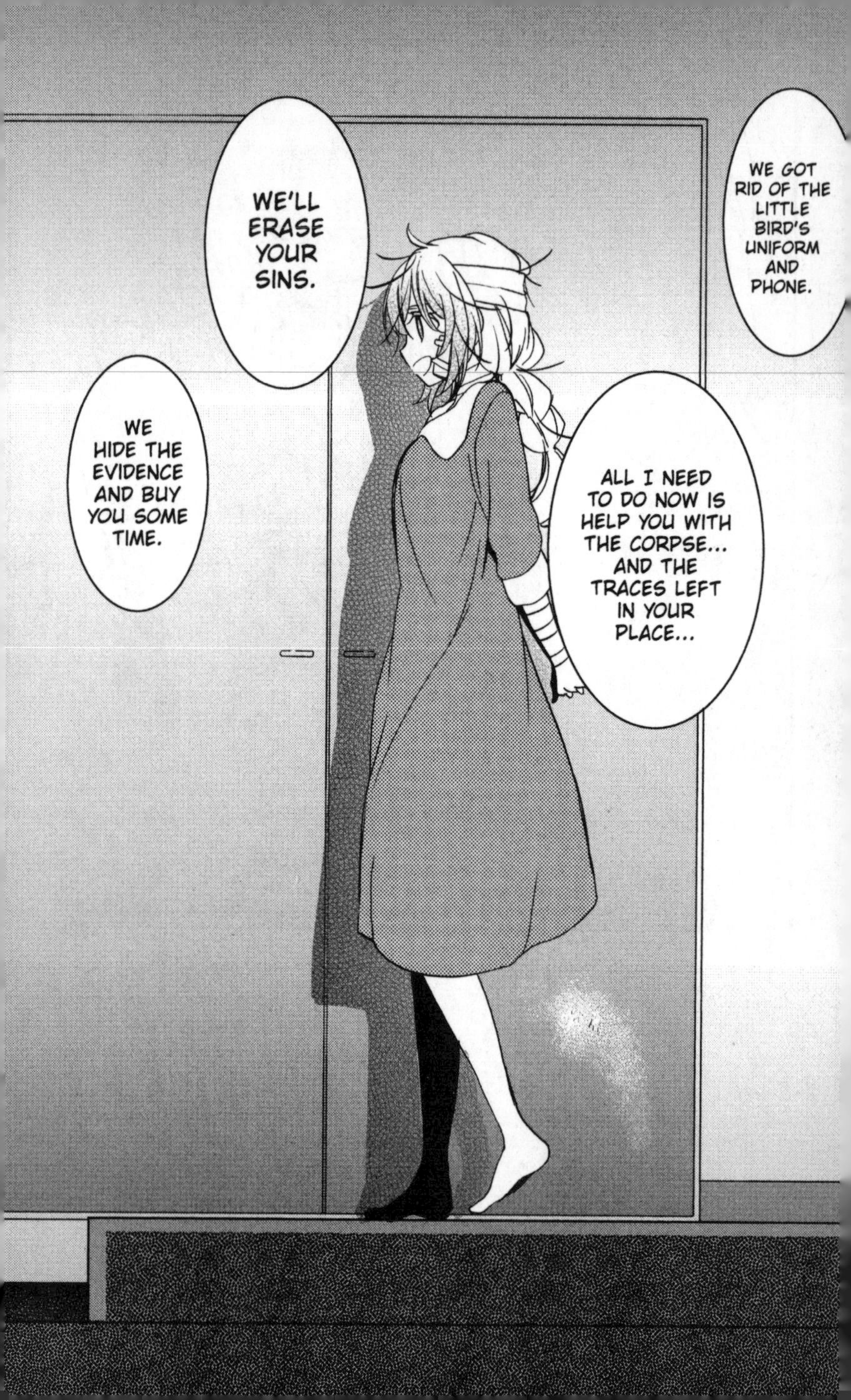
WE GOT RID OF THE LITTLE BIRD'S UNIFORM AND PHONE.
ALL I NEED TO DO NOW IS HELP YOU WITH THE CORPSE... AND THE TRACES LEFT IN YOUR PLACE...
WE'LL ERASE YOUR SINS.
WE HIDE THE EVIDENCE AND BUY YOU SOME TIME.

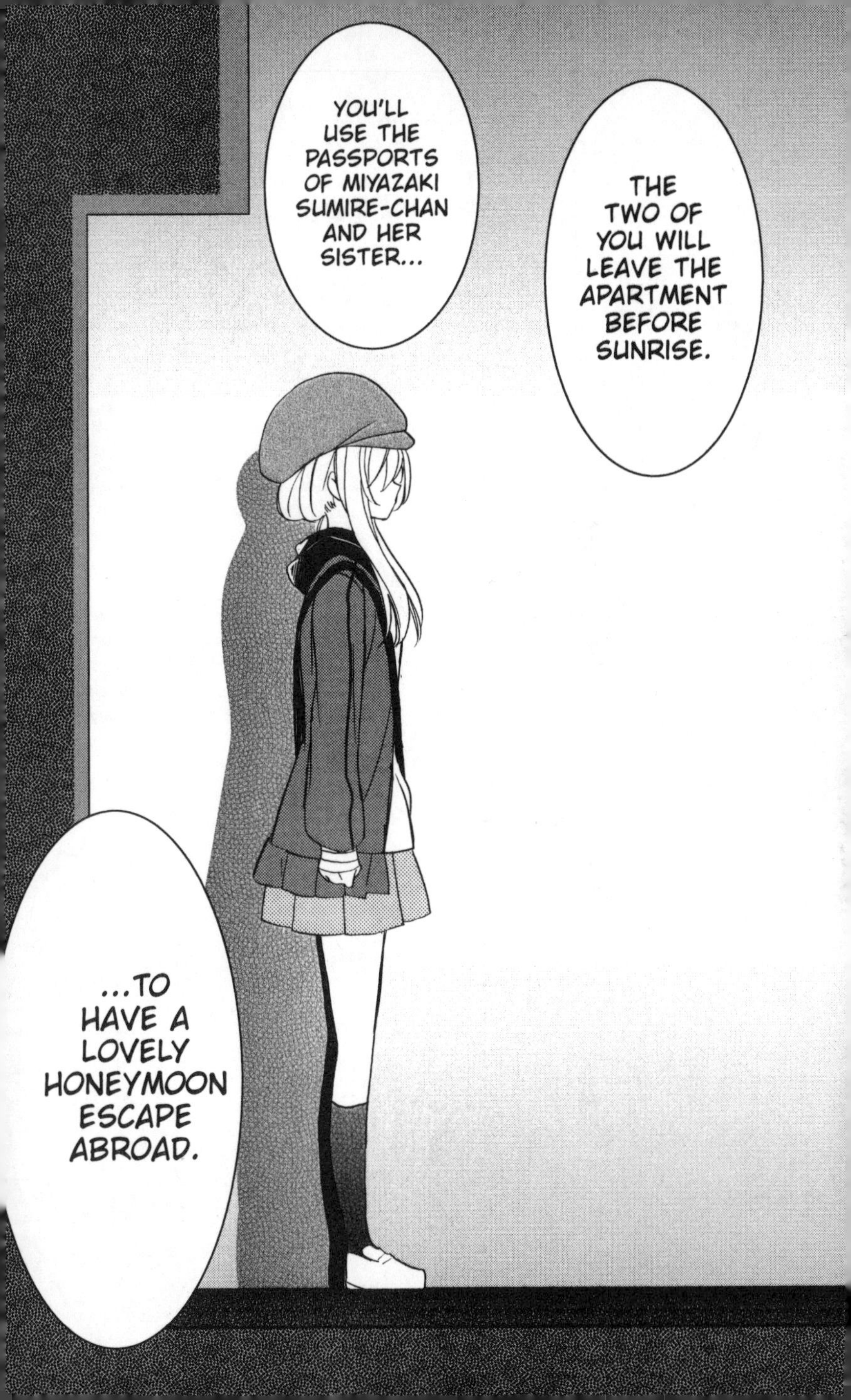
THE TWO OF YOU WILL LEAVE THE APARTMENT BEFORE SUNRISE.
YOU'LL USE THE PASSPORTS OF MIYAZAKI SUMIRE-CHAN AND HER SISTER...
...TO HAVE A LOVELY HONEYMOON ESCAPE ABROAD.

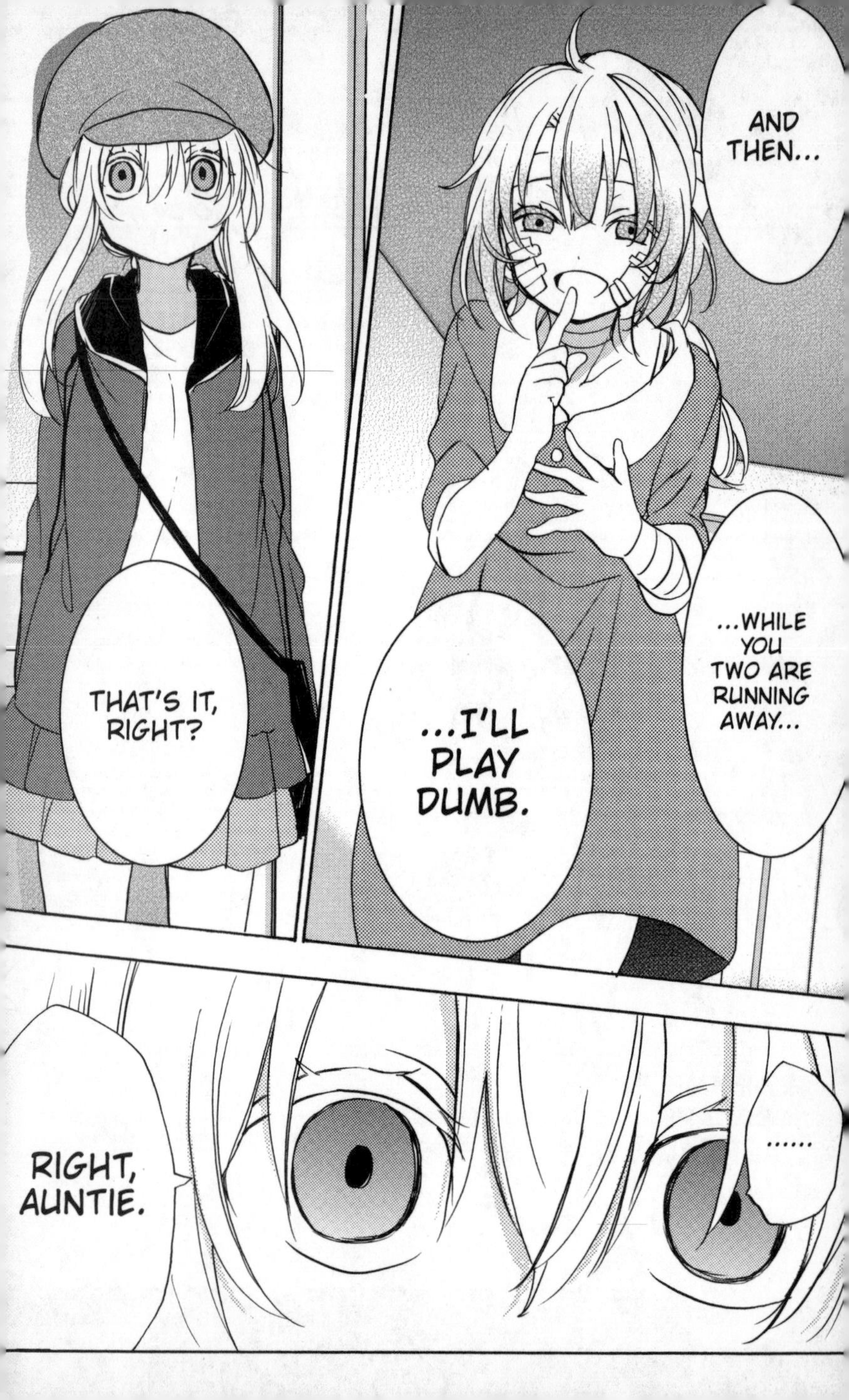
AND THEN...
...WHILE YOU TWO ARE RUNNING AWAY...
...I'LL PLAY DUMB.
THAT'S IT, RIGHT?
......
RIGHT, AUNTIE.

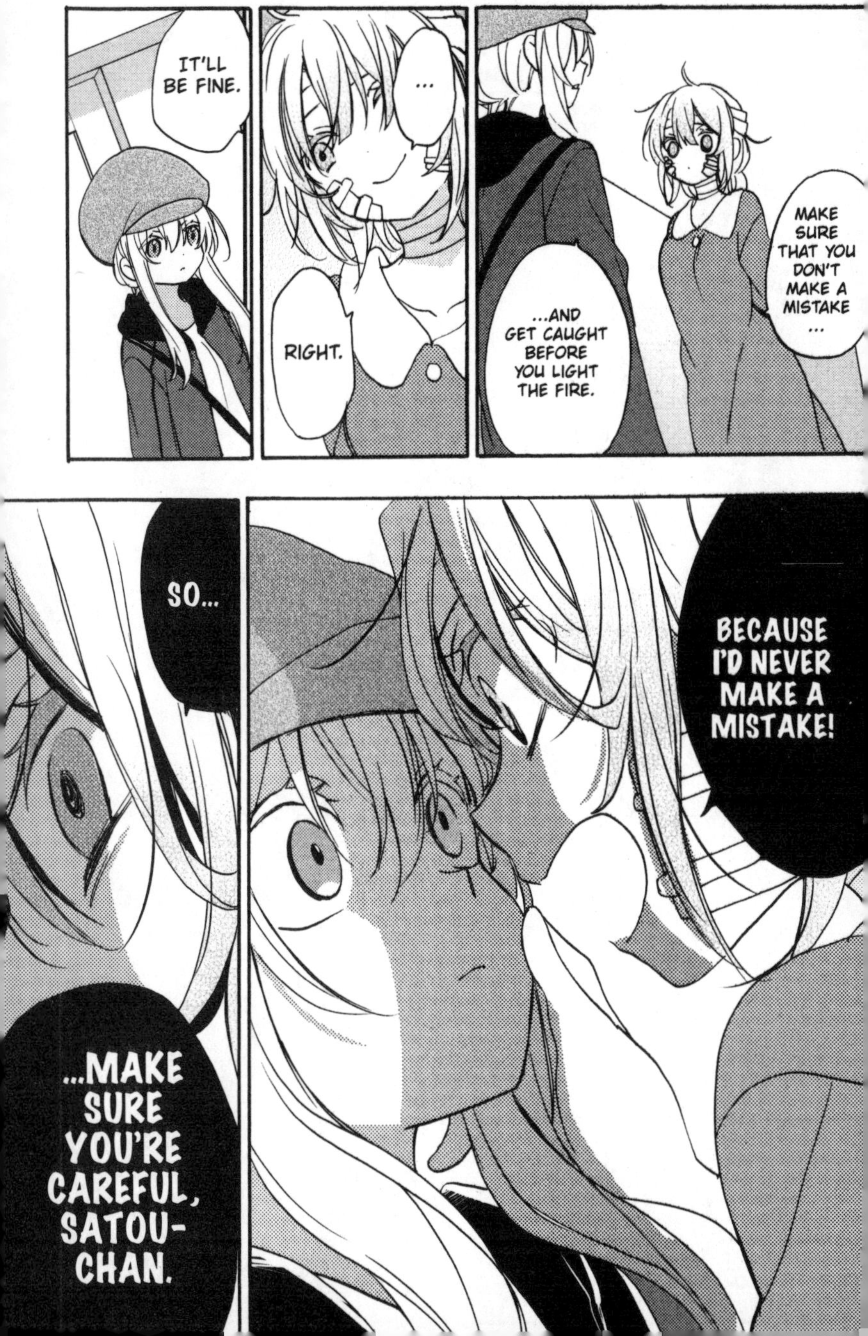
MAKE SURE THAT YOU DON'T MAKE A MISTAKE ...
...AND GET CAUGHT BEFORE YOU LIGHT THE FIRE.
...
RIGHT.
IT'LL BE FINE.
BECAUSE I'D NEVER MAKE A MISTAKE!
SO...
...MAKE SURE YOU'RE CAREFUL, SATOU-CHAN.

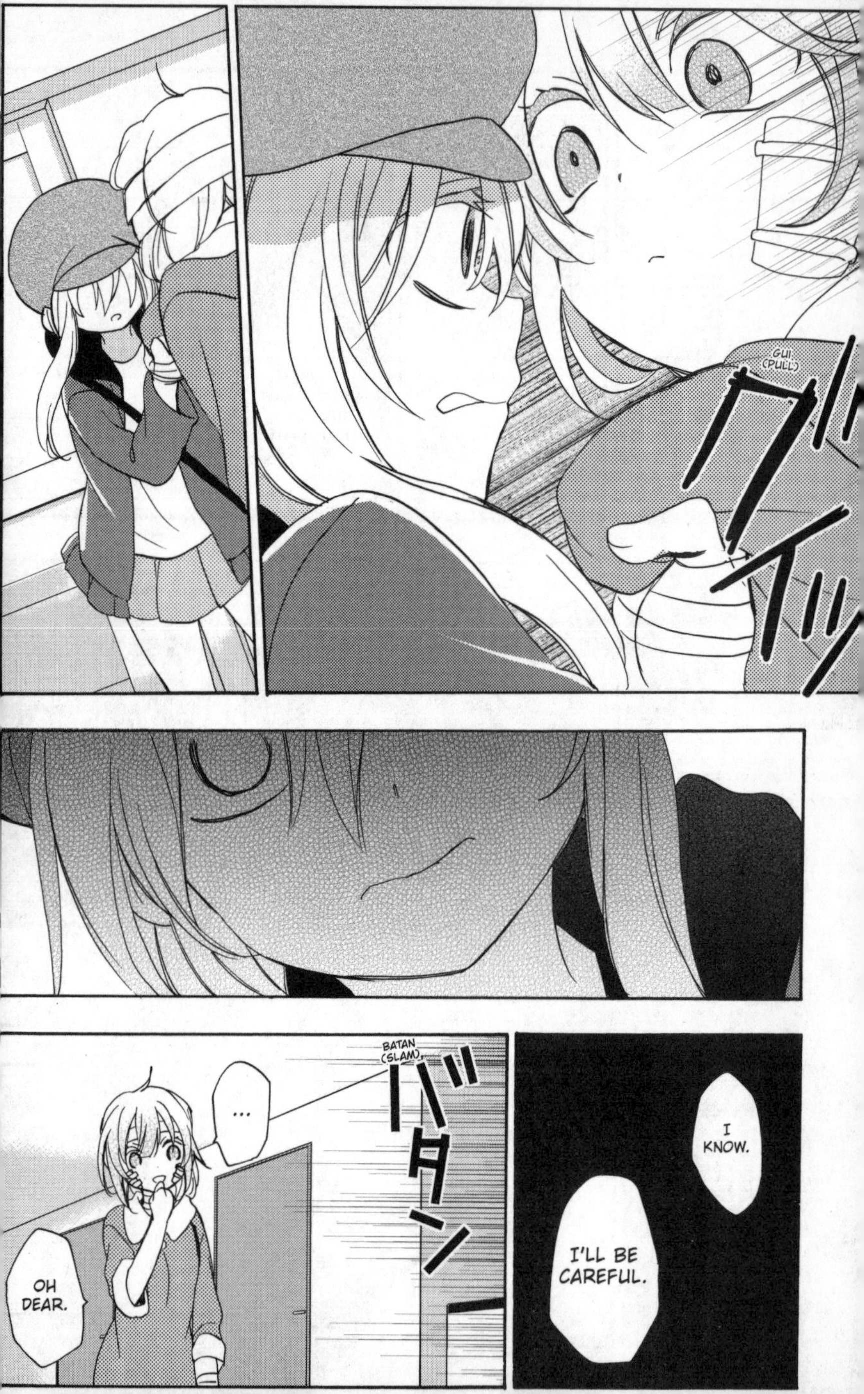
GUI (PULL)
I KNOW.
I'LL BE CAREFUL.
BATAN (SLAM)
...
OH DEAR.

SHE'S AT SUCH A DIFFICULT AGE.

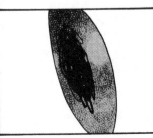

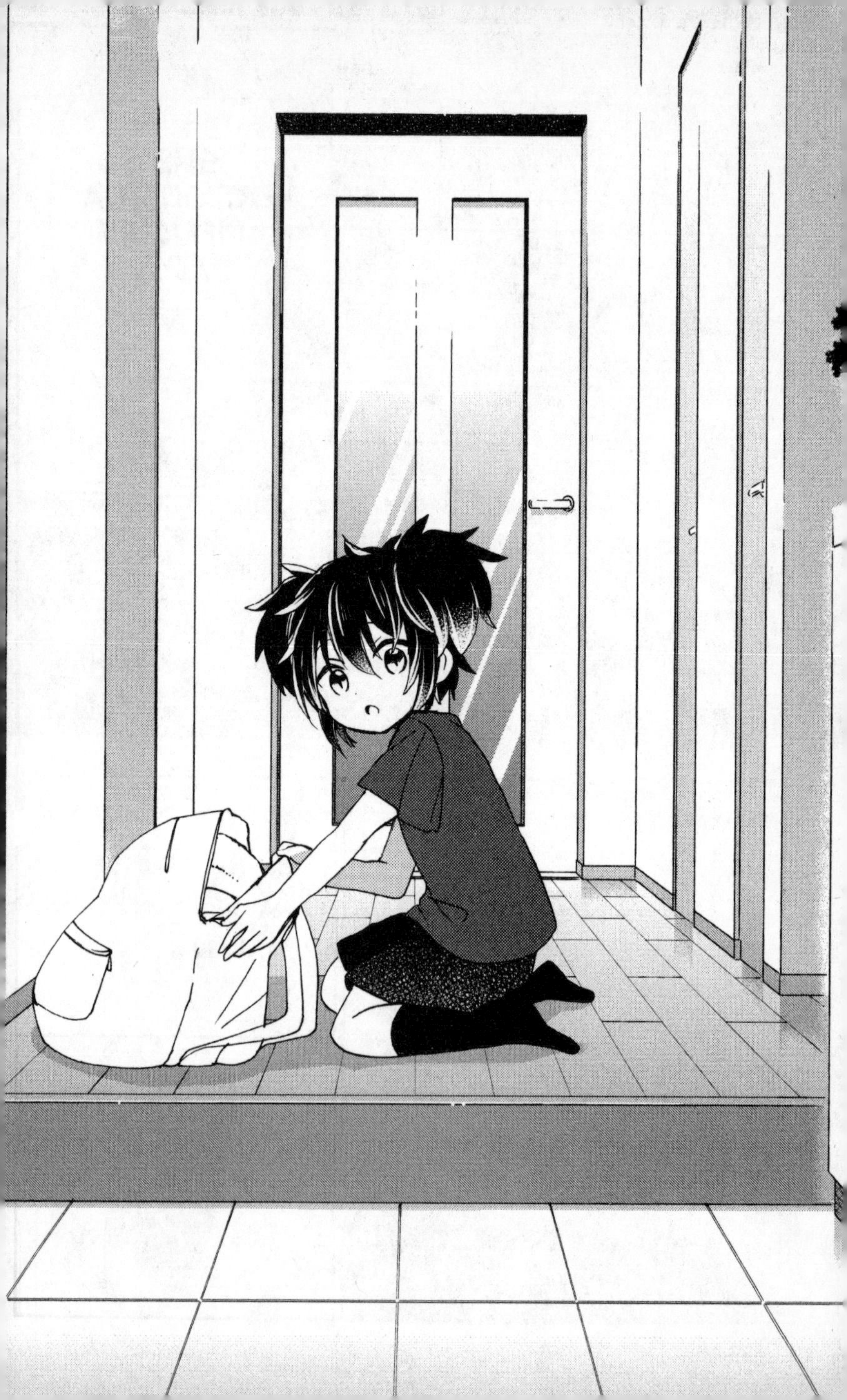

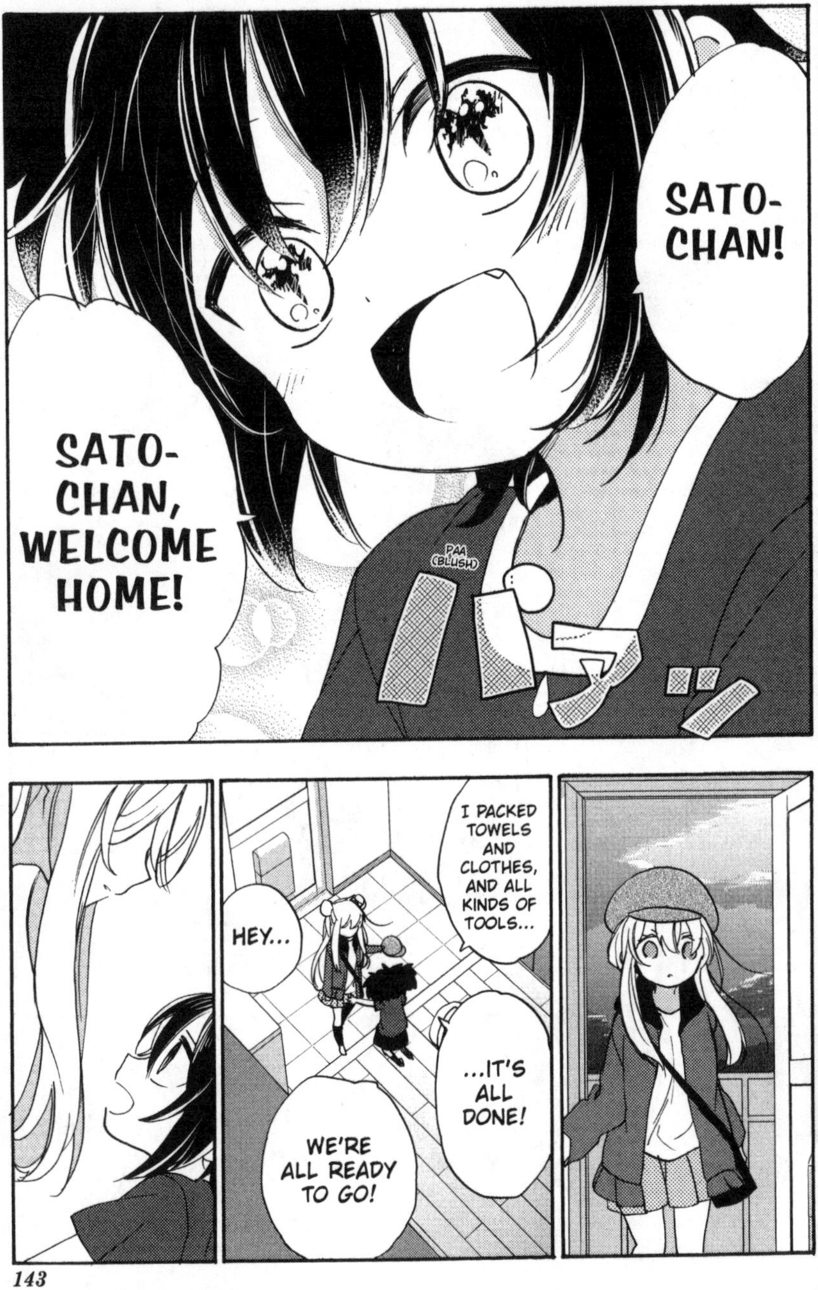
SATO-CHAN!
SATO-CHAN, WELCOME HOME!
PAA (BLUSH)
I PACKED TOWELS AND CLOTHES, AND ALL KINDS OF TOOLS...
HEY...
...IT'S ALL DONE!
WE'RE ALL READY TO GO!

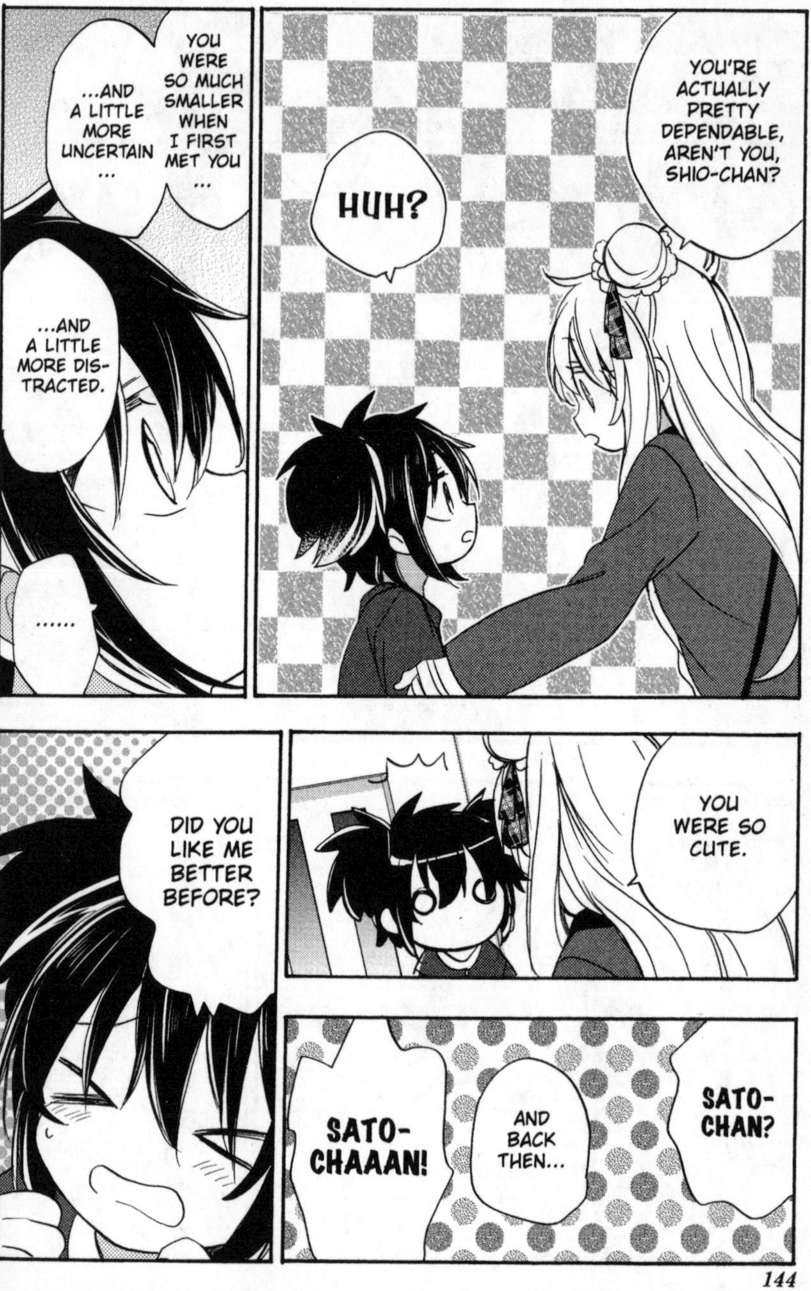
YOU'RE ACTUALLY PRETTY DEPENDABLE, AREN'T YOU, SHIO-CHAN?
HUH?
YOU WERE SO MUCH SMALLER WHEN I FIRST MET YOU...
...AND A LITTLE MORE UNCERTAIN...
...AND A LITTLE MORE DIS-TRACTED.
......
YOU WERE SO CUTE.
SATO-CHAN?
AND BACK THEN...
SATO-CHAAAN!
DID YOU LIKE ME BETTER BEFORE?

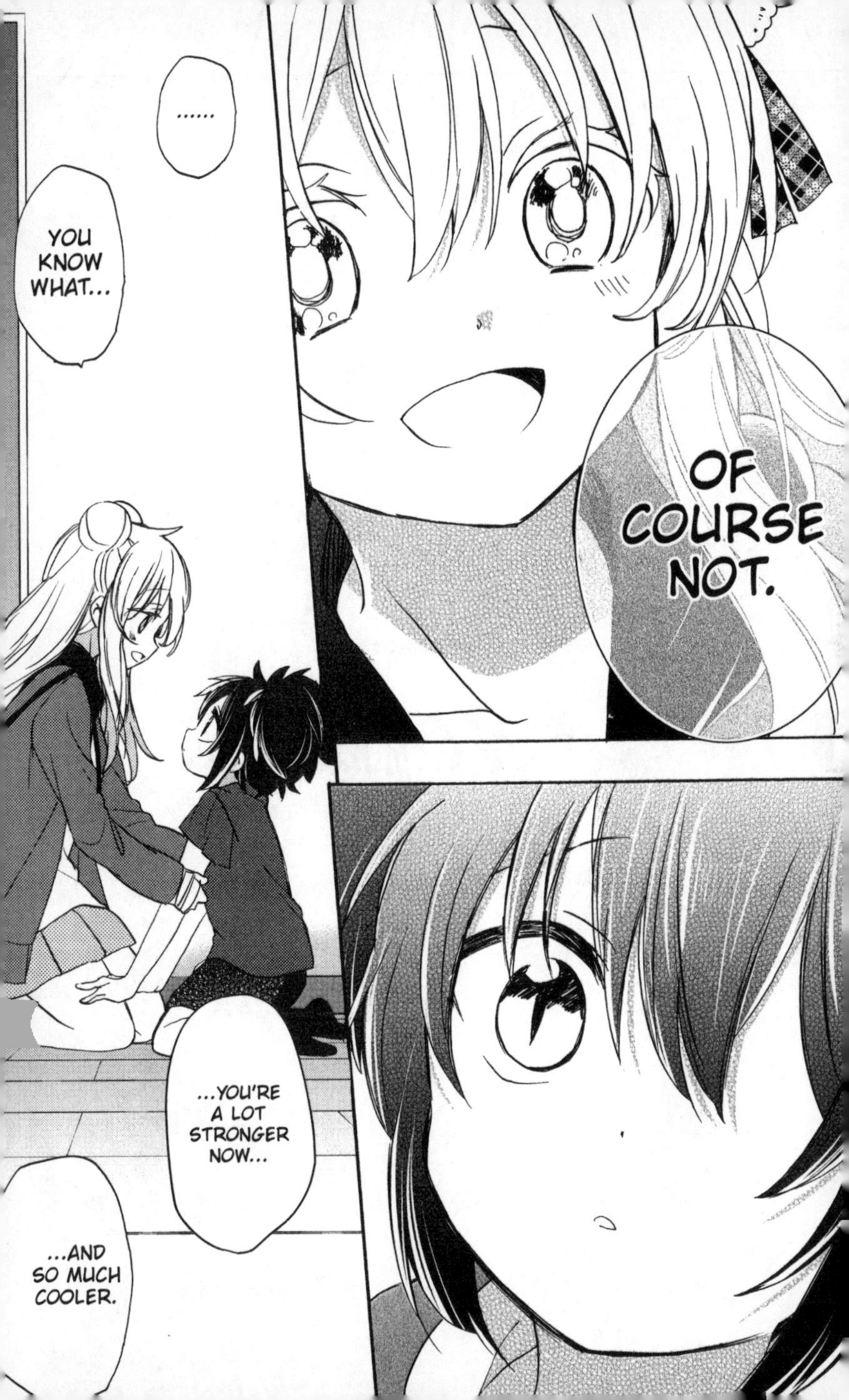
OF COURSE NOT.
......
YOU KNOW WHAT...
...YOU'RE A LOT STRONGER NOW...
...AND SO MUCH COOLER.

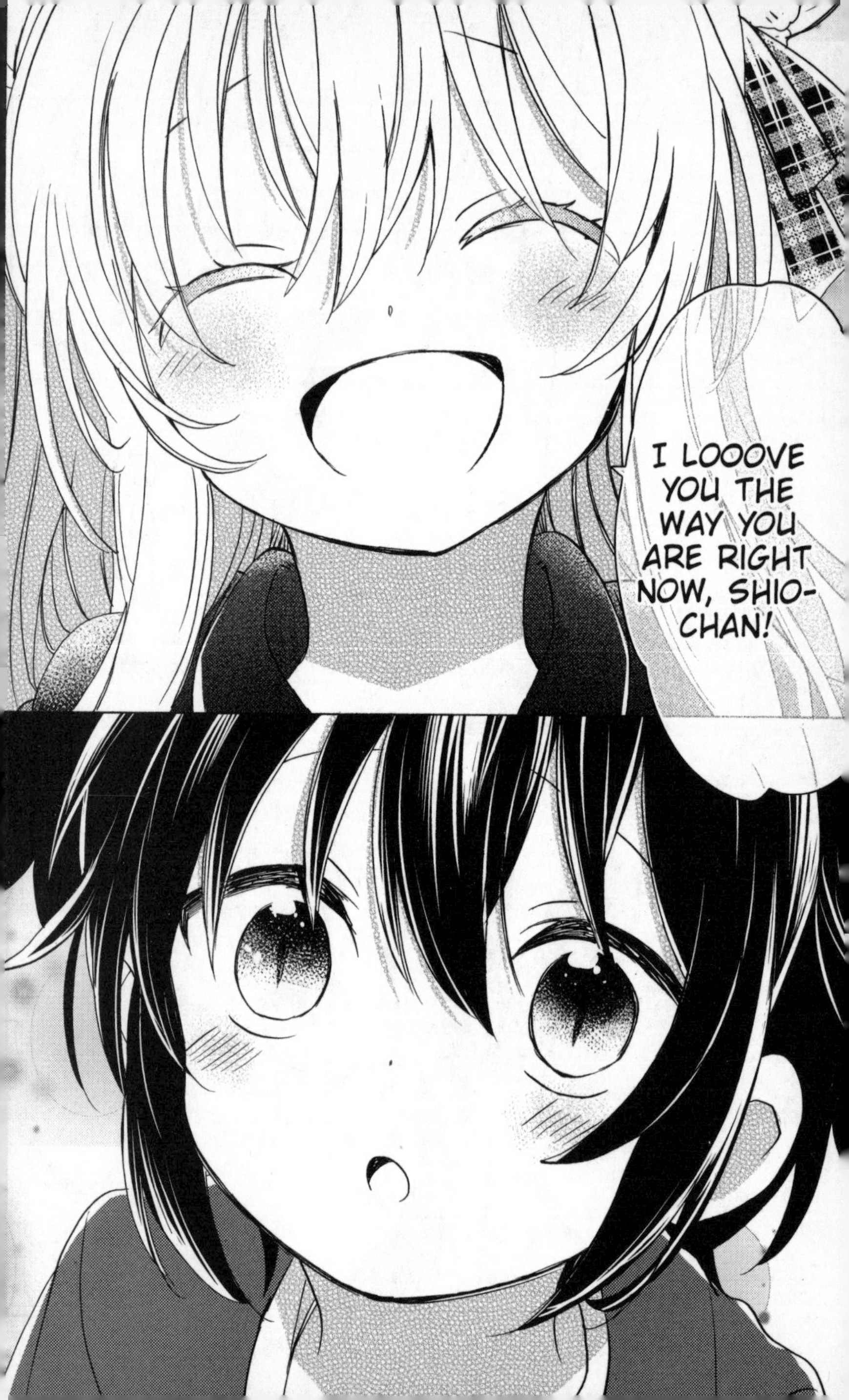
I LOOOVE YOU THE WAY YOU ARE RIGHT NOW, SHIO-CHAN!

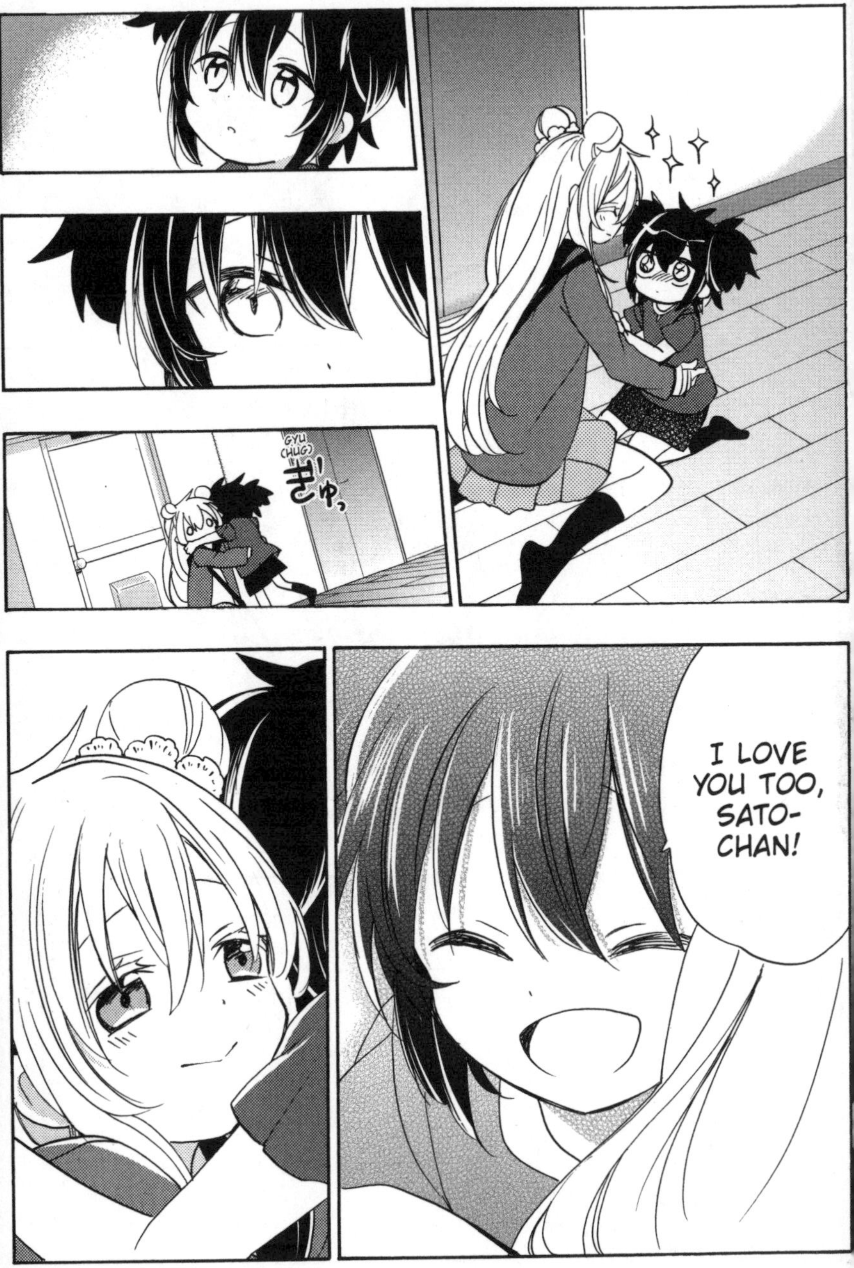
GYU (HUG)
ぎゅっ
I LOVE YOU TOO, SATO-CHAN!

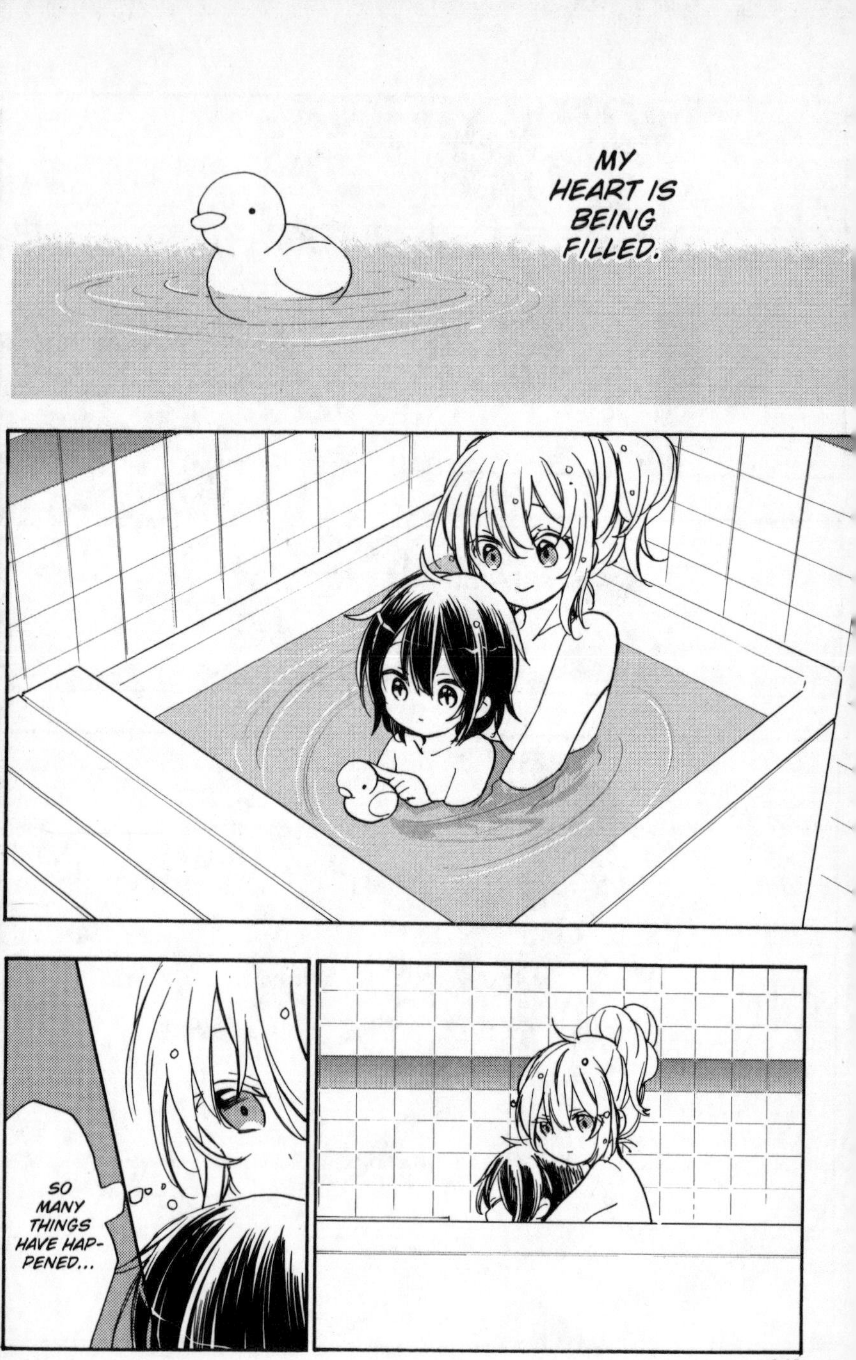
MY HEART IS BEING FILLED.
SO MANY THINGS HAVE HAPPENED...

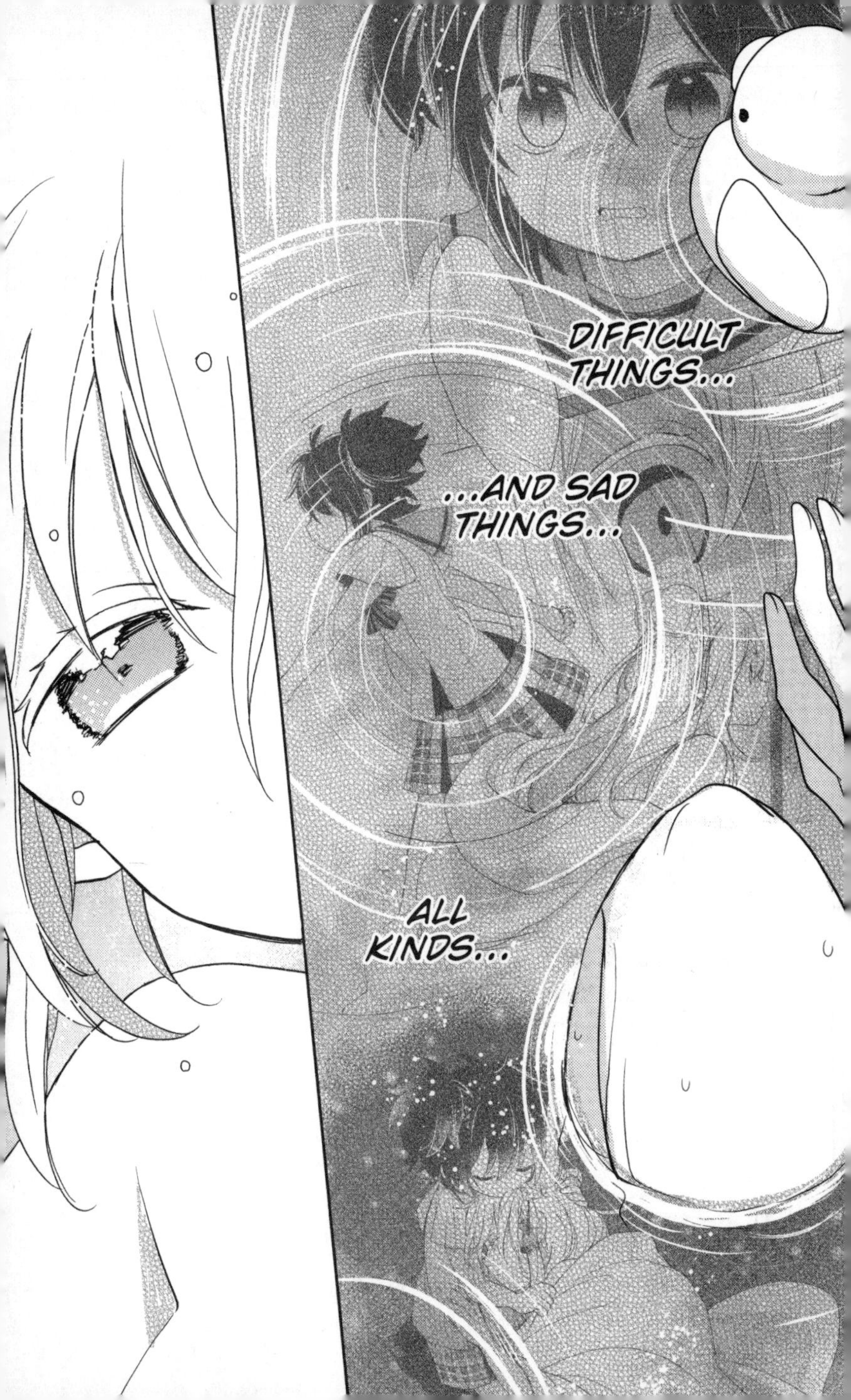
DIFFICULT THINGS...
...AND SAD THINGS...
ALL KINDS...

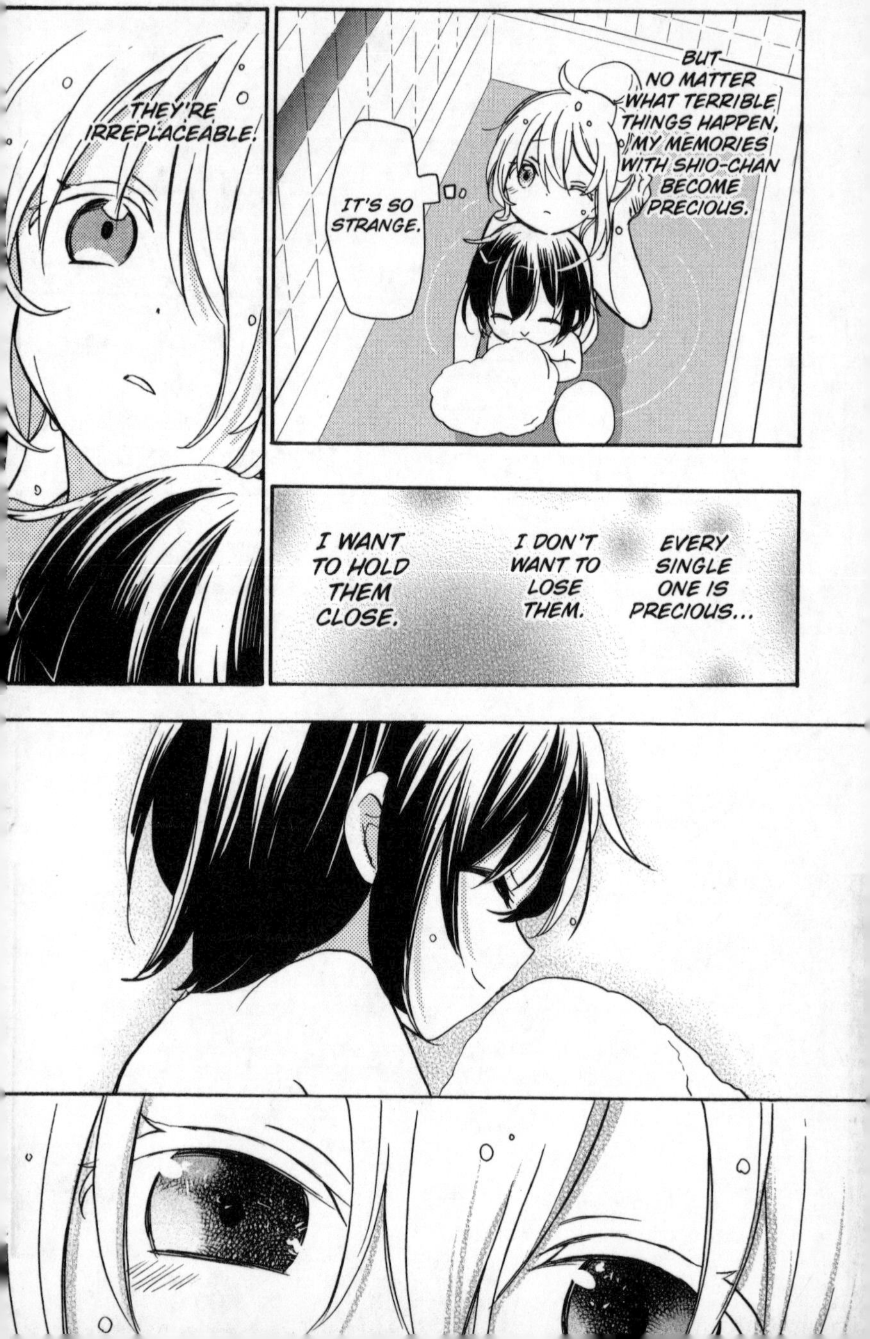
BUT NO MATTER WHAT TERRIBLE THINGS HAPPEN, MY MEMORIES WITH SHIO-CHAN BECOME PRECIOUS.
IT'S SO STRANGE.
THEY'RE IRREPLACEABLE.
EVERY SINGLE ONE IS PRECIOUS...
I DON'T WANT TO LOSE THEM.
I WANT TO HOLD THEM CLOSE.

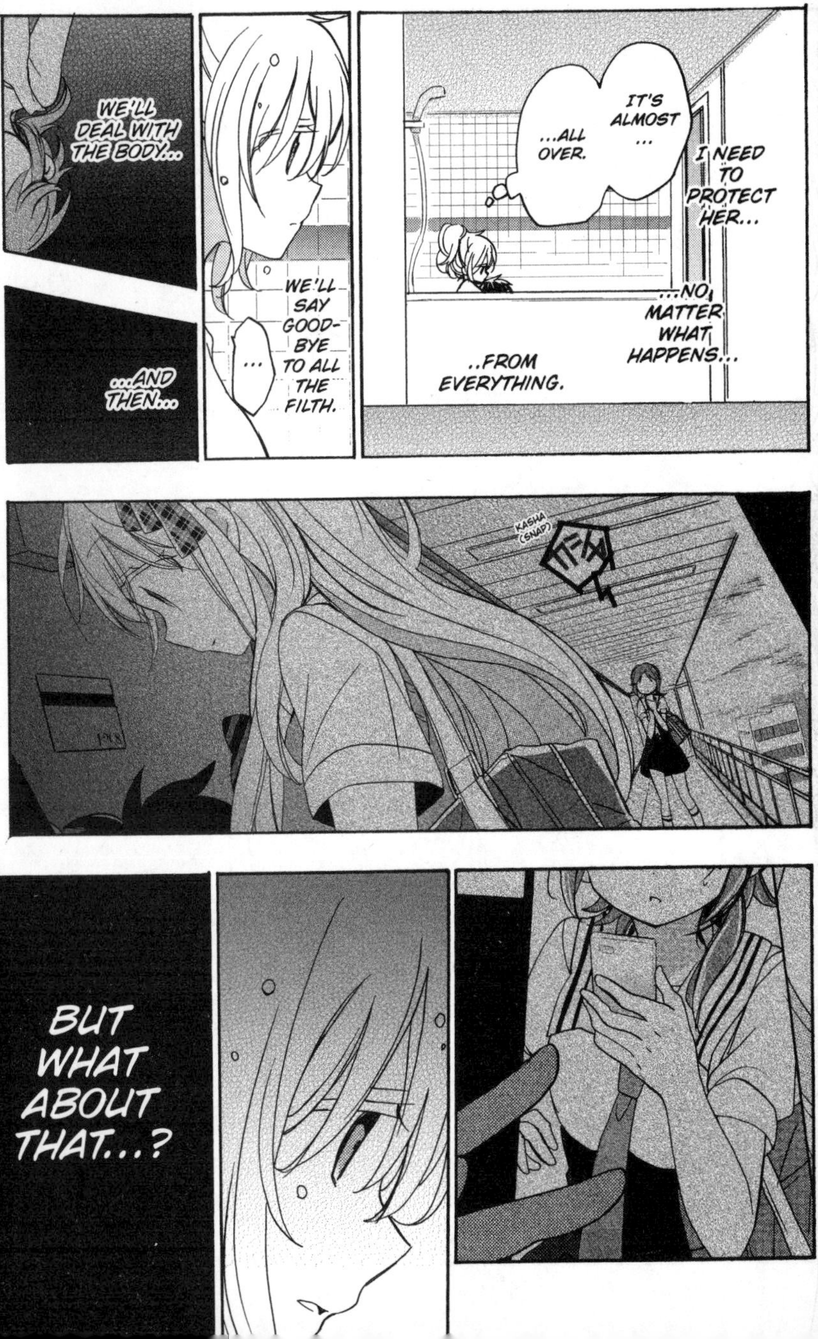
IT'S ALMOST ...
...ALL OVER.
I NEED TO PROTECT HER...
...NO MATTER WHAT HAPPENS...
..FROM EVERYTHING.
WE'LL SAY GOOD-BYE TO ALL THE FILTH.
...
WE'LL DEAL WITH THE BODY...
...AND THEN...
KASHA (SNAP)
BUT WHAT ABOUT THAT...?

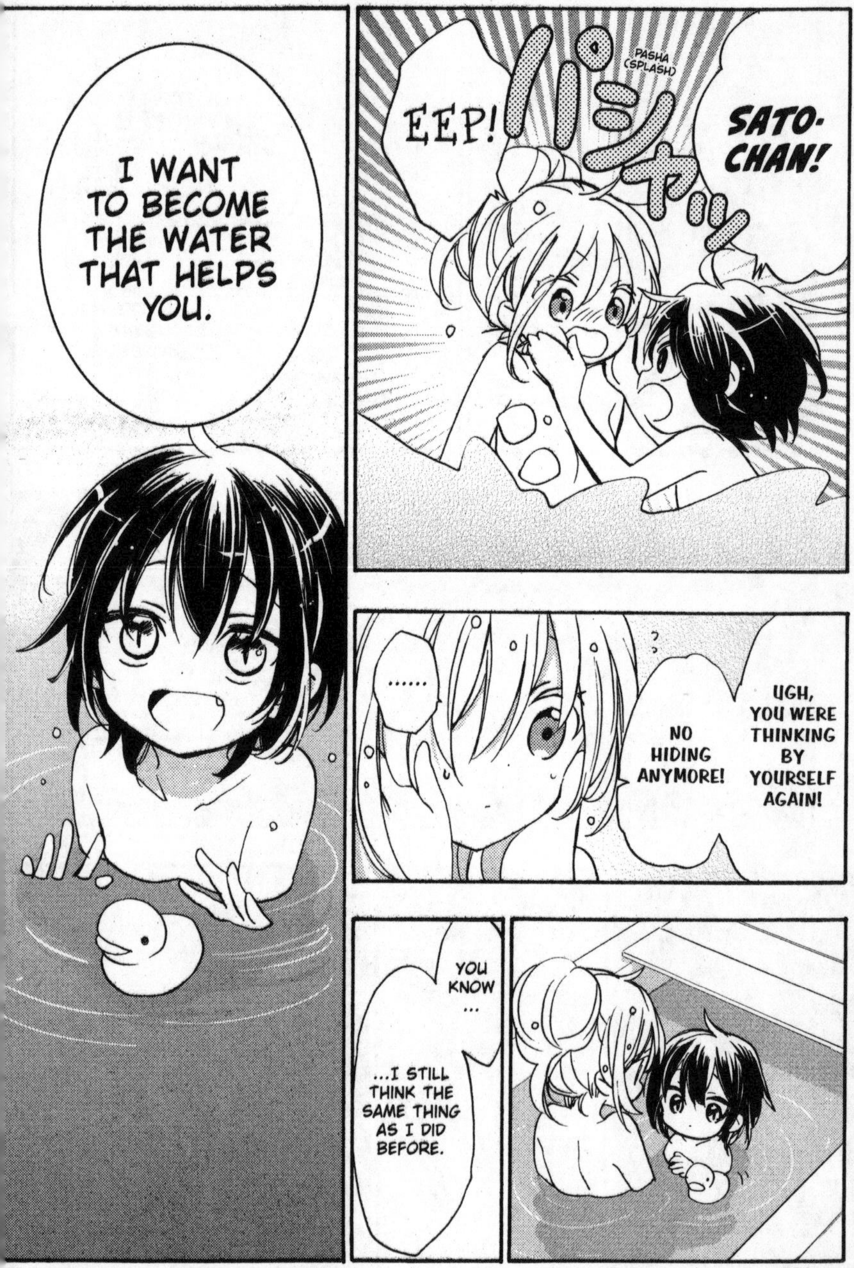
SATO-CHAN!
PASHA (SPLASH)
EEP!
UGH, YOU WERE THINKING BY YOURSELF AGAIN!
NO HIDING ANYMORE!
......
YOU KNOW ...
...I STILL THINK THE SAME THING AS I DID BEFORE.
I WANT TO BECOME THE WATER THAT HELPS YOU.

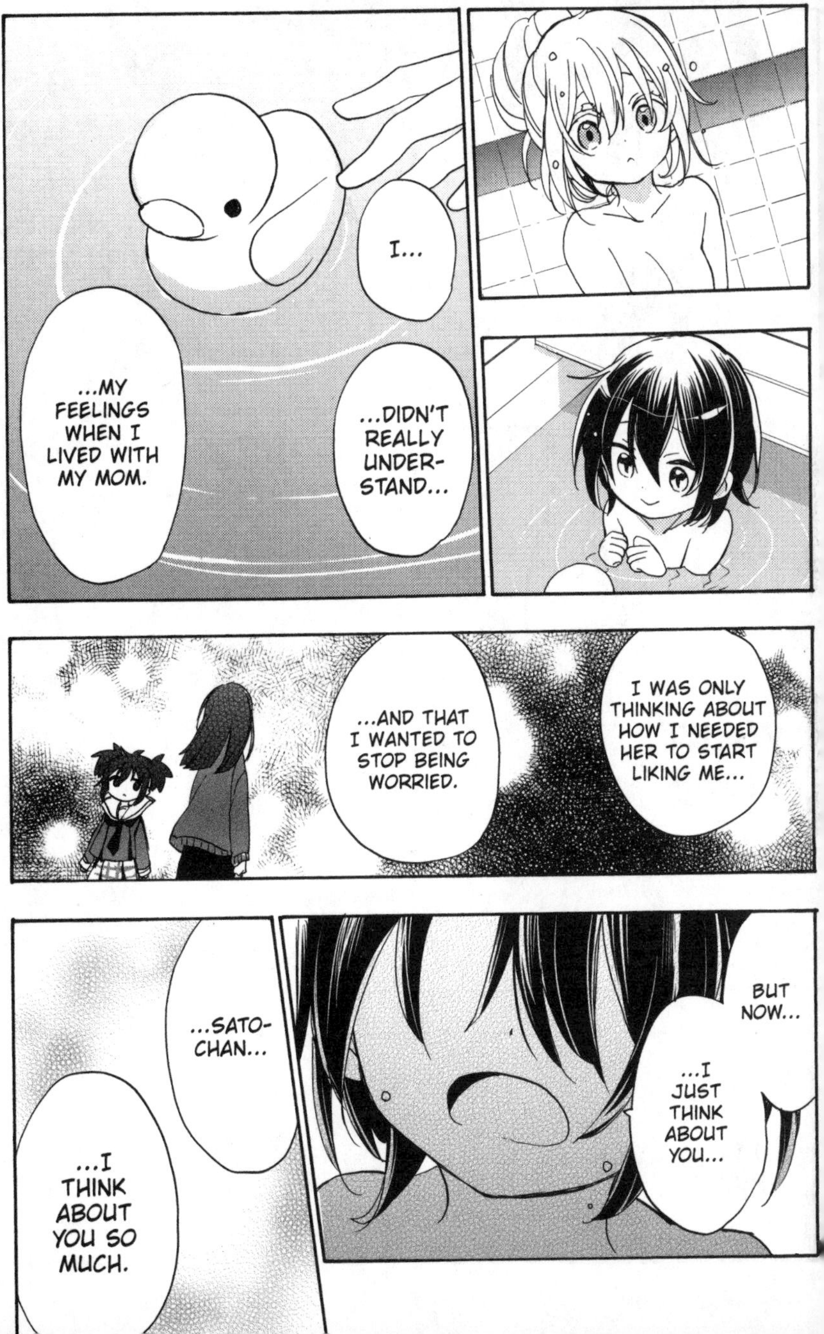
I...
...DIDN'T REALLY UNDER-STAND...
...MY FEELINGS WHEN I LIVED WITH MY MOM.
I WAS ONLY THINKING ABOUT HOW I NEEDED HER TO START LIKING ME...
...AND THAT I WANTED TO STOP BEING WORRIED.
BUT NOW...
...I JUST THINK ABOUT YOU...
...SATO-CHAN...
...I THINK ABOUT YOU SO MUCH.

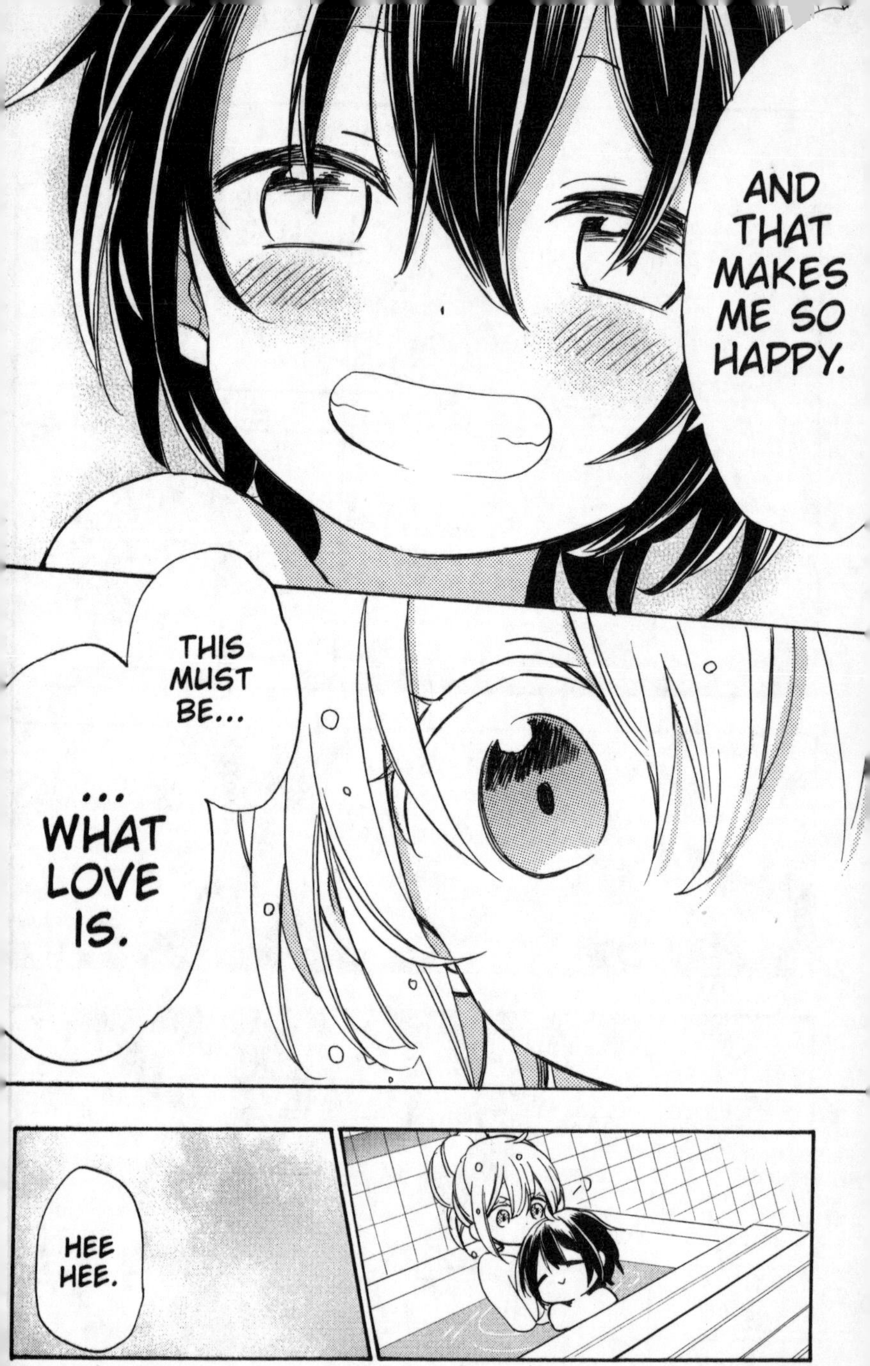
AND THAT MAKES ME SO HAPPY.
THIS MUST BE...
... WHAT LOVE IS.
HEE HEE.

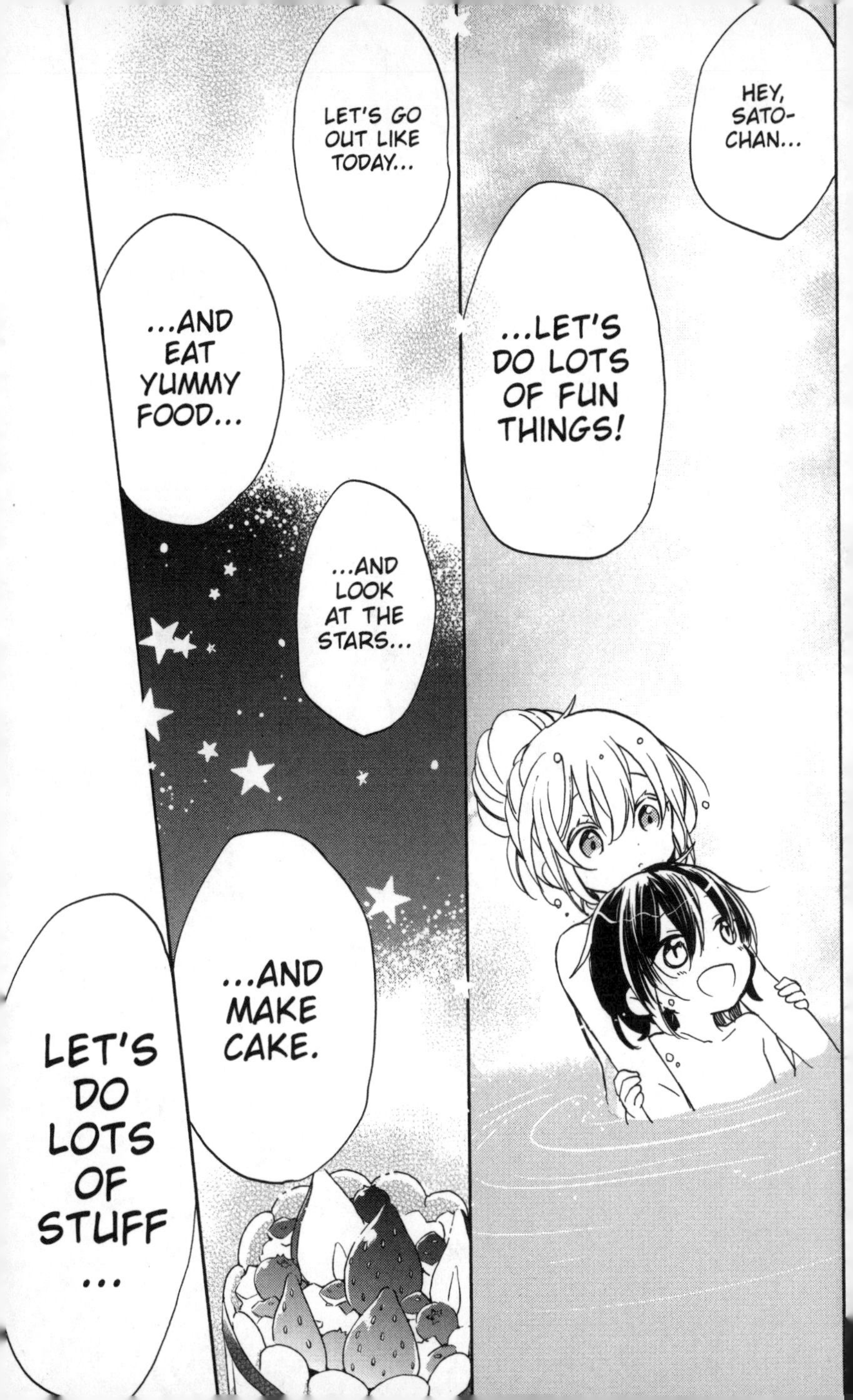
HEY, SATO-CHAN...
...LET'S DO LOTS OF FUN THINGS!
LET'S GO OUT LIKE TODAY...
...AND EAT YUMMY FOOD...
...AND LOOK AT THE STARS...
...AND MAKE CAKE.
LET'S DO LOTS OF STUFF...

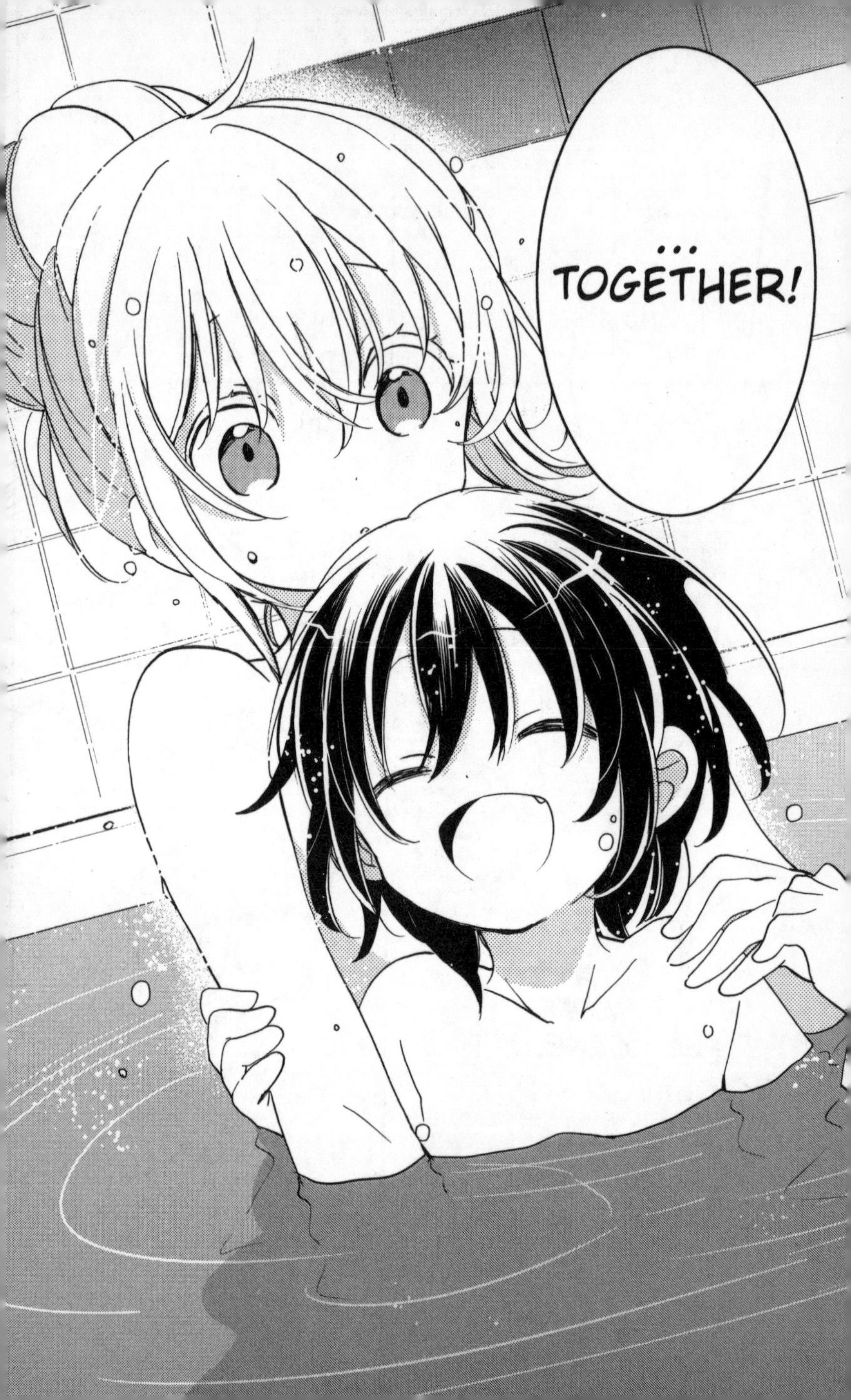
...TOGETHER!

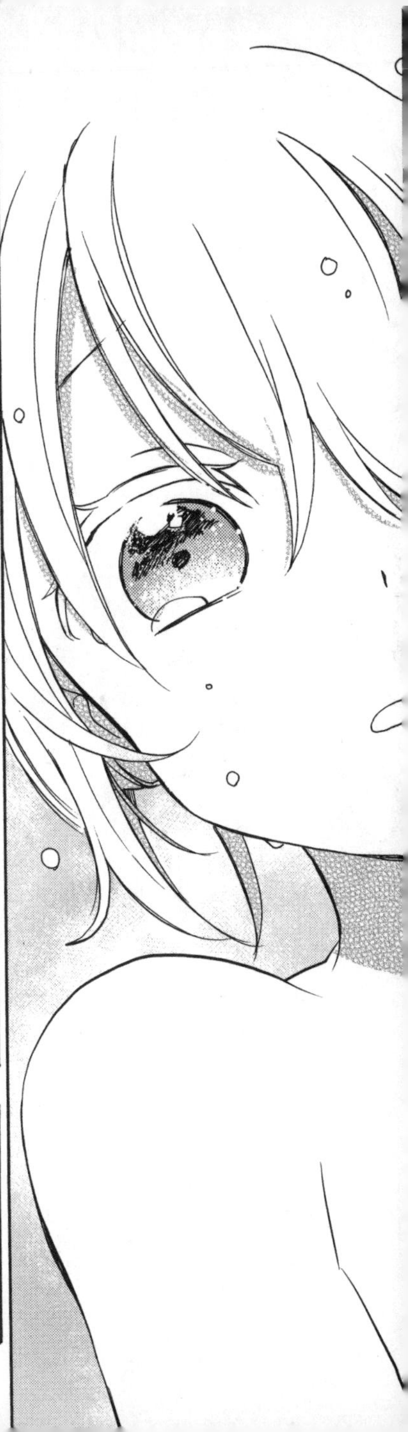

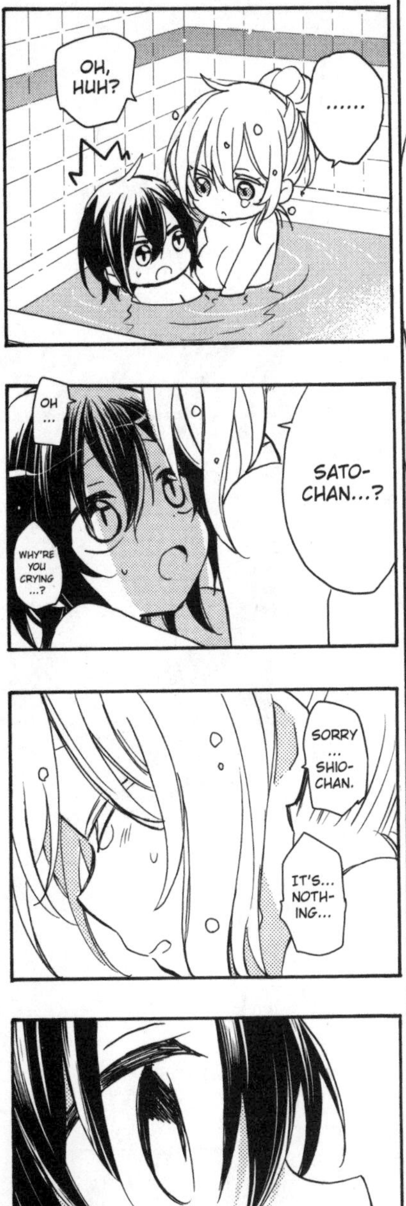
......
OH, HUH?
SATO-CHAN...?
OH ...
WHY'RE YOU CRYING ...?
SORRY ... SHIO-CHAN.
IT'S... NOTHING...

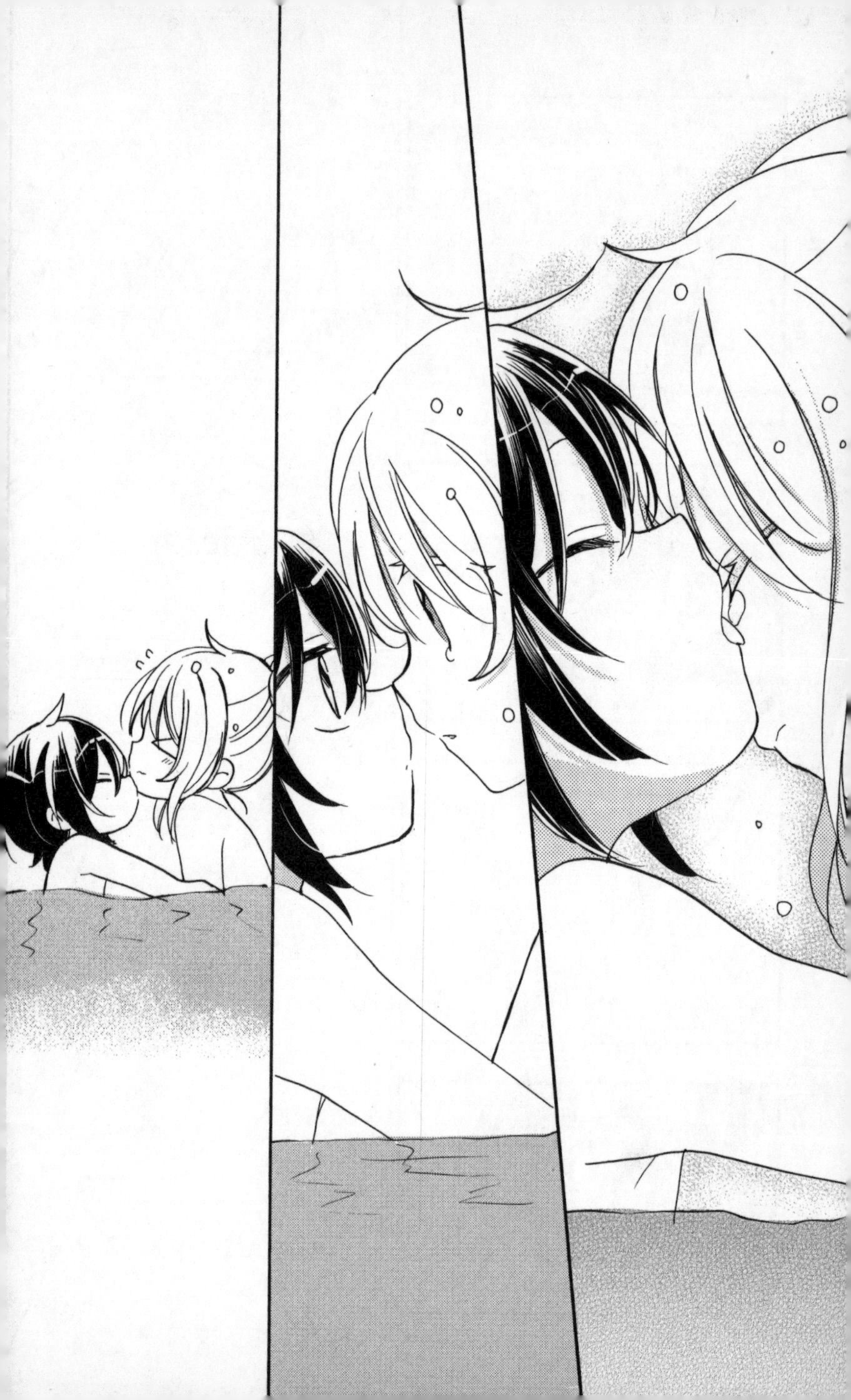

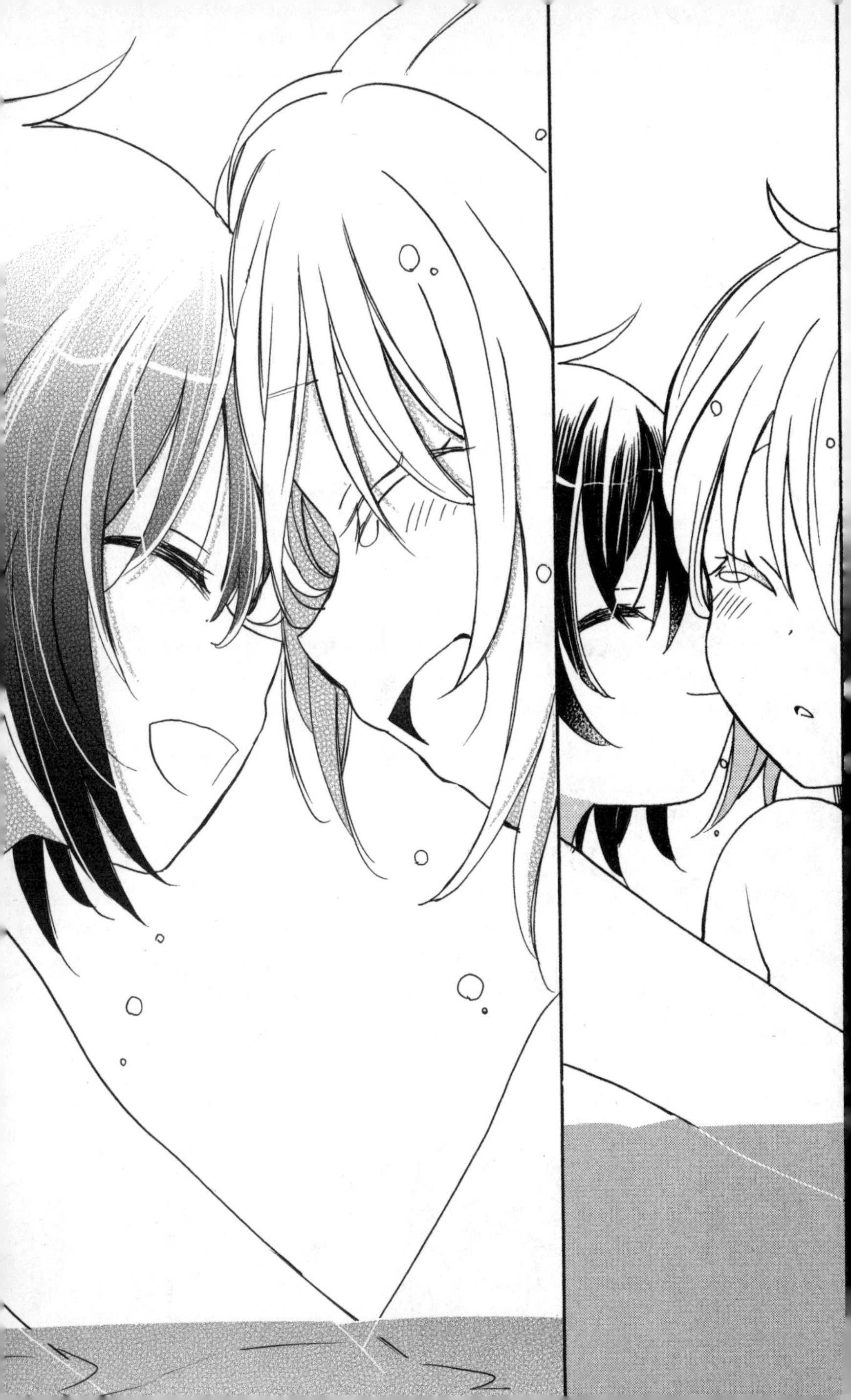

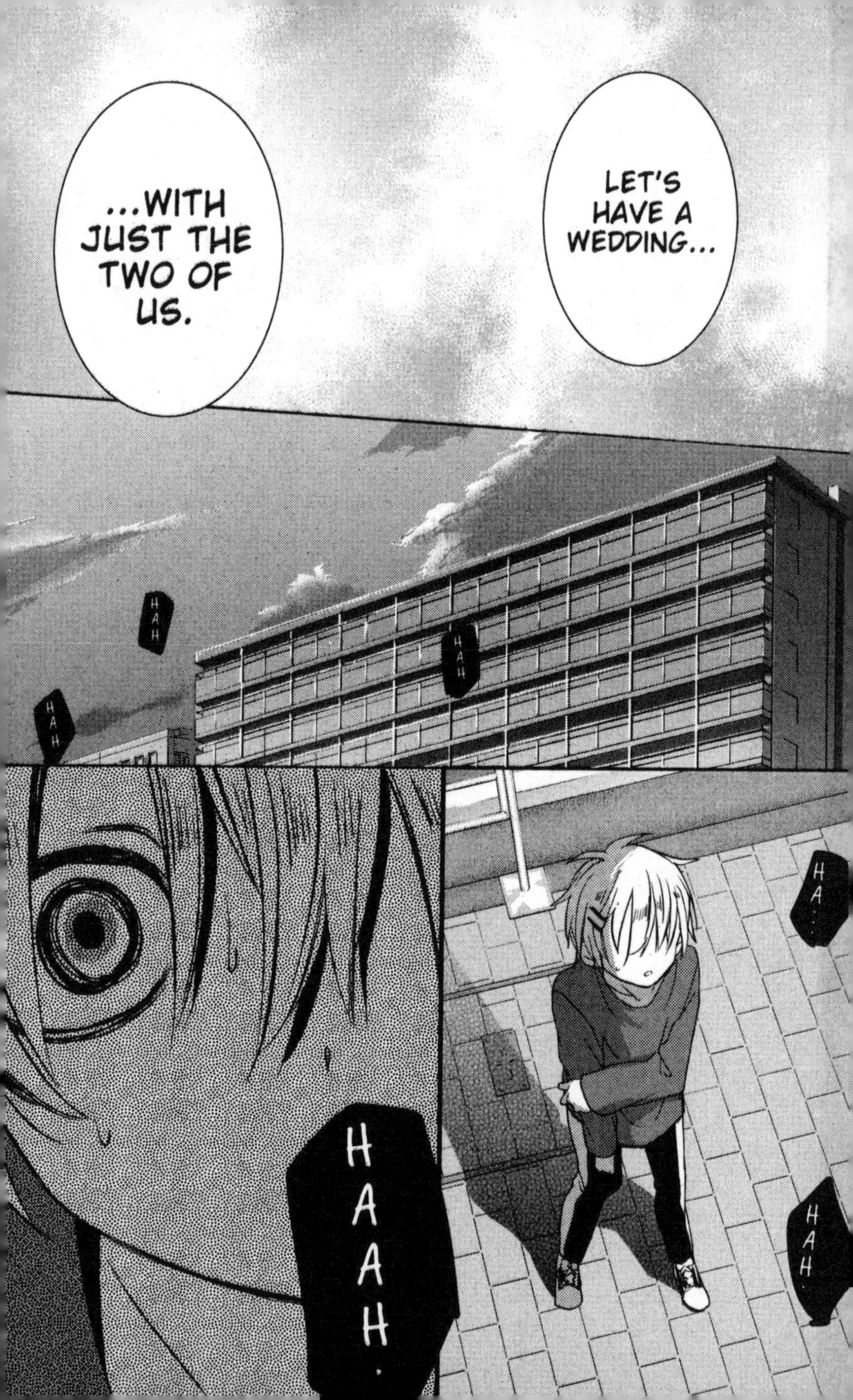
LET'S HAVE A WEDDING...
...WITH JUST THE TWO OF US.
HAH
HAH
HAH
HA...
HAH.
HAAAH.

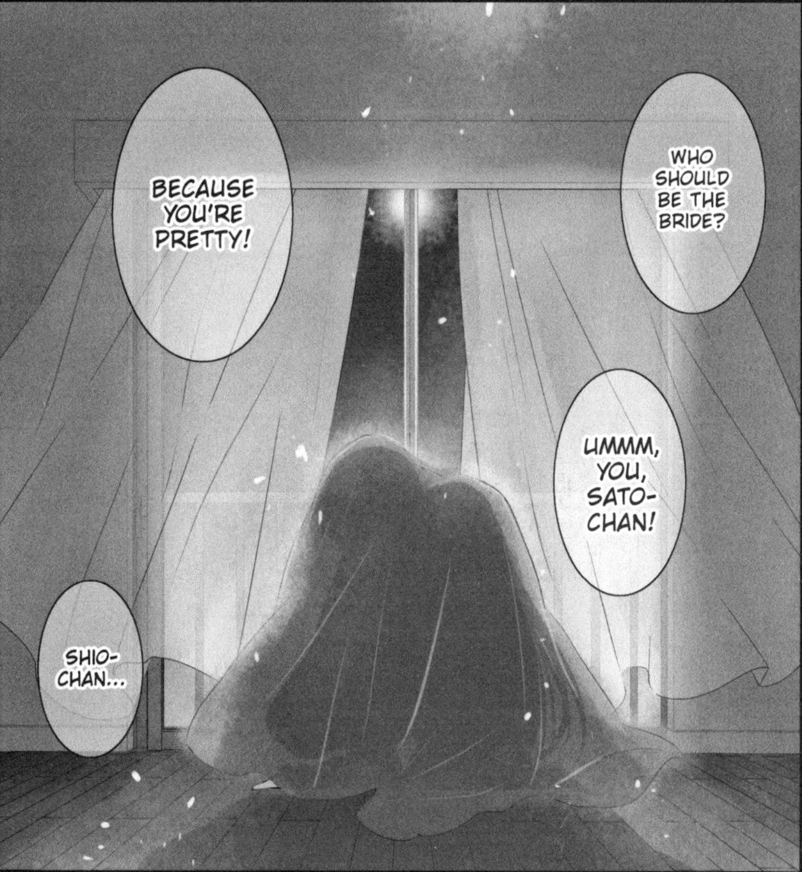
WHO SHOULD BE THE BRIDE?
BECAUSE YOU'RE PRETTY!
UMMM, YOU, SATO-CHAN!
SHIO-CHAN...

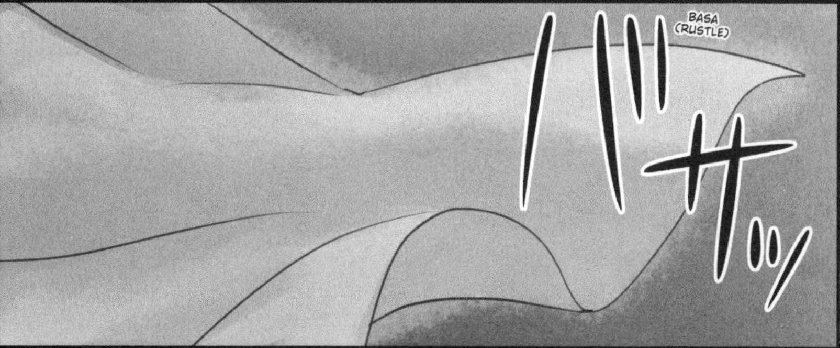
BASA (RUSTLE)

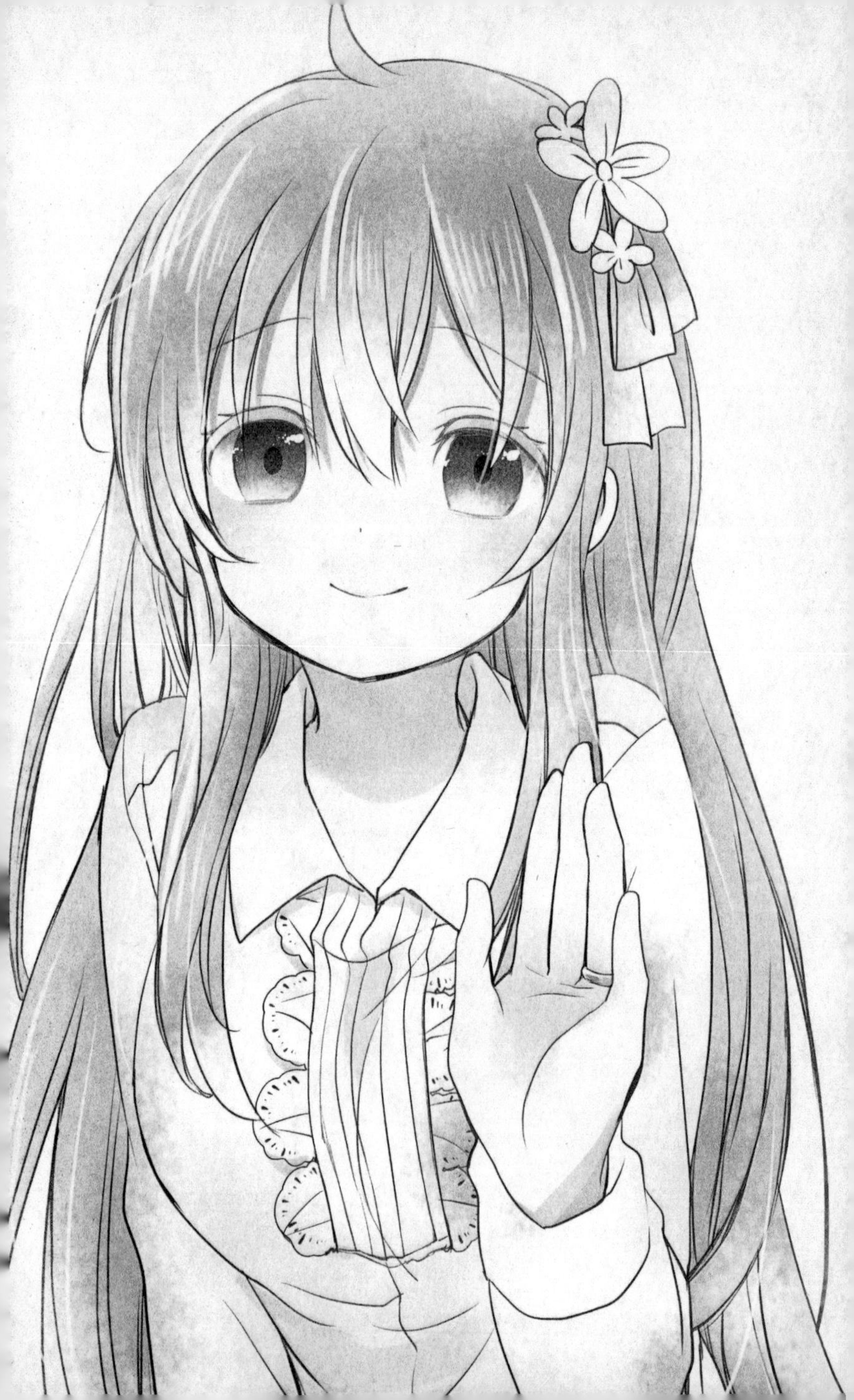

37TH LIFE: A MOMENT WITH YOU, FOREVER.

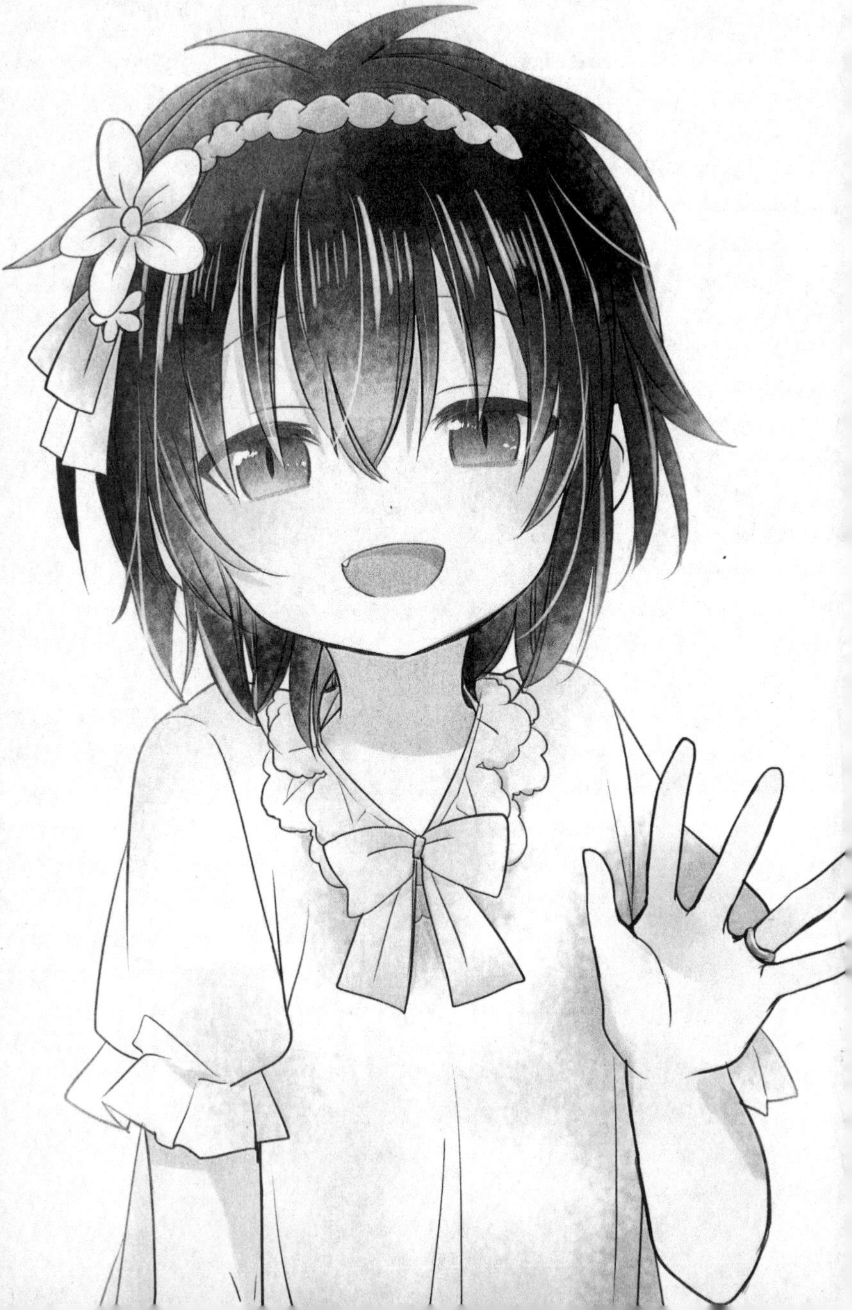

Happy
Sugar
Life

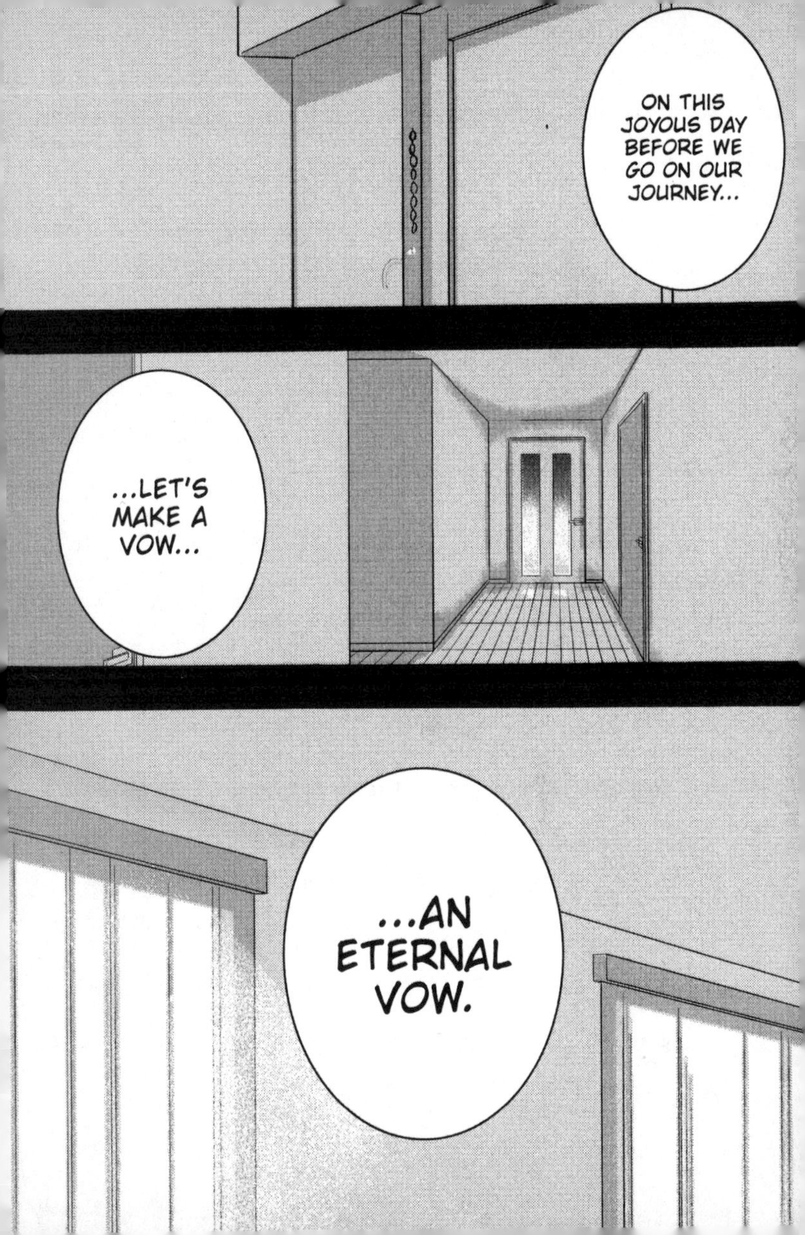
ON THIS JOYOUS DAY BEFORE WE GO ON OUR JOURNEY...
...LET'S MAKE A VOW...
...AN ETERNAL VOW.

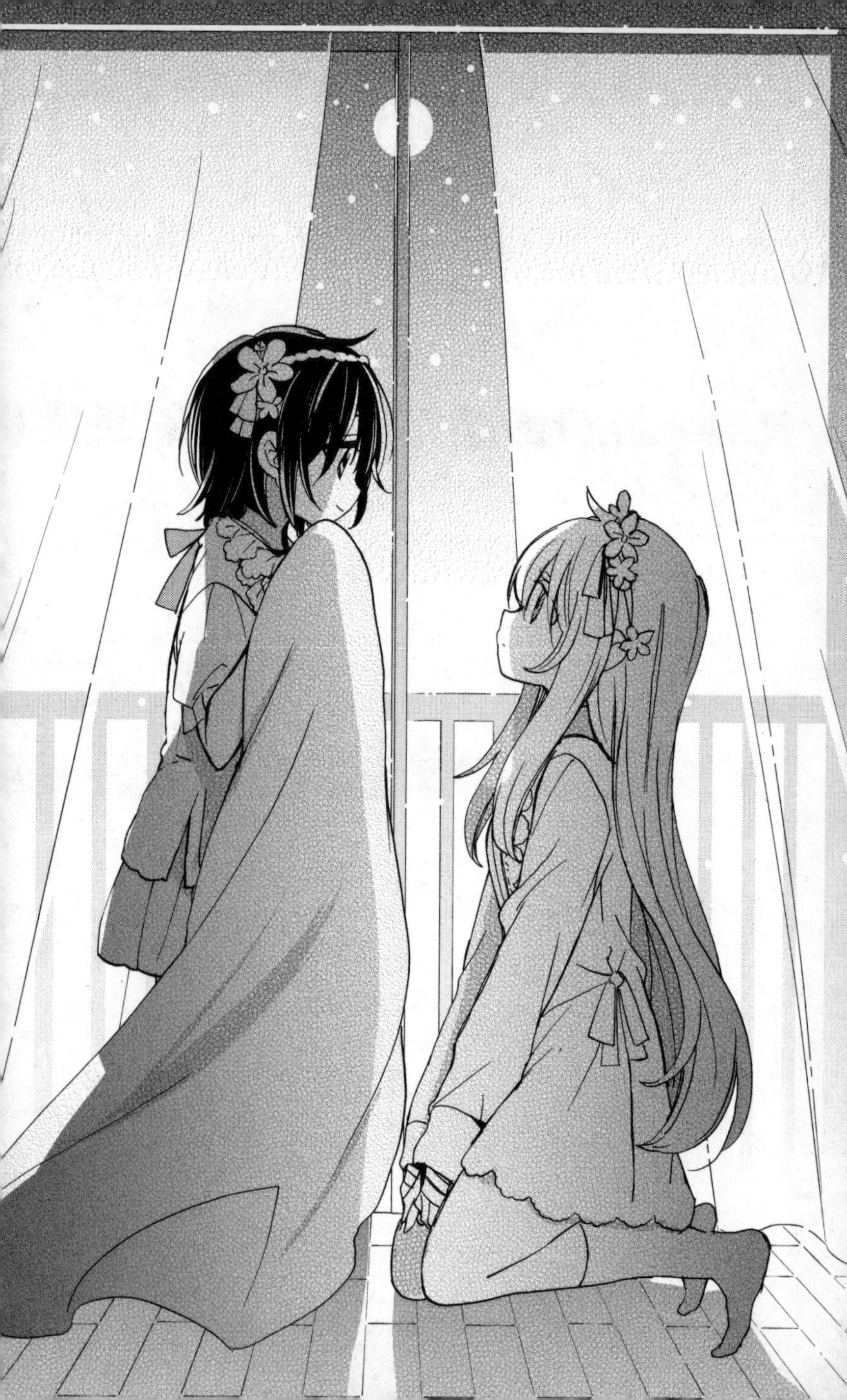

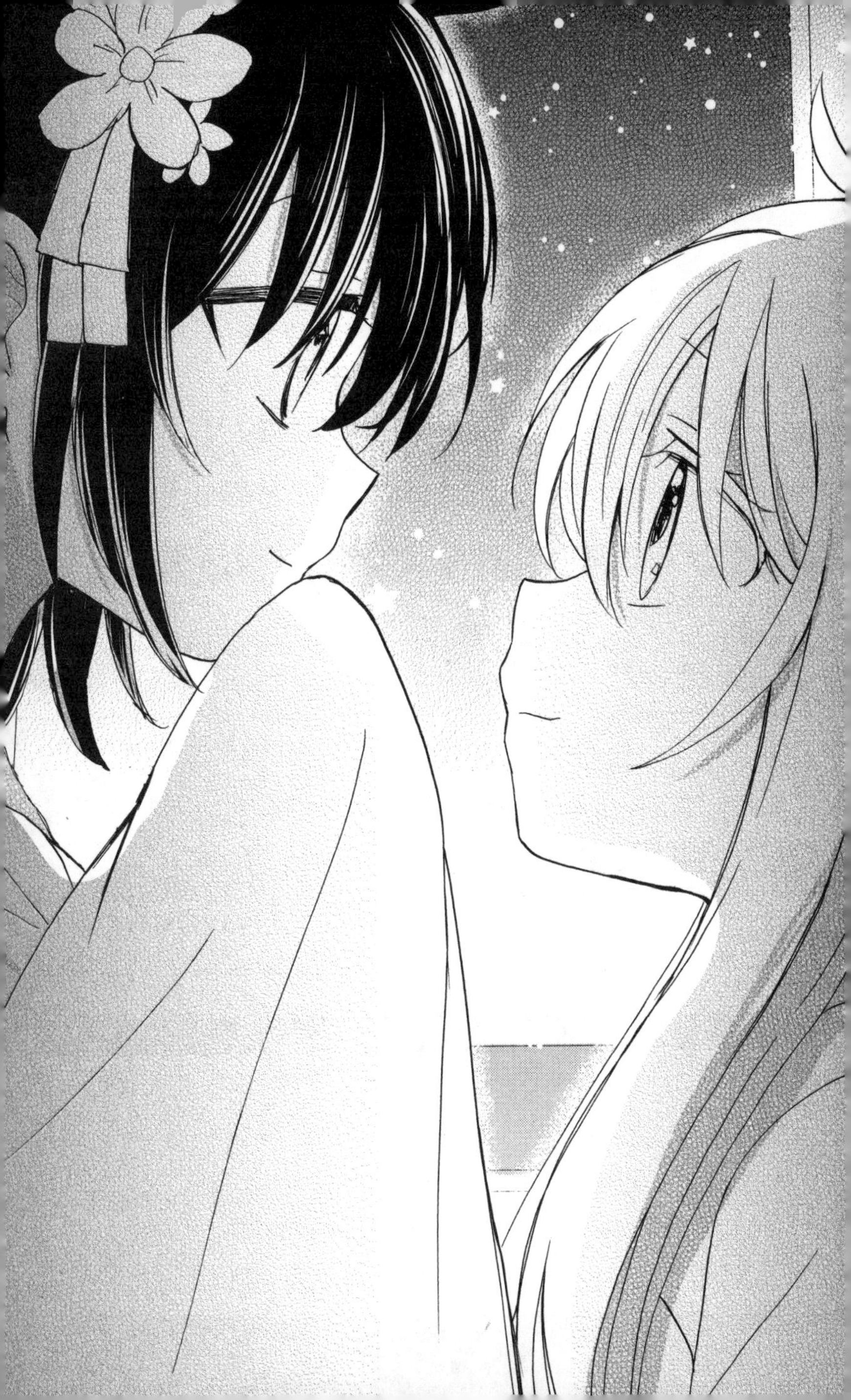

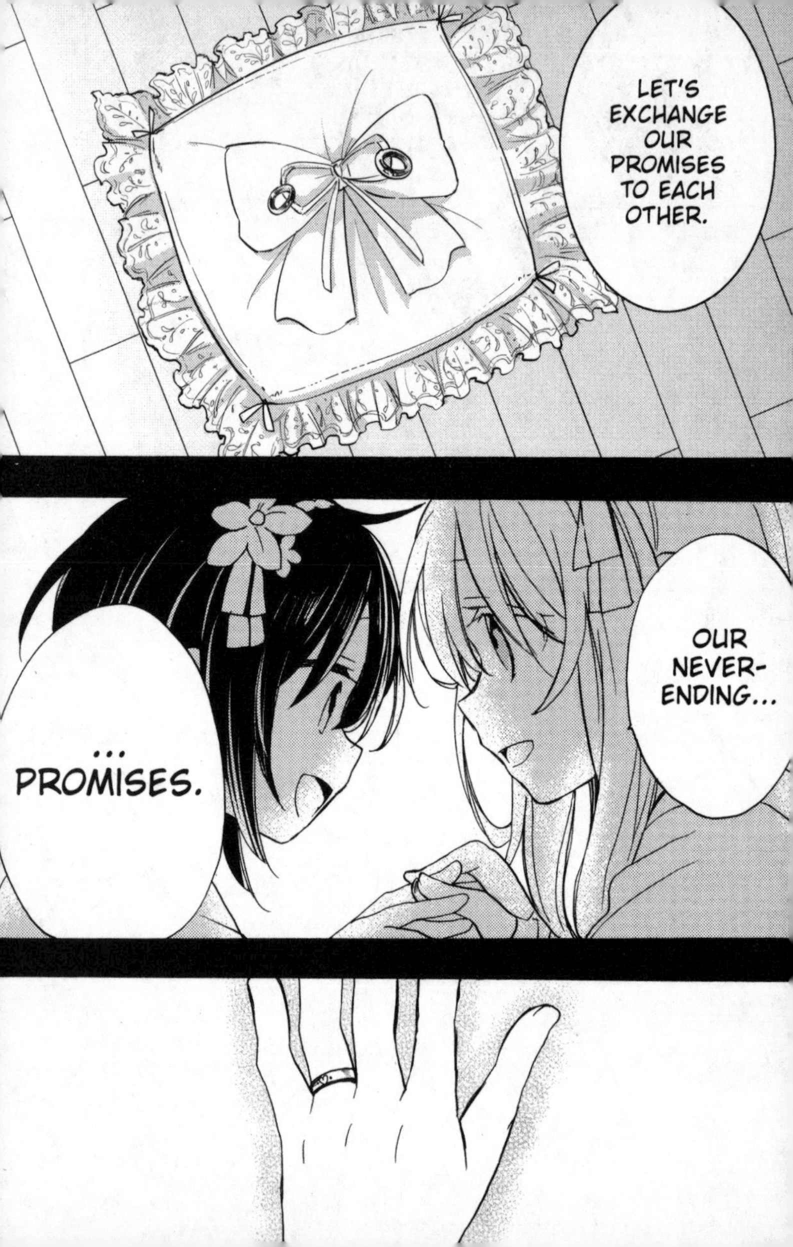
LET'S EXCHANGE OUR PROMISES TO EACH OTHER.
OUR NEVER-ENDING...
...PROMISES.

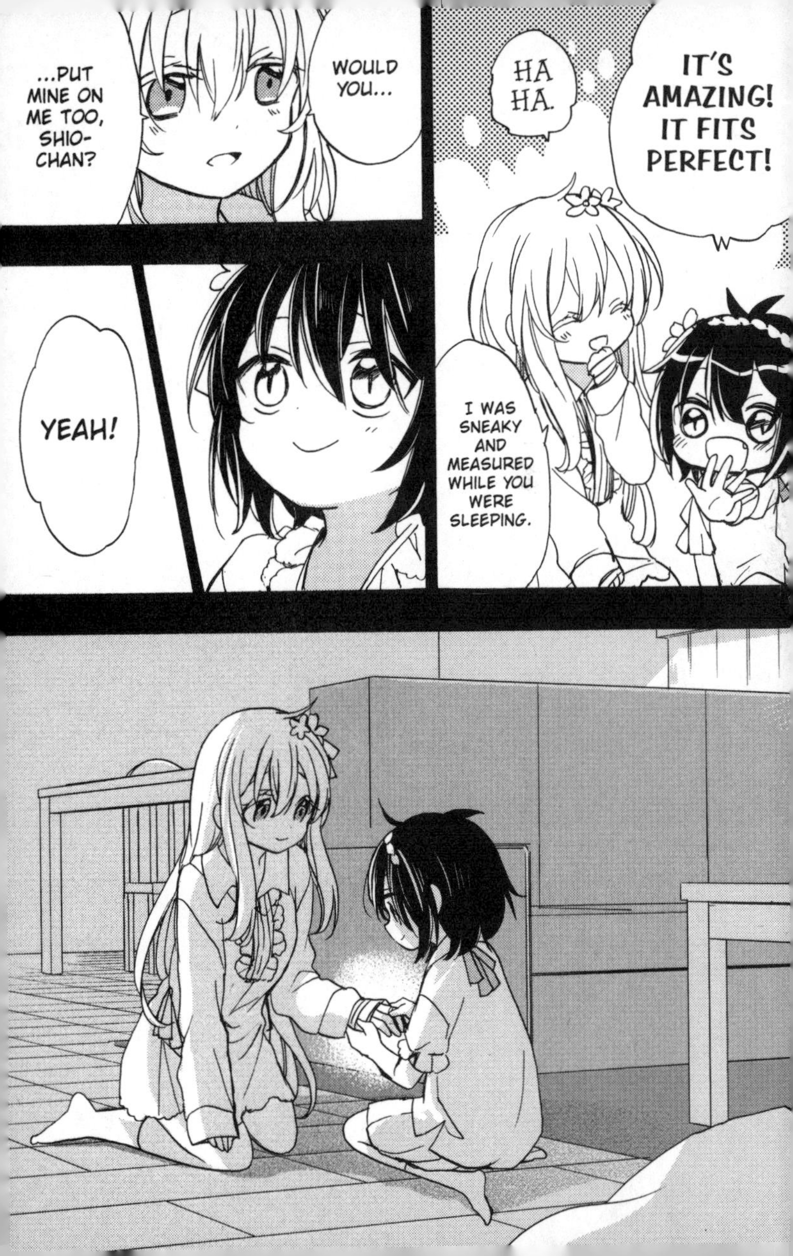
IT'S AMAZING! IT FITS PERFECT!
HA HA.
I WAS SNEAKY AND MEASURED WHILE YOU WERE SLEEPING.
WOULD YOU...
...PUT MINE ON ME TOO, SHIO-CHAN?
YEAH!

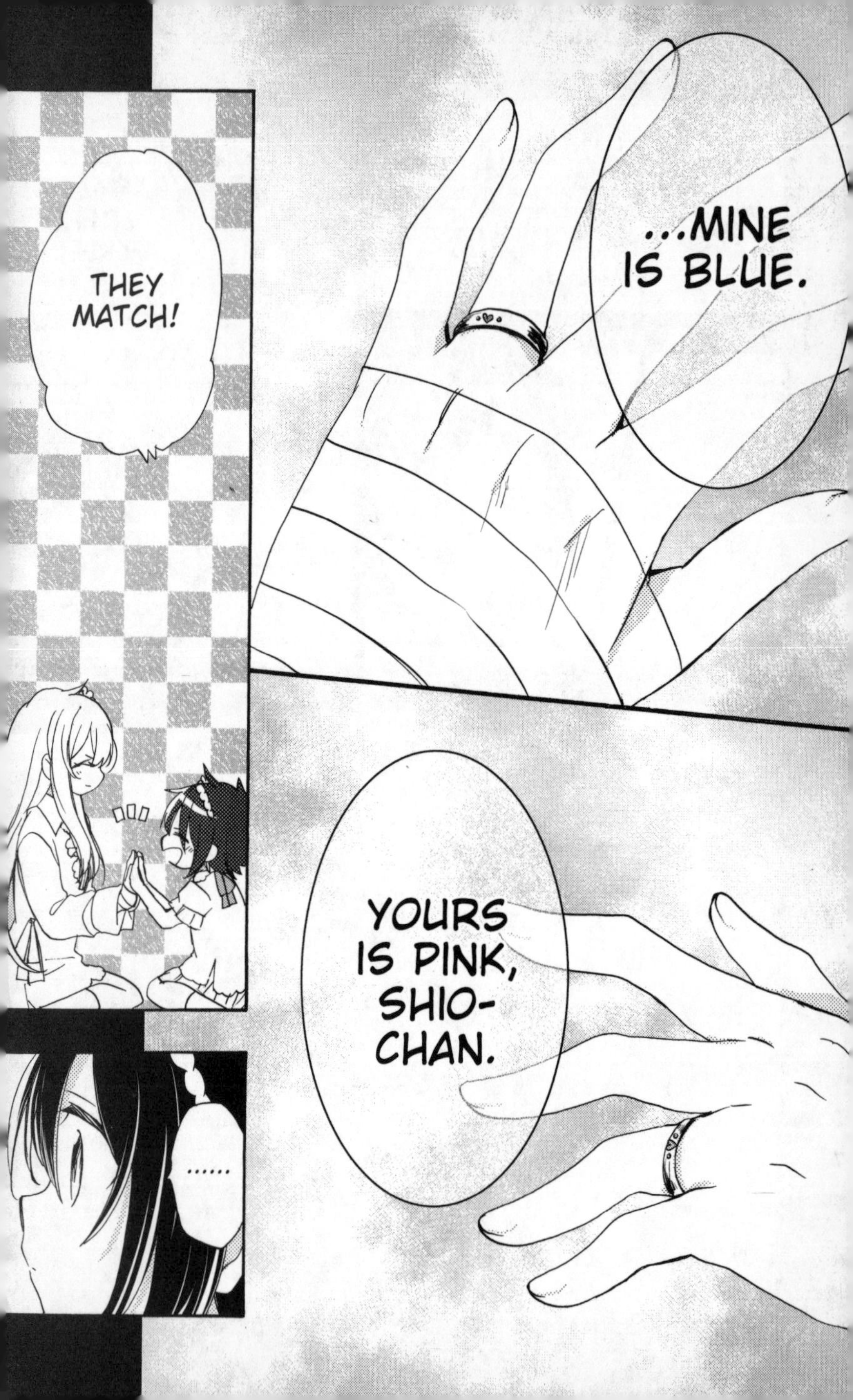

...MINE IS BLUE.
YOURS IS PINK, SHIO-CHAN.
THEY MATCH!
......

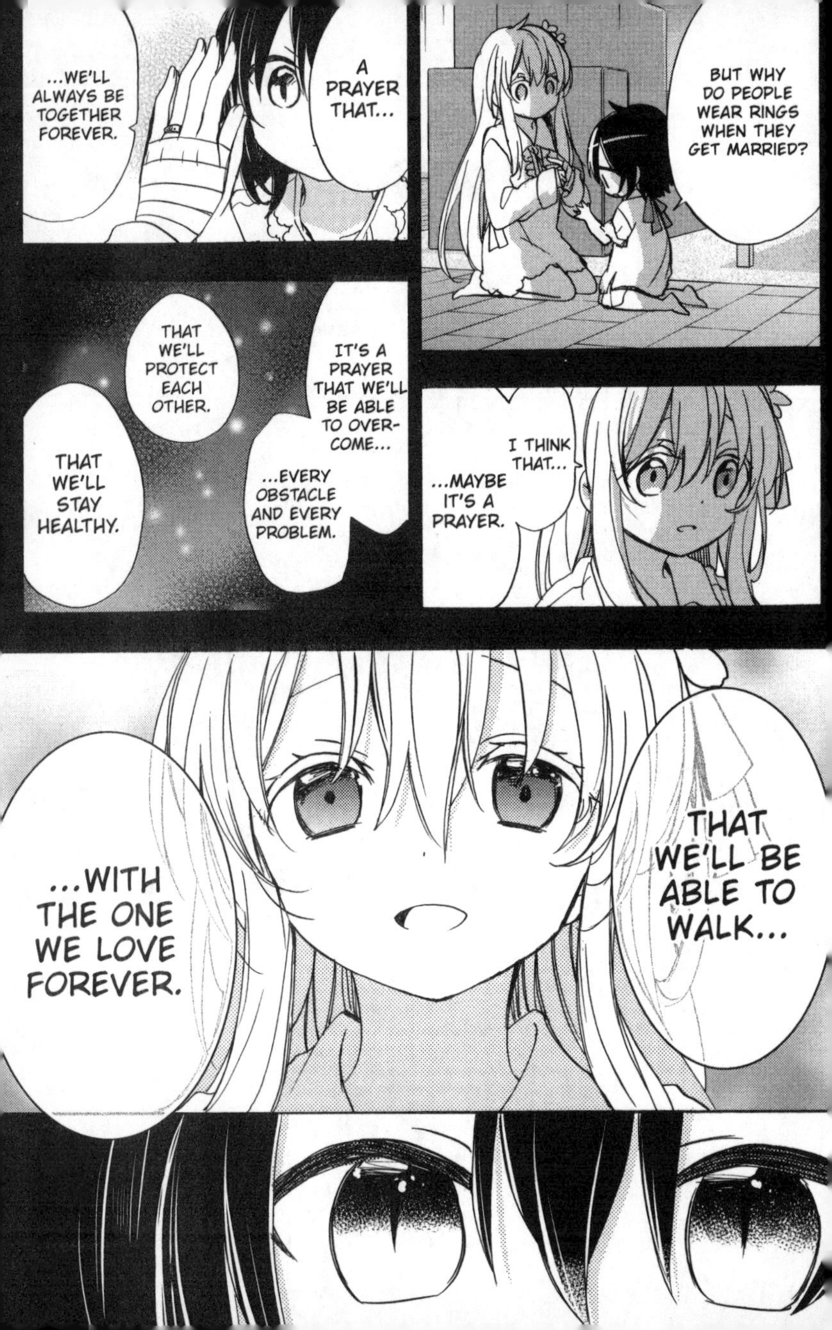
BUT WHY DO PEOPLE WEAR RINGS WHEN THEY GET MARRIED?
A PRAYER THAT...
...WE'LL ALWAYS BE TOGETHER FOREVER.
I THINK THAT...
...MAYBE IT'S A PRAYER.
IT'S A PRAYER THAT WE'LL BE ABLE TO OVER-COME...
...EVERY OBSTACLE AND EVERY PROBLEM.
THAT WE'LL PROTECT EACH OTHER.
THAT WE'LL STAY HEALTHY.
THAT WE'LL BE ABLE TO WALK...
...WITH THE ONE WE LOVE FOREVER.

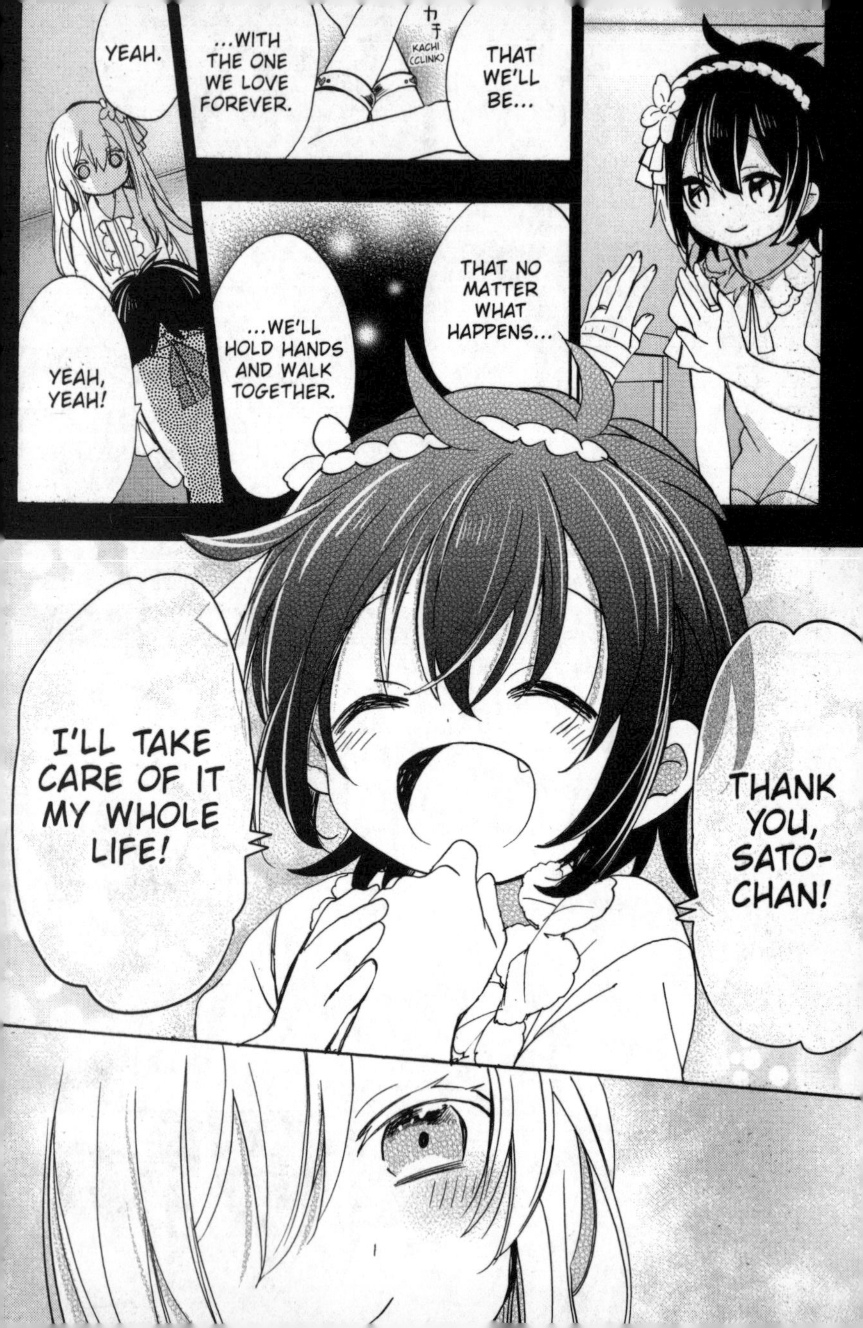
THAT WE'LL BE...
カチ KACHI (CLINK)
...WITH THE ONE WE LOVE FOREVER.
THAT NO MATTER WHAT HAPPENS...
...WE'LL HOLD HANDS AND WALK TOGETHER.
YEAH.
YEAH, YEAH!
THANK YOU, SATO-CHAN!
I'LL TAKE CARE OF IT MY WHOLE LIFE!

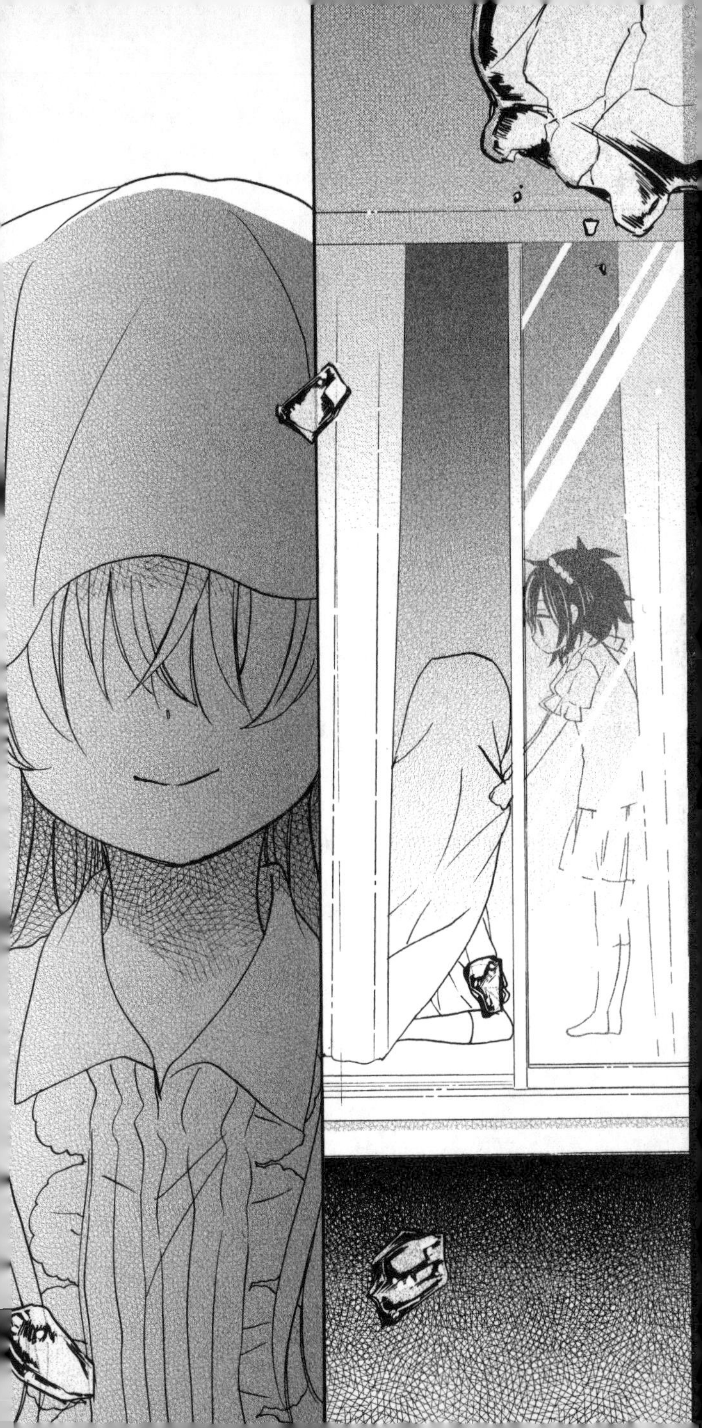

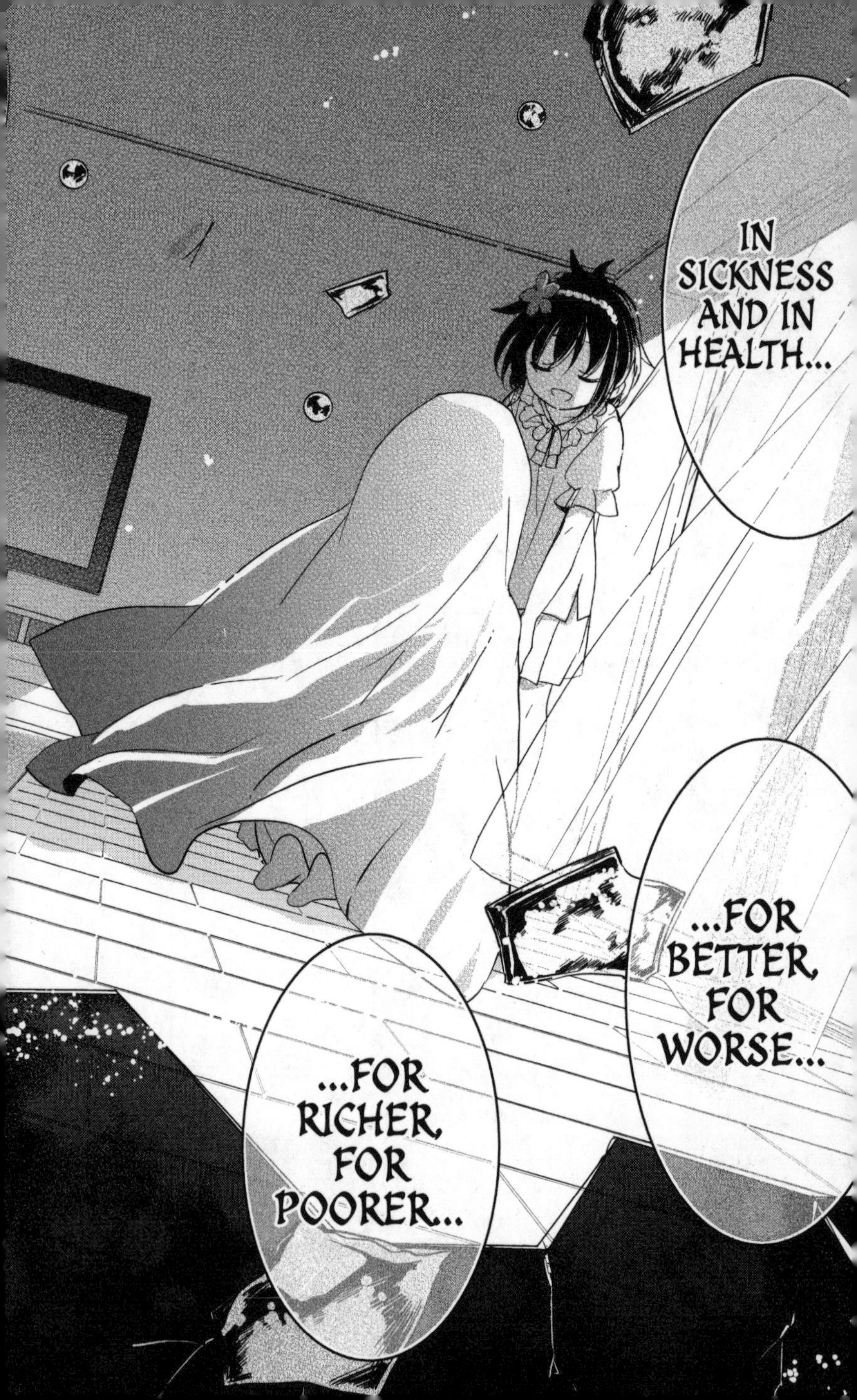
IN SICKNESS AND IN HEALTH...
...FOR BETTER, FOR WORSE...
...FOR RICHER, FOR POORER...

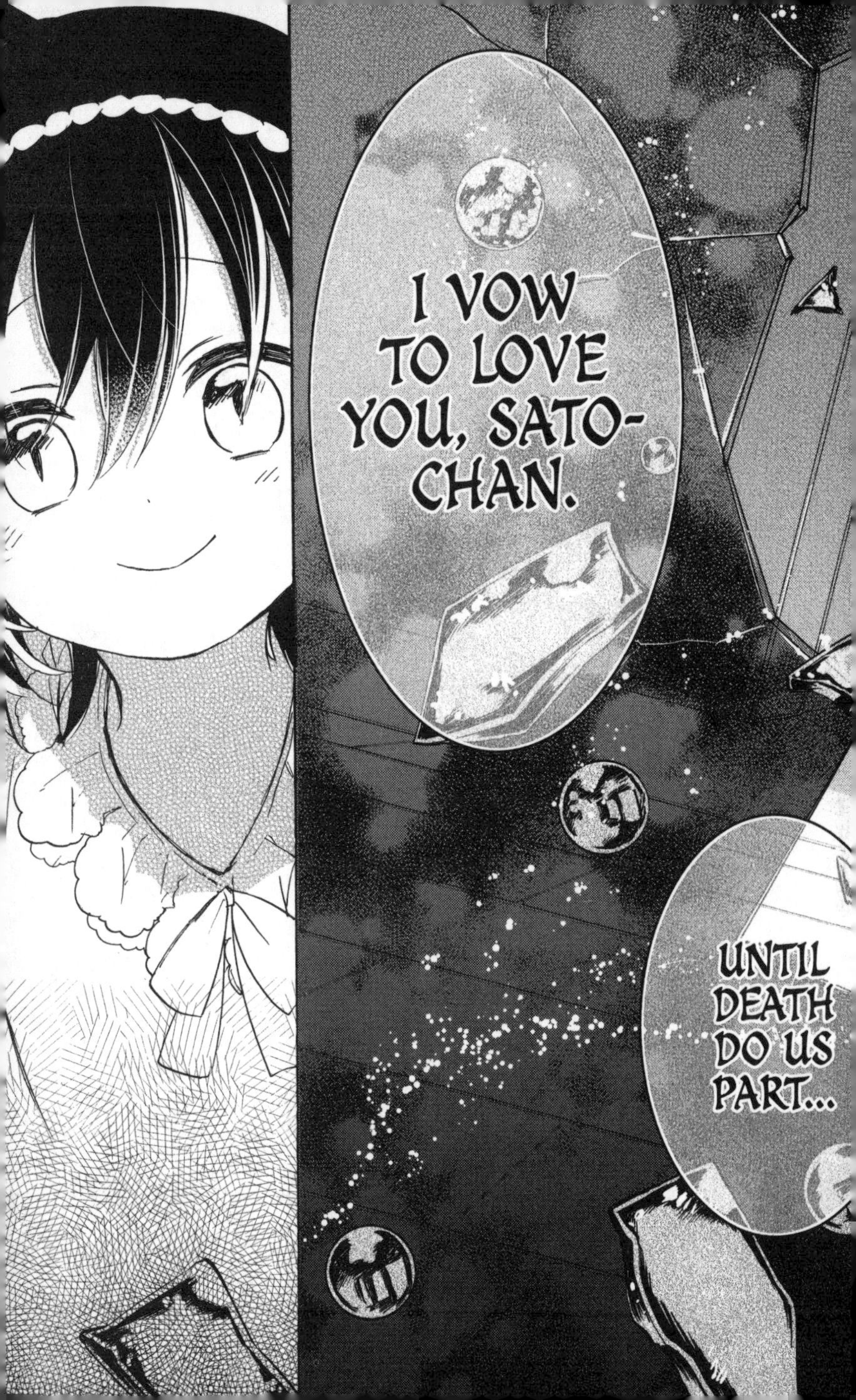
I VOW TO LOVE YOU, SATO-CHAN.
UNTIL DEATH DO US PART...

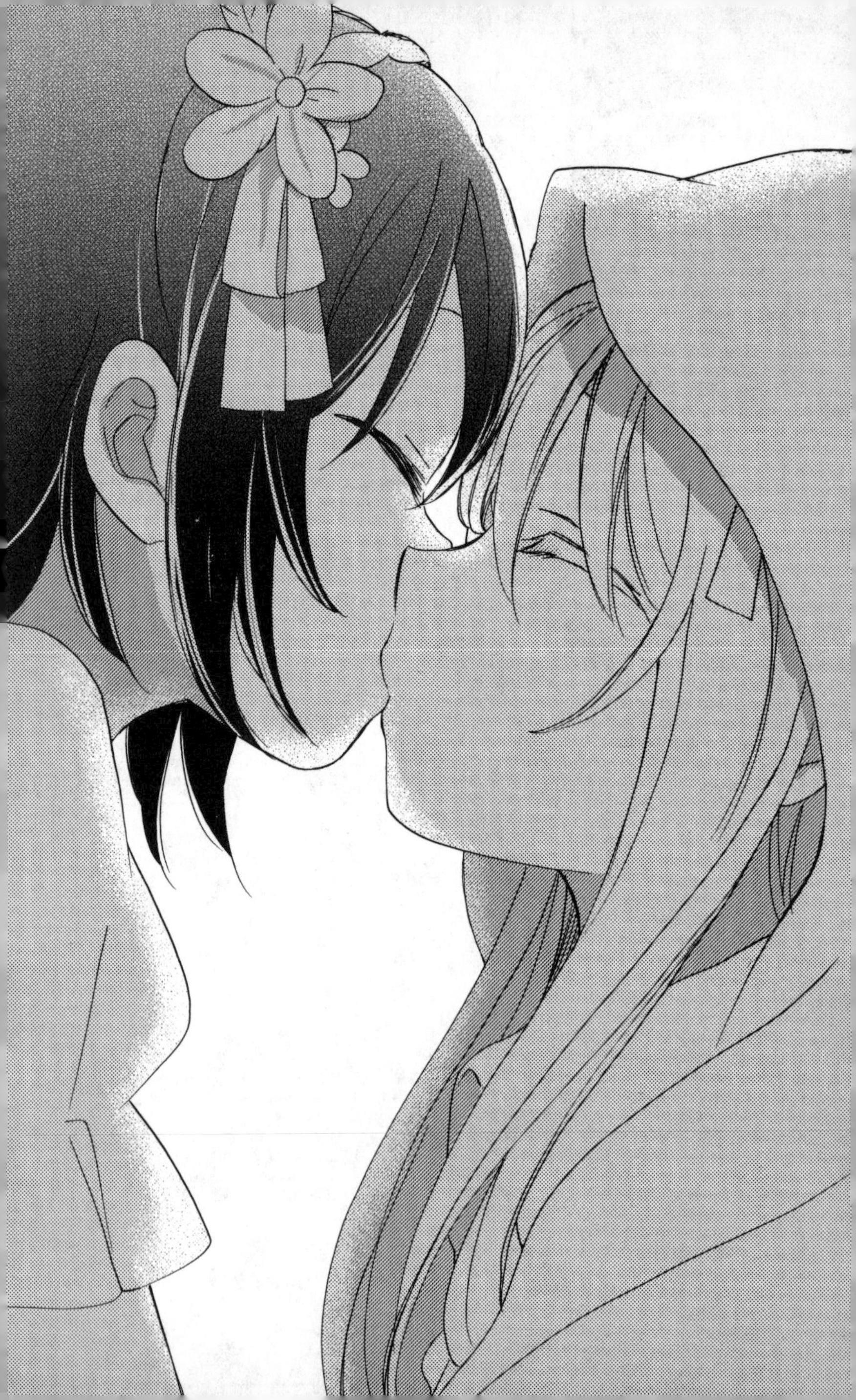

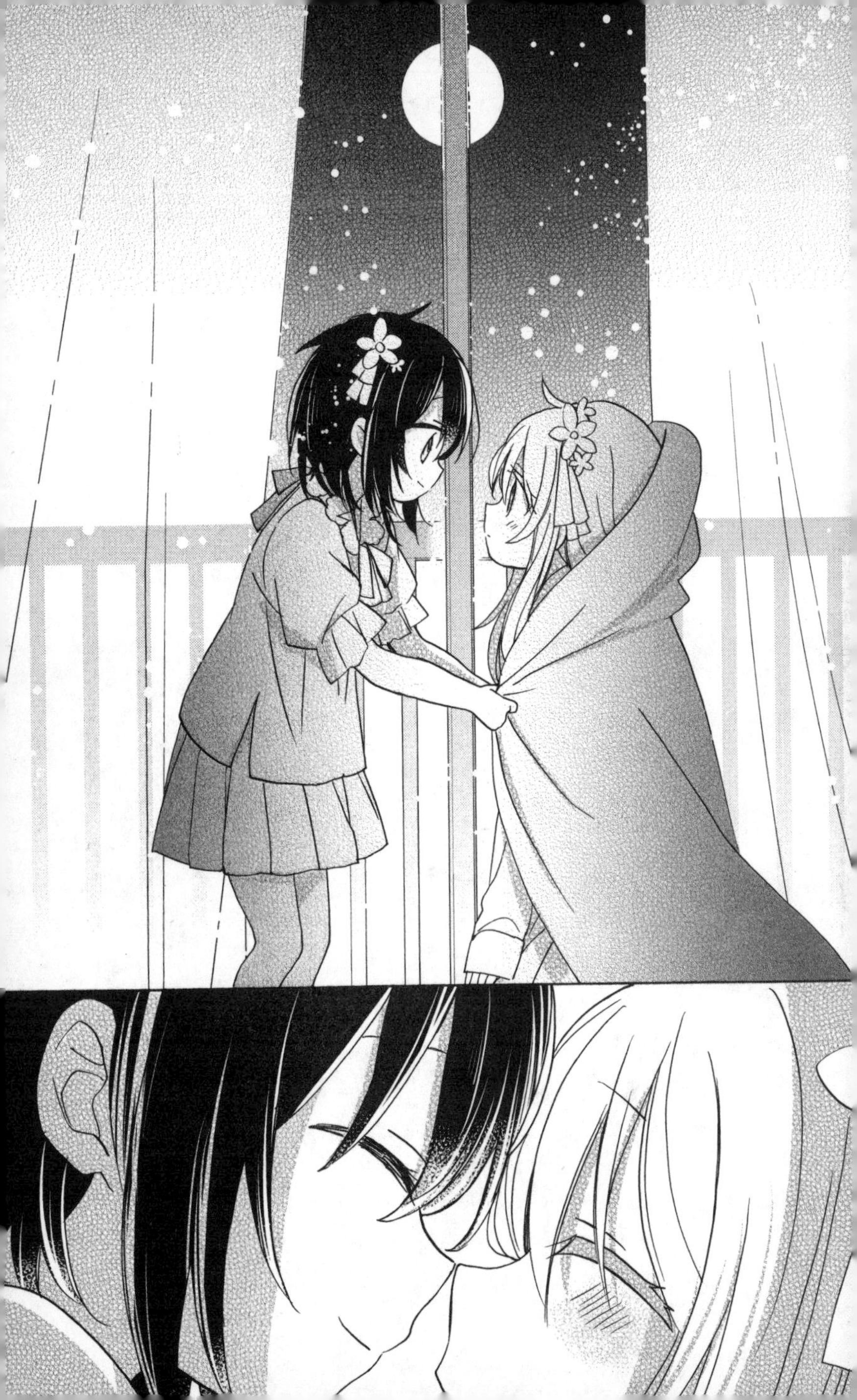

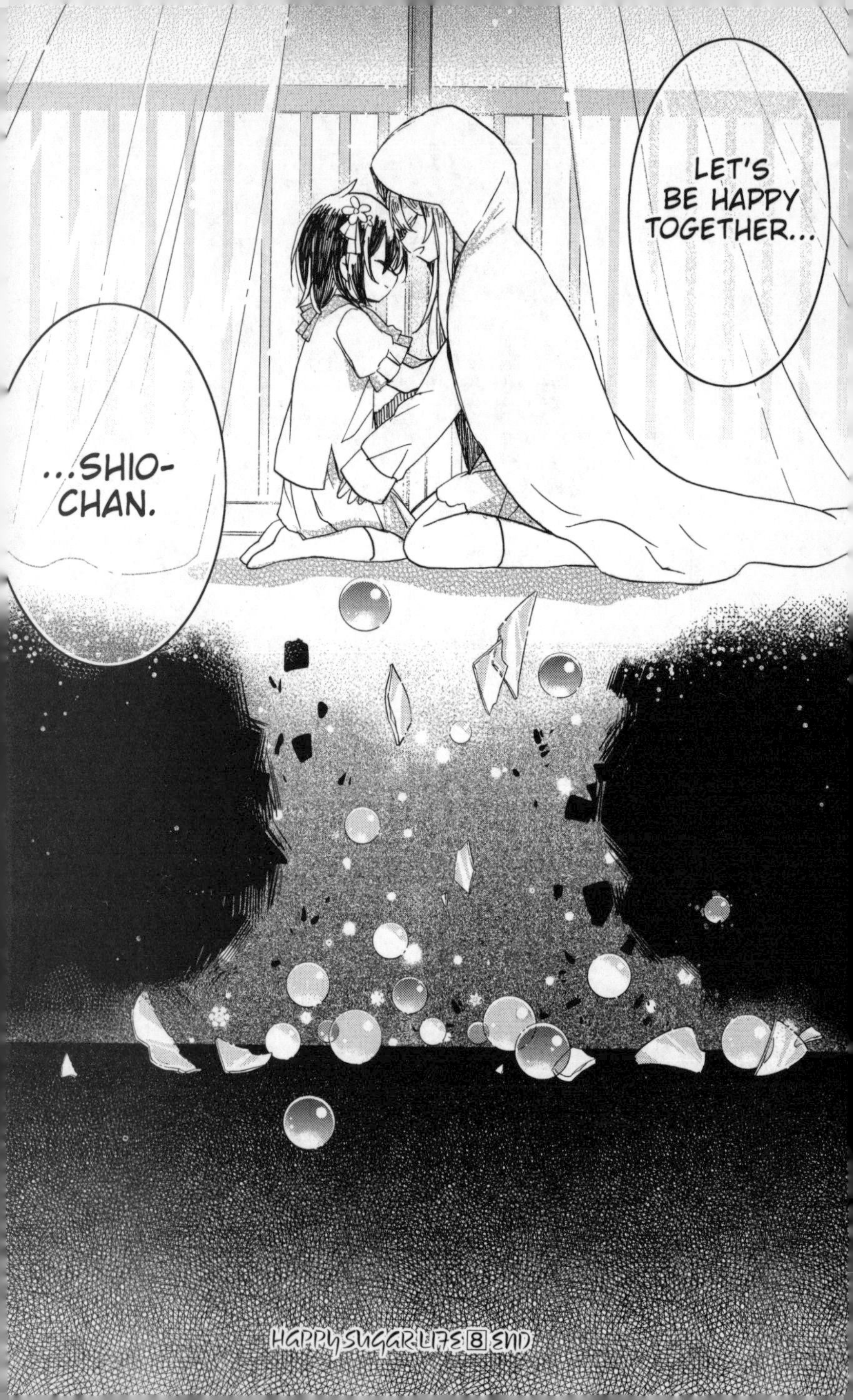
LET'S BE HAPPY TOGETHER...
...SHIO-CHAN.
HAPPY SUGAR LIFE 8 END

Happy
Sugar
Life

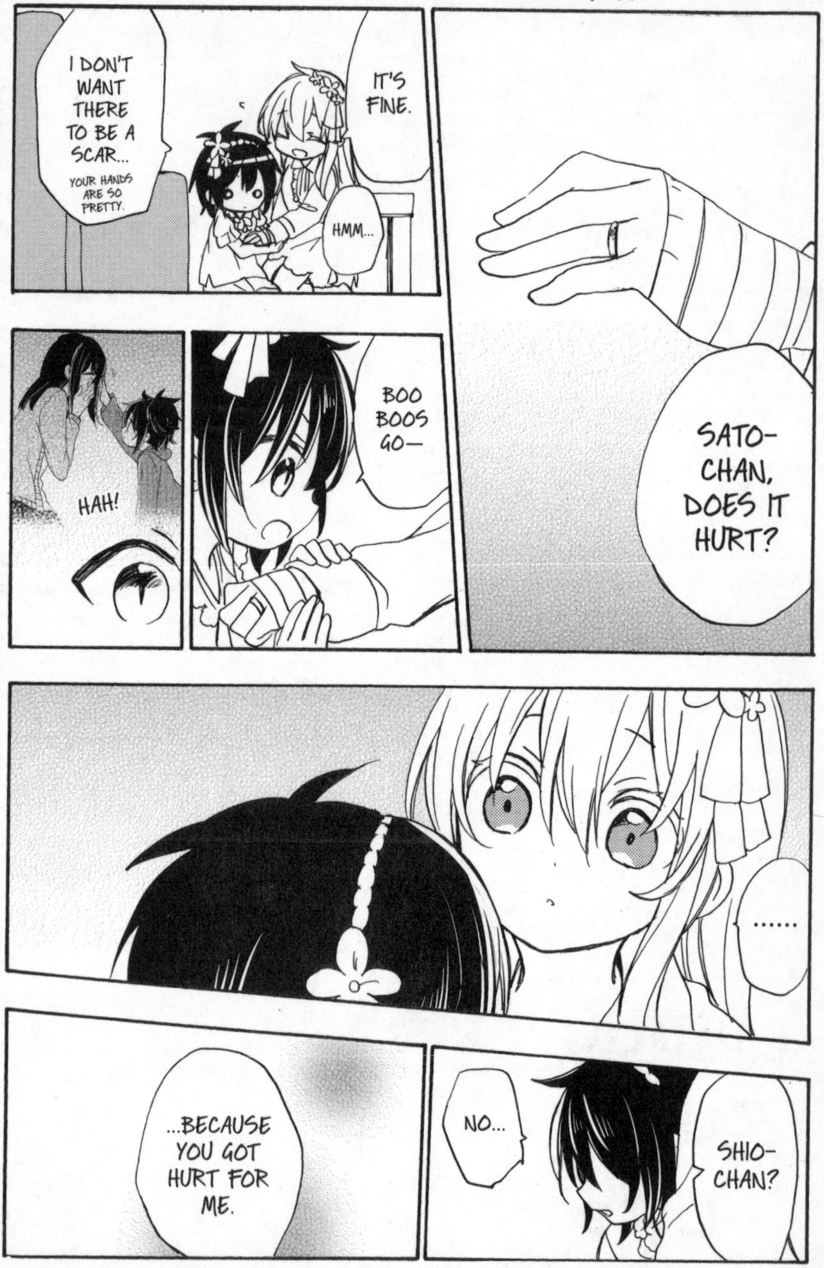
SATO-CHAN, DOES IT HURT?
IT'S FINE.
I DON'T WANT THERE TO BE A SCAR...
YOUR HANDS ARE SO PRETTY.
HMM...
BOO BOOS GO—
HAH!
......
SHIO-CHAN?
NO...
...BECAUSE YOU GOT HURT FOR ME.

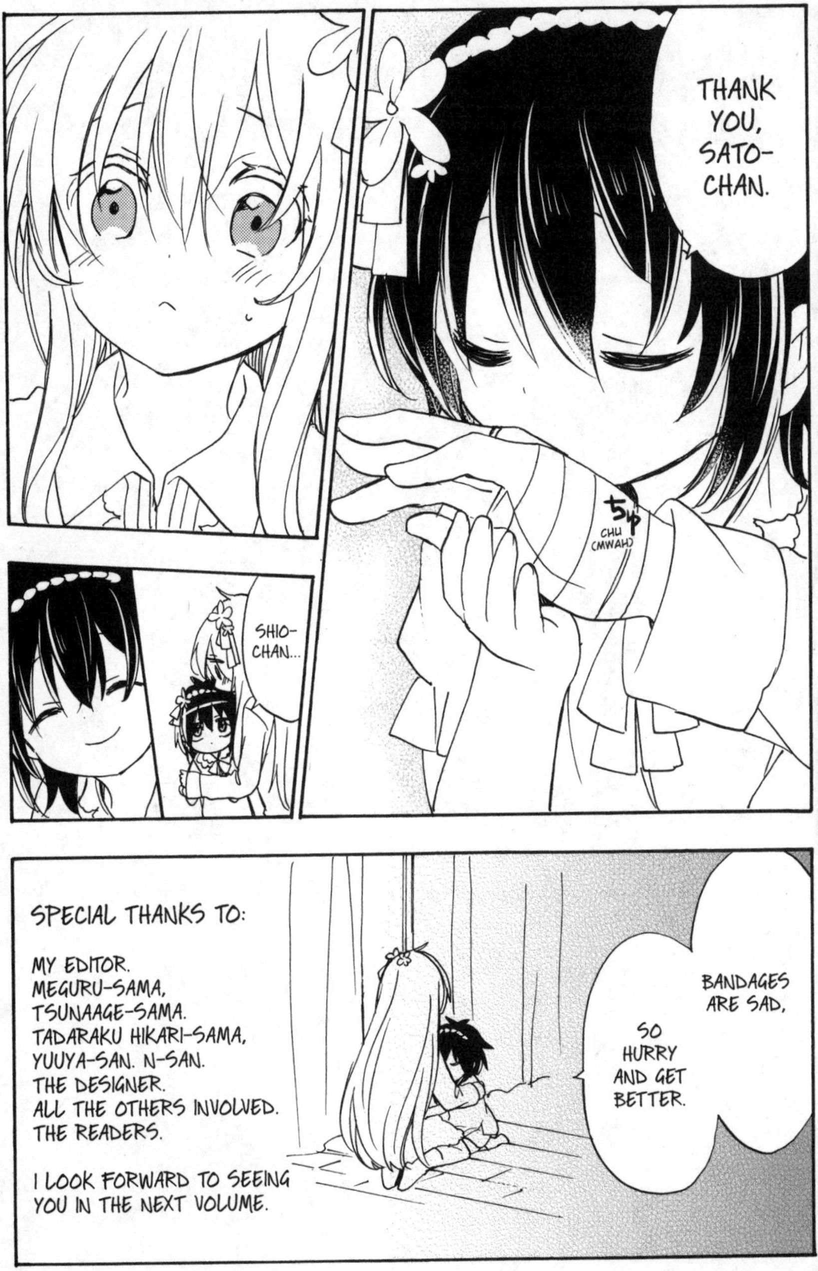
THANK YOU, SATO-CHAN.
ちゅ
CHU (MWAH)
SHIO-CHAN...
BANDAGES ARE SAD,
SO HURRY AND GET BETTER.
SPECIAL THANKS TO:
MY EDITOR.
MEGURU-SAMA,
TSUNAAGE-SAMA.
TADARAKU HIKARI-SAMA,
YUUYA-SAN. N-SAN.
THE DESIGNER.
ALL THE OTHERS INVOLVED.
THE READERS.
I LOOK FORWARD TO SEEING
YOU IN THE NEXT VOLUME.

es on.

Volume 9 coming February 2021!

Life go

Happy Sugar Life

Tomiyaki

SQUARE ENIX

Kagisora

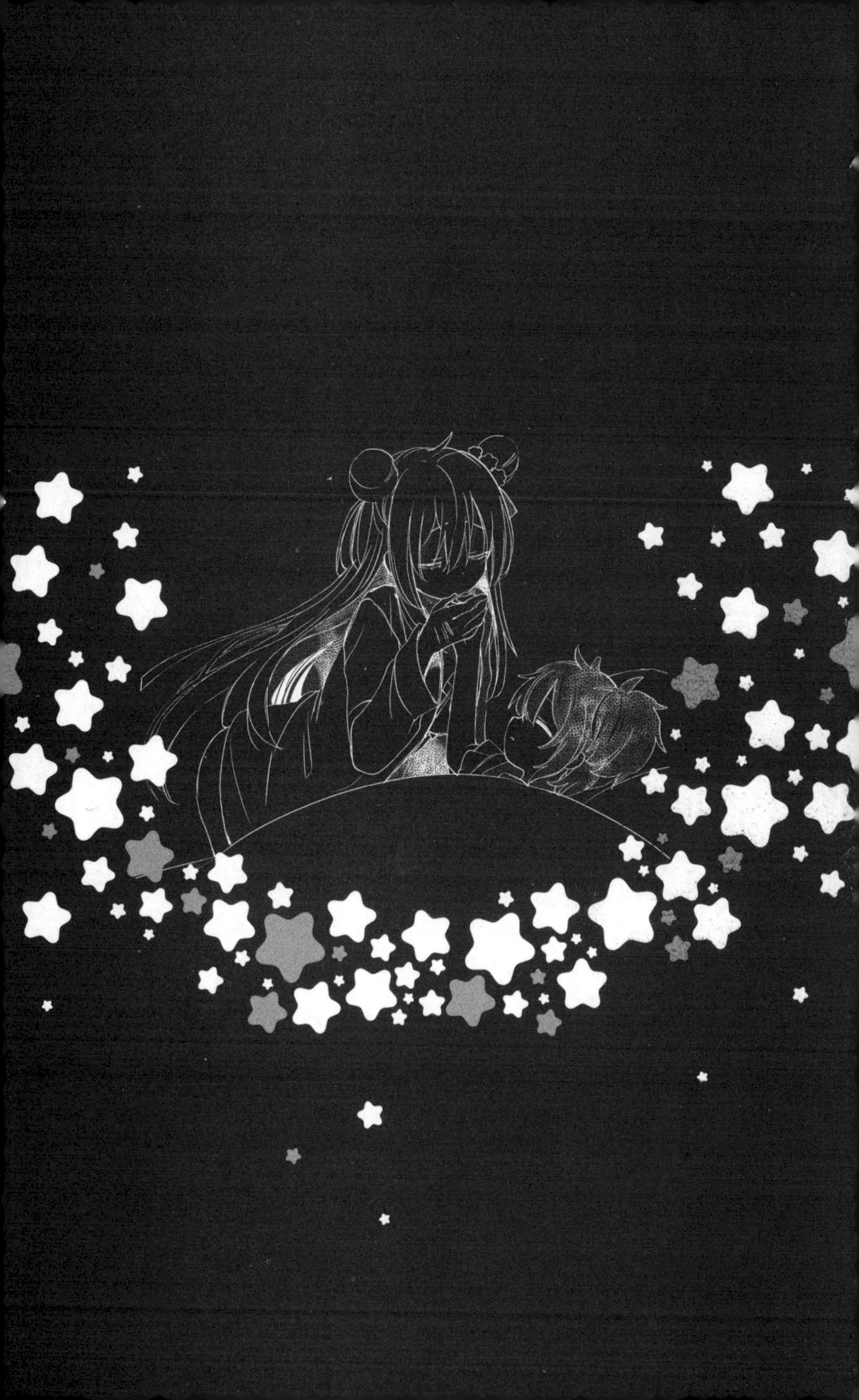

©Aidalro/SQUARE ENIX

VOLUMES 1-7 **IN STORES NOW!**

VOLUMES 1-13 AVAILABLE DIGITALLY!

Toilet-bound Hanako-Kun

At Kamome Academy, rumors abound about the school's Seven Mysteries, one of which is Hanako-san. Said to occupy the third stall of the third floor girls' bathroom in the old school building, Hanako-san grants any wish when summoned. Nene Yashiro, an occult-loving high school girl who dreams of romance, ventures into this haunted bathroom...but the Hanako-san she meets there is nothing like she imagined! Kamome Academy's

Now read the latest chapters of BLACK BUTLER digitally at the same time as Japan and support the creator!

The Phantomhive family has a butler who's almost too good to be true...

...or maybe he's just too good to be human.

Black Butler

YANA TOBOSO

VOLUMES 1-29 IN STORES NOW!

Yen Press
www.yenpress.com

BLACK BUTLER © Yana Toboso / SQUARE ENIX
Yen Press is an imprint of Yen Press, LLC.

OLDER TEEN
OT

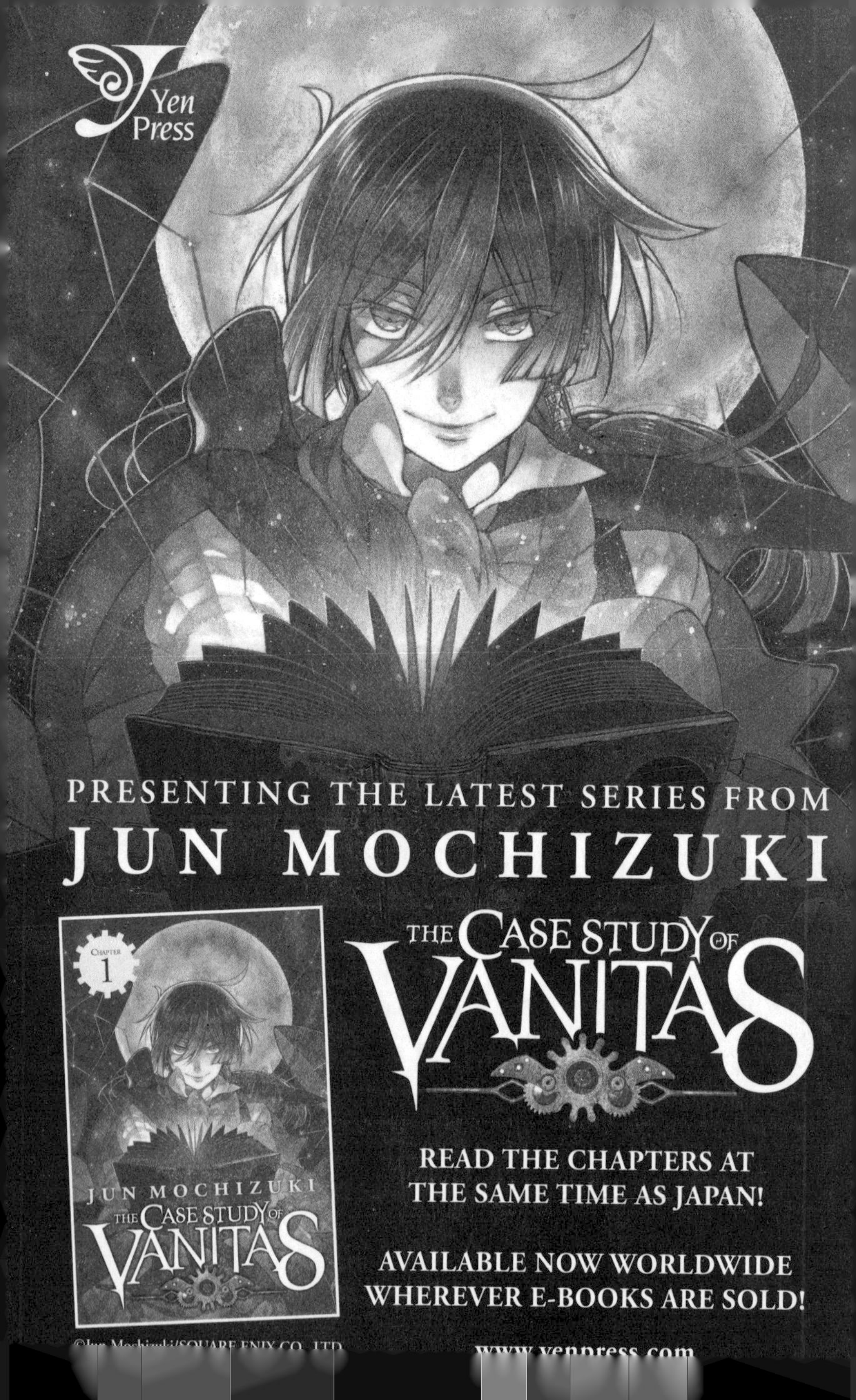
Yen Press
PRESENTING THE LATEST SERIES FROM
JUN MOCHIZUKI
CHAPTER 1
JUN MOCHIZUKI
THE CASE STUDY OF VANITAS
THE CASE STUDY OF VANITAS
READ THE CHAPTERS AT THE SAME TIME AS JAPAN!
AVAILABLE NOW WORLDWIDE WHEREVER E-BOOKS ARE SOLD!
www.yenpress.com

I've Been Killing SLIMES for 300 Years and Maxed Out My Level

It's hard work taking it slow...

After living a painful life as an office worker, Azusa ended her short life by dying from overworking. So when she found herself reincarnated as an undying, unaging witch in a new world, she vows to spend her days stress free and as pleasantly as possible. She ekes out a living by hunting down the easiest targets—the slimes! But after centuries of doing this simple job, she's ended up with insane powers... how will she maintain her low key life now?!

IN STORES NOW!

Light Novel Volumes 1-7

Manga Volumes 1-4

SLIME TAOSHITE SANBYAKUNEN,
SHIRANAIUCHINI LEVEL MAX
NI NATTEMASHITA
© 2017 Kisetsu Morita
© 2017 Benio / SB Creative Corp.

SLIME TAOSHITE SANBYAKUNEN,
SHIRANAIUCHINI LEVEL MAX
NI NATTEMASHITA
©Kisetsu Morita/SB Creative Corp.
Original Character Designs:
©Benio/SB Creative Corp.
©2018 Yusuke Shiba
/SQUARE ENIX CO., LTD.

For more information, visit www.yenpress.com

WELCOME TO IKEBUKUR
WHERE TOKYO'S WIL
CHARACTERS GATHE

BOY WHO
ABOUT T

NAIVE
TALKE

A SHUT-IN
QUESTIONA
E MOST
MAN IN

"HEADLES
CH-BLACK

AS THEIR PATHS CROSS, THIS ECCENTRIC
WEAVES A TWISTED, CRACKED LOVE STO

AVAILABLE NOW

MURDERER
IN THE STREETS, KILLER IN THE SHEETS!

MURCIÉLAGO

VOLUMES 1-16
AVAILABLE
NOW!

www.YenPress.com

Mass murderer Kuroko Koumori
has two passions in life: taking
lives and pleasuring ladies. This
doesn't leave her with many career
prospects, but Kuroko actually has
the perfect gig—as a hit woman
for the police!

Murciélago © Yoshimurakana / SQUARE ENIX

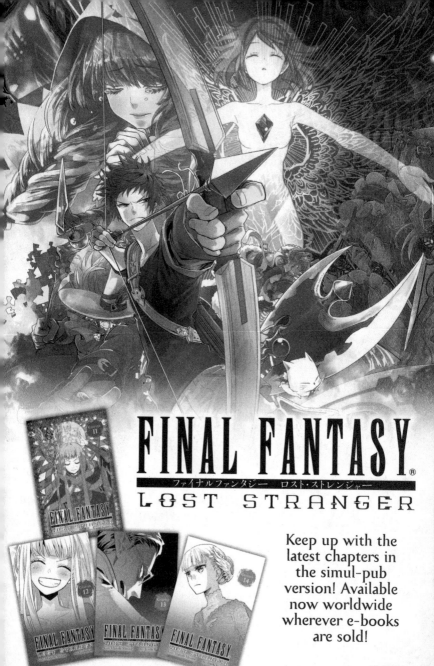

Great Priest Imhotep

VOLUMES 1-7 IN STORES NOW!
VOLUMES 1-11 AVAILABLE DIGITALLY!

From the sands of ancient Egypt to the streets of modern Japan, being displaced by thousands of miles and years won't distract the newly resurrected Great Priest Imhotep from his hunt for the Magai, devious beings who impersonate the gods and have an appetite for destruction! When schoolgirl Hinome crosses paths with this illustrious ancient, is her loner lifestyle about to change for the better...or the worse?!

For more information
visit www.yenpress.com

Yen Press

Happy Sugar Life 8

Tomiyaki Kagisora

Translation: JAN MITSUKO CASH

Lettering: CHIHO CHRISTIE

This book is a work of fiction. Names, characters, places, and incidents are the product of the author's imagination or are used fictitiously. Any resemblance to actual events, locales, or persons, living or dead, is coincidental.

HAPPY SUGAR LIFE vol. 8 ©2018 Tomiyaki Kagisora / SQUARE ENIX CO., LTD.
First published in Japan in 2018 by SQUARE ENIX CO., LTD. English translation rights arranged with SQUARE ENIX CO., LTD. and Yen Press, LLC through Tuttle-Mori Agency, Inc.

English translation ©2021 by SQUARE ENIX CO., LTD.

Yen Press, LLC supports the right to free expression and the value of copyright. The purpose of copyright is to encourage writers and artists to produce the creative works that enrich our culture.

The scanning, uploading, and distribution of this book without permission is a theft of the author's intellectual property. If you would like permission to use material from the book (other than for review purposes), please contact the publisher. Thank you for your support of the author's rights.

Yen Press
150 West 30th Street, 19th Floor
New York, NY 10001

Visit us at yenpress.com
facebook.com/yenpress
twitter.com/yenpress
yenpress.tumblr.com
instagram.com/yenpress

First Yen Press Edition: February 2021

Yen Press is an imprint of Yen Press, LLC.
The Yen Press name and logo are trademarks of Yen Press, LLC.

The publisher is not responsible for websites (or their content) that are not owned by the publisher.

Library of Congress Control Number: 2019932474

ISBNs: 978-1-9753-0337-2 (paperback)
978-1-9753-8720-4 (ebook)

10 9 8 7 6 5 4 3 2 1

BVG

Printed in the United States of America